Great Outdoor Guide to Southern New England

Also Available:

Frommer's Great Outdoor Guide to Northern California
Frommer's Great Outdoor Guide to Southern California & Baja
Frommer's Great Outdoor Guide to Washington & Oregon
Frommer's New England
Frommer's Cape Cod, Nantucket & Martha's Vineyard
Frommer's USA

Frommer's®

Great Outdoor Guide to Southern New England

by Peter Oliver

IDG Books Worldwide, Inc.
An International Data Group Company
Foster City, CA • Chicago, IL • Indianapolis, IN • New York, NY

IDG Books Worldwide, Inc.

An International Data Group Company
919 E. Hillsdale Blvd.
Suite 400
Foster City, CA 94404

Find us online at **www.frommers.com**

ISBN: 0-02863518-3
ISSN: 1522-8126

Editor: Naomi P. Kraus
Production Editor: Jenaffer Brandt
Photo Editor: Richard Fox
Design by Madhouse Studios
Staff Cartographers: John Decamillis and Roberta
Stockwell
Page creation by Natalie Evans, Julie Trippetti

Special Sales

For general information on IDG Books
Worldwide's books in the U.S., please call our
Consumer Customer Service department at
1-800-762-2974. For reseller information, including discounts, bulk sales, customized editions,
and premium sales, please call our Reseller
Customer Service department at 1-800-434-3422.

Manufactured in the United States of America

5 4 3 2 1

photo credit: Barrie Fisher

About the Author

Peter Oliver has been exploring the
wilderness of southern New England
since childhood. When he isn't pursuing
a new outdoor adventure, he writes
award-winning pieces on sports and the
outdoors. A contributing editor at Skiing
and *Aspen* magazines, his work has also
appeared in *Backpacker, Bicycling,
Outside,* the *Boston Globe,* and the *New
York Times.* He is the author of several
books, most recently *Bicycling: Touring
and Mountain Biking Basics,* and is cur-
rently working on a guide to skiing
around the world.

Contents

FEATURES

FEATURES

Jerimoth Hill   253
Serving Up Winners at the Newport Casino   260

List of Maps

Map Legend

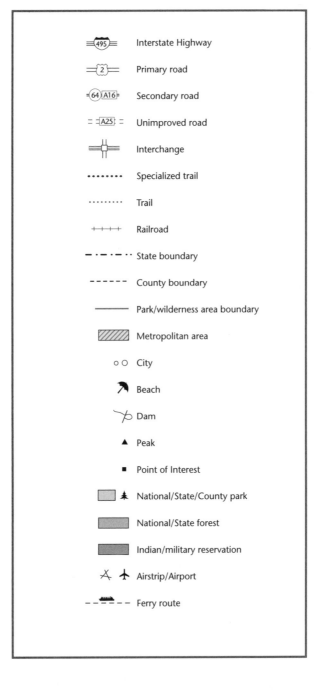

495	Interstate Highway
2	Primary road
64 A16	Secondary road
A25	Unimproved road
	Interchange
•••••••	Specialized trail
········	Trail
+++++	Railroad
— · — · ··	State boundary
— — — —	County boundary
————	Park/wilderness area boundary
//////	Metropolitan area
○ ○	City
	Beach
	Dam
▲	Peak
■	Point of Interest
▲	National/State/County park
	National/State forest
	Indian/military reservation
✗ ✈	Airstrip/Airport
– –□□□ – –	Ferry route

Acknowledgements

I owe Steve Jermanok, author of *Outside Magazine's Adventure Guide to New England,* a world of thanks. Steve's New England guide served as a model for this book, and much of the research that Steve did for that book gave me a huge head start in my own research, organization, and writing. I would also like to thank Naomi Kraus, the Frommer's editor who patiently and thoughtfully saw this book through to completion.

An Invitation to the Reader

In researching this book, I criss-crossed southern New England in search of the very best places to get outside. I'm sure you have your own favorite spots, or at least will find new ones as you explore. Please share your secrets with me, so I can pass them on in upcoming editions. If you were disappointed with a recommendation, we'd love to know that, too. Please write to:

Peter Oliver
Frommer's Great Outdoor Guide to Southern New England
Frommer's Travel Guides
1633 Broadway
New York, NY 10019

An Additional Note

Please be advised that travel information is subject to change at any time—and this is especially true of prices. We therefore suggest that you write or call ahead for confirmation when making your travel plans. The authors, editors, and publisher cannot be held responsible for the experiences of readers while traveling. Outdoor adventure sports are, by their very nature, potentially hazardous experiences. In doing any of the activities described herein, readers assume all risk or loss that may accompany all such activities. The Publisher disavows all responsibility for injury, death, loss, or property damage which may arise from a reader's participation in any of the activities described herein, and the Publisher makes no warranties regarding the competence, safety, and reliability of outfitters, tour companies, or training centers described in this book.

Find Frommer's Online

www.frommers.com offers up-to-the-minute listings on almost 200 cities around the globe—including the latest bargains and candid, personal articles updated daily by Arthur Frommer himself. No other Web site offers such comprehensive and timely coverage of the world of travel.

Introduction

I have in my collection of photos at home a picture of a marsh on Cape Cod taken in the early light of day. The sun has barely risen above a far-off island, and its reflection is smeared across the water in a golden swath, interrupted only by a curtain of marsh grasses. The picture evokes a serenity that I swear can take your breath away. There is no hint of anything other than undisturbed, pristine wilderness—some preternaturally perfect piece of the world.

It's an idealized vision, of course, and something of an illusion. If you were able to pan left and right of the photo's frame, you would see summer homes along the water's edge. You would see cars and docks and telephone lines and most of the usual signs of human settlement and civilization. This is simply the way it is in southern New England: the natural world and the civilized world coexisting in close proximity, neighbors in a sometimes uneasy but still workable alliance.

So as much as I might like to imagine otherwise in my photograph, the fact is that there is really no such thing as true wilderness any more in southern New England. This is not something I report with any deep sense of remorse, sadness, or deprivation, and I don't mean to imply that open and undeveloped land has ceased to exist. But true wilderness—unspoiled, untouched, and unmanaged by human intervention—hasn't existed in southern New England for hundreds of years.

The entire landscape has been tilled, logged, built upon, torn down, uprooted, smoothed over, processed, and reprocessed in the nearly four centuries since the Pilgrims set foot on Plymouth Rock. There is good reason for that, beyond the fact that this simply was the first land settlers encountered upon arriving from Europe in the 1600s and 1700s. This has always been land almost ideally suited for human habitation: sweeping forests to provide building materials; plentiful water; temperate climate; tillable soils full of nutrients; and a coastline pocked with numerous natural havens and ports, for trade and transportation. For nearly four centuries, people have made the most of nature's bounty; it is as though the entire landscape has been repeatedly rendered through a giant sieve, refined and remade to suit the needs and whims of its human inhabitants.

So in looking at the natural world—the great outdoors—of southern New England, we're looking at something that, like the rest of the landscape, has come through that rendering process. Yet this shouldn't necessarily make it any less inviting or inspiring, and I think of my photograph as proof of that. I am still moved by a walk in the Berkshire woods, or a mountaintop view, or a fish at the end of my line as I stand in some clear-running stream. Southern New England's natural landscape may have undergone continual reinvention over the centuries, and it might not be real wilderness, but it can be a great place to bide one's time, nonetheless.

Perhaps I inherit this point of view from the likes of Henry David Thoreau and Ralph Waldo Emerson, who in the 19th century—a boom time for development in New England—still managed to appreciate the persistence of a wilderness ethic. Emerson and Thoreau saw water, trees, and sky and were able to perceive that, even as mechanization and cultivation churned all around them, nature still had room to spread its wings and assert itself.

The vitality of the natural world manages to persist today throughout southern New England. Of course nature and human development wage an ongoing battle, and there is no foreseeable end to that. But it would be wrong for even the most hardened environmental cynic to presume that nature is the preordained loser. The numbers suggest otherwise.

Over 60% of the area's land is now classified as forested, a dramatic change from a century ago, when forests covered less than 30% of the land. The Sierra Club lists 179 "natural areas" in the three southern New England states, totaling roughly 600,000 land acres. And I know this list to be incomplete, because I have visited other natural areas that aren't on it.

In addition, all that acreage does not include hundreds of thousands of acres of water—lakes, ponds, rivers, and coastal bays and inlets. Nor does it account for such highlights as the Appalachian Trail, which passes through western Connecticut and Massachusetts, or lesser-known "long trails," such as the Metacomet–Monadnock Trail and the Midstate Trail. On the land-use grid of southern New England, wild spaces have won a hard-earned right to exist, if for no better reason than a widely shared belief that the preservation of undeveloped land is essential to the psychic well-being of the public.

Of all of southern New England's natural areas, perhaps none illustrates the synthesis of nature and civilization more dramatically than Quabbin Reservation in central Massachusetts. Here, in the form of Quabbin Reservoir, is the largest body of fresh water in southern New England. The reservoir is surrounded by roughly 60,000 undeveloped, unspoiled acres. Moose, bears, and bald eagles reside here, and lake trout in the reservoir weigh in at as much as 20 pounds.

Yet, as pristine a natural environment as Quabbin is, I find it ironic that it is also entirely a man-made construct. The reservoir contains the main supply of drinking water for Boston, and exists only because of a dam built in 1927. Were it not for the raging thirst of greater Boston, there would be no Quabbin Reservation or Reservoir. There would undoubtedly be towns and roads and farms, just as there are in the surrounding areas of central Massachusetts. Were it not for the demands of southern New England's largest city, one of the region's great natural wonders would not exist.

So civilization and nature have somehow come to terms with one another, and in some cases the deal tips in favor of nature, Quabbin being a prime case in point. But it hasn't always worked out that way. In years past, people have been incredibly abusive of southern New England's natural resources, its rivers in particular. The Blackstone, Housatonic, Hoosac, and Millers rivers were all at one time lined by mills and factories, and industrial effluvia discharged into these waters made the rivers national poster children for pollution. It was not so long ago that the Housatonic was a chameleon of a river, literally changing colors according to the dyes discharged into the water by paper mills in Pittsfield.

Nevertheless, it says a good deal about the value that southern New Englanders have historically put on the preservation of nature—perhaps a moral descendant of the philosophy propounded by Emerson and Thoreau—that these rivers are making a remarkable comeback. And perhaps no body of water has made a more remarkable recovery than Boston Harbor, which just a decade ago was a cesspool and the butt of national ridicule. Thanks to a swift-moving clean-up effort, the harbor is now a first-rate place to fish, sail, kayak, and even swim.

Perhaps because it was one of the first parts of the country to be broadly developed, southern New England has, in response, also been a national leader in the galvanization of environmental advocacy and action. The Trustees of Reservations, which now can claim 33,000 protected acres in Massachusetts, was founded in 1891. The Massachusetts Audubon Society, established in 1896, is the oldest Audubon Society in the country. Around the same time, the Metropolitan District Commission in Boston was formed as the first parks commission in the country.

A recreational enthusiasm has gone hand in hand with this environmental sentiment. The Appalachian Mountain Club, the foremost hiking organization in the country, is based in Boston. Newport is probably the spiritual epicenter of sailing in America. The Boston Bicycle Club, formed in 1878, was the first bike club in America. Thanks to the volunteer-driven Connecticut Forest and Parks Association, the blue-blazed trail system used throughout Connecticut is considered a national model of a recreational-trail network.

All the efforts to preserve natural spaces and to promote outdoor recreation in this region have transpired in the face of incredible and continuing developmental pressures. According to the Massachusetts Audubon Society and other sources, 44 acres a day in Massachusetts succumb to development. Among the 50 states, Massachusetts, Connecticut, and Rhode Island are surpassed only by New Jersey in population density. In the three states combined, there are more than 700 people per square mile, and that figure that doesn't include metropolitan New York City, the most densely populated patch of land in America, which sticks to the southwestern corner of the region like a tumorous appendage.

Without some sort of specific intent and concerted effort to preserve land from development, I can easily imagine the landscape of southern New England transformed into a lazy, haphazard sprawl of settlement and industry. With a population of close to 10 million, there are certainly enough people in the region to make it happen. Instead, you still have enough open spaces—enough forests, lakes, beaches, wetlands, etc.—to separate yourself completely from that populous world and to feel inspired for while.

Although I have never lived in southern New England, I nonetheless have many ties to the area. My mother was born and raised in Pittsfield, and my grandparents lived all of their adult lives in Pittsfield and Williamstown. I spent summers as a kid on Cape Cod, working odd jobs there when I was old enough to do so, and, in winter, I often skied in the Berkshires during my childhood. Members of my family have attended various colleges in Connecticut and Massachusetts, and other members continue to live in the region.

So as I began traveling and researching this book, I felt I knew southern New England reasonably well. I figured that I had spent enough time in the region—and had enough of a personal attachment—to write about it with some authority and passion. Little did I know, however, how limited my knowledge was—at least when it came to the great outdoors. The outdoor world of southern New England is much more difficult to come to intimate terms with than I ever expected it to be.

The reason for that, I think, has much to do with the fragmentation of southern New England, a puzzle made up of thousands upon thousands of tiny, disparate elements. Just try to imagine the hundreds of small towns and the countless private home sites and lots—who knows how many—of an acre or less. Imagine all the commercial complexes, the industrial parks, the colleges and universities, the churches, and the public lands designated for myriad uses. And then imagine all of this crammed into a three-state space so compact it could fit into Alaska 40 times over, with room to spare. If you don't pay careful attention, southern New England can pass by in a blur, and you can miss a lot.

So despite the many times I visited Williamstown or Pittsfield, for example, I never even knew of the existence of Bartholomew's Cobble, an enchanting refuge just a few miles away. I knew almost nothing of the spectacular estuarial wilds of the Essex River basin and Parker River National Wildlife Refuge, north of Boston. I never knew that a section of the Farmington River in northern Connecticut had been officially designated "wild and scenic" by the federal government, and once I got there to witness the river for myself, it was easy enough to see why.

The outdoor world of southern New England, then, fits in with all the other tracts of land as part of an incredibly complex mosaic. You could say that the process of discovering this outdoor world resembles rummaging around in an over-filled closet. You might eventually find what you're looking for, but you'll spend most of your time fascinated by stuff you never expected to be there.

The rummaging process can produce both surprise and disappointment. On a hot July day, I visited Walden Pond—Thoreau's inspirational bailiwick—with some degree of heightened expectation. What I discovered was not much more than a fairly ordinary (although pleasant enough) swimming hole. Visiting Walden was not the transcendent moment I might have wanted it to be. Later that afternoon, I happened upon the Great Meadows National Wildlife Refuge, just a few miles from Walden and a hard find even if you know what you're looking for. Wildflowers bloomed, songbirds sang, and cattails in the marshes nodded gracefully in the breeze. The pervading hush of the place was resonant. Everything I might have expected to find at Walden seemed to have been transported to Great Meadows.

What you won't find in the southern New England mosaic are any constituent pieces of mind-bending dimension. You won't find million-acre forests or mountains 14,000 feet high. There is no Grand Canyon, Mississippi River, Denali, or Yellowstone National Park. I suppose the closest thing there is to some take-your-breath-away, natural wow is Cape Cod National Seashore, with its dunes, sandy bluffs, and miles of unspoiled beaches.

This absence of knock-your-socks-off grandeur, I think, is a big part of the reason southern New England fails to appear on the great-outdoor radar screen of America. I understand that. But I also understand that the natural allure of the region comes mainly from its diversity and subtleties. Visit almost any wildlife sanctuary in southern New England, and you can expect to encounter a bird-sighting list with between 150 and 300 entries. Walk in the forests and exhaust yourself in trying to catalogue the many different trees and wildflowers. In Bartholomew's Cobble, less than 300 acres in all, there are more than 40 different species of ferns, 500 species of wildflowers, 100 different kinds of trees, and close to 250 species of birds. I wonder how the Grand Canyon stacks up against that.

Now I don't mean to suggest that southern New England is entirely lacking in natural grandeur. The panorama from the summit of Mt. Greylock or Mt. Everett in the Berkshires; the setting sun on the cliffs of Gay Head on Martha's Vineyard; the endless sands of the dunes of Provincetown—all insist upon a long moment's pause for appreciation. But I really think such spectacular displays are essentially overtures to a more complex and compelling drama. Take all of southern New England's natural variety and then throw in the changing seasons and the overlapping of ecosystems and habitats, and you've got a full kaleidoscope of natural wonders.

And that's just your backdrop, the stage on which your interaction with the outdoor world takes place. There are many ways, of course, to interact with nature here—by hiking, canoeing, fishing, kayaking, cycling, skiing, snowshoeing, hang-gliding, horseback riding, camping, etc. The grand dimensions might be lacking, but still, this is a region where, if you choose to do so, you could be surfing in the morning and skiing in the afternoon. I'm not saying it is either easy or convenient, but there aren't many places in America where you can do something like that.

To maintain what there is of the great outdoors in southern New England, a certain amount of stewardship and management must come into play. Forests and wildlife areas are "managed," meaning, euphemistically, that logging and hunting are permitted as a means of maintaining some theoretical natural balance. Rivers are controlled and dammed, for both flood-control and hydroelectric purposes, and are artificially stocked with fish raised in hatcheries.

Certain areas are, from time to time, closed off entirely to human visitation, as a means of protecting wildlife habitats or allowing forests and vegetation to regenerate. Structures of various sorts are built along the shore to prevent beach erosion. The clearing and maintenance of trails and roads in undeveloped places must adhere to specific ordinances and guidelines, which vary depending on whatever state agency or private organization happens to oversee the land.

In short, human control, even in so-called wild places, for the most part supersedes natural law. I doubt there is any way around that, and I believe that without that kind of control and vigilance, the outdoor world of southern New England would surely suffer. It is easy to envision a world of over-logged forests, a world where wildlife has been all but eliminated due to over-hunting and habitat destruction, and where rivers have been over-fished and possibly polluted, etc.

It's easy to envision this because it has already happened. There is, after all, essentially no old-growth forest left in southern New England, and logging is largely responsible for that. It has only been in the past few years that such wild animals as moose and bears, once native to the region, have returned in small numbers. Rivers *have* been over-fished—the reason stocking is necessary—and horribly polluted, as I have mentioned. I'll bet that if you were able to return to the industrial New England of the early 20th century while equipped with early 21st-century sensibilities as to how the environment should be treated, you would be appalled.

Keep this perspective in mind as you face the kinds of regulations you will inevitably encounter in the southern New England outdoors. Trails are often closed to mountain bikers. Hunting is permitted in what might seem idyllic and ideal wildlife habitat. Campfires are prohibited in backcountry camping areas. Beaches are closed to protect nesting birds. Off-trail hiking is prohibited to curb erosion. These are just a few of the regulations I have encountered, and I can't deny having been frustrated by them from time to time.

At the same time, I am obviously not alone in wanting a robust, clean, and fecund natural world to endure and thrive in southern New England. If it takes various forms of regulation and management to ensure that, then so be it. I want to continue to be able to take long walks in the woods; to fish in healthy, clear rivers; to ride my bike through a countryside filled with bucolic scenery. I want to continue to be surprised by the natural places that can be found here, and to be surprised when I pick up the paper to read stories like the one about the remarkable clean-up of Boston Harbor. And I want to continue to be able to take photos of the sunrise on the Cape, to be able to indulge myself at least in the fantasy that a wilderness in southern New England still survives.

—*Peter Oliver*

Chapter 1

The Basics

This book is divided into seven geographical regions, spanning southern New England from the northeast corner of Massachusetts to the southwest corner of Connecticut. All the regional chapters include an in-depth list of sports, categorized alphabetically from bird-watching to whitewater rafting. Under each sports heading, I feature detailed descriptions of specific trails, routes, and waterways that I have tried personally. The time required, level of difficulty, location, and the availability of maps are all addressed in the individual listings. Of course, *time* and *level of difficulty* are relative terms, but I base these categorizations on an average adult who is in relatively good shape. For example, I labeled all walks and rambles as either easy or moderate, since they are inherently shorter and/or less strenuous than a hike. "Easy" can also differ from one sport to the next. An easy cross-country skiing trip, for example, generally involves more effort than an easy flatwater canoe outing.

If you haven't taken a hike, been on a bike, paddled a canoe or kayak, or skied in the last 12 months, you'll probably find the easy outings challenging but still doable. On the other hand, if you're a dedicated cyclist, hiker, paddler, or skier, the strenuous outings should provide a genuine test of your ability and stamina.

I am not, however, particularly worried about those of you who are fit and are veterans of the outdoors. Rather, I want to be sure that those of you with couch-potato tendencies don't get in over your heads. If, in the last 10 years, your longest hike has been to the nearest Seven-Eleven for a bag of chips, don't head out for a climb up Mt. Greylock. Start with an outing that's listed as easy, and work your way up to the more strenuous stuff as your fitness and ability allows.

For some sports, such as fishing and surfing, the hot spots I list are based primarily on the recommendations of local fishermen, local outfitters, owners of sporting-goods stores, sporting clubs, schools, chambers of commerce, and other knowledgeable and experienced folk. As you travel through southern New England, I suggest that you also make a point of tapping into the expertise of such people. A complete listing of outfitters and schools, as well as some helpful hints regarding your options, can be found in this chapter. Each regional chapter concludes with the top campsites, inns, and resorts that cater to sports enthusiasts.

This introductory chapter will help you plan your trip, whether you're on your own or with an outfitter. Here you'll find information on everything you'll need to plan a successful outdoors vacation in southern New England. You'll also find a listing for every sport found in the regional chapters, discussing in detail the equipment, logistics, and conditioning necessary to perform a particular activity. I also list the top destinations in southern New England for each sport. Finally, at the end of this chapter you'll find a list of pertinent books, and of bookstores specializing in books and maps on the outdoors. I'd like to think that this book contains almost everything you'll ever need for traveling in the outdoors of southern New England. But, a little more information from other resources never hurts.

Before You Go

GETTING THERE

There are three major airports in the southern New England region: Boston's **Logan International Airport,** Providence's **T. F. Green International Airport,** and **Bradley International Airport,** about halfway between Hartford and Springfield. Another good option, especially for people visiting the Berkshires, is to fly into **Albany, New York.** Airports in the metropolitan New York area may also be convenient for arriving and departing in the region.

Major airlines that serve southern New England include **American** (☎ 800/433-7300; www.aa.com), **Continental** (☎ 800/525-0280; www.continental. com), **Delta** (☎ 800/ 221-1212; www. delta-air.com), **Northwest** (☎ 800/225-2525; www. nwa.com), **TWA** (☎ 800/ 221-2000; www.twa.com), **United** (☎ 800/241-6522), and **US Airways** (☎ 800/428-4322; www.usairways.com).

Some of the smaller cities in southern New England also have commercial airports, served mostly by commuter or charter air service. For the most part, however, it is less expensive and just as convenient to fly to one of the major airports and drive to your destination. The notable exceptions are the airports of **Hyannis, Martha's Vineyard,** and **Nantucket.** Particularly if you are coming from New York (rather than Boston), flying to the Cape or the islands can save a considerable amount of drive time and/or ferry time.

Carriers to the Cape and Islands include all of the above except TWA, plus **Cape Air** (☎ 800/352-0714 or 508/

771-6944; www.flycapeair.com), **Colgan Air** (☎ 800/272-5488 or 508/775-7077; www.colganair.com/), **Island Airlines** (☎ 800/248-7779 or 508/775-6606; www.nantucket.net/trans/islandair/), and **Nantucket Airlines** (☎ 800/635-8787 or 508/790-0300; www.nantucketairlines. com).

Amtrak (☎ 800/USA-RAIL; www. amtrak.com) has excellent rail service between New York and Boston and between New York and Albany. Rail service into the heart of the region is much more sporadic. If you want to travel by bus, **Greyhound** (☎ 800/231-2222; www.greyhound.com) connects Boston with the rest of the country, and **Bonanza Bus Lines** (☎ 800/556-3815 or 508/548-7588) covers a good portion of southern New England.

Major rental-car companies, of course, operate out of all the major airports. Companies represented in the area include **Avis** (☎ 800/331-1212), **Budget** (☎ 800/527-0700), **Hertz** (☎ 800/654-3131), **National** (☎ 800/227-7368), and **Thrifty** (☎ 800/367-2277).

In almost all cases, you'll need a car to get around the region. The notable exceptions are the islands—**Block Island, Martha's Vineyard,** and **Nantucket.** All are compact enough so that it is possible (and in many ways more convenient) to get around by bicycle or public transportation. Using public transportation (buses and trains) is also an option in the Greater Boston area.

VISITOR INFORMATION

I've included information sources for specific activities under the headings for those activities in this chapter. For general tourist information, however—and they're always a good place to start—state tourism offices are listed here.

CONNECTICUT For general tourist information, contact the **Department of Economic & Community Development,** 505 Hudson St., Hartford, CT

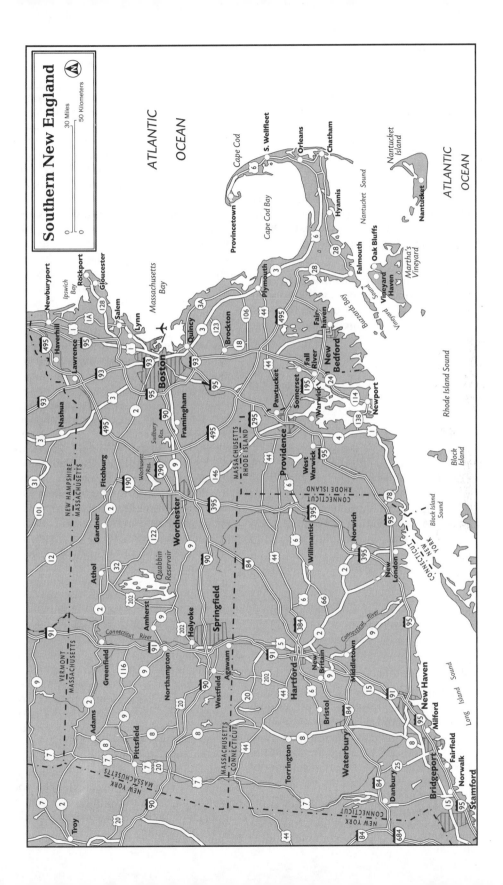

06106 (☎ **800/CTBOUND**). For parks and recreational information, contact the **Department of Environmental Protection,** Office of Parks and Recreation, 79 Elm St., Hartford, CT 06106 (☎ **860/424-3200**). You can also try the **Connecticut State Parks & Forests** Web site (**http://dep.state.ct.us/rec/parks.htm**), or surf over to the home of the **Friends of Connecticut's State Parks** (**www.friendsctstateparks.net/**).

MASSACHUSETTS   The main source for tourist information is the **Office of Travel and Tourism,** 100 Cambridge St., Boston, MA 02202 (☎ **800/447-6277**). The **Massachusetts Department of Environmental Management** (Office of Public Information, 100 Cambridge St., Boston, MA 02202; ☎ **617/ 727-3180;** www.magnet.state.ma.us/dem/) manages the state's parks and forests.

RHODE ISLAND   For tourist information, call the **Department of Economic Development, Tourism Division,** 7 Jackson Walkway, Providence, RI 02903 (☎ **800/556-2484**). Another useful contact is the **Rhode Island Department of Environmental Management, State Parks & Recreation Division,** 2321 Hartford Ave., Johnston, RI 02919 (☎ **401/222-2632**).

On the Web, **GORP** (Great Outdoors Recreations Page) has excellent listings for online information about recreation activities in southern New England. Head for **www.gorp.com,** then search the site by state or by outdoor activity.

WHEN TO GO

Southern New England is a world defined by four distinct seasons. In an average winter, snowfall totals in the Berkshires, the snowiest region of southern New England, are generally in the neighborhood of about 80 inches. Hence, for winter activities, the Berkshires are the place to be. Decent natural snow coverage—for cross-country skiing or snowshoeing—typically lasts from about mid-December

to mid-March. That season, however, varies considerably, depending largely on latitude (the more northerly, the more snow), elevation, and exposure (north-facing slopes hold snow longer). Snowmaking enables downhill ski areas to stay open from about the first of December to the end of March.

Snow sports such as skiing, snowboarding, and snowshoeing aren't the only winter activities possible in the region. Winter is often the best time for birders to spot the bald eagles that come south to escape the Canadian cold and, in some cases, to nest. Fishing in some streams and rivers in the southern half of the region is possible year-round. And even surfing, for the truly hardcore, is possible when powerful winter storms churn up big swells along the Rhode Island coast.

Spring is the best time for whitewater enthusiasts. As winter snows and ice melt, stream and river levels swell. Streams that in summer might not be not much more than trickles are often raging torrents for a few weeks in March. Beginning in April, spring migrations are one of the highlights of the bird-watching year, particularly around wetland areas along the coast. As the weather begins to warm, spring can also be a good time for road biking. Roads are clear of ice and snow, daytime temperatures begin to nudge into the 60s, and the nightmarish traffic that comes with the influx of summer tourists has yet to appear.

Summer, of course, is prime time throughout the region. From Nantucket to the Berkshires, just about every activity that isn't snow dependent is possible. Yet summer has obvious drawbacks, too. You can expect crowds on the roadways and at the beach, and most lodging rates increase dramatically. At the same time, if you want to head into the woods, hiking or mountain biking can quickly take you away from the crowds, and trails that in spring are often muddy have usually dried by early June.

New England falls are justifiably famous. Maple trees, a major constituency of the region's forests—particularly in the western hills and mountains—put on the most dramatic shows. Maple leaves can turn anywhere from deep purple to vivid pink, or bright orange to Day-Glo yellow, before succumbing to the chill of an impending winter. Fall lodging rates in the Berkshires and the Litchfield Hills remain high through October, as foliage fanatics come in droves before the leaves finally disappear by early November. The foliage season is far less dramatic as you move toward the southeast—toward Cape Cod and the islands—where forests composed primarily of oak and pine simply don't undergo the same chromatic transformation as do the forests farther inland.

SAFETY

In the absence of true wilderness, southern New England might seem a relatively safe place to enjoy the outdoors, and it is. At the same time, there are inherent dangers any time you pull yourself away from the safe couch of civilization, even to take a short walk in the woods. Something as minor as a sprained ankle can become a serious problem if, say, you're miles from a trailhead on some remote trail in the Berkshires. The Boy Scouts have it right—be prepared.

For any trip of more than a couple of miles into the backcountry—to hike, fish, bike, canoe, ski, or whatever—there are a few safety items you ought to bring along. A basic first-aid kit is the most obvious, and you should also pack a small toolkit or all-in-one tool (such as a Leatherman or a Swiss Army knife). For a detailed backcountry equipment list, see the "Backpackers Equipment List" on page 22. Having these things with you, of course, is not in itself protection against injury. Be prepared to use them, and be resourceful. For example, a couple of trimmed branches secured by tape can act as a makeshift brace or splint to enable

you or a companion to at least get to a trailhead for medical assistance.

Be prepared also for changes in weather, particularly drops in temperature. In the forested hills of New England, it is often difficult to get a good read on the sky and thus impending weather changes. A nice warm walk in the woods can turn into sudden misery, especially at higher elevations, should an unexpected storm move in. Hypothermia—a sudden drop in the body's temperature—is a problem all backcountry travelers should be aware of and prepared for. Similarly, anyone out on the water on a hot summer's day should be prepared for a squall that can cause a sudden temperature drop of as much as 30°.

Pack along a lightweight fleece and some rainwear, even on a hot summer day, and you should be in good shape. In winter, of course, you'll need more substantial layers, as well as a warm hat and gloves. The operative concept is this: You can always remove unnecessary clothing if you're too warm, but it is hard to put on clothing you don't have if you become cold or wet. One other weather-related item you should always have with you is a sunscreen with an SPF factor of 15 or higher.

Drinking water is the ultimate essential. Dehydration can lead to all sorts of problems (muscle cramps, headaches, hypothermia, fatigue, etc.). The water you see running in those beautiful, free-flowing mountain streams might look refreshing and inviting. Unfortunately, the pesky and resilient giardia parasite has made its way into most of the streams and rivers in New England. Giardia can cause all sorts of intestinal unpleasantries that you simply don't want to know about. So unless you have a water filter or purification tablets, or boil water for at least 10 minutes, don't ever drink the water—bring your own.

Three other potential problems lurk in the New England woods. Poison ivy is particularly prevalent in the woods of the southeast. While the consequences of an encounter with poison ivy are not going to be life threatening, a severe reaction can be incredibly unpleasant and last for several days. Familiarize yourself with poison ivy's three-leaf pattern, and steer clear of it. If you expect to head off-trail, wear long pants as an additional precaution.

A more odious problem is Lyme disease, borne by tiny deer ticks. Southern New England is not only the prime territory for the disease, it is the place where it was first diagnosed (in eponymous Lyme, Connecticut). Wearing long pants— especially long pants tucked into your socks—is a good preventive measure against ticks, but it is no sure thing. After a day in the backcountry, particularly if you've been walking or biking through long grass and underbrush, check yourself thoroughly for ticks. And if you've got kids, be sure to check them, too.

Last of all, and the rarest of the potential health hazards, is rabies. Over the past 10 years, rabies has been spreading northward from New Jersey into southern New England. The disease is spread by animal saliva and is always fatal if left untreated in humans. Infected animals tend to display erratic aggressive behavior, so you're best off keeping a safe distance between yourself and any wild animal you may encounter. If you are bitten, wash the wound as soon you can and seek immediate medical attention. Treatment for the disease is no longer as painful as it once was, but still involves a series of shots.

So who are you going to call in an emergency? Throughout the region, ☎ **911** is the general emergency number. A local forest, park, or wildlife-refuge ranger can also be an invaluable resource. Particularly in the era of cellular-phone technology, knowing the phone number of the headquarters of the park, forest, or refuge you're in may prove the surest way to get a quick response to an emergency. Always stop in at a park's headquarters before heading out and find out who to call in case of an emergency.

I don't mean to employ scare tactics here. The vast majority of outdoor outings in southern New England come off smoothly, with only a few sore muscles to worry about after a day of activity. The chances of your encountering a serious problem are minimal. By taking a few, simple precautions, you'll not only be able to reduce risks, you'll also raise the enjoyment factor of your trip.

Getting Underway: A Primer

In this section, I've included write-ups of only the principal sports found throughout the region. That does not mean that other activities such as ballooning, hang gliding, or scuba diving are being left out entirely. But in the big picture of the southern New England outdoors, they are minor players, and you'll find listings for them in the regional chapters, where appropriate.

Here, then, are some of the basics— equipment you'll need, skills you might need, hazards to expect, and so on—to get you up and running in any particular activity. Under each activity heading you'll also find a starter kit on where to go in the region. I have chosen to mention briefly the top four or five places in southern New England for each activity. As in any "best of" compilation, however, my choices are highly selective and, depending on your interests, you might favor a different spot. This chapter represents only the tip of the iceberg in exploring what's possible in the region. If there were nothing more to talk about, after all, there would be no need for seven additional chapters in this book. If a selection highlighted in this chapter whets your appetite, turn to the regional chapters for more detailed descriptions—or for other options not mentioned here.

Finally, I've also included useful resources—noteworthy outfitters, books, schools, and organizations. I'm just trying to rev your engine here; books have been written on the subjects that I've devoted only a few pages to. So if you need more information or guidance, I hope I've given you enough tools and leads to do the job. These resources also represent something of a best-of list. You'll find additional resources included in the regional chapters.

BIRD-WATCHING

Of all the activities possible in the outdoors of southern New England, none is more accessible than bird-watching. The environment—or variety of environments—is exceptionally conducive to attracting birds. Beaches, coastal wetlands and marshes, river valleys, forests of various compositions, mountains—there is a little something here for almost any bird imaginable, which is why well over 300 species have been sighted in the region.

With winters not as harsh as the winters of northern New England, resident species flourish. At the same time, migrant species pass through by the thousands during the changing of the seasons. During the course of an average year, something like 500,000 migrating waterfowl pass through the so-called Atlantic Flyway, a corridor of migration along the East Coast.

Zeroing in on the best bird-watching spots in the region is to some degree dependent on what kind of birds you're looking for. For birds that favor coastal environments, **Parker River National Wildlife Refuge** north of Boston and **Monomoy National Wildlife Refuge** off the southeast coast of Cape Cod would have to top my list.

Inland, **Quabbin Reservation,** surrounding Quabbin Reservoir in central Massachusetts, provides more than 100,000 acres for more than 250 species to fly wild. Prominent on anyone's Quabbin list should be the bald eagle. At last report, there were at least six resident pairs of eagles nesting on the reservation, and the coming of winter brings other eagles migrating from the north.

In the Berkshires, the hills and meadows of **Bartholomew's Cobble** are literally alive with sound of songbirds in the spring. The exotically decorated bobolink is a common sighting, as it nests in the tall meadow grasses.

Because of migration patterns, spring and fall are probably the best birding seasons in the region. But again, it depends on what you're looking for. Bald eagle sightings are most common in late fall and early winter, for example. Each state has one or more birding hotlines that announce unusual sightings: Connecticut: ☎ 203/254-3665; Rhode Island: ☎ 401/949-3870; Cape Cod: ☎ 508/349-9464; Western Massachusetts: ☎ 413/253-2218; Eastern Massachusetts: ☎ 781/ 259-8805.

One of the great things about bird-watching is that it is a relatively uncomplicated, inexpensive activity. The one big-ticket item should be a good pair of binoculars, but even these aren't necessary. All you need is a good pair of eyes and ears, and a decent field guide to help identify what you're seeing. Oh, yes—don't forget the sunblock and bug spray; they always help make a long outing more pleasant.

Books

The twin kings of the field-guide world are Audubon and Peterson. *A Field Guide to the Birds: A New Guide to All the Birds of Eastern and Central America,* by Roger Tory Peterson and Virginia Marie Peterson, and the *National Audubon Society Field Guide to North American Birds, Eastern Region,* by John Bull et al, are probably the best general guides. Peterson also publishes audio guides with eastern birdcalls in both cassette and CD versions.

Organizations

When you think bird-watching, it's hard not to think Audubon. The **National Audubon Society** (700 Broadway, New York, NY 10003; ☎ 212/979-3000) is essentially the captain of the Audubon ship, and is the best place to go for general birding information and publications, including *Audubon,* the society's first-rate magazine that goes to all members. For local and regional activities, contact the **Connecticut Audubon Society** (613 Riverville Rd., Greenwich, CT 06831; ☎ 203/869-5272), the **Massachusetts Audubon Society** (208 South Great Rd., Lincoln, MA 01773; ☎ 800/AUDUBON), or the **Audubon Society of Rhode Island** (12 Sanderson Rd., Smithfield, RI 02917; ☎ 401/949-5454).

BOARDSAILING

The best boardsailing in the region is undoubtedly off the southern and western shores of Cape Cod. **Nantucket Sound** and **Buzzard's Bay** are both exposed to the steady, southwestern winds of summer, and both are relatively shallow bodies of water, meaning the wind-driven swells can build up in a hurry. Along Nantucket Sound, **Kalmus Beach** south of Hyannis is considered a boardsailing mecca, but its renown can also draw crowds on weekends. If Kalmus is too busy, there are plenty of other beaches along the Cape's southern shore that can provide a decent launching pad.

If you're just learning how to sail, of course, the big winds and waves of the Cape are going to be more intimidating than inviting. You'll probably do better in more protected waters, such as **Duxbury Bay** south of Boston, **Edgartown Harbor** on Martha's Vineyard, or **Nantucket Harbor.**

A big bonus of sailing in Nantucket Sound and Buzzard's Bay is that summer water temperatures there usually climb into the 70s. If you plan to spend extended time in the water, you'll still want some

kind of wet-suit protection, but on a typically windy, sunny day you can easily spend a couple of hours on the water without getting uncomfortably chilled. The same can't be said about sailing in Cape Cod Bay, in the ocean off the Cape, or north of Boston. Water temperatures in these locations rarely rise above the low 60s, and are often in the 50s.

Instruction

Nauset Sports (Route 6A, Orleans, MA 02653; ☎ 508/255-4742) offers rentals and instruction on the Cape. On Martha's Vineyard, the place for rentals and instruction is **Wind's Up** (199 Beach Rd., Vineyard Haven, MA 02568; ☎ 508/693-4252). On Nantucket, head to **Force 5** (☎ 508/228-0700) on Jetties Beach. In Rhode Island, **Island Windsurfing** (86 Aquidneck Ave., Middletown, RI 02842; ☎ 401/846-4421) offers rentals and lessons for all ability levels. **Sail Newport** (60 Fort Adams Dr., Newport, RI 02840; ☎ 401/846-1983) conducts 1-week classes for young people during July and August.

Books

Let's Go Windsurfing, by Algis Steponitis (Hearst Marine Books), leans heavily on illustrations to explain basic boardsailing techniques.

Charts

See "Sailing," below, for information on nautical charts.

CANOEING/FLATWATER KAYAKING

With plenty of ponds, lakes, and reservoirs with boat ramps, along with a variety of gently flowing rivers, the basic concept in southern New England is this: Have car with boat-rack and boat, will travel. It is pretty hard to travel more than, say, 10 miles in southern New England without passing some body of water that can make for at least a couple of hours of pleasant canoeing.

CHOOSING AN OUTFITTER

Before getting involved in an organized tour—most likely hiking or biking—there are a few questions you might want to ask the outfitter, or yourself, before signing up.

1. **What does it cost, and what's included?** The options vary considerably, particularly when it comes to lodging and meals. Overnights in elegant country inns, with full breakfasts and fancy dinners, may make a tour more expensive, but may also be well worth the price of admission. Ask about potential hidden costs, particularly transportation to and from the airport and equipment rentals.

2. **What level of fitness is required?** Many tours include options. On a typical day of bicycling, for example, a tour company might include two or three ride options ranging between 15 and 60 miles. You might not be fit enough to complete the 60-mile route, but if you think you can ride 15 miles, you're good to go. In general, then, you don't have to be a world-class triathlete to participate in tours in southern New England. But if you fall short of minimal fitness requirements, you're going to be miserable.

3. **What is the guide-to-guest ratio?** I'd say that on a cycling or hiking tour, a ratio of 10 guests for each guide is about the acceptable limit. But for other activities, the limit might be much lower. Use your own judgment. For example, would you want to go fly-fishing with a guide and 10 other anglers? I wouldn't.

4. **What are the guides' credentials?** Just being a good cyclist or hiker doesn't make a person a good guide. Ask about the guides' experience level and age. Ask about whether he or she is a naturalist; it's a real plus if someone can identify plant life or a birdcall when walking in the woods. Ask about certification by a professional organization. In some sports, such as rock climbing or sailing, such certification can be meaningful. Finally, ask about emergency medical training. Any guide lacking basic first-aid and CPR skills is simply not a guide.

5. **What equipment is required?** Bike-tour companies usually have bike and helmet rentals available, but you'll probably have to reserve a rental bike in advance. In most cases, you'll be expected to bring your own clothing and footwear, although there is the occasional outfitter that may have, say, hiking boots or rain gear to rent or borrow.

6. **What will the weather be like?** No outfitter, of course, can answer this question with precision. But when packing for the trip, you'll need to know what clothing to bring. Even in midsummer, the temperature at the top of Mt. Greylock in the Berkshires can drop into the 40s. Rainy weather is a possibility at almost any time of year anywhere in New England, so rain gear is a must. Trip itineraries might be modified if the weather is uncooperative, but don't expect any rainchecks.

7. **How far in advance do I need to book?** Plan on at least 7 weeks, possibly more. Some popular tours get filled up months in advance. On the other hand, tours are occasionally cancelled several weeks before the tour date if the bookings are insufficient.

8. **Who else will be in the group?** Some outfitters and tours cater to singles, some to seniors, some to families. If you're uncomfortable with the people in the group, you're missing out on one of the real advantages—companionship—of joining a group in the first place.

If I had a day to play on the water in southern New England and could be anywhere I wanted in an instant, I would probably choose one of the coastal ponds on Martha's Vineyard or Rhode Island. **Edgartown Great Pond** on the Vineyard and **Ninigret Pond** in Rhode Island are two of the most scenic, but they aren't alone. These places can be truly magical in the morning, with mists rising from the marshes. They're also great for bird-watching.

If I were to choose a river for a day of paddling, it would be either the **Housatonic** or **Farmington** in northwestern Connecticut. Both move at a manageable pace for canoeists of intermediate skill or better, and offer great scenery for continuous stretches of about 20 miles.

Overnight trips are possible on the **Connecticut** and **Housatonic** rivers, but in most cases, they require considerable planning. Both rivers are heavily dammed, and some of the portages are demanding—we're not talking about quick, 100-yard jaunts around a dam complex. So if you're ambitious and want to travel the full length of either river (about 140 miles for the Housatonic; more than 400 miles for the Connecticut from its start in northern Vermont), keep at least two things in mind. First, you'll have to make arrangements to portage, and that may require contacting the authority in charge of any particular dam. Second, the pace of both rivers slows considerably as they near Long Island Sound. You might be able to paddle more than 20 miles a day in the north, with the flow of the river helping you along. Plan on a lot more time and effort, however, as you go south.

For a good, 2-day paddle, probably the best section of the Connecticut is the 21-mile stretch from **Vernon Dam** to **Barton Cove.** About halfway along, there's a campground for boaters only at Munn's Cove. It is also possible to portage past Turner's Falls Dam below Barton Cove for another 20-mile paddle to Northampton.

If you were to pick an ideal time of year to go canoeing, it would probably be June. Water levels in rivers and streams are still relatively high, so you don't have to worry too much about getting stranded in shallows, as you might later in the summer or fall. By June, air and water temperatures have warmed up enough to be pleasant without being uncomfortably hot.

For paddling in lakes and ponds or in estuaries along the coast, water levels remain relatively constant throughout the year. Estuaries, of course, are fed by the tides, and you need to be alert, at any time of year, of tidal movements. Getting stranded for hours deep in some marsh is a real possibility if you fail to keep track of the tides.

One other thing to watch out for is wind, particularly if you're paddling on open shallow water. The sudden onset of a strong wind can kick up big waves in a hurry, and, particularly if the waves are coming at you broadside, this can become a treacherous situation. If you're planning to explore a lake or pond that's known to be exposed to wind, then the best time of day to go is in early morning, before the wind has had a chance to pick up steam.

What equipment do you need? Obviously you'll need a canoe (or kayak) and paddles, but you don't necessarily need to have your own gear. Canoe rentals are usually available in areas where canoeing is popular. There are, however, a couple of obvious drawbacks to renting a canoe. One is that your options are automatically limited; if you see a great place to paddle but there's no canoe-rental outlet nearby, you're out of luck. Second, you're not apt to get a high-performance vehicle when you rent. In most cases, that might not make a heck of a lot of difference. But if you're going to face any kind of rapids, having a well-balanced, maneuverable craft is a major bonus.

The basic day-trip gear list should include life jackets, sunblock, hat, rain gear, and plenty of fresh drinking water. A small dry sack—available at most out-door-supply stores—is also a good invest-ment. That way, you can bring along a camera, binoculars, and perhaps a dry item of clothing such as a fleece pullover, just in case you manage to tip over and become chilled.

When it comes to the question of whether you need a guide, there are actu-ally three options to consider. The first is a fully guided trip, and there are several reasons why this option makes sense. If you're planning a river trip, there are a lot of logistics to consider—where to put in, where to take out, how to shuttle vehicles from the put-in point to the take-out, etc. It's awfully nice to have someone who knows the river take care of those logis-tics for you.

Furthermore, a guide can keep you apprised of the nuances of the river and possible hazards, including rapids, sweepers, shallows, or branches of the river that may take you far off your intended course. And if you are a less than expert paddler, a guide can provide helpful instructional tips.

A second option is a self-guided trip. In this case, an outfitter supplies all the necessary gear, arranges for a pickup at the take-out, and can give you a rundown of just what to expect on your trip. A self-guided trip is usually less expensive, and is a good option for experienced paddlers who don't happen to have their own canoes with them.

Finally, of course, you can simply head out on your own. If you're paddling on a still body of water—a pond or a lake—this is a sensible way to go. If you're able to keep track of where you started from, you shouldn't have to worry too much about getting lost. The great advantage to going on your own, of course, is the flexibility. You can go where you want, on your schedule. Still, no matter where you go, it's smart to acquire some local knowledge if you can get it. If there's a local outdoor shop around, drop in and ask a few questions.

Quirky currents, characteristic weather patterns, various legal restrictions (for example, in some areas, beaching your boat is not permitted), are the kind of things worth knowing before heading out.

One of the trickiest issues you must deal with in canoeing, particularly if you're paddling in open water, is the wind. A sudden surge of wind can quick-ly turn a seemingly benign lake into a treacherous body of water. If you're plan-ning an outing on a body of water exposed to wind—and the coastal ponds I highly recommend are extremely exposed—I'd suggest setting out in the early morning, when the wind is usually light. Whenever you go, however, avoid getting caught miles from your destina-tion with a strong headwind blowing. I guarantee you that having to paddle for a couple of hours into 1- to 2-foot seas is one of the most exhausting things you'll ever do.

Outfitters

Clarke Outdoors (163 Route 7, Cornwall, CT 06753; ☎ **860/672-6365**) guides day trips and arranges self-guided trips along the Housatonic in northwest-ern Connecticut. In Massachusetts, the place to go is **Gaffer's Outdoors** (216 Main St., Sheffield, MA 01257; ☎ **413/229-0063**). **Adventure In, Adventure Out** (Box 474, Monson, MA 01057; ☎ **413/283-2857**), an organization that focuses on environmental education as well as recreation, leads day trips (and sometimes moonlight trips) for flatwater canoeists and kayakers on the Quaboag and other rivers.

Instruction

In addition to Clarke Outdoors (see "Outfitters," above), **Charles River Canoe & Kayak** (2401 Commonwealth Ave., Newton, MA 02466; ☎ **617/965-5110**) offers instructional programs in the Boston area.

Books

The *Quiet Water Canoe Guide: Massachusetts, Connecticut, Rhode Island,* by Alex Wilson (AMC Books), is a great guide to lakes and ponds in the region. The Appalachian Mountain Club's *River Guide: Massachusetts, Connecticut, Rhode Island* (AMC Books) is a useful handbook to getting started on river paddling in the area.

Organizations

Local chapters of the **Appalachian Mountain Club** (5 Joy St., Boston, MA 01208; ☎ **617/523-0655**) regularly organize canoeing and kayaking trips in the region; its Southeastern Massachusetts chapter's Web site (**www.cris.com/~Ndrma/canoe.htm**) offers numerous tips on canoeing in the area. The club is also a good clearinghouse for general information on the New England outdoors. The Rhode Island Canoe/Kayak Association (**www.ricka.org/**) offers information on canoeing and kayaking on its Web site. Among its many, wide-ranging activities, the **American Canoe Association** (7432 Alban Station Blvd., Suite B-232, Arlington, VA 22150; ☎ **703/451-0141;** www.aca-paddler.org) certifies instructors, promotes river conservation, and generally acts as a clearinghouse for paddling information. The ACA publishes *Paddler* magazine.

CROSS-COUNTRY SKIING

Wherever there is snow, there exists the possibility of cross-country skiing (also known as Nordic skiing). In some ways, it is the most versatile and accessible of all the outdoor activities. On cross-country skis, you can go places you can't even go when hiking in summer or fall. Streams freeze, making stream crossings easier. Underbrush in the forest lies dormant and covered in snow, making for easier off-trail exploring. And, in some ways, it's harder to get lost when you do venture off-trail because it's usually easy to find your way back—a clearly defined set of tracks left in the snow shows the way. Perhaps the only activity more versatile and accessible is cross-country skiing's cousin, snowshoeing. Almost anywhere that you can go cross-country skiing, you can go snowshoeing.

Cross-country skiing divides basically into two types—backcountry skiing and track skiing. The former is the go-anywhere sport described above. The latter requires groomed tracks at a cross-country skiing (or touring) center. While the two are obviously related, they are also very different.

In some ways, the difference is comparable to the difference between mountain biking and road biking. Track skiing, like road biking, tends to be faster and more continuously aerobic. Equipment, as in road biking, tends to be lighter and more streamlined. Track skiing itself has two subcategories—classical skiing, with its straight-ahead, kick-and-glide motions, and skate skiing, where skiers move forward using side-to-side skating motion. I highly recommend the latter; once you get the hang of it, it's much faster than classical skiing.

Backcountry skiing is less clearly defined. It could include anything from cruising around on open meadows behind your house to wandering deep in the woods on forest roads to descending steep, mountainous trails on telemark skis. But it's probably fair to say that for most people, backcountry skiing falls somewhere in the middle, an activity comparable to going for a hike in the woods in winter.

It should almost go without saying that the best cross-country skiing in southern New England will be found in the area with the most abundant natural snowfall. On that score, the Berkshires must rank at the top of the heap. **Notchview Reservation, October Mountain State Forest,** and **Savoy Mountain State Forest** are particularly good areas to spend a few hours in the backcountry. In addition to having extensive trail networks, all are blessed with relatively high elevation, where colder temperatures are a key factor in improving snow quality. **Northfield Mountain Recreation Center** in central Massachusetts is another area with a good trail network and relatively high elevation.

Unfortunately, cross-country ski centers, in southern New England and elsewhere, don't usually have the extensive snowmaking systems that downhill ski areas do. So, while downhill ski areas can still keep more than three-quarters of their trails covered when the natural snow cover is lean, cross-country ski centers aren't so lucky. A handful of ski centers—most notably the **Weston Ski Track** near Boston—do have limited snowmaking, but most must rely on natural snowfall.

The first rule of cross-country skiing in New England should be fairly obvious by now: Go where there's snow. Even in the snowy Berkshires, this can be an iffy proposition in some winters. But generally speaking, the mid-winter months of January and February are the most reliable months for finding decent snow coverage. Keep tuned to the weather, too, particularly if you can be flexible in your travel planning. If there has been a lot of snow, or the forecast is for snow, you're going to have a much more enjoyable skiing experience.

It is one of the real shortcomings of cross-country skiing that, for a relatively simple sport, it can be incredible gear intensive. You would think you could get one pair of skis, one pair of boots, and one pair of poles and you'd be good to go. But because cross-country skiing is not a single sport, but many, you need all sorts of equipment. Classical track skiing, skate skiing, backcountry touring, telemarking—you might think (or wish) that one setup would work for everything. It just isn't so. For example, skate skis and boots would flounder in the deep snow or ice of the backcountry. Conversely, using a backcountry-touring setup on groomed tracks would be like driving a tank on the highway.

So before you go—or before you buy or rent gear—decide what kind of skiing you want to do and make sure you get the right gear for the job. Some setups are more versatile than others are. Light touring gear works reasonably well for track skiing and for skiing on backcountry trails, as long as you don't expect to encounter difficult snow conditions or rugged terrain.

If you do plan to spend time in the mountainous backcountry, with a lot of climbs and descents, you'll probably want a more robust pair of skis with metal edges. You'll also want to make sure your skis have reasonably robust bindings. The light, toe-connected bindings you find on most track skis are liable to break under the extra stress of going up and down hills. And if you expect to encounter a lot of long, steep uphills, you'll want climbing skins, which attach to the bottoms of your skis and grip the snow so that you can easily walk straight uphill. Whatever gear setup you do choose, make sure all of it is compatible. Certain boots won't fit into certain bindings, and there is no better way to spoil an outing than to discover at the trailhead that your boots won't fit into your bindings.

Clothing yourself properly can be a tricky thing, particularly for backcountry skiing. You don't want to be cold, but overheating can be a problem, too, not only because it consumes excess energy, but also because you'll sweat, which in turn will cause you to become chilled. Many people, overly worried about being cold, overdress while cross-country skiing, unaware of how quickly they can warm up while engaged in such vigorous exercise. The next thing they know, they're sweating profusely, only to become more prone to being chilled as a result.

The solution is layering. A typical layering scenario for a day of backcountry skiing might go like this: Start with a polypropylene shirt (good for wicking away sweat from your skin), cover that with a second, light layer, then a fleece vest, and finally a shell for outerwear. A shell with zippered vents is a particularly good idea; open the vents to cool off, and close the vents to stay warm. Also, bring a comfortable wool or fleece hat—most of your body heat is lost through your head.

As you warm up, simply remove layers and stow them in a day pack. As you become chilled, add layers. You might want to bring along two pairs of gloves, if there's room in your pack—a thin pair for when you're warm, and a well-insulated pair for when you're cold.

Dressing right for track skiing is less complicated, particularly in light of the fact that you are usually not far from a lodge or warming hut. You might notice experienced, cross-country jocks gliding around the trails in what looks to be little more than Lycra underwear. The fact of the matter is that track skiing at a high aerobic rate can produce an incredible amount of body heat. Once you've warmed up, it's amazing how comfortable you can feel, even on a sub-freezing day, in just one thin layer.

Whether track skiing or backcountry skiing, be sure to drink plenty of water. Although winter might not bring on the same kind of thirst that summer heat can, you can become dehydrated just as quickly in winter as in summer. In fact, some doctors say that your system consumes more water in winter, as the lungs try to make up for the lack of moisture in the typically drier, cold air. So keep drinking even if you don't think you're thirsty.

One bonus of cross-country skiing is that the cost, once you've geared up, is minimal. Backcountry skiing is in most cases a freebie, although you might have to pay a nominal parking or entry charge at some areas. And rare is the cross-country center that charges more than $12 for a daily trail pass.

Instruction

Any Nordic ski center should have instructors to teach you the basics of track skiing. The **Weston Ski Track** (200 Park Rd., Weston, MA 02493; ☎ **781/ 891-6575**) is a good place to go, as is **Brodie Mountain Cross Country**

Touring Center (Route 7, New Ashford, MA 01237; ☎ **413/443-4752**). As far as backcountry basics are concerned, Nordic centers may be of some help, but backcountry skiing instruction in New England is pretty ad hoc. You'll probably have to rely on the expertise of those with whom you go touring, or simply figure it all out on your own through trial and error.

Books & Web Sites

Cross Country Skiing New England, by Lyn and Tony Chamberlain (Globe Pequot Press), is a good introduction to cross-country skiing in both southern and northern New England. *Classic Backcountry Skiing,* by David Goodman (Appalachian Mountain Club), might be hard to find, but it's a good guide to backcountry skiing throughout New England.

The Alpine Zone (**www.alpinezone. com/**) is an exceptionally good source of information on both skiing and hiking activities in southern New England. It offers links, a message board, trip reports, weather forecasts, and information on lodging.

Maps

The **U.S. Geological Survey** and **Topaz** (see "Maps" under "Hiking/Backpacking," below) are your best bets for topographical maps. *A note of warning:* Even in well-settled southern New England (particularly in the Berkshires) it is possible to get incredibly lost, particularly if you ski off marked trails. Getting lost on a summer hike can be annoying, but in winter it can literally be life threatening. Get good maps and be absolutely sure where you're going if you head off-trail.

DOWNHILL SKIING/ SNOWBOARDING

Big mountains do not exist in southern New England as they do farther north, nor do big-mountain snows or big-mountain resorts. Yet there are a number of reasons why skiing in southern New England might be preferable. There is something to be said for the relaxed intimacy of skiing at a smaller ski area, particularly if you've got a bunch of kids in tow.

For starters, prices are commensurately lower at smaller ski areas. If you are a novice or intermediate skier who isn't likely to ski long steep runs anyway, why spend an extra $20 or more a day for trails and lifts you'll never use? The big-mountain experience can also be a little misleading, if you look at the way lifts are laid out in Vermont and New Hampshire. The majority of those runs cover 1,200 vertical feet or less, and the average skier rarely tackles a run much more vertical than that. Well, you can find the same kind of vertical in the Berkshires; the mountains might be smaller, but the runs aren't necessarily shorter.

The big selling point for smaller ski areas, however, is unquestionably character. I have skied all over the world, but skiing at a resort like **Jiminy Peak** or **Catamount** renders the unrivaled feeling of coming home. All services—rentals, food, ski school, parking, even lodging—are right at the base of the lifts. A low-key, family atmosphere rules. These are the kinds of places I like coming with first-time skiers; there's a lot less intimidation (in the form of fast skiers and steep slopes) built into smaller ski areas than you inherently find at big-mountain resorts. Pocket-sized areas like **Bousquet** or **Mohawk Mountain** in Connecticut are that much less intimidating

And the skiing is often pretty darned good. For all its small-resort character, for example, Jiminy Peak has some serious, big-mountain steeps. If you like long, cruising runs, **Brodie Mountain,** with the region's longest vertical drop of 1,250 feet, is the place to go. Snowmaking throughout the region is extensive, with 90% coverage being more the norm than the exception. So even when Mother Nature has not been forthcoming, you can expect to find decent snow from December into March.

Where southern New England areas do come up short, compared to their northern neighbors, is in slope-side lodging. Jiminy Peak has a slope-side hotel, but elsewhere the pickings are slim. You can regard this as a plus or a minus. If you're trying to mobilize a family for a day of skiing, it's a lot easier to dress up the kids and walk right out the door to the slopes. At the same time, there is something satisfying about skiing on mountains not cluttered up with condos alongside the trails. Also, staying away from the slopes at a centuries-old country inn—an easy find in southern New England—can be a lot more pleasant and memorable than shacking up in some sterile condo that just happens to be conveniently located.

Most ski areas have rental shops right at the base of the mountain, so all you need to go skiing or snowboarding is warm clothing. Every ski area has some kind of ski school, too, so you don't even have to know what you're doing when you show up. Someone will teach you how. If you're a beginner, ask about beginner packages that include lifts, lessons, and rentals. Such packages are usually dirt cheap; ski areas are looking to get more people hooked on the sport, and they don't want price to be a barrier—at least at first.

Snowmaking has helped guarantee a ski season in southern New England that runs from December into March. Depending on how cold the weather is—sub-zero temperatures being essential for snowmaking—or how abundant the natural snowfall, the season might extend somewhat in either direction. But if you expect to go skiing in southern New England in early December or April, expect the action to be limited.

The most popular times of the year for skiing are between Christmas and New Year's, and on President's Day weekend. At those times, you might find all that wonderful, small-area intimacy overcome by excess humanity. On the other hand, if you're able to get away for a mid-week outing, you might find the ski areas so deserted that you may actually feel a little bit lonely. To encourage mid-week business, ski areas often package together deals with local inns that are incredibly reasonable. If you thought skiing was expensive—which it can be—check out a mid-week package in the Berkshires.

Incidentally, pretty much all the downhill terrain in southern New England is open to snowboarders and skiers alike. Even so-called "terrain parks," once strictly the province of snowboarders, are usually open to skiers as well.

Books

There are a number of instructional manuals for downhill skiing, but for my money, the best of the bunch is *Breakthrough on Skis,* by Lito Tejada-Flores (Vintage Books). It's also available in a video format.

FISHING

Two categories of fishing are available in southern New England—freshwater fishing and saltwater fishing. The main game fish in freshwater streams, rivers, lakes, and ponds are trout and bass, whereas the main saltwater game fish are bluefish and striped bass. Of course, there are many, many other types of fish to be caught out there; there's a lot of water in New England. But when most sport fishermen head out onto the water, the four species mentioned above are mainly what they're after.

Freshwater fishermen can thank the states of Connecticut and Massachusetts in particular for ambitious fish-stocking programs. There may be a lot of other fishermen out there, but extensive stocking ensures there are a lot of fish, too. Rainbow trout, brown trout, and smallmouth bass are the principal species stocked, although salmon are also stocked in some bodies of water. A few native (as in non-stocked) fish still survive in the waters of southern New England,

and many dedicated fly fishermen insist that landing a native trout, no matter how small, is a real accomplishment. Native fish, they say, are smarter about evading the catch.

Three rivers in the region deserve special mention—the **Deerfield** in northwestern Massachusetts, and the **Farmington** and **Housatonic** in northwestern Connecticut. All have widespread reputations within the community of fly fishermen, and there are a few reasons they're great rivers to fish. For starters, of course, they are well stocked. Second, all three rivers have long catch-and-release areas, meaning the fish that live there get to stay there and become larger fish and can be caught by other anglers on other days.

Third, the environmental components of the rivers—the stream beds, the insect life, the flow and temperature of the water, etc.—are ideal for fish to thrive in. Fourth, the river water is surprisingly clear and clean. This is not something that could have been said 20 years ago, particularly in the case of the Housatonic. But clean-up efforts on many rivers in southern New England have been remarkably successful. Even the **Blackstone River,** which runs through Worcester and Providence and was once reputed to be one of the most polluted rivers in America, can now claim to be a reasonably good fishery.

Finally, the Deerfield, Farmington, and Housatonic are attractive settings in which to fish. When you're standing around waist-deep in cold water and maybe or maybe not hooking your dream fish, it makes a difference to be able to look up at scenery that can steal your breath away.

Of course, rivers aren't the only place to find good freshwater fishing. Ask any three fishermen in southern New England what their favorite pond or lake is for fishing, and you're apt to get three different answers. Who knows—there is probably some tiny, undiscovered pond out there with a 15-pound monster trout waiting to be caught. But until that pond is discovered, you'll have to satisfy yourself with these hot spots:

Twin Lakes in northwestern Connecticut has a reputation for producing trophy-sized trout. In eastern Connecticut, **Mashapaug Lake** has produced record largemouth bass. The bass fishing on **Worden's Pond** in central Rhode Island is also reputed to be top-notch. How good the fishing in any of these places is—and the same goes for rivers and streams—largely depends on water temperature. In general, trout are more active in cool water (in the 50s), whereas bass prefer warmer water. Midsummer, then, is usually better for bass fishing, and the trout action is often better in spring and fall.

The hot sport in the angling world these days is saltwater fly-fishing. In some ways, saltwater "fly"-fishing is a misnomer. The lures for saltwater fly-fishing are usually designed to imitate small baitfish rather than insects. Yet the fishing gear and technique—the basic casting method and the relatively light tackle—are close cousins to the gear and technique used in freshwater fly-fishing. If you really want to impress your buddies, tell them about the 15-pound striper you reeled in on an 8-pound test line off the Monomoy Islands near Cape Cod.

Fly-fishing, of course, isn't the only way to go after saltwater fish; in fact, saltwater fly fishermen are a considerable minority among all the fishermen out on the water. Most fishermen use heavier, spinning gear and troll for their catch. As previously noted, bluefish and striped bass are the main game fish, but there are plenty of other fish out there. Fishermen willing to go well offshore—in craft sturdy enough to do so—can fish for tuna, shark, cod, and halibut.

The remarkably successful clean-up of **Boston Harbor** has returned this once horribly polluted body of water into a hive of fishing activity. The fishing near **Monomoy National Wildlife Refuge** can also be superb. For deep-sea fishing, **Gloucester,** with fishing roots that reach back centuries, is an excellent harbor to choose as your starting point.

To fish offshore, or even relatively close to shore, obviously requires a boat. Fear not if you don't happen to have your own; fishing charters operate out of marinas all along the southern New England coast, from Stamford to Gloucester. I'd recommend staying away from the bigger boats—sometimes called "party" boats—on which dozens of anglers, side by side, hang over the rails. You stand a reasonable chance of catching plenty of fish, but somehow the sport gets lost in the process. Charter boats that typically carry six passengers or less aren't cheap, usually running $125 a person and up for a half-day of fishing or more, but the extra expense is worth it.

There is one other option—surfcasting. Probably the greatest shortcoming of surfcasting is the lack of mobility; surfcasters generally pick a spot on the beach and stay there, hoping that schools of fish might come their way. But the most successful surfcasters don't simply rely on hope and luck. They stay tuned to fishing reports on local radio stations and are aware of when and where schools of bluefish are running. Among the surfcasting hot spots in southern New England are **Parker National Wildlife Refuge** north of Boston, **Cape Poge** on Martha's Vineyard, and **Ninigret Conservation Area** on the southern shore of Rhode Island. Even if you don't catch a fish, there is something supremely peaceful about standing on the beach with your pole planted in the sand and with the sound of the surf rolling in.

Guides & Outfitters

Points North (Box 146, Adams, MA 01220; ☎ 413/743-4030) is the premier guiding service for the Deerfield River, as well as other rivers in western Massachusetts. Also head to Points North for Orvis equipment and hand-tied flies. **Housatonic River Outfitters** (Route 128, West Cornwall, CT 06796; ☎ 860/672-1010) is exactly what its name suggests, an outfitter and guide service for the Housatonic River. If you show up gearless and happen to get an urge to fish, Housatonic River Outfitters will also rent you everything you need to get out on the river.

Charters

Dozens—perhaps hundreds—of boats are available in marinas throughout coastal southern New England for fishing charters. In Rhode Island, call the **Rhode Island Party & Charterboat Association** (☎ **401/737-5812**) for information on charters. For fishing charters in the other southern New England states, check out the charter information in the regional chapters, or call state tourism offices for a list of charter contacts.

Instruction

Both **Points North** and **Housatonic River Outfitters** offer clinics in freshwater fly-fishing. For saltwater fly-fishing instruction, **Fishing the Cape** (Harwich Commons, East Harwich, MA 02645; ☎ **508/432-1200** or ☎ 800/235-9763 for Orvis Fishing School reservations) conducts 2½-day courses on the Cape under the Orvis aegis.

Books

Trout Streams of Southern New England, by Tom Fuller (Countryman Press), describes where and how to successfully fish the rivers and streams in the region. *Housatonic River: Fly Fishing Guide,* by Jeff Passante (Frank Amato Publications), gets even more specific, giving detailed descriptions of the Housatonic and its hatches. If you're into surfcasting, *Striper Surf,* by Frank Daignault (Globe Pequot), will not only help you find hot spots, but also stoke your passion for the sport.

Organizations

Trout Unlimited (150 Wilson Blvd., Suite 310, Arlington, VA 22209; ☎ **703/522-0200**) is primarily devoted to the protection and conservation of fisheries in North America. The organization also publishes *Trout* magazine.

HIKING/BACKPACKING

Hiking is both simplistic and pure. You don't need to learn any complex skills to be able to hike. If you can put one foot in front of the other, you are a hiker. You don't need to invest hundreds or thousands of dollars in fancy hiking gear—unless you choose to do so, of course. For the most part, you don't have to pay an admission fee to hike. You can hike almost any time of year, even in the deep snow of winter; just put on a pair of snowshoes, and you're good to go. Great hikes are everywhere; I'll bet you that within an hour of your home, there are several fine walks in the woods that you didn't even know about. There are no age restrictions involved. It seems to me that in many places I hike, kids and seniors outnumber the 20- to 50-something crowd.

Hiking, in short, is the sport for everyone and anyone. Heck, there are many parks, state forests, and refuges with trails that are handicapped-accessible. So although you might be able to drum up excuses not to get involved in many activities in the outdoors of southern New England, you'd be hard-pressed to come up with an excuse not to go hiking.

Backpacking is a different story. I still think it is incredibly accessible to most people, but it does require a certain level of fitness and a certain amount of gear. It might not require any great skills, but common sense and backcountry smarts go a long way toward making an overnight trek in the mountains safer and more enjoyable. Often, you learn the nuances of smart backpacking the hard way—by doing something wrong before learning how to do it right. I know; I am a master of doing things wrong. I've had campsites raided by bears and raccoons because I failed to stow away my food properly. I've suffered through miserable nights in a tent because I failed to lay down a ground cloth. I've suffered a sore back because I didn't bother to adjust my backpack to fit properly. And so on.

Southern New England might lack the majestic, mountain wilderness that you'll find in northern New England, but don't sell it short as a hiking destination. Two aspects of southern New England hiking particularly appeal to me. The first is accessibility. Hitting the trail does not require a long drive to some remote trailhead. Within 2 hours of Midtown New York, for example, you can be deep in the forests of western Connecticut, embarking on a 100-mile backpack north through the Berkshires. In less than a half-hour from downtown Boston, you can be scrambling around Blue Hills Reservation, with something like 200 miles of hiking trails.

The other thing I like about southern New England hiking is that it comes in so many different forms. A hike in the hills and forests of the Berkshires is a completely different experience from a long walk along the beach on Cape Cod or Martha's Vineyard. From dunes and marshes to mountaintop vistas—that kind of variety in such close proximity is a rare find anywhere in North America.

Certainly for strenuous mountain hiking, with climbs of more than 1,000 vertical feet, the Berkshires are the place to go. What makes **Mt. Greylock Reservation,** north of Pittsfield, a premier hiking spot is not so much its trail network, which is vast, but that Mt. Greylock is made up of several different micro-environments. Of particular interest to me is the so-called Hopper, a glacial cirque that is being preserved in a pristine, natural state.

The views from Mt. Greylock are stunning, as you might expect on the highest mountain in southern New England. But in some ways, I find the views from **Mt. Everett** and **Race Mountain** in the southern Berkshires even more satisfying. The views to the west, of the Taconic and Catskill Mountains, are particularly impressive from Mt. Everett. And you don't have to share the view with

motorists who have driven to the top, as you do on the summit of Mt. Greylock.

Not all great hikes, of course, involve reaching summits with sweeping views. For a long, quiet walk in the woods, much of it along the shores of a pond, I'd probably head for the loop around **Breakneck Pond** in Bigelow State Park in eastern Connecticut. In fact, eastern Connecticut in general, with three large state forests (**Pachaug, Natchaug,** and **Cockaponset**), is a surprisingly easy place to lose yourself in the woods for a while.

Finally, there are the beaches—long, undeveloped stretches of 6 miles and more. A walk on the beach might not fit into the typical notion of a hike, which so often conjures up images of mountains and woods. But I like the simplicity of it—land on one side, sea on the other. And I like the rhythmic sound of waves rolling in, as soul-soothing a sound as there is in this world. Forced to choose a couple of favorite places for beach walks, I'd probably have to go with **Cape Poge Wildlife Refuge** on Martha's Vineyard and **Parker River National Wildlife Refuge** on Plum Island north of Boston.

Any hike, whether in the mountains or at the edge of the ocean, is always more enjoyable if you're in reasonably good shape. Obviously, the more strenuous the hike, the higher your level of fitness should be. Start easy, then, and work your way up. Unless you feel confident that you're in great shape, for example, I wouldn't recommend choosing a hike up Mt. Greylock as your introduction to hiking in the Berkshires. Start with a 2- or 3-mile hike on more gentle terrain, assess how you feel afterward, then go on to something more challenging if you think you're up to it.

Don't assume that all the hard work on a hike is in the climbing. Hiking downhill, while it may be less aerobically taxing, can be surprisingly stressful on your muscles and bones. The sorest I have ever been after a hike was after I rushed down a steep slope near Winter Park, Colorado. For the next few days, I felt as if concrete had been poured into my quadriceps.

To make the most of whatever your fitness level might be, when you go out on any hike, be sure to bring along plenty of drinking water and snacks to munch on. Dehydration can cause cramps and fatigue, and once you become dehydrated, you can't simply drink a gallon of water and expect to be good to go. It takes a while for all that water to migrate to the parts of the body where it's needed.

Many people, of course, look to hiking as a means to lose weight. As a result, they are reluctant to eat much on the trail. You can probably get away without eating on a hike of an hour or less. But for any hike much longer than that, you'll need fuel to prevent your body from shutting down (or bonking) after a couple of hours on the trail. Gorp, the ubiquitous hiker's snack of raisins, nuts, and chocolate, is perfect for a couple of reasons. It's easy to eat on the go, and it's high in carbohydrates, the key component to getting energy-boosting glycogen to the muscles quickly.

Hiking, as I've said, is a fairly easy sport to get geared up for. If you plan to do a fair amount of hiking, or if you're thinking of an extended backcountry trip, I would highly recommend getting a pair of sturdy hiking boots. Now I've seen people successfully complete week-long backpacking trips in sneakers, so I'm not saying hiking boots are essential. But the extra support, a sole that provides good traction through mud and over rocks, and a reinforced toe to avert the pain that comes from accidentally (and inevitably) kicking roots and rocks—all these are features you'll come to appreciate in a good pair of boots.

Leather, waterproof boots will cost at least $100, although you can get a decent (although not necessarily durable) pair of light hiking boots for less. And as long as you're investing in a pair of boots, you might as well invest in some decent socks, too. Cotton socks are usually a bad idea; they tend to bunch up inside a boot and get damp (with water or sweat). As a result, the skin of your feet can chafe and peel, eventually causing painful blisters. Outdoor stores sell a variety of synthetic-material socks that do a much better job than cotton of wicking moisture away from the foot and reducing friction within the boot that might cause blisters. When in doubt, simply go with a reliable pair of wool socks.

Other than that, all you really need is the standard outdoor gear—rainwear, hat, multi-tool knife, sunblock, and a small pack to carry it all in. As long as you've got a pack, you might as well toss in a few extras: binoculars, a camera, and maybe a fancy picnic lunch. If you're hiking in the cooler weather of spring or fall, of course, you'll need extra clothing. Several thin layers of clothing are preferable to, say, a single, insulated jacket. Layering allows you to make small clothing adjustments as the air temperature or your body temperature changes. If you do it right, you'll never be too hot or too cold.

Backpacking, of course, has far greater gear requirements. In addition to good hiking boots, the main thing you need is a good pack. There are many, many packs out there. Packs come in different sizes, different framing (internal or external), and with different configurations of compartments and pockets. Many come with attachments to hold such items as technical climbing gear, ice axes, and skis. Most have an array of straps that can be cinched up or loosened to improve the fit of the pack on your back.

So it's up to you to decide what size and type of pack you need and to make sure you don't spend more for a pack that's too big or one with lots of extras you'll never use. The critical issue is to find a pack that fits well, and toward that end, a knowledgeable salesperson can go a long way. You want a pack that fits snugly on your back, that's comfortable, and that doesn't shift or sway as you walk. No matter what kind of pack you get, you can expect it to weigh somewhere between 30 and 50 pounds when you hit the trail. With a pack that fits properly, that's a burden you ought to be able to haul without too much discomfort. With an ill-fitting pack, you'll feel like you're hauling around 300 pounds.

Exactly what is that 30- to 50-pound load composed of? I always find it hard to pack light, but it's amazing how little you can get by with. For a 3-day trip, you don't need three changes of clothes, for example. (In fact, among the great pleasures of backpacking are the shower and clean clothes at the end of a trip.) Be willing to leave behind that extra shirt and those three extra camera lenses. For a list of essentials, check out the "Backpacker's Equipment List" on page 22. The one item you must have is a decent water filter, available at most good outdoor stores. Even deep in the woods and high in the mountains, where crystal-clear streams have a look of undefiled purity, you need to be sure to filter (or boil for at least 10 minutes) any water you expect to drink.

Don't expect to find many week-long treks in the wilderness in southern New England, but also don't assume no great backpacking trips are out there. The **Appalachian Trail** (AT) runs for about 140 miles through Connecticut and Massachusetts, and it comes with a distinct bonus. It is a hikers-only trail, meaning mountain bikers and horseback riders are supposedly not allowed. If I were to spend 3 days hiking the AT in southern New England, I'd probably focus on the southern Berkshires, where the trail runs through Sages Ravine before climbing over Race Mountain and Mt. Everett. There is a real sense of wilderness here.

The Appalachian Trail is not the only long trail that traverses the region. To the east is the **Metacomet–Monadnock Trail,** which runs north from around Meriden, Connecticut for about 150 miles to the New Hampshire border, on its way to New Hampshire's Mt. Monadnock. It doesn't pass through as much wild country as does the AT, but sections of the trail through central Massachusetts, particularly in crossing the Holyoke Range, give the AT a run for its money.

Still farther east is Massachusetts's **Midstate Trail,** which connects with Rhode Island's **North-South Trail.** These trails, like the Metacomet–Monadnock Trail, pass through well-settled areas as well as undeveloped lands, so if you were to plan an extended trip, don't expect a nonstop wilderness experience. Still, by starting at the southern end of the North-South Trail and continuing on the Midstate Trail, you could go from the Rhode Island shore to New Hampshire. In fact, you could keep going right through New Hampshire all the way to Canada.

Outfitters

New England Hiking Holidays (Box 1648, North Conway, NH 03860; ☎ **800/869-0949** or 603/356-9696) leads 3-day, weekend trips in the Berkshires. Daily hiking distances generally range between 6 and 10 miles. **North Country Adventures** (1385 Bernardstown Rd., Greenfield, MA; ☎ **413-775-0080**) leads overnight trips on the Metacomet–Monadnock Trail.

Books & Web Sites

There are a number of good guidebooks on hiking in southern New England. *Hiking Southern New England,* by Rhonda and George Ostertag (Falcon Press), does a good job of mixing descriptive prose with nuts-and-bolts trail information and mileages. The *Connecticut Walk Book,* published by the Connecticut Forest and Parks Association, is something of a legend—*the* guide book to Connecticut hiking published by the organization primarily responsible for maintaining the state's blue-blazed trail network. The Appalachian Mountain Club's *Massachusetts & Rhode Island Hiking Guide* (AMC Books) makes for

BACKPACKER'S EQUIPMENT LIST

If you're just going out for 1 night, there are a few things here you might be able to do without. But for any extended trip, the list below includes what I'd recommend bringing along for a 2- or 3-day summer trip. If you're hiking with a group, of course, much of the gear can be divvied up. Things like cameras, binoculars, and books are heavy and technically not essential, but the enjoyment they add to a trip makes every extra ounce seem worthwhile.

COOKING & EATING

Food. You'll quickly grow sick of instant oatmeal, but as lightweight and filling food, it's hard to beat. Cheese, trail mix (gorp), and hard sausage are foods that keep reasonably well and are easy to eat on the go. Pasta—especially with those just-add-water sauces—is a good lightweight and filling dinner entree. For dessert, chocolate is a great minimal-bulk, high-energy food.

- [ ] water filter
- [ ] 2 quart-sized water bottles
- [ ] mess kit or cook set
- [ ] backpacking stove (GAZ-fueled stoves work well at all but sub-20° temperatures)
- [ ] matches (in a waterproof bag)
- [ ] scouring pad
- [ ] biodegradeable soap

- [ ] towel (to double as potholder)
- [ ] Ziploc bags, for storing food

SLEEPING

- [ ] light backpacking tent
- [ ] waterproof ground cloth
- [ ] sleeping bag rated to at least 20°
- [ ] sleeping pad

CLOTHING

- [ ] baseball cap
- [ ] wool ski cap
- [ ] extra socks
- [ ] extra shorts
- [ ] rainwear (top and bottom)
- [ ] fleece pullover
- [ ] extra T-shirt

---

pretty dry reading, but is an excellent just-the-facts guide book and includes precise trail mileages between trail junctions. The book also comes with a small but helpful collection of topographical maps. For a how-to manual, *Hiking and Backpacking,* by Karen Berger (W.W. Norton), does a great job of covering the basics.

The Leisurely Backpacker (**www. leisurelybackpacker.com/**) offers links to hiking clubs and organizations, outfitters, gear companies, and weather forecasting sites. It also features trip reports and gear reviews.

Maps

The **U.S. Geological Survey** is the chief producer of topographical maps for hikers and backpackers. Either call the USGS (☎ **800/ASK-USGS**) or check in at any well-stocked outdoor store for maps. **Topaz Outdoor Travel Maps,** available in many outdoor stores in the region, have an advantage over the usual USGS topo maps in that most are waterproof. The **Appalachian Mountain Club** (see "Organizations," below) and its affiliated chapters can also be a good source for maps.

Organizations

The **Appalachian Mountain Club** (5 Joy St., Boston, MA 01208; ☎ **617/523-0655;** www.outdoors.org/) is the king of hiking and backpacking organizations in America. The club is a major publisher of books on hiking and the outdoors, and

- [ ] long-sleeved, polypropylene under-shirt
- [ ] light gloves
- [ ] bandana
- [ ] sunglasses

ESSENTIALS

- [ ] maps
- [ ] compass
- [ ] sunscreen
- [ ] bug repellent
- [ ] toiletries
- [ ] headlamp
- [ ] multi-tool knife (e.g., Swiss Army knife)
- [ ] rope—at least 60 feet long, for hanging food
- [ ] toilet paper
- [ ] flashlight

FIRST-AID KIT

- [ ] 2-in. x 3-in. moleskin
- [ ] pair small shears

- [ ] thermometer
- [ ] safety pins
- [ ] OTC pain reliever (such as aspirin or acetaminophen)
- [ ] diarrhea pills
- [ ] antacid tablets
- [ ] sting relief pads
- [ ] iodine solution
- [ ] iodine ointment
- [ ] triple antibiotic ointment
- [ ] antiseptic towelettes
- [ ] single-edge razor blade
- [ ] 1-in. × 3-in. fabric bandages
- [ ] fabric knuckle bandages
- [ ] sterile wound closure strips
- [ ] 4-in. × 4-in. sterile gauze pads
- [ ] adhesive tape
- [ ] elastic bandage
- [ ] irrigation syringe
- [ ] wire mesh splint

its local chapters organize guided hikes and backpacking trips. The **Appalachian Trail Conference** (Box 807, Harper's Ferry, WV 25425; ☎ **304/535-6331**) can supply you with information on the Appalachian Trail.

HORSEBACK RIDING

There are plenty of great places to ride in southern New England, particularly in the state forests of Connecticut and Massachusetts. Of these, perhaps none are more inviting than **Natchaug** and **Patchaug** state forests in eastern Connecticut, both of which have camping areas specifically designed for people with horses.

Unfortunately, southern New England significantly lacks in outfitters to get you saddled up and take you on a ride on the trails and back roads of the region. In most cases, you're obliged to bring your own horses if you really want to escape deep into the woods. A few riding stables in the region offer trail rides, most notably **Lee's Riding Stable** (57 E. Litchfield Rd., off Route 118, Litchfield; ☎ **860/567-0785**) in western Connecticut and **Eastover Resort** (430 East St., Lenox, MA 01240; ☎ **800/822-2386**) in the Berkshires. But in most cases these rides are relatively short and near the stables.

One particularly enticing option is riding on the beach, which is about as romantic as horseback riding gets. At least a couple of companies in Rhode Island, **Rustic Rides Farm** (on West Side Road, Block Island; ☎ **401/466-5060**) and **Newport Equestrian Academy** (see "Instruction," below) offer guided rides on the beach. These rides too, however, are relatively short. Guided daylong or overnight outings are a hard find indeed. **Western Riding Stables** (see "Outfitters," below) is the rare company that offers anything comparable to the kind of pack trip you might experience in the mountains of the West. Too bad—it seems like there is an opportunity here for other stables or outfitting companies to seize.

Riding instruction, on the other hand, is not an especially hard find. Plenty of stables in the region offer riding lessons. Just be sure to specify the style of riding—English or Western—you want to focus on.

Outfitters

Western Riding Stables (Sawchuk Road, Millerton, NY 12456; ☎ **518/789-4848**) offers guided full-day and overnight rides in Mt. Washington State Forest, as well as other guided trips.

Instruction

If the weather is uncooperative, the **Newport Equestrian Academy** (287 Third Beach Rd., Middletown, RI 02842; ☎ **800/8HORSES** or 401/848-5440) has an indoor ring for riding instruction.

MOUNTAIN BIKING

You can call it a matter of attitude, a matter of neglect, or the travails of a sport still moving upward on its growth curve. For whatever reason, mountain biking in southern New England is a fairly disorganized affair. Go to other mountain-biking hot spots in the country—northern New England, Colorado, California—and you'll find mountain-biking schools, well-mapped and marked trails, and outfitters to organize and guide trips. In other words, there are support systems in place.

That's not the case in southern New England, and it's certainly not because of a lack of terrain to ride. Great trails can be found in state forests and parks from Rhode Island to the Berkshires, covering the full gamut of riding. Long rides, short rides, technical single track, wide-open dirt roads—you name it, you can find it here. It would even be possible, using paved roads to connect with backcountry roads and trails in some cases, to do a multiday mountain-biking tour through southern New England. Yet planning such a ride would tax your ingenuity and time, and finding adequate maps would be as much of a challenge as riding the route.

Efforts to improve the infrastructure are in motion, but they're moving slowly. There is a central organization, the New England Mountain Biking Association, that with its local chapters is doing an admirable job of spurring the growth and development of mountain biking in southern New England. But one organization, minimally funded, can't do it when it is trying to service a region that encompasses the three northern New England states as well.

So for mountain-biking entrepreneurs, opportunities beckon. You'd think one of the Berkshire ski areas—Jiminy Peak would be a logical choice—would follow the lead of ski areas to the north and set up a mountain-biking center or school to lure summer business. And maybe one or more of them will. For someone looking to organize, say, inn-based mountain-biking trips in the Berkshires or Connecticut, the field is wide open.

Mapping issues here are improving, but finding your way around is still anything but easy. For some terrific rides, the best available maps—if they exist—are often hand-drawn by local riders. In some areas, local riders resist mapping, simply as a way of reducing traffic on their favorite trails. The bottom line: Your chances of getting lost while mountain biking in southern New England are very, very good. The dense foliage of southern New England's forests—one of its great attractions—also has a tendency to obscure landmarks (mountain peaks, roads, villages, etc.), so your orienteering skills can be tested. If you plan on venturing deep into the woods on your own, bring a compass.

So . . . that's the bad news. The good news is that there is plenty of good riding in southern New England, with some of the best places described below. You'll also be happy to know that local bike shops are usually eager to share trail information and are also great sources of information on group rides. If you don't know where you're going, it's not a bad idea to join up with a group of people who do.

For locally organized group rides, the public is almost always welcome. Occasionally—very occasionally—a small donation might be requested, usually to support the local bike club or to help with trail maintenance. The common procedure for most group rides is to segregate riders according to ability. If you're a novice rider, you don't want to get thrown into a pack of single-track jocks who "hammer" (biking lingo for going as hard as possible) the hardest terrain they can find. Conversely, you don't want to be moseying along with a group of novices if you're a fit and aggressive rider. Ask at the local bike shop, be realistic about your abilities, and you'll probably be able to find a group ride that fits the bill.

While year-round riding is possible in much of the region, especially if you don't mind negotiating through snow and ice from time to time, the prime time for riding is realistically in late summer and early fall. In spring, and sometimes in early summer, trails can be wet and muddy, particularly in mountain areas. Riding on wet trails can not only be difficult, but also cause severe trail damage and erosion. Although it can be cool to return from a ride with your face and bike caked with mud, in the long run you might be doing yourself and other riders a disservice. Concerns about (or evidence of) erosion are among the leading reasons trails end up being closed to bikers.

By late summer, however, trails in all but the boggiest areas are usually dry enough (unless there's been a recent rainstorm) to make for good riding. When leaves start falling in late October, however, you might run into problems if you're riding steep or technical terrain. The reason is simple: Leaves can be slippery.

Before going into my favorite riding spots in southern New England, a definition is probably in order. "Mountain biking" can mean different things to different people and can, in fact, *be* very different from one riding area to the next. For example, the mountain biking on Cape Cod can be very good and very challenging, but obviously there are no mountains there. So riding on the Cape is a different experience from the true *mountain* biking you might experience in the Berkshires.

Mountain biking—in this book and according to most definitions—basically covers riding off of paved roads (although the occasional stretch of pavement might come into play to complete a loop). That means riding on well-maintained dirt roads; rougher fire roads and forest roads; "double track," meaning wide trails that once were roads and may still be used by four-wheel-drives and off-road vehicles; and single track—trails not much wider than the width of a tire tread that often double as hiking trails.

This basically represents a gradation of difficulty, from the easiest kind of riding to the hardest. Dirt-road riding is something that novice mountain bikers and kids should be able to handle, whereas single-track riding generally requires deft bike-handling skills. But there can be exceptions, of course. A flat, straight, and smooth single-track trail is a lot easier to deal with than a steep, sandy road. So don't assume that just because something marked on a map is a road, it's going to be easy riding.

I personally am one who enjoys mixing things up. While experienced mountain bikers thrive on challenging single track, I often find that the intense concentration required, the complete focus on the trail, can be mentally draining. I appreciate the chance to lift my eyes from the trail from time to time to take in the beauty of my surroundings. Single-track riding tends to be more of an athletic experience, whereas riding wider roads and trails often becomes a more aesthetic one.

So the places in southern New England that I choose as my top spots are a mixed lot. For sheer challenge, there's probably no ride more difficult than the loop around **Mt. Greylock** in the Berkshires. The ride involves something like 4,000 vertical feet of climbing, and it's a long ride. But what I like is the variety here; the riding runs the gamut from single-track to stretches of pavement. For the same reason—variety—I also like the riding in nearby **Savoy Mountain State Forest.** There are loops here on dirt roads that are suitable for novice riders, as well as double- and single-track trails for more advanced riders. The extensive network of roads and trails makes a vast array of loops possible.

A vast array of loops is also possible in neighboring **Acadia Management Area** in Rhode Island and **Pachaug State Forest** in Connecticut. These places offer more than 35,000 acres, a lot of room to roam. I only wish trails and roads were marked a little better in those areas, and maybe that will happen as more and more mountain bikers ride there. Finally, I'd include **Maudslay State Park,** situated just north of Boston, on my list because it so completely goes against the hard-core image of athletic mountain biking. Wide, gentle trails along the banks of the Merrimack River are easy enough for young kids to negotiate. Maudslay proves that mountain biking doesn't have to be all about testosterone overdrive.

Wherever you choose to ride in southern New England, there are a couple of important issues to keep in mind. First, there is a lot of private land out there, and you must respect the rights of landowners. Many landowners are very gracious about granting bikers rights of way across their property, but if you don't have clear and explicit permission to cross someone's land, ride elsewhere.

The second issue you have to tackle is shared trail use. Many (perhaps most) trails and roads are used by hikers, horseback riders, other mountain bikers, and motorized vehicles. With a little bit of courtesy, all trail users should be able to co-exist pretty easily. Slow down when you encounter other trail users, and I'd recommend coming to a full stop around horses. Be friendly. I assure you that a little courtesy will not ruin your ride, and if you find you're encountering so many other trail users that you're spending an entire ride starting and stopping, I would suggest simply going somewhere else.

Over the past several years, mountain biking has been swept away in an orgy of new technology. That has made selecting a bike—either to rent or to buy—more complex than ever. Mountain bikes basically come in four categories: hybrids (part mountain bike, part road bike), standard mountain bikes, front-suspension bikes, and full-suspension bikes. There are many variations on all these, of course, and you can spend anywhere from $150 to $5,000 on a new bike. But consider these categories as your starting point when selecting a bike.

If you plan to do most of your riding on roads, and a lot of it on paved roads, a hybrid bike is a good choice. Hybrids are versatile, relatively inexpensive, and much better for riding on pavement than mountain bikes. For most people just getting into the sport, I'd recommend a standard mountain bike. (By standard, I don't necessarily mean mediocre or ordinary; I simply use the term to differentiate a standard bike from a bike with suspension.) These bikes come with anywhere from 18 to 27 gears, along with wider tires that usually have deeper treads than hybrids.

A standard mountain bike is better than a hybrid at handling off-road terrain. It's also, in general, going to be less expensive than a bike with suspension. If you don't want the shock absorption that suspension provides, and many world-class racers think bikes without suspension give them a better feel for the terrain, then a standard bike is the way to go.

There is no question that front-suspension bikes provide a comfortable ride on rough, rocky terrain. If, after bouncing along a rough trail, your arms and hands feel as though they had been run through a meat grinder, you might want to try a front-suspension bike. Finally, full-suspension bikes can offer a Cadillac-smooth ride, but they do have drawbacks. They're expensive and usually heavy (not good if you plan to do a lot of climbing), and the ride is often so soft and mushy that bike-handling in tight places may be more difficult.

If you think this is more information on bikes than you need, just visit a well-equipped rental shop and face the full array of options you'll be offered. You can spend as little as $12 a day on a hybrid or more than $35 a day for a full-suspension bike. You can save a lot of money by not renting more bike than you need.

The one essential piece of equipment you will need (other than a bike) is a helmet. When you rent a bike, a helmet is almost always included. But whether you rent a helmet or own one, make sure it fits properly—snugly over the brow of your head. I often see riders with loose-fitting helmets propped on the back of their heads, and vicariously I can almost feel the pain potential. Most falls are forward; if the helmet doesn't cover the front part of your head or slips out of position as you fall, it isn't going to be much help.

Books

Probably the two most useful ride guides are *Mountain Biking Southern New England,* by Paul Angiollo (Falcon Press), and *25 Mountain Bike Tours in*

Massachusetts, by Robert Morse (Countryman Press). There are a number of how-to books out there on mountain biking technique; one that I'd recommend is *Mountain Bike! A Manual of Beginning to Advanced Technique,* by William Nealy (Menasha Ridge Press).

Maps

Rubel BikeMaps (Box 1035, Cambridge, MA 02140) show most back roads and some trails, but in most cases the scale is too large to be of help if you're concentrating your riding in one particular area. State-forest and state-park maps are usually available at headquarters and often at the trailhead. A local bike shop may have a trail map for a particular area, but don't be surprised if it's hand-drawn by some local rider. It might be helpful, but don't expect it to be scientifically accurate. **U.S. Geological Survey** topographical maps (12201 Sunrise Valley Dr., Reston, VA 20192; ☎ 888/ASK-USGS) are scientifically accurate, but they don't always show all trails. Topo maps are available in many outdoor stores.

Organizations

The **New England Mountain Biking Association** (Box 2221, Acton, MA 01720; ☎ 800/57-NEMBA; www.nemba. org/nemba.html) is certainly the organization to turn to for riding information in New England. It's your starting point for learning about rides, bike shops, local clubs, and organizations in the region. There are also a number of local NEMBA chapters in the region with information on local group rides. The **Appalachian Mountain Club** (5 Joy St., Boston, MA 01208; ☎ 617/523-0655; www.outdoors.org/) and its affiliated chapters can also be helpful, particularly when it comes to trail information.

ROAD BIKING

I am a road cyclist who pedals several thousand miles a summer and occasionally races when the competitive urges within me build up. I have ridden in many parts of the country, so I think I have a reasonably good idea of where southern New England riding stands in the grand scheme of things. The variety of terrain, the many possible loops, the scenery, the history and heritage, the inns and restaurants along the way—all combine for one of the most enjoyable riding experiences possible.

That's the good stuff, of course. The downside is traffic, which in places—particularly around Boston and in southwestern Connecticut—can be horrendous. The thought of riding along Route 2 into Boston, say, on a weekday at 8am positively frightens me. Such riding, or anything like it, would be far from enjoyable. So the first rule in making the most of southern New England riding is to avoid traffic.

This might be less challenging than you think. For starters, simply steering clear of major population centers is an automatic traffic-reduction strategy. In general, traffic in the region is probably lightest in the **Berkshires, northwestern Connecticut,** and **eastern Connecticut,** although you'll obviously find places where the traffic flow can be pretty obnoxious at certain times of the day.

That raises a second traffic-avoidance strategy—timing. In the major tourist regions, traffic is heaviest in midsummer and, in some cases, in the fall, when the foliage season is in high gear. If I were planning an extended tour through the Berkshires or Martha's Vineyard or some other tourist hot spot, I'd probably choose May as the month to go. The weather is relatively warm and the tourist influx has yet to pick up.

Choosing the best time of day for riding can be trickier. I happen to like riding in the late afternoon and evening, a time when traffic is often pretty light. But by riding at that time of day, you can run into an extended rush hour, even around such small cities as Great Barrington in the Berkshires or Mystic in eastern

Connecticut. Riding in the middle of the day can be a way of avoiding rush hour. At the same time, in tourist areas in midsummer, the middle of the day is often when traffic peaks. So you'll have to make the call depending on where you are riding and the time of year.

Choosing a relatively traffic-free loop is obviously a smart thing to do, but don't automatically assume that bigger roads with steadier traffic flows should be avoided. Major roads usually have shoulders, back roads usually don't. Sometimes I find that the few cars passing me on a narrow back road are more obnoxious or hazardous than the steady stream of cars passing by on a road with a substantial shoulder. Often what I do, if I have the time, is to drive a loop before riding it to see what kind of traffic (and of course what kind of terrain) I might encounter.

The loops I've chosen to include in this book range in length from about 15 miles to 50 miles. For most people, those lengths compute to about 1 to 5 hours in the saddle, depending on how fast you ride, how hilly the terrain is, and how often you stop. For the average recreational cyclist in reasonable shape, that should be a manageable amount of riding. But in no way does this mean that 50 miles a day is the limit in southern New England. Much longer rides are obviously possible, and there's no rule against doing the same loop twice if you feel that 20 or 30 miles of riding aren't enough.

Eastern Connecticut, with which I was not especially familiar before researching this book, was a real revelation. The riding here, over rolling terrain on back roads that are relatively lightly traveled, is wonderful. In particular, the 20-mile loop along the Connecticut River between **Hadlyme** and **East Haddam** proved to be one of my favorite rides in the entire region. Because I've ridden it often, I'm also a fan of the **Williamstown** loop in the Berkshires, through the rolling forests and farm country at the foot of Mt. Greylock. And after joining a Vermont

Bicycle Touring group on **Martha's Vineyard,** I am convinced that seeing the Vineyard on a bike is not only a good way to go, it's the only way to go.

As far as gearing up for a ride is concerned, let me offer a few suggestions. First, get a bike that best suits the kind of riding you expect to do. That's not always easy, particularly if you rent a bike, where you pretty much have to make do with what's available at a local bike shop. Typically, bike shops rent what are called "hybrids," which try to blend the best features of a road bike with the best features of a mountain bike. Indeed, these are pretty versatile machines, but they are also inherently a compromise.

If you expect to be doing a fair amount of riding on dirt roads (of which there are many in the region) as well as paved roads, a hybrid might be the best choice. The thin tires of a road bike often make for awkward, uncomfortable riding on rough, unpaved surfaces. But if you want to combine your road riding with off-road trail riding, you're probably best off on a mountain bike. It is a lot easier taking a mountain bike on the road than it is taking a road bike on a rough, back-country trail.

If you plan to do a lot of paved-road riding, particularly if there are hills involved, you'll be happier on a lighter, more streamlined road bike. Many people gag when they see the curved, so-called "drop" handlebars of a road bike, thinking that they'll be forced to ride in an uncomfortable, bent-over riding position. In fact, the beauty of drop handlebars is that they allow you to ride in several different positions, including sitting upright as you would with the kind of straight handlebars you find on mountain bikes and most hybrids. Being able to vary your position on the bike during a long ride does wonders for relieving muscle strain and stiffness.

In addition to the bike, I'd recommend three other pieces of equipment. A helmet, of course, is a must, and you should make sure it fits properly. A pair of bike shorts with a soft, padded insert around the crotch is less essential than a helmet, but for any ride of more than a couple of hours, you'll be much more comfortable than in a regular pair of shorts or pants. Pant seams can chafe, leading to blisters and saddle sores. Finally, if you're going to be doing any extended riding, a pair of cycling shoes with a stiff sole go a long way toward improving riding efficiency. In a 4- or 5-hour ride, the slightly higher force you deliver to the pedal with each stroke really adds up.

Probably nothing can improve your riding efficiency more than drinking and eating sensibly while you ride. On a 40-mile ride on a hot summer day, I can easily go through more than a quart of water. As for food, I find I can only go about 2 hours without having literally to refuel. Marathon runners talk of bonking or hitting the wall, and if you don't eat enough on a long ride, the same debilitating phenomenon can happen on a bike.

Gearing up for an extended, multiday tour is obviously more complicated than gearing up for a 2- or 3-hour ride. I go by a simple philosophy: When in doubt, throw it out. In other words, pack light; there is little reason to bring along much more than an extra set of cycling wear, a normal (non-cycling) shirt and a pair of pants, walking shoes, rain gear, and toiletries. I see touring cyclists with their bikes heavily laden with stuffed panniers, and I feel for them. The amount of effort hauling all that stuff around looks brutal. But because there are so many country inns in southern New England—and there is no better part of the country for inn-to-inn touring—there's no reason to bring along camping gear and lots of food. Stop for the night in a nice inn and enjoy civilization before setting off on the next leg of your tour.

What might a long-distance ride in the area look like? If I were to plan a 3-day trip in the region, my first choice would probably be to ride from roughly Danbury, Connecticut north to Williamstown,

Massachusetts, approximately paralleling Route 7. There are many, many fine inns along this route, so there's no shortage of places to overnight. One advantage to riding in a mostly north-south direction (as opposed to east-west) in New England is that most of the mountain ranges run north-south. As a result, the climbing tends to be less severe.

Another fine 3-day ride might be a loop starting in Mystic, Connecticut, bearing northwest toward East Haddam, northeast to Woodstock, and finally due south back to Mystic. There aren't any big mountains here, but you can expect lots of rolling and scenic terrain. One good strategy that many touring groups use on longer rides is to have a support vehicle, with driving duties split among the riders. With a support vehicle you don't have to lug your baggage and supplies on your bike, and on a one-way ride, you've got a means of getting back to your starting point.

An option to organizing your own ride, of course, is to join a group tour. The three main reasons to join a tour are 1) all the trip and route planning is taken care of for you, 2) you can travel incredibly light (the tour operator will take care of transporting your bags, if necessary), and 3) there's usually a "sag wagon" to pick you up whenever you feel you've had enough riding. It's also nice to be in the company of other cyclists and to benefit from the local knowledge of the tour guides.

One final long-distance ride you might want to consider in the region is the Pan-Mass Challenge (☎ **800/WE-CYCLE**). The ride is usually held the first weekend in August and is organized to raise money for cancer research. There are various 1- and 2-day route options, with distances ranging from 88 to 192 miles between Sturbridge and Provincetown, Massachusetts. It's a fund-raiser, so you (or your sponsors) will be obliged to do your share, but if you like company on your rides, you'll literally have a cast of thousands to share in the experience.

Outfitters

Vermont Bicycle Touring (Box 711, Bristol, VT 05443; ☎ **800/245-3868**) is one of the real pioneers of organized group bicycle tours. The company leads popular tours in summer and fall on Martha's Vineyard and Nantucket. **Easy Rider Tours** (Box 228, Newburyport, MA 01950; ☎ **800/488-8332** or 978/463-6955) leads 5-day fall tours through the Berkshires. The **Bicycle Tour Company** (Box 381, Kent, CT 06757; ☎ **888/711-KENT**) leads 3-day, weekend trips in summer and fall in the southern Berkshires and northwestern Connecticut, starting in New Marlborough.

Instruction

Once you've learned how to ride, you never forget, right? Maybe so, but a few tips here and there never hurt. One way to bone up on the basics is to join an organized tour (see "Outfitters," above). Tour leaders might not have you doing wheelies without hands after a few days of riding, but they can help you with basic techniques that will improve your riding efficiency, bike-handling skills, and confidence.

Books

Perhaps the best ride guide for the region is *Best Bike Rides: New England,* by Paul Thomas (Globe Pequot Press). The "25 Bicycle Tour" series published by Backcountry Guides (☎ **800/233-4830**) outlines some worthy tours on Cape Cod and the Islands. And I'd be remiss not to mention my own book, *Bicycling: Touring and Mountain Biking Basics,* by Peter Oliver (W.W. Norton), a primer on everything from clothing to riding technique.

Maps

Even if you aren't a cyclist, you'll probably want to stock up on the detailed road maps produced by **Rubel BikeMaps** (Box 1035, Cambridge, MA 02140;

☎ **617/776-6567**). In addition to showing (and naming) most back roads, the maps indicate hills and their steepness and list bike shops and—for whatever reason—ice cream shops. The maps are usually available in local bike shops and bookstores.

Organizations

The **Massachusetts Bicycle Coalition** (44 Bromfield St., Suite 207, Boston, MA 02108; ☎ **617/542-BIKE**), a.k.a. Mass-Bike, is the leading bicycling-advocacy group in Massachusetts. The organization can also provide planning assistance for extended tours of the state. The **Connecticut Bicycle Coalition** (One Union Place, Hartford, CT 06103; ☎ **860/527-5200**) organizes numerous rides in eastern Connecticut, some free, some requiring a fee. For group rides and local route information, local bicycle clubs are hard to beat. Club and ride information is usually available at local bike shops.

ROCK CLIMBING

Rock climbing is obviously not a sport to enter into cavalierly. Without expert guidance, without personal expertise, and without the proper equipment, you are exposing yourself to an incredible level of risk. Falling from an 80-foot wall of rock can be catastrophic. One of the great challenges of rock climbing, in fact, is turning an activity that is inherently dangerous into one that is relatively safe.

If you don't know the basics skills of rock climbing—from knot-tying on up—I'm not about to try to give you a primer here. A little knowledge, as the saying goes, can be dangerous. I'll say just one thing: Seek out an expert instructor and learn the sport literally from the ground up. This doesn't have to be as logistically difficult as it might seem. Many urban gyms have indoor climbing walls, where you can learn to climb in a controlled environment. Stop by the gym for an hour or two after work and go climbing—it can be as easy as that.

Still, climbing in a gym is not climbing outdoors. In the outdoors, you need to know how to use all the hardware—and no sport uses more hardware than climbing—that goes into securing a safety rope on a rock face. Being a successful climber is less about spectacular climbing technique than it is about knowing how to use ropes, to tie knots, secure anchors and screws, etc. I don't mean to use scare tactics here; rock climbing done properly can be exhilarating and surprisingly safe. But in a sport where one small mistake can lead to serious injury or even death, it is essential to know how to do things right.

As far as rock climbing in southern New England goes, here's the real surprise—just where you'd probably least expect to find it, in populous southwestern Connecticut, is some of the best climbing in the region. Walls of exposed "traprock," the solid, igneous rock that forms Connecticut's terrestrial foundation, rise up as cliffs up to 100 feet high. Places like **Ragged Mountain** near Southington and **Sleeping Giant** near Hamden have routes that range anywhere from an easy 5.2 difficulty rating to a very challenging 5.12. In central Massachusetts, you'll also find some decent climbing in the **Northfield Recreational and Environmental Center** and **Purgatory Chasm** south of Worcester.

Much of this climbing is possible year-round, although occasional accumulations of snow and/or ice in winter may make the going tricky. In choosing a good time to go, weather conditions probably affect southern New England climbing more than the season does. Obviously, a clear, dry day is best. Climbing wet, slippery rock is really no fun at all.

Be forewarned before you get hooked by the rock-climbing bug: It can be a surprisingly expensive sport. A good rope alone can cost $200—undoubtedly a wise investment when your life is literally on the line, but still a fair chunk of change. When you start adding all the other required gear to your shopping cart, you'd better hope you have a healthy credit line on your charge card.

Guides & Instruction

Go Vertical (727 Canal St., Stamford, CT 06902; ☎ **203/358-8767**) offers group and private instruction both outdoors and on an indoor climbing wall. **Connecticut Mountain Recreation** (119 Jessica Dr., East Hartford, CT 06118; ☎ **203/ 569-3113**) also offers climbing instruction both indoors and outdoors. The place to go for rock-climbing clinics in central and western Massachusetts is **Zoar Outdoor Adventures** (Mohawk Trail, Box 245, Charlemont, MA 01339; ☎ **800/ 532-7483**).

Books

Rock Climbing, by Don Mellor (W.W. Norton), is a great primer for those just getting into the sport.

Organizations

The Appalachian Mountain Club (5 Joy St., Boston, MA 01208; ☎ **617/523-0655;** www.outdoors.org/) and its regional affiliates may be helpful with information about climbing hot spots.

SAILING

Talk to any well-traveled sailor, and he or she is likely to tell you that when it comes to cruising, the New England coast is hard to beat. Farther to the south, the bays and sounds from New Jersey to the Carolinas are more sheltered and the winds often less reliable. The California coast has few coves and harbors to explore, and the same is true of most of the Florida coast.

The New England coast, however, has hundreds of coves and harbors, many gorgeously framed by old homes, sandy bluffs, and rocky shores. The winds (except for those in Long Island Sound) are usually reliable, at least during the summer months. If you've got a week or more and a fair amount of disposable cash, a cruise along the New England coast during July or August is a great way to vacation.

It is not cheap, however. So-called bareboat charters—boats you sail yourself without the help of a crew—usually start at around $1,500 per week for a boat that sleeps four or more, and from there the sky is the limit.

No one, of course, should head off on an extended cruise without having a solid knowledge of sailing fundamentals. Toward that end, New England again comes up with the goods. There are a number of good sailing schools, particularly around Newport, Rhode Island and the greater Boston area, that teach both adults and kids everything from the basics to open-ocean sailing.

To me, extended cruises are the real highlight of New England sailing, but I don't mean to suggest that is the only kind of sailing there is. There are plenty of harbors where you can rent a boat for a half day or full day of sailing. If I were to head off on a day trip in southern New England, I'd probably head out into **Vineyard Sound** from Wood's Hole. A sail to pristine Tarpaulin Cove on Naushon Island is an easy sail of less than 2 hours (depending on the wind, of course). And if you push it, a round-trip to the wonderful, weather-worn island of Cuttyhunk is possible in a day, although I'd make it a 2-day trip if I had the time.

A day or two to explore **Narragansett Bay** is also time well-spent. Newport is arguably America's sailing capital, having for many years been the home of America's Cup racing. If I did have time for an overnight trip, I'd probably head out to **Block Island,** a popular stop for yachts cruising up and down the coast. Finally, the north shore of Boston around **Marblehead** and **Manchester** is a place where sailing is taken very seriously. When I see bios on America's top racers, I am never surprised to see the north shore well represented.

I have sailed in the waters off southern New England in April and May, so I know that it is possible to do so at that time of year. But I don't necessarily recommend it. It can be chilly, of course, but that's not the only discouraging factor. Many smaller harbors and marinas aren't really up and running until late May or early June.

The prime summer months—June through August—are clearly the prime sailing months. The waterways may be busy, but it is a rare day when you pull into even the most popular harbors and can't find some place to drop anchor. September can be a great time to sail, too, but watch the weather forecasts carefully. September is the heart of hurricane season, and wind and waves can pick up considerably even if the eye of the hurricane is hundreds of miles away. The closest I have come to being swept overboard was in trying to bring down a jib in a 50-m.p.h. gale and 10-foot seas in Buzzard's Bay in September.

Outfitters

Offshore Sailing School (16731 McGregor Blvd., Fort Myers, FL 33908; ☎ 800/221-4326) operates from several harbors around the country, including Newport. While it bills itself as "the Ivy League of sailing schools," Offshore is really as much a luxury-tour operator as it is a school. The 3-day "Live Aboard Cruising" course mixes instruction with tour stops on islands from Block Island to Martha's Vineyard, where fine dining, shopping, and other non-instructional enticements are part of the package.

Instruction

The **Boston Sailing Center** (The Riverboat at Lewis Wharf, Boston, MA 02110; ☎ 617/227-4198) offers courses that range in length from 4 days to 5 weeks, for everyone from beginners to advanced offshore sailors. **J World** (Box 1509, Newport, RI 02840; ☎ 800/343-2255), with "campuses" in Annapolis, San Diego, and Key West as well as Newport,

is consistently rated one of the top sailing schools in the country. Two- to 5-day courses (with 6 hours a day of on-water time) are offered for everyone from the landlubber novice to the blue-water expert. **Newport Sail School & Tours** (Goat island Marina, Dock 5A, Newport, RI 02840; ☎ 401/848-2266) offers 5- to 13-hour courses for beginning, intermediate, and racing sailors.

Books

A Cruising Guide to the New England Coast, by Roger F. Duncan and John P. Ware, is the indispensable guide for sailors planning extended trips along the coast. If you want to get started on learning how to sail, pick up a copy of *Sailing Fundamentals,* by Gary Jobson (Fireside Books), the official how-to guide of the American Sailing Association.

Charts

Most nautical charts are based on the surveys and soundings of the **National Oceanographic and Atmospheric Administration** (for charter orders, call ☎ 800/638-8975 or 301/436-6990). They are available at many marinas or through most marine-supply stores. Another good source is **Waterproof Charts Inc.** (320 Cross St., Punta Gorda, FL 33950; ☎ 800/423-9026). As the name implies, charts are waterproof and hence more durable than the usual paper charts.

Charters

Yacht charters are available at numerous marinas up and down the coast, particularly in Boston and Newport. Refer to regional chapters for charter-company suggestions, or contact state tourism agencies (see "Visitor Information," above).

SEA KAYAKING

Sea kayaking has been growing in popularity in recent years, and for good reason. It is a relatively easy sport to pick up—mastering the fundamentals of propelling a boat forward with a paddle and steering it with foot pedals should take even an unathletic person less than an hour. Sea kayaks are fairly roomy as kayaks go, so you can head off on a trip with extra clothing, food, and even—why not?—a bottle of wine for a picnic on the beach. If you are a bird-watching enthusiast, sea kayaking is one of the best ways imaginable to get into the heart of prime avian habitats.

Finally, sea kayaking opens up an enormous world of exploratory possibility. Sea kayaks can negotiate tidal marshlands, shallow bays, and coastal ponds as easily as a canoe. But unlike canoes, they are usually sturdy enough to take into open water, where a good-sized wave might swamp a canoe.

For all these reasons, sea kayaking is a particularly good way to explore the coast of southern New England. From the western end of Long Island Sound to the New Hampshire coast north of Boston, the number of nooks and crannies to explore—the many inlets, bays, marshlands, islands, and beaches—is all but infinite. To me, embarking on a sea-kayaking trip is like stepping through a looking glass and gaining a whole new perspective of southern New England. If you thought that southern New England, particularly along the coast, was one of the most developed parts of the country (and you are right), look again from the vantage point of a sea kayak. The places you can go in a sea kayak—wetlands and open water—are, generally speaking, places that are inherently undevelopable.

Ozzie Osborn, who heads up Essex River Basin Adventures north of Boston, boasted to me that the terrain he covers in his sea-kayak tours "is one of the most pristine areas of coastal land and open marshland anywhere." He is absolutely right. And yet, as I ventured along the coast in doing research for this book, I found many more areas equally compelling. Welcome, then, to the looking-glass world of southern New England sea kayaking.

I'll endorse Osborn's enthusiastic praise of the **Essex River** area. Marshes and beaches laced with small rivers and inlets stretch northward from Essex to the New Hampshire border, opening up an astonishing world of wetland discovery. The islands of **Boston Harbor,** undergoing a recreational rebirth with the successful clean-up efforts of recent years, are also great for a day or two of exploration.

For open-water paddling, I'd head for the **Elizabeth Islands,** which form a chain stretching southwest from Cape Cod. An overnight trip from Woods Hole to Cuttyhunk, the tiny, soulful island at the end of the Elizabeth chain, is about as good as sea kayaking gets. In Long Island Sound, the **Great Island** area at the mouth of the Connecticut River is a place I'd head to if bird-watching were a prime objective. For the adrenaline rush of surf riding, the southern beaches of **Rhode Island** are where you'll want to go. (If you are into surf riding, you'll want a lighter, quicker boat, more like a whitewater kayak than a standard sea kayak.)

Now that I've painted such a rosy and positive picture of the sport, let me temper it with a few cautionary words. Basic paddling and steering may be something you can learn in an hour or less, but before heading out into open, exposed water you need more than the basics. You need to be able to navigate a boat through rough seas if necessary, and you need to know how to self-rescue should the unexpected happen.

In addition, three natural forces (other than plain bad weather) can turn a great sea-kayaking trip into a nightmare: winds, currents, and tides. For any extended trip into open water, you should plan carefully. Powerful winds that kick up from the southwest in the summer can create big seas in the shallow waters of Nantucket Sound, Buzzard's Bay, and Narragansett Bay. Having to battle into the wind, or even worse, having the wind come at you broadside, can be not only draining but treacherous.

The hazards of strong currents can be even more insidious. In such places as Woods Hole and the Race, a channel between the Rhode Island coast and Fisher's island, currents can exceed three knots. The surface of the water might appear placid enough, but when the current gets hold of your boat, you'll feel like you're trying to reign in an ill-tempered bronco.

Currents are, of course, driven by the tides, and hence they are predictable. Therefore, with astute trip planning, you should be able to time your passage through (or across) any channel when the current is either favorable or slack. Wind is less predictable, but typically it is lightest in the morning. So if any part of your trip might be exposed to strong winds, you'll do well if you can plan to do that segment of your trip in the morning.

Tides can be a concern if you're poking around in marshes and estuaries. A channel that is 2 feet deep at high tide might be no more than a strip of mud at low tide. Being stranded for several hours in the middle of some marsh, waiting for the tide to come back in, might not be life threatening, but it's no fun, either. Again, tides are predictable, so if you plan properly and stay alert to tidal levels, you shouldn't have any problems.

There is one other hazard to consider—other human beings. Sea kayaks have a relatively low profile on the water, and particularly when waves rise to a foot or higher, they might be hard for people in other boats to see. It's a smart idea to avoid a lot of time paddling in busy channels with a lot of power-boat traffic. Take advantage of the shallow draft of the kayak and, if possible, head for water outside the channel where deeper-draft boats can't go.

For the time being, if you're interested in a long-distance trip along the southern New England coast, you're on your own. To the best of my knowledge, there is no outfitter that offers, say, a week-long guided trip from Rhode Island to the Cape. But there's no reason why such a trip wouldn't be possible. Hugging the coast, you can find harbors and marinas every 5 to 10 miles, usually with an inn or campground not far away. It is a trip I can easily imagine myself trying some day.

Outfitters

Essex River Basin Adventures (66R Main St., Box 270, Essex, MA 01929; ☎ **800/KAYAK-04** or 978/768-3722) leads half-day and full-day trips in the Essex River area, as well as off the coast of Cape Ann. **Sakonnet Boathouse** (169 Riverside Dr., Tiverton, RI 02878; ☎ **401/624-1440**) leads half-day and full-day trips along the Sakonnet River south of Bristol, Rhode Island.

Instruction

The Kayak Center (9 Phillips St., Wickford, RI 02852; ☎ **401/295-4400**) conducts clinics in open-ocean paddling and surf riding, as well as basic kayaking technique. **Sakonnet Boathouse** (see "Outfitters," above) conducts clinics in rolling, open-water paddling, and basic paddling technique.

Books & Web Sites

Complete Sea Kayak Touring, by Jonathan Hanson (McGraw-Hill), is a good place to start for those just getting into the sport. A worthwhile guidebook is *Sea Kayaking Along the New England Coast,* by Tamsin Venn (AMC Books).

For information on clubs, educational material, planning tips, and gear and outdoor equipment dealers, try the **Ultimate Directory of Kayaking Links** (**www.cstone.net/users/winter/Kayakmain.htm**). If you plan on going to Connecticut, the **Connecticut Sea Kayakers** Web site (**www.mindspring. com/~connyak/**) is another good place to look for information.

Charts

See "Sailing," above for information on nautical charts.

Organizations

Sea kayaking also comes under the aegis of the **American Canoe Association** (see "Canoeing/Flatwater Kayaking," above).

SURFING

I would certainly not consider surfing to be one of southern New England's strong suits. There are a number of areas along the East Coast—the Outer Banks of North Carolina and the New Jersey shore—that come to mind as having larger, more consistent surf. Many are the summer days at the beaches of Rhode Island and Massachusetts when the wave action is not much more than a gently rolling trickle. Big surf days are like days of fresh powder in skiing—unpredictable and uncommon, but incredibly welcome when they do happen.

Actually, there are New England surfers who insist that the winter surf in Rhode Island is more consistent and reliable than the surf in summer. They show up at Watch Hill in January, something that strikes me as guaranteed misery. If you're game, I encourage you to go for it, but don't expect me to be there to join you.

When the surf is up in southern New England, I'd guess an average wave would come in at around 3 to 4 feet. But when there's a storm brewing out in the Atlantic, waves of 8 feet and higher sometimes roll in. Experienced surfers know how to make sense of weather forecasts and buoy reports—reports of swell sizes and wind directions from National Weather Service buoys at sea—and figure out where and when the surf is going to be best.

The best surfing in the region is probably along the **Rhode Island coast.** Exactly where the best breaks are, however, often depends on the wind direction. Your best strategy for finding the hot spots is to check at local surf shops or with local surfers. This is another good reason to surf Rhode Island—there is a fairly active and knowledgeable surfing community. You might not be introduced to the super-secret, special places right off the bat, but surf shops are usually willing to steer you in a good direction and often post wave reports. Good surf can also roll in on the ocean beaches of the southern New England Islands— **Block Island, Martha's Vineyard,** and **Nantucket.** However, the local support system is not as well formed as it is in Rhode Island.

By the way, you don't have to be an expert or experienced surfer to get into the thrill of riding waves. First-time surfers are often frustrated by the difficulty of learning to catch a wave and then standing up and staying balanced on a board. Enter, then, bodyboarding—the easier intro to surfing. Bodyboarding involves surfing waves while lying down on a small board; within a few hours, you should be able to get the basic knack of it. And if waves are on the small side, bodyboarding is a good way to make the most of them.

Instruction

The Watershed (396 Main St., Wakefield, RI 02879; ☎ 401/789-3399; surf phone ☎ 401/789-1954) offers free lessons every summer Wednesday at noon.

Surf's Up?

If your vacation plans call for hitting the waves in Massachusetts or Rhode Island, surf over to the **Shore.Net Beach Guide (www.shore.net/cgi-bin/tidechart/tide/tideform.html)**, where you can view tidal charts for both states' beaches.

SWIMMING

There are plenty of long, sandy beaches along the southern New England coast, but for my money the best of the bunch are the ocean beaches on the islands: **Block Island, Martha's Vineyard,** and **Nantucket.** Dunes and bluffs form the backdrop, and the endless sea lies on the foreground. From time to time, the surf builds sufficiently for some decent body-surfing. And because these are island beaches, they are almost by definition more remote than mainland beaches. As a result, you rarely encounter crowds.

The ocean beaches of Cape Cod, with their own dunes and bluffs, are beautiful, too, but the cold water can be a turn-off. It takes a hot summer day for me to want to spend more than a minute or two in water that is not much above 50°. The water is warmer along the Rhode Island beaches, but I find that these beaches can become more crowded than I like.

Of course, the social activity on the beach is one of the reasons some people go to the beach in the first place. So if that's your scene, by all means, head for southern Rhode Island or the ocean beaches of Cape Cod. On the other hand, if you want to steer clear of other beach-goers, I'd recommend trying **Parker River National Wildlife Refuge** on Plum Island north of Boston. I was there on a sunny day in June, and I doubt there were more than two dozen other people along the 6-mile beach. One reason crowds can be scared off is that the beach is often closed to leave nesting piping plovers (an endangered species) undisturbed. So if you decide to go to the refuge, call first to make sure the beach is open.

Inland, the lakes and ponds of southern New England must surely number in the thousands. On Cape Cod alone, there are said to be more than 500 freshwater "kettle" ponds, leftover glacial remnants now primarily fed by rainwater. If I had to pick one lake as a favorite, it would probably be **Lake Waramaug** in western Connecticut. It's not only pretty, but it comes with a choice. You can go swimming at the state-park beach, or you can stay at one of the terrific country inns along the lake's shore and swim at the inn's private beach.

You might also want to take a dip in **Walden Pond** in Concord, west of Boston. I can guarantee that it will not be a solitary experience; this is a popular swimming hole. But Walden is where Henry David Thoreau hung out, enraptured by the splendor of the great outdoors. So from a spiritual point of view, taking a dip in Walden Pond—with all the other swimmers—might be something of a great-outdoors baptism.

Remember that southern New England has a legitimate winter. Most lakes and ponds aren't completely ice-free until late March or early April, which ought to give you some idea of the water temperature at that time of year. Even in May, the water can be uninvitingly chilly. Not surprisingly, then, the prime swimming time is June through August. But the ocean off the beaches of the Vineyard and Nantucket, close to the warming influences of the Gulf Stream, can be relatively pleasant in September and even in early October. That's another reason to rank them at the top of my list.

WALKS & RAMBLES

What makes a walk a walk and a hike a hike? I'm not sure even I know the difference. A hazy line separates the two: on one side there's longer and more strenuous hiking, on the other is easier, less time-consuming walking (or rambling). But exactly where that line is drawn, I don't know. One person's hike is another's ramble, and vice versa. So as you read the descriptions of walks in this book, read carefully and determine for yourself.

Actually, I can be of a little more help than that by at least offering my own approximate take on the subject. Generally speaking, I would say that a walk or ramble shouldn't last more than 2 hours, unless you decide to take your own sweet time with bird-watching or picnicking interludes. That means the walks and rambles in this book generally max out at about 5 miles. Also, a walk or ramble shouldn't include much climbing, and if there is climbing, it should be fairly easy. A few walks in this book might involve a short, steep scramble, but those walks are rare.

Basically, I look for a walk (as opposed to a hike) to be able to pass the 10-year-old-kid test. If it is something that a 10-year-old could handle (complaining a little bit, perhaps, but still able to go the distance), then it's a walk. Anything longer or harder than that probably deserves being called a hike.

Southern New England is perfect country for walks and rambles. So many sanctuaries, preserves, parks, and refuges here provide havens of natural or pastoral retreat in the midst of an otherwise well-developed world. A bird sanctuary or state park may constitute no more than a few acres, yet I'm often amazed at how quickly one can absorb the spirit of natural isolation after only a few minutes on the trail. I think of places like **Canoe Meadows** in Pittsfield or **Devil's Den** in Weston, Connecticut, where the roar and incessancy of traffic, industry, and mechanization might be just a stone's throw away. Yet as you look across placid ponds, or try to single out the call of some particularly rare songbird, or just wander for a while in the woods, all that other stuff seems far, far away.

To choose a favorite among all these places is not easy, but I feel partial to **Bartholomew's Cobble** in the southern Berkshires. There is an enchantment to the place that I doubt could be done real justice in any written description. The meadows and forests and the Housatonic River ambling by; the aura of history; and the strange cobble itself, a peculiar outcropping of rock now overgrown with plant life—it all adds up to something special.

There's also something pretty magical about the cliffs of **Gay Head** on Martha's Vineyard at sunset. The tourist hordes that arrive at the cliffs in the middle of the day can be a bit disheartening, but when they disappear in the evening and the setting sun highlights the subtle variations of color in the cliffs, a whole different sentiment wells up. A couple of other favorite spots are **Great Meadows National Wildlife Refuge** outside Boston and **Sachuest National Wildlife Refuge** near Newport, because they are, in both physical and metaphysical ways, what they claim to be—refuges.

Obviously, for anything that can be considered a walk or a ramble, you won't need the kind of equipment you might need for a more extended hike. In fact, I'd recommend thinking very little about whether you're properly geared up. Chief among the real appeals of a walk are that it is perhaps the least gear-intensive of all outdoor activities and that it can happen on a whim. You pass by some park or refuge, it looks good, so why not? Park the car and go away for an hour.

Nevertheless, a few things can make any walk more enjoyable. Robust hiking boots might not be necessary, but a comfortable pair of running, walking, or "cross-training" shoes are a good idea. Many shoe manufacturers produce what are called light hiking boots, in most cases not much more than a high-cut walking or running shoe with a little extra ankle support built in. For most walking or rambling in southern New England, such boots are probably just about right.

If you expect to be on the trail for more than an hour, bring drinking water. A fanny pack that can hold a water bottle along with a few other choice items—a camera, sunblock, hat, perhaps a light rain jacket—is the sort of thing you might want to keep in the back of the car, ready to go at a moment's notice.

Finally, after any walk in southern New England between May and October, don't forget to check for ticks. And if you bring the kids along, check them, too.

Outfitters

See "Hiking/Backpacking," above. Many of the walks included in the itineraries of hiking tour operators are relatively easy, and easier options are usually available on days when a more strenuous hike is scheduled. Both the Nature Conservancy and state Audubon societies (see "Organizations," below) organize regular bird-watching or nature walks on the lands under their aegis. At most, a nominal charge of a few dollars is all you have to pay.

Books

In addition to the books listed under "Hiking/Backpacking" above, *Walks and Rambles on Cape Cod and the Islands,* by Glenda Bendure and Ned Friary (Backcountry Publications), is well written, detailed, and well worth the price of admission.

Maps

The **U.S. Geological Survey** (see "Hiking/Backpacking," above) produces topographical maps that may be helpful. For a short walk, however, these maps are often overkill and might confuse more than help. At most parks, reservations, and refuges in the region, a trail map is either posted or available at headquarters, and is probably preferable to a detailed topo map.

Organizations

The **Connecticut Audubon Society** (613 Riverville Rd., Greenwich, CT 06831; ☎ 203/869-5272). the **Massachusetts Audubon Society** (208 S. Great Rd., Lincoln, MA 01773; ☎ 800/AUDUBON). and the **Audubon Society of Rhode Island** (12 Sanderson Rd., Smithfield, RI 02917; ☎ 401/949-5454) all help organize nature walks in sanctuaries under their aegis. **The Nature Conservancy** (International Headquarters, 4245 N. Fairfax Dr., Arlington, VA 22203; ☎ 703/841-5300) has been an important force

for preserving undeveloped land throughout the country, including southern New England. Call headquarters for information on state and local chapters, which are responsible for organizing most outings on Conservancy lands.

The **U.S. Fish & Wildlife Service** oversees the national wildlife refuge system. You can get a visitors' guide to the system by calling ☎ 800/344-WILD. The **Trustees of Reservations** (Long Hill, 572 Essex St., Beverly, MA 01915; ☎ 978/921-1944) is responsible for the protection of more than 80 reservations, covering 33,000 acres in Massachusetts.

WILDLIFE VIEWING

When naturalists single out reasons for vanishing wildlife, invariably habitat destruction is at the top of the list. Probably nowhere in the country has wildlife habitat, both on land and at sea, been bulldozed over and ravaged more often and completely than in southern New England.

Still, many habitats—forests, rivers, harbors, etc.—are making a comeback, and in some places wildlife is thriving. The cleanup of Boston Harbor has received a fair amount of press in recent years, and according to the Massachusetts Audubon Society, between 1988 and 1997 state land was being protected for wildlife habitat at a rate 48% faster than land was being developed.

No wonder deer, coyotes, moose, bear, and other animals are gaining a foothold in southern New England and, in some cases (such as deer and coyotes), flourishing. At sea, humpback whales are thriving, thanks in large part to the designation of Stellwagen Bank, 25 miles off the Massachusetts coast, as a National Marine Sanctuary in 1993.

So . . . you stand a reasonable chance of spotting wildlife of some sort in almost any walk in the woods. I won't dare to make any guarantees, but so healthy is the deer population in the western hills and mountains of southern New England that your chances of seeing deer on a day-long hike are incredibly good. Operators of whale-watching cruises are more confident than I am; most guarantee you will see a whale on a 4-hour tour.

Generally speaking, I would say your chances of seeing wildlife improve in almost direct proportion to the size of the undeveloped tract of land you might be exploring. You're less likely to see deer, moose, or bear in a 50-acre sanctuary than you are in a 25,000-acre state forest.

If my main objective, then, were to see wildlife, I'd probably head for **Quabbin Reservation** in central Massachusetts. At something like 60,000 acres, the reservation, surrounding the reservoir of the same name, is the largest tract of undeveloped land in southern New England. One of the main objectives of the reservation is to provide a haven for wildlife, and moose, bears, and deer are regularly sighted here. **Savoy Mountain State Forest** in western Massachusetts and **Pachaug State Forest** in eastern Connecticut are also likely places for wildlife sightings.

Offshore, **Stellwagen Bank** is where whale-watching cruises usually go. As previously stated, tour operators are so confident of whale sightings that cruises usually come with a guarantee. Your chances of sighting dolphins are also extremely good. Taking a cruise to **Monomoy National Wildlife Refuge,** off the southeastern coast of Cape Cod, provides an opportunity to see harbor seals and dolphins in addition to a vast array of bird life.

Incidentally, wildlife viewing can in many ways be more enjoyable and rewarding in winter. Identifying tracks in the snow can be a source of great entertainment if you bring along your kids on a snowshoeing or backcountry-skiing tour. Conversely, it is usually ill-advised to go wandering around the woods in late fall, when the hunting season is in full swing.

Outfitters

Among the reputable whale-watching operators, the **New England Aquarium** (Central Wharf, Boston, MA 02110; ☎ 617/973-5281 for reservations) runs tours from Rowe's Wharf near Logan Airport. The **Cape Cod Museum of Natural History** in Brewster (☎ 508/896-3867) offers naturalist-led tours to Monomoy National Wildlife Refuge.

Books

A Field Guide to Animal Tracks, by Olaus Murie and Roger Tory Peterson (Chapters Publishing), is probably the best book out there on the subject. *Whales, Dolphins, and Porpoises,* by Carwardine et al (Checkmark Books), tells you in words and pictures pretty much everything you ever wanted to know about whales, and maybe a bit more.

WHITEWATER RAFTING/ KAYAKING

The absence of big mountains and long, steep rivers and streams sets an obvious limit on the whitewater experience in southern New England. If you envision anything like, say, a week-long ride through the Grand Canyon, you will end up sadly disappointed. But for a few hours of whitewater fun in the region, there are several excellent options. In a couple of places, on a couple of rivers, at certain times of year, rapids can rise to Class V ferocity and even higher, as much whitewater as even the most experienced—or crazed—kayaker can handle.

Exactly how does the classification of rapids work? Class I is little more than fast-moving water, with a few riffles or small waves. With just a little bit of instruction, even a first-time kayaker should be able to hand Class I. In Class II water, waves begin to emerge with whitecaps, with the slight potential of flipping an inexperienced paddler who might get caught in an awkward position. But Class

II rapids are generally uncomplicated—no big rocks to maneuver around or tricky bends in the river. If you line your boat up properly and steer a straight course, you shouldn't have any problem.

Class III is really when rapids start to get "technical," as kayakers say. Class III rapids are the level at which paddlers in open canoes begin to think about portaging. Waves are big enough to swamp a boat, and there may be tricky turns, short drops, unpredictable currents, and large rocks or ledges to deal with. Beginning with Class III, you should scout rapids before running them.

Class IV is both technical and big. To negotiate Class IV rapids requires a high level of paddling skills. Channels are often narrow, the waves big, and the hydraulics (or powerful washing-machine action) of the water can be treacherous. Class V is similar to Class IV, except the scale of everything—the size and power of the waves, the length of the rapids, the drops, the technical difficulty of the channels—is increased. Running anything above Class V rapids can be extremely dangerous. To run Class VI rapids requires either extraordinary paddling skills or a screw loose in your head—or both.

The ratings are the same for kayaks and rafts, but obviously rafts, being larger and more stable crafts, can handle bigger water more easily. Under the guidance of an experienced rafting outfitter, Class III and even IV rapids are manageable for most healthy, fit adults with no river experience. If you're willing to get wet and chance the slight possibility of taking an unexpected swim, you're ready for Class IV rapids in a raft. The same cannot be said, however, for kids under 14. For trips into anything exceeding Class II rapids, most outfitters set a cut-off age, typically around 14.

Rapids also change, depending on the water level. A stream that might be a mere trickle in the fall can be a raging, Class IV monster for a few short stretches in the spring. A good example of a river that operates like this is the **Cold River,** which runs eastward out of the Berkshires along Route 2. Drive by it in midsummer, and you might think it's not a particularly fearsome stretch of water. But in March it is considered by local kayakers to be one of the best and most challenging whitewater runs in Massachusetts.

There are basically three different sources of water that can change the level of a river and, consequently, the rating of its rapids. The first is melting snow in the spring, second is a heavy rainfall at any time of year, and the last is a dam release. Because all major rivers in southern New England are dammed to some degree, the flow of water is a fairly controlled event. While it might lessen opportunities for a wild ride after a particularly big rainstorm, the controlled flow is generally good news for kayakers and rafters. Regular dam releases extend the whitewater season well into the summer on a river like the **Deerfield** in northwestern Massachusetts. Were it not for the dam releases, a summer whitewater adventure on the Deerfield would be an unlikely proposition other than after a period of heavy rain.

So where are the best whitewater spots in southern New England? Ironically, a section of the Deerfield called the **Dryway** offers up whitewater that is about as good as it gets. The 3-mile section of the river below Monroe Bridge is usually just what it is billed to be—a dry riverbed. But regularly scheduled dam releases during the course of the spring and summer turn the Dryway, for brief periods, into whitewater heaven.

Probably the biggest whitewater in the entire region is on the **Housatonic River** just above Bull's Bridge in Connecticut. Depending on the water level, this brief stretch of rapids approaches Class VI—not something to be taken lightly even by expert paddlers. Below Bull's Bridge, the river eases up a bit, and rapids top out at around Class IV. This is a terrific place to go for raft trips in the spring. Another good spring run is the **Millers River** in central Massachusetts.

Wherever you go in spring, be prepared for cold water with waterproof outerwear. (Some outfitters may be able to help you out, but don't count on it.) Much of the water in March and April is, after all, just recently melted snow. Even in summer, the water can be colder than you might expect. Most dam releases draw water from the bottom of the dammed reservoir—much colder water than that warmed by the sun near the surface. On a hot summer day, the cold water might be refreshing, but at any other time it can cause a serious chill.

One equipment item (in addition to the obvious stuff such as a life jacket, helmet, and paddle) that can be a real blessing is a good pair of river sandals or old sneakers for walking in the water. Stretches of any river with fast-moving water are almost always rocky; the powerful flow washes away softer, looser sediment. Being able to walk comfortably on the rocks can save you from stumbling into an unexpected and chilly swim. Sandals are preferable; sneakers fill with water and can make swimming difficult should you end up out of your boat in a rapid.

Outfitters

Zoar Outdoor Adventures (Mohawk Trail, Box 245, Charlemont, MA 01339; ☎ 800/532-7483) guides rafting trips on the Deerfield and Millers rivers. **Clarke Outdoors** (163 Route 7, Cornwall, CT 06796; ☎ 860/672-6365) guides spring rafting trips on the Housatonic, below Bull's Bridge. In summer, raft trips on a different section of the Housatonic, where rapids top out at around Class II, are suitable for bringing along younger kids.

Instruction

Both **Zoar Outdoor** and **Clarke Outdoors** offer first-rate instruction in whitewater kayaking. Bruce Lessels of Zoar and Mark Clarke of Clarke Outdoors

have impressive credentials. Lessels is a former world whitewater champion, and Clarke has won the national championship in the open-canoe category eight times.

Books

Classic Northeastern Whitewater Guide, by Bruce Lessels (Appalachian Mountain Club), is the manual of choice for whitewater enthusiasts in New England.

Organizations

American Whitewater Affiliation (1430 Fenwick Lane, Silver Spring, MD 20910; ☎ 301/589-9453) promotes river conservation and access and is a clearinghouse of whitewater information. The Affiliation has numerous local chapters and publishes the magazine *American Whitewater.* (See also the **American Canoe Association** under "Canoeing/Flatwater Kayaking," above.)

Campgrounds & Other Accommodations

CAMPGROUNDS

One man's campground is another man's trailer park, and one man's shelter might be another man's palace. In other words, what people are looking for and expecting in a campground varies widely. In general, I've steered clear in this book of campgrounds that cater primarily to the RV crowd. Call me a snob, but somehow it seems that a place to hook up your Airstream isn't quite a campground, just as touring the country in your RV is not something that I think can properly be called camping. I'm not knocking it—I just don't think it's camping.

Camping to me serves two purposes. First, it's a way to get out into the outdoors—to cook a meal in the fresh air, to tell campfire stories, and to sleep in a tent. Second, it provides economical lodging. If there is a campground that costs more than $15 a night for a site, I don't know of it, and most public campgrounds charge far less than that. Furthermore, if you want to camp in the backcountry (usually at designated backcountry sites), it's pretty much a free world out there.

I haven't discriminated in this book against non-tent camping; in fact, most of the campgrounds I've included in regional chapters are drive-in campgrounds. I've also included campgrounds that, while they might not be the most soulful or scenic, are conveniently located to take advantage of nearby recreational activities.

Camping in southern New England is, for the most part, a seasonal activity. Unfortunately, the "season" is not the same everywhere. In some cases, the season runs from Memorial Day to Labor Day, although it might also extend for a month or two in either direction. On the other hand, a few campgrounds do stay open throughout the winter, particularly in the southern part of the region. If you plan to camp in any season other than summer, be sure to call ahead to make sure the campground is open.

During the summer, and particularly on weekends, many campgrounds are booked well in advance. I was told, for example, that to ensure yourself a space in Savoy Mountain State Forest in western Massachusetts, you have to book 6 weeks in advance. I'm not sure if that's true or not, but it gives you some idea of how popular certain campgrounds can be. The campground in Nickerson State Forest on Cape Cod also gets booked up well in advance. The best suggestion I have to offer is to be sure to have a Plan B in case things don't go as expected. For example, there are other campgrounds relatively nearby that can handle the Nickerson and Savoy Mountain overflow.

Massachusetts has taken the camper-friendly step of setting up a single toll-free number (☎ 877/422-6762) for reservations at all state forest and park campgrounds. For general information (but not reservations) on public campgrounds in Connecticut and Rhode Island, you can call the main state tourism numbers (see "Visitor Information," above). The most useful camping guidebook I've found is *New England Camping,* by Carol Connare and Stephen Gorman (Foghorn Press), with thumbnail write-ups of thousands of public and private campgrounds in the region.

RESORTS & SPAS

Southern New England is the land of the centuries-old country inn, particularly in northwestern Connecticut and the Berkshires. For recommended inns, check out the regional chapters in this book, but I'd also suggest you get a good guidebook to inns in the region. One of the best that I've found is *Inn Spots & Special Places in New England,* by Nancy Webster and Richard Woodworth (Wood Pond Press). *Frommer's Wonderful Weekends from Boston,* by Marylin Wood (IDG Books Worldwide, Inc.), also has some good suggestions for inns to stay in, and there are a number of other books you might find useful.

I'd say there is little question that the king of spas in southern New England is **Canyon Ranch** (165 Kemble St., Lenox, MA 01240; ☎ 800/742-9000). The spa combines guided outdoor activities (hiking, biking, canoeing, and so forth) with all the stuff you'd expect at a spa—fitness programs, massage, hydrotherapy, healthy meals, etc. It's a pretty impressive place, where a week's stay also comes at a pretty impressive price, well over $2,000 per person.

One of the things I like about the **Norwich Inn & Spa** (607 W. Thames St., Route 32, Norwich, CT 06369; ☎ 800/ASK-4-SPA) is that you don't have to commit to a specific spa program. You can simply stay at the inn as though you were a guest at any other resort, and you won't be required to pick at some spartan, low-calorie meal. Or you can pick and choose how you want to make use of the spa facilities—a massage, a body wrap, whatever. Or you can immerse yourself in a full-on, week-long program to get fit and healthy. The choice is yours, but as at Canyon Ranch, be prepared to pay for it.

The **Spa at Grand Lake** (Route 207, Lebanon, CT 06429; ☎ **203/642-4306**) is in the heart of eastern Connecticut's Quiet Corner. The place might not be as fancy as Canyon Ranch or Norwich, but then neither is the price, and the atmosphere is decidedly low-key.

Because there are so many great inns in the region, it seems unfair to those omitted to select just a few here. But I'm going to go ahead with it anyway—under the assumption that before booking anywhere, you'll check regional chapters for other options. When it comes to seaside resorts, it's pretty hard to beat **The Wauwinet** (Wauwinet Road, Nantucket, MA 02554; ☎ **800/426-8718** or 508/228-0145). The weather-shingled inn with its sprawling porches, the manicured grounds with the backdrop of dunes and sea—this is exactly what an inn on Nantucket is supposed to look like. Such perfection, however, can be costly; room rates start at $195 a night and go way up from there.

Bascom Lodge (Box 1800, Lanesboro, MA 01237; ☎ **413/443-0011**), the AMC lodge at the summit of Mt. Greylock, is neither the most luxurious nor expensive place to stay in southern New England. But if you're a hiker on the Appalachian Trail who has been slogging around in the woods for several days, you may consider it a five-star resort. And what a place to wake up to the sunrise—literally, at the top of southern New England.

The **Boulders Inn** (East Shore Road, Route 45, New Preston, CT 06777; ☎ **800/55BOULDERS** or 860/868-0541), on the shores of Lake Wampanaug in western Connecticut, is just one of a number of great inns in this part of the state.

A particularly good restaurant and a private beach are the kind of extras that draw me in. Like The Wauwinet, however, the Boulders Inn is pricey—from $175 to close to $400 a night with meals included.

It is certainly not necessary in southern New England to drop that kind of change for a stay in a fine country inn. In fact, it might seem a bit silly to spend a bundle for lodging when presumably you'll be spending most of your time out and about in the great outdoors. So shop around and research your options. There are plenty of inns that charge well under $100 a night, and they may be as quaint, comfortable, and soulful as inns charging twice as much or more.

Keep in mind that the inn business can be seasonal. Not all inns near the coast shut down in winter; in fact, I'm surprised at how many on Martha's Vineyard and Nantucket stay open year-round. But many inns do close for business in the off-season, so your choices are more limited than in summer. The ski season, of course, keeps most inns in the mountains of the Berkshires and western Connecticut open in winter. But during the "shoulder seasons"—essentially April and November—some inn-keepers shut down. You might have fewer inns to choose from, but you're likely to be treated to reduced, off-season rates at any place that remains open.

Further Reading

For general travel information, as well as dining and accommodations listings, *Frommer's New England,* by Wayne Morris et al (IDG Books Worldwide, Inc.) and *Frommer's Cape Cod, Nantucket & Martha's Vineyard,* by Laura M. Reckford (IDG Books Worldwide, Inc.), are hard to beat. The *Sierra Club Guide to the Natural Areas of New England,* by John

Perry and Jane Greverus Perry (Sierra Club Books), provides thumbnail sketches (and not much more) of the parks, forest, sanctuaries, and refuges of New England.

If you're looking for a visual armchair tour, *The Smithsonian Guides to Natural America: Southern New England,* by Robert Finch et al (Random House), takes a photographic look at the natural wonders of the region. On the other hand, if you like having a guidebook along with you in the woods, *A Guide to Natural Places in the Berkshire Hills,* by Rene Laubach (Berkshire House), is almost like having a naturalist in your pocket when hiking in the Berkshires.

Walden, by Henry David Thoreau, might seem a bit ponderous, but if you're into the natural world of southern New England, it seems as though it should be required reading. And you might as well go ahead and read Thoreau's *Cape Cod,* too.

BOOKSTORES

Adventurous Traveler Bookstore (245 S. Champlain, Burlington, VT 05401; ☎ **800/282-3963**) is the rare bookstore that specializes exclusively in exactly the kind of activities covered in this book. If it is a book that has anything to do with the outdoors, Adventurous Traveler either has it or can get it for you. I have also found **Eastern Mountain Sports** (**www.emsonline.com**), the first-rate outdoor retail chain, to be a good place to go for books on the outdoors.

Chapter 2

The Berkshires

My familial connection to the Berkshires goes back several generations. My mother was born and raised in Pittsfield, at the edge of what is now the Canoe Meadows Wildlife Sanctuary. In fact, my family always referred to my grandparents' home—its blue awnings and structured lawns overlooking a supremely pastoral setting—as Canoe Meadows. I had assumed the name was simply the one my grandparents had chosen to give to the house. It had never occurred to me as a child that the "canoe" of Canoe Meadows might have had something to do with Native American history—that centuries earlier, the Housatonic tribe had held this place in sacred regard.

My grandfather, an incorrigibly loyal Williams College alumnus, skied the slopes of Sheep Mountain, just outside Williamstown, at least 20 years before ski lifts came into being in the '30s. Sheep Mountain seems barely a hill now; the arrival of lift-serviced skiing and the opening of other ski areas in the region have rendered its nearly 200-foot-high sloping pastures obsolete. But what impressed me in my youth—and still does now—was this corner of the country's robust outdoors heritage, predating even those nascent days of downhill skiing, when the materials of choice were hickory and wool (not carbon fiber or Gore-Tex), and men went skiing properly dressed in jackets and ties.

Williams, with its illustrious Outing Club already active in the early 19th century, had a zeal for adventure that may well have been unsurpassed by any institution in the country. Williams students built the first observation tower on Mt. Greylock's summit in 1831, and it was the Outing Club that did much of the early trail-clearing work on Mt. Greylock and the surrounding territory. Those of us who now venture into the Berkshire outback are the beneficiaries of their efforts. The club survives today and is as active as ever, with organized hiking, climbing, canoeing, and mountain-biking programs. It is this kind of continuity that instills in me a real respect for the time-honored and energetic commitment to the outdoors that characterizes residents of the Berkshires. The landscape elsewhere in the East (Vermont, Maine, New Hampshire) might be more rugged, but outdoors enthusiasts in the Berkshires—the Williams Outing Club is just one of many—traditionally make the most of all available opportunities.

I never skied Sheep Mountain; when, many decades after my grandfather's expeditions, my family went skiing on Christmas vacations, ski areas such as Jiminy Peak and Brodie were going strong—and had lifts to ride, thank goodness. But I may have captured the spirit of my grandfather's early skiing experiences when I embarked on my first backcountry excursions; although I don't recall the term "backcountry" being in vogue, or even in existence, in the early '60s. My cousins and I would venture out along a woodsy loop called the Brooks Trail, and while the results—getting tangled in saplings, falling into brooks—were often more comical than skillful, we truly felt we were getting closer to the soul of the forest and hills. It was, perhaps, my first intimate contact with the Berkshires outback.

My grandparents moved to South Williamstown in their later years, and the farm fields visible from the front porch of their house provided a foreground for the hulking mass of Mt. Greylock: a curvaceously symmetrical summit dome flanked by equidistant ridges. I was awestruck by this near-perfect example of Eastern mountain geography. But it was only when I ventured onto Greylock itself—a drive to the top and a hike down was my family's modus operandi—that I realized just how large the mountain really was and that the Berkshires, for all of their reputation as hills, were so much more than that.

It would be incorrect to call the Berkshires big-mountain country, but they are not a mere collection of insignificant hills either. I would label them something of a hybrid, borrowing in part from the orderly, gentrified sensibilities that characterize the land and villages of northwestern Connecticut, and the more rugged, in-country spirit of southern Vermont. The gentility of, say, Stockbridge appears Connecticut flavored, while the brawn of Mt. Greylock seems to be a spillover from Vermont. The world of western New England is not so Balkanized that merely crossing a state border means encountering a radical redefinition of culture and landscape.

Yet for all that they exhibit many of the qualities of their neighbors, the Berkshires are truly a world of their own. In part, the allure of their natural wonders stems from the realization that they inspired a number of this country's earliest literary giants: Nathaniel Hawthorne, Herman Melville, and Henry David Thoreau. Melville, envisioning whale-like shapes in the hills, wrote *Moby Dick* in his Pittsfield home. Hawthorne, in his

American Notebooks, was effusive in his praise of the Berkshires: "I have never driven through such romantic scenery, where there was such a variety and boldness of mountain shapes." The region's romantic scenery also inspired the creation of perhaps America's most famous outdoor music forum—Tanglewood in Lenox. Every summer, Tanglewood's sloping lawns, dense hedges, and views of the Berkshire countryside attract luminary artists from the worlds of classical, folk, popular, and operatic music. It is a setting worthy of the best in music, and vice versa. (For more on Tanglewood, see "A Little Night Music," on page 70.)

Although inspiring to literati and outdoor enthusiasts, historically, not all people have held the beauty of the Berkshires in high regard. Instead, the region was prized mainly for the value of its natural resources, especially its timber. Beginning in the 18th century, heavy logging began to decimate the Berkshire forests, and by the end of the 19th century, only about 20% of the land was classified as forested. Factories and mills indiscriminately polluted rivers and streams, primarily the Housatonic and the Hoosac, in an age predating ecological consciousness. In what many regard as one of the great engineering feats of the 19th century, the 4.75-mile Hoosac Tunnel was bored through Hoosac Mountain, at the cost of $15 million and 195 human lives during its 24 years of construction. Upon its completion, it was the second longest tunnel in the world, providing a convenient conduit for transporting people and raw and refined materials to and from the Berkshires. The industrial wheels spun, feeding the insatiable needs of a growing nation, and ravaged the landscape in the process.

Trees have since returned to the once-denuded hills, and forests now cover roughly 75% of the land in the Berkshires. They are young forests, of course, with few trees large enough to be of much commercial value. Logging continues in

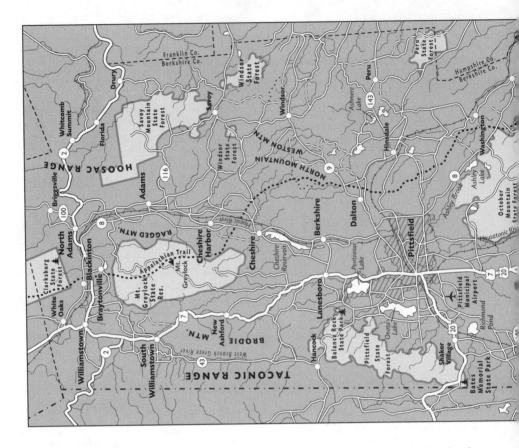

isolated pockets, but at least until the trees grow to full maturity, the industry is largely a nonentity. The economics of the late 20th century are not what they were a century or two ago; tourism now supersedes logging as the real breadwinner of the Berkshire economy. And as tourist attractions, forests are more valuable left standing, creating a natural setting that attracts summer visitors, foliage fanciers in the fall, and skiers in winter.

Once-abused rivers are also gradually returning to a fresher, more natural state. Through the first half of the 20th century, the Housatonic, the Hoosac, the Green, and several others were regarded as little more than waste receptacles, or power sources for mills and factories. Downstream of Pittsfield's paper mills, it was said you could tell what sort of paper was being produced on any given day by the color of the dye in the water.

But the federal Clean Water Act of 1972 and Massachusetts's visionary Wetlands Protection Act of that same year were giant legislative leaps toward cleaning up the watersheds of the Berkshires. While it may be many years before resident PCBs can be flushed entirely from the riverbeds' soil, Berkshire rivers are now canoeable, fishable, and in many cases swimmable. Thirty years ago, this would have been unimaginable.

So in many ways, today's Berkshires may be approaching a natural splendor not seen for centuries. The landscape about which Hawthorne rhapsodized in the early 1800s would likely appear even more inspiring to him today. My own memory, of course, does not go back far

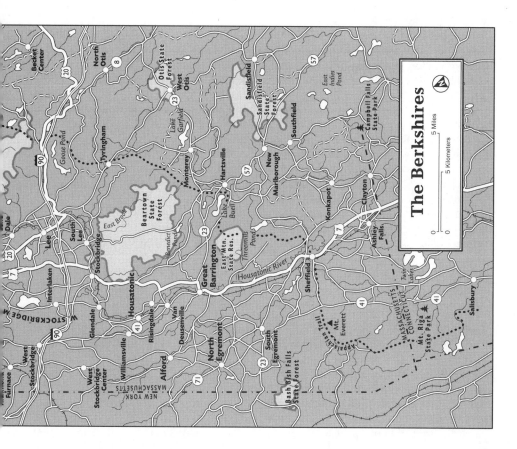

The Berkshires

5 Miles

5 Kilometers

enough to make such a comparison, but what does impress me, in my 4 decades of traveling in the Berkshires, is how unchanging a world it is. It is an area that has borrowed from its past—from Hawthorne, from the Williams Outing Club, from the Colonial sensibilities that created Stockbridge and Lenox—and incorporated and encapsulated the best of that past, in an all but immutable way, into its present.

Sure, there are shopping malls and new-home developments and other crude eyesores of the latter half of the 20th century. But there are also some 100,000 acres or more of protected lands, and, perhaps driven by the power of the tourist dollar, there is a marked sentiment that natural beauty is a good thing worth preserving. For anyone wishing to ven-

ture off into the great outdoors of this region, this nod toward preservation is a welcome development.

The Lay of the Land

The Berkshires are ancient hills indeed. At one time, millions of years before man stood erect, they looked something like the Rocky Mountains—tall, jagged, and fierce. But the Berkshires have suffered the ravages of time, as all mountains do eventually. They have shrunk in size and softened in shape, due primarily to the erosive influence of glaciers and the weather. (If any of us has the stamina to hang around this world for another few hundred million years, the Himalayas will probably look something like the Berkshires.)

The young forests that cover the prehistoric hills are a mix of hardwoods and conifers. Among the conifers, spruce, hemlock, and fir predominate, while the primary hardwood species are maple, ash, beech, and birch. In settlements such as Lenox and Stockbridge, many old-growth maples and poplars tower majestically above the streets; spared from the early logging onslaught, they provide some idea of what the forests might have looked like had the logging and nation-building of previous centuries been deemed unnecessary.

From late spring until fall, the forest floors play host to dense ground vegetation, ferns, laurel, wild herbs, and wildflowers. This blanket of rich green is made possible by a healthy dose of precipitation; the average annual precipitation of Pittsfield is roughly 40 inches. The forests' numerous streams and waterfalls seek out paths of least resistance through the granite and limestone that are the principal constituents of the bedrock. The inhospitable nature of the shallow soil and brisk weather at higher elevations allows for only stunted mixed-forest growth. As a result, high points in the region—notably the summits of Mt. Greylock, Mt. Everett, and Mt. Race—often afford sweeping panoramic views.

Sitting on a plateau, the Berkshires, with the notable exception of Mt. Greylock, are not marked by rugged, sharply upthrust mountains. Summits for the most part are soft rolling domes that rise not much more than 1,000 feet above the plateau. The plateau drains to the east into the Connecticut River, with the Deerfield River forming an important watershed. To the south and west, feeder streams spill into the Housatonic, the residual stream left by the glacier that 10,000 years ago carved out the wide, flat Housatonic Valley. To the north, the Hoosac watershed is the principal drainage. Interspersed among the mountains and forests are numerous natural lakes and ponds as well as man-made reservoirs, an ideal environment for canoe exploration.

More than 100,000 acres of public land, protected from development, offer in the Berkshires what is perhaps the closest thing to a backcountry world in southern New England. Principal among these protected lands are state forests, the largest tract occupied by the 17,665 contiguous acres of Savoy Mountain State Forest and Mohawk Trail State Forest. (Unlike in northern New England, national forests are a nonentity here.) Put it this way: If you want to get lost deep in the woods of the Berkshires, it can be done. As the mountains begin to recede toward the south, giving way to the broad plains of the Housatonic Valley, the forests give way to farmland that lines the banks of the Housatonic River

This is a land of four well-defined seasons. Unlike those in the milder Connecticut hills to the south, winters in the Berkshires are robust. Snow is a constant, at least at higher elevations, from early December to mid-March, and the mean February temperature is 26°F. Yet, unlike Vermont to the north, where spring can seem to pass in a matter of days, the Berkshires are awash in blossoming trees and flowers from late April until late May.

Summer comes to the Berkshires warmly, but rarely oppressively. The mean summer temperature is about 77°F, and lakes and ponds warm to ideal swimming temperatures. Fall here is justly famous; from late September until well into October, the hillsides burn with the radiance of autumnal New England. It is only in April and November—the shoulder seasons—that a dullness settles on the region; the hills are gray, the trees leafless, and neither the white of snow nor the green of abundant flora covers the forest floor.

Orientation

The Berkshires occupy a well-defined quadrant of western Massachusetts. To the south is the Connecticut border, to the north, the Vermont border, and to the west, the New York border. Where the Berkshires' eastern border lies is less clear; it's defined differently by natural features, county lines, or the needs of a guidebook writer to determine where one chapter begins and another ends. The Pioneer Valley, on the eastern periphery of the Berkshires, is essentially the Connecticut River watershed. But that watershed also includes the Deerfield River and its upper reaches, which are included here as part of the Berkshires instead of in the Central Massachusetts chapter.

The road system of the Berkshires is also well defined. The major north-south routes are **Routes 7 and 8,** while **Route 2** (also known as the **Mohawk Trail**), **Route 9,** and **Route 20** complete the latticework as the major east-west trails. The **Mass Pike (Interstate 90)** also passes through the heart of the region, but as a limited-access highway, it is not a fixture of day-to-day life.

While Route 8, connecting **Pittsfield** and **North Adams,** is probably the primary thoroughfare of commerce and industry in the region, Route 7 could probably be considered its tourism aorta. It is along Route 7 that you are more likely to encounter the sorts of things that attract visitors in great numbers to the Berkshires during the summer: antiques shops, museums, inns, and B&Bs, as well as less soulful attractions such as soft-ice-cream stands and go-kart tracks.

If you seek the soul of the Berkshires, you'll do best setting up camp—figuratively or literally—in **Stockbridge** or **Lenox.** Here is where the idyllic image of the Berkshires—the stately, colonial houses (a good many converted to elegant inns), the picket fences, the old-growth tree canopies arcing over streets—is so

perfectly executed you might be led to believe it is a movie set or theme park, not the real thing. Pittsfield, by contrast, is the commercial and legislative center of the region—not surprising, given that it also lies roughly at the geographical center. It is characterized by a functional, turn-of-the-century look, with streets lined by squared-off mercantile and office buildings. For the Berkshire traveler, however, Pittsfield serves a purpose. If you're looking for basic supplies, from groceries to fishing tackle, you'll likely have your best luck finding them here.

South of Pittsfield are **Egremont** and **Sheffield,** the smaller but equally spirited equivalents of Stockbridge and Lenox, while **Great Barrington** is somewhat the commercial equivalent of Pittsfield. The antiques culture, so much a part of summer life in the Berkshires, finds its ground zero in Sheffield, where no doubt hundreds of thousands of antiques-driven dollars change hands during the course of an average tourist season. In the far north is North Adams, its history steeped in blue-collar industry, and **Williamstown,** which exists primarily because of Williams College. It is neither extraordinarily quaint nor especially commercial, but is instead an attractive, quiet, and orderly place—its tidy lawns and brick colonial buildings defining the quintessential small-college town. Many trails in this area now used by hikers, skiers, and mountain bikers exist due to the energetic trail work of the Williams Outing Club, which was formed more than a century ago to take advantage of the northern Berkshires' considerable natural assets.

Parks & Other Hot Spots

Appalachian Trail
From Connecticut, the trail enters Massachusetts through Mt. Washington State Forest and exits, on its way into

Vermont, through Clarksburg State Forest. The Berkshire chapter of the Appalachian Mountain Club is at the Mt. Greylock headquarters (☎ **413/443-0011;** www.fred.net/kathy/at.html).

The exact length of the Massachusetts portion of the famous trail, stretching from Georgia to Maine, is between 83 and 90 miles, depending on who is doing the walking, talking, or counting. Maintained by the Appalachian Mountain Club, the trail has been designated a National Scenic trail by the National Park Service. The trail is routed to take advantage of the panoramic views offered by the high ridgelines, but because of this, the trail, as it rises from valleys to ridges, features considerable elevation changes. Short sections of the "AT," particularly in Mt. Greylock Reservation and Mt. Washington State Forest, make for excellent day hikes or can be traversed in 2-day overnights. Long-distance and overnight hikers should be aware that trailside shelters are located only about every 18 to 22 miles, with less substantial lean-tos in between. The trail also crosses major roadways from time to time, so the occasional night's stay in a motel is not necessarily a bad idea. Just ask any Georgia-to-Maine through-hiker, who is desperate for a shower and the comfort of a mattress.

Beartown State Forest

From Great Barrington, head east on Rte. 23 to Blue Hill Rd. Turn left, continue for about 2 miles, then right for .5 mile to the forest headquarters. Headquarters: Monterey (☎ 413/528-0904).

Somewhat smaller (10,852 acres) than its northern neighbor, October Mountain State Forest, Beartown is an elevated plateau, situated mostly above 1,600 feet, with the 2,155-foot Mt. Wilcox as its high point. Its network of paved and unpaved roads and multiuse trails make it a terrific spot for mountain biking in summer and cross-country skiing and snowmobiling in winter. Interestingly, its northern half features dense conifer groves—hemlock,

pine, and fir—and a primarily deciduous forest covers its southern half. Trail work in recent years has made Beartown somewhat more user-friendly than October Mountain, where a shortage of road and trail markings makes getting lost a likelier proposition.

Deerfield River

For the popular upper sections of the river, head west from Charlemont on Rte. 2 about 2 miles. Look for a right turn onto River Rd. at a sign for Yankee Atomic Energy. Sections of the river south of Charlemont are also good for fishing and boating. For dam release schedules, call ☎ 888/356-3663.

The Deerfield forms from a couple of branches into a single, fast-moving river at the Massachusetts–Vermont border. The river north of Charlemont, fed by fresh rushes of water throughout the summer, thanks to dam releases, features perhaps the best whitewater in southern New England. The trout fishing is also first-rate. Below Charlemont, the river slows down and widens as it makes its way toward the Connecticut River and the rapids ease up somewhat. Here the river is better for canoeists and novice kayakers and rafters. And fishermen will still get what's coming to them—the river abounds with trout.

Dubuque State Forest

From Adams, take Rte. 116 west through Savoy. Turn left onto Rte. 8A north. Forest headquarters are on the left side of the road. For information, call Mohawk State Forest (☎ 413/339-5504).

With the nearby Savoy State Forest attracting more attention, Dubuque is often the overlooked outsider among state forests in the Berkshires. For that reason, it can be a terrific place to spend a day or even a weekend; there are four trailside shelters within the park, all far from the summer crowds. Forest-service roads and multiuse trails make for excellent mountain biking, yet there is also an extensive network of trails reserved for hiking only.

Stillwater canoeists and fishermen will get their share of the action too, with three small ponds near park headquarters to explore. Lower elevations and extensive forestation help keep Dubuque naturally air-conditioned in the summer heat. At the same time, that means this is not the park to visit if you're looking for panoramic vistas of the Berkshires.

Housatonic River
Accessible from Rte. 7 at various bridge crossings. For information, contact the Berkshire office of the Housatonic Valley Association (☎ 413/637-3188), located in the Berkshire Scenic Railway Museum in Lenox.

The headwaters of the Housatonic (*Hoo-satonic*) join forces in Pittsfield to flow south into Connecticut as a mostly slow-moving, meandering river. It is the remnant stream of what was once a mighty glacier of the last ice age (10,000 to 12,000 years ago) that carved out the Housatonic River Valley. Passing through an alluvial flood plain of cornfields and cow pastures, this is the primary river in the Berkshires for a mellow, flatwater paddle. Considerable work has been done in the past 3 decades to clean up the Housatonic, and the effect has been remarkable. Nevertheless, it may be many years before all the PCBs can be flushed from the silt and soil of the river's bed. So although good sport fishing can be had along the river, fish should be released.

Mt. Greylock Reservation
From Pittsfield, head 5 miles north on Rte. 7 through Lanesboro. Look for signs for a turnoff to the right to reservation headquarters. Headquarters: Lanesboro (☎ 413/499-4262).

At 3,491 feet, Mt. Greylock is the highest mountain in Massachusetts (and in all of southern New England). Two paved roads—one from Lanesboro from the south, and one from North Adams from the north—make the summit accessible

by motor vehicle, meaning a hike to the summit on a warm summer's day won't necessarily yield a private mountaintop experience. Yet a summit trip, by whatever means of transportation, is well worthwhile; Nathaniel Hawthorne called the summit view "a daydream to look at." Visitors to the summit will also find Bascom Lodge, an Appalachian Mountain Club facility welcomed in particular by hikers along the Appalachian Trail, which passes over Mt. Greylock.

Numerous trails—some exclusively for hiking, others on which mountain bikes and horses are permitted—make get-aways into the forests of the mountain's sizeable flanks an easy proposition, even on a busy summer weekend. Among the noteworthy features of the mountain is an area called the Hopper, a glacially formed cirque, now heavily forested and preserved—through limitations on hiker, biker, and camper access—in a pristine natural state.

Mt. Washington State Forest
From South Egremont, take Rte. 41 south. Turn right on Mt. Washington Rd. just south of town, and continue for about 10 miles to forest headquarters. Headquarters: Mt. Washington (☎ 413/528-0330).

This is something of an oddball state forest. It is, in fact, three parcels of land separated by intervening plots of private land, and while there are several noteworthy mountains—Mt. Everett, Mt. Race, and Alander Mountain—there seems to be no Mt. Washington, except for a tiny, barely extant town of that name. This is a terrific spot for hiking and overnight backpacking—the best in southwestern Massachusetts—yet some trails, particularly those connecting the three forest sections, venture briefly out of state and into Connecticut to the south and New York to the west. Highlights of the forest are the hike up Mt. Everett, the open views from the Mt. Race ridgeline, and the short hike to Bash Bish Falls.

Notchview Reservation

From Pittsfield, take Rte. 9 east and look for signs to the reservation (on your left) past Windsor. Maintained by the Trustees of Reservations. Western Regional Office: The Mission House, Box 792, Sergeant St., Stockbridge, MA 01262; ☎ 413/298-3239.

This 3,000-acre reservation sits on a plateau above Windsor, at an elevation almost entirely above 2,000 feet. A well-defined trail system through mixed forest and open meadows makes for fine day-hiking in the summer; when trails pass through meadows, mountain views can be superb. In winter, Notchview is also a terrific place for cross-country skiing and snowshoeing. The high elevation helps to ensure a consistent snowpack, and steep ups and downs are minimal; the high point of the park is Judges Hill at 2,297 feet, while the visitors' center sits at approximately 2,000 feet. One more bonus for hikers and winter travelers: The reservation is off-limits to off-road vehicles and snowmobiles.

October Mountain State Forest

Head east from Lee on Rte. 20. Turn left on East St., then right on Willow Hill Rd. to forest headquarters. Headquarters: Lee (☎ 413/243-1778).

At 15,710 acres, this is one of the heftier chunks of public land in Massachusetts, outsized only by the contiguous Mohawk Trail and Savoy Mountain state forests. With the forest sitting on a relatively flat plateau (by mountain standards, anyway), elevations here generally run between 1,800 and 2,000 feet. With a sizeable network of unpaved roads and multiuse trails, October Mountain can be a great place for mountain biking and cross-country skiing—with a couple of caveats. Roads and trails are often not well marked, and a navigational error can result in a visitor not only getting lost but also facing a brutally steep climb (by biking or skiing standards) to reattain the elevations at the heart of the forest. Also, this can be wet land, meaning mountain bikers can find themselves almost literally in over their heads, especially in spring.

The presence of moisture does have its rewards, however. There are several attractive lakes and reservoirs within the forest, and a recently developed interpretive trail around Washington Mountain Marsh has been a superb addition. On the downside, selective logging in the forest is an ongoing operation. While the visual aesthetic of pristine forest has not, for the most part, necessarily been impaired, logging vehicles can churn up the forest roads, making mucky roads even muckier.

Pittsfield State Forest

From Pittsfield take West St. west to Churchill St. Turn right on Churchill, then left onto Cascade St., leading to the forest entrance. Headquarters: Pittsfield (☎ 413/442-8992).

Crisscrossed by an extensive network of multiuse trails and old roads, Pittsfield State Forest is probably best for mountain biking and horseback riding. The Taconic Skyline Trail, which runs for roughly 20 miles through the state forest, is a good option for a 2-day hike, with the campground at Berry Pond, at the approximate halfway point, an ideal spot for an overnight. Unfortunately, the trail has not been well maintained, and the going can be rough in some places. Views along the high ridges of the park, particularly to the west, are superb.

Savoy Mountain State Forest

From North Adams, take Rte. 2 east to Florida (Massachusetts). Turn right on Center Shaft Rd. to reach forest headquarters. Headquarters: North Adams (☎ 413/663-8469).

At over 11,000 acres, this is one of the largest state forests in Massachusetts. A network of dirt roads and multiuse trails make it a terrific spot for mountain biking and horseback riding in summer. In winter, the higher elevations of the park (much of it around 2,000 feet) make finding a reliable snowpack for cross-country skiing and snowmobiling relatively easy.

The potential downside: Campsites tend to be in high demand on weekends. Also, because many trails are open to off-road vehicles in summer and snowmobiles in winter, deep-forest serenity is far from a sure thing.

What to Do & Where to Do It

BIRD-WATCHING

The dense forests of the Berkshires, the many small bodies of water, and—sometimes unfortunately—the often abundant bug life, attract a wide variety of species to the region. At **Bartholomew's Cobble,** on the Massachusetts–Connecticut border, 240 species have been sighted and recorded. On a spring day, when insect hatches abound and avian hormones run rampant, the woods and meadows are a symphony of thrush and warbler song, punctuated by the occasional screech of a hawk, the caw of a turkey vulture, or the trumpeting of passing geese.

Not surprisingly, some of the best places to settle in with a pair of binoculars are the sanctuaries managed by the Massachusetts Audubon Society at **Canoe Meadows** in Pittsfield and **Pleasant Valley** in Lenox. The sanctuaries provide an excellent habitat for lower-elevation songbirds. In the meadows of **Greylock Glen** (in Adams at the western base of Mt. Greylock), look for robins and finches. Trails descending from the summit of **Mt. Greylock** offer a number of spurs to overlooks, from which you can spot hawks and ravens. In recent years, sightings of bald eagles have increased along the **Housatonic River.** Migratory birds, notably Canada geese, seem, for whatever reason, to like using **golf courses** as layover spots in their journeys north and south. Apparently the fairways make for comfortable takeoffs and landings.

Guides

The **Massachusetts Division of Fisheries & Wildlife** (Field Headquarters, Westborough, MA 01581; ☎ **508/792-7270**) publishes a wildlife viewing guide as well as a bird checklist for Massachusetts. Checklists are also available at its headquarters at Pleasant Valley Sanctuary and Bartholomew's Cobble. The **Massachusetts Audubon Society** organizes guided outings throughout the region. Contact the Society's **Berkshire Wildlife Sanctuaries** (472 W. Mountain Rd., Lenox, MA 01240; ☎ **413/637-0320**) for a schedule.

CANOEING

Canoeing in the Berkshires is largely a day-outing affair. Long stretches of interconnected, undammed waterways simply do not exist, although small ponds ideal for a few hours of exploration are numerous.

Benedict Pond

Moneterey, in Beartown State Forest. Access: From Great Barrington, take Rte. 23 approximately 5 miles to Blue Hill Rd. Turn right. After about 2 miles, turn right onto Beartown Rd. for the parking lot and boat launch.

In the world of quiet-water canoeing, bigger is not always better. This 35-acre pond is just a speck of water compared with, say, the 1,000-acre Otis Reservoir about 10 miles to the east. Yet on a busy summer weekend, when Otis Reservoir is buzzing with water skiers, Jet Skis, and generally youthful mayhem, Benedict Pond remains its own haven of quietude. Hemlocks hug the shore. In spring, azaleas bloom, and in late summer, blueberries are ripe for picking. Beaver dams are highlights for waterborne exploration, and when you're done with that, a network of hiking trails allows for exploration on land. If you have young kids, make a weekend of it; there's a campground that reaches to the water's edge, although with just 12 sites, it can fill up in a hurry.

Bog Pond

Florida, in Savoy Mountain State Forest. Access: From North Adams, take Rte. 2 east to Florida (Massachusetts). Turn right on Center Shaft Rd. Continue past North and South ponds and turn left at sign for Bog Pond.

Don't expect a great expeditionary outing here. This is a small pond, great for a half-day paddle of poking around the forested shoreline and through the shallow marshes that lent the pond its name. In summer, crowds tend to migrate to North and South ponds nearby; they're more readily accessible, with better swimming. But by traveling just a few minutes farther, you'll find the relative serenity of Bog Pond. The surrounding woodlands are entirely undeveloped—no lakeside homes, no nearby highways—so the awareness of your separation from civilization and your celebration of nature is accentuated. This is a great place to while away a few hours with a picnic lunch and the kids.

Buckley Dunton Lake

Becket, in October Mountain State Forest. Access: From Lee, take Rte. 4 east 4 miles to Becket Rd. Turn left and continue for 2.5 miles to the lake access, on your left (look for the sign BUCKLEY DUNTON LAKE—DAY USE ONLY).

When is a pond large enough to be a lake, or a lake small enough to be a pond? Buckley Dunton exists as perhaps the size in between and, as such, is ideal for canoeing in many ways. At 195 acres, it is large enough for a full day of exploration, yet small enough to be only minimally affected by the winds that sometimes sweep across bigger bodies of water.

In fact, Buckley Dunton is technically a reservoir, created by damming Yokum Brook more than a century ago. Some houses line the lakeshore along its southern extremes; otherwise, the surrounding state forest invokes the spirit of the wilderness. Toward the north end, the lake becomes marshier—a world of waterlilies, cattails, and frogs that is great for poking around in. Just be sure to navigate the water with care to avoid such obstacles as rotting stumps. On weekends, the lake can be a popular fishing spot for bass, pickerel, and perch, but to call it overcrowded would be a gross overstatement. On weekdays, you're likely to have the place to yourself.

Housatonic River, Housatonic to Sheffield

Allow 3–4 hours. Easy–moderate. Access: From Great Barrington, take Rte. 41 north about 2 miles to Division St. Turn right and continue for less than .5 mile to a bridge. Parking along the road is permitted. Takeout is at the covered bridge north of Sheffield.

The Housatonic is, for the most part, a slow-moving river through the Berkshires. But for those seeking at least some white-water thrill, this section of the river features a short but sometimes tricky stretch of rapids between Housatonic (the town) and Great Barrington. The trip begins as a gentle ride through pretty countryside, but as you near Great Barrington, the pace quickens and you must be deft in maneuvering your craft through what, depending on the water level, may approach Class II conditions. Be on the lookout, just after the Cottage Street Bridge in Great Barrington, for what canoeists sometimes call a thank-you-ma'am—a particularly sudden but short drop. From here the river resumes its easygoing ways, passing through the scenic farmlands of the southern Berkshires. If you make this trip early in the morning, do not be surprised to see deer grazing near the river's edge—you will certainly see cows in the pasturelands nearby. Also, be wary of blown-down trees—a freak tornado in 1995 dumped trees in the river, and while most have since been removed, you may still encounter an obstacle or two. And as you near the last part of your trip, watch out for the covered bridge (see description, below) that marks the end of your ride. Or perhaps it doesn't—if you want to make a long day of it, you can continue on the section of river described below.

Housatonic River, Sheffield to Bartholomew's Cobble

Allow 3–4 hours. Easy. Access: From Sheffield, head north on Rte. 7 .5 mile. Turn right on Covered Bridge Lane, and park near the bridge. Takeout at the Rannapo Road Bridge.

You can make this a half-day or full-day trip, depending on your need for expedience. The river here moves so slowly you won't be at the mercy of a robust flow that would thwart your efforts to pull along shore and hold the boat steady for a moment of rest or reflection. This is not a river that ought to be rushed, as it twists and loops back and forth through the farmlands of the Housatonic plain.

The covered bridge at the put-in long held the claim of being the oldest covered bridge in Massachusetts. Alas, the original 1837 bridge burned in 1994, and what exists today, although some of the original elements have been incorporated, is essentially a replica. In its first few miles, the river seems a study in navigational indecision as it passes east of Sheffield. It loops back and forth from north to south as if unable to determine its own course or the directional slope of the land. Evidence of oxbows—former loops in the river that have now been cut off as a new, more direct channel forms—is widespread. Watch for blown-down trees; you might be obliged to execute a quick portage or two to avoid obstacles. In doing so, be careful about stepping boldly from your craft; the silty soil can seize an unwary boot with quicksand-like suction.

In the distance, the low hills that mark the edge of the Housatonic River Valley are an ever-present backdrop. Keep an eye out for swallows nesting in the river banks, for cows grazing in riverside pastures, and, if you are particularly fortunate, a bald eagle. The reinvigoration of the national emblem has been a triumphant showcase of the past 2 decades' efforts for endangered-species protection, and while eagles are hardly common along the Housatonic, they aren't exceedingly rare, either. You might spot an osprey—that supremely athletic hunter of fish—as well. If you have energy at the takeout at Rannapo Road, take a walk over to Bartholomew's Cobble, just south of the bridge. It is one of the Berkshires' premier sites for short hikes and bird-watching.

Westfield River, North Branch

Allow 2 hours. Moderate. Access: In Cummington, put in at the Rte. 9 bridge that crosses the river east of town. Takeout at the Rte. 143 bridge west of Chesterfield.

The North Branch of the Westfield River offers a great ride for experienced canoeists. There are rapids here, but they max out at around Class II—too mild-mannered for whitewater kayakers, but robust enough to give open-boat canoeists a charge. Perhaps the best part of the trip is the relative remoteness of the location. Although the first couple of miles are along Route 9, the river dips southward into a largely roadless and undeveloped countryside after its confluence with the Swift River. This region is locally known as the Pork Barrel, and as the scenery of hills and forest close in, so do the rapids. There is nothing here that should intimidate a paddler confident of his or her skills, but this is also not an area where you want to be overturning or pinballing off rocks. Should you encounter troubles, you might be facing the prospect of bushwhacking for a couple of miles before reaching help. Be sure to bring along a fly rod if you're inclined to fish; because this is a relatively inaccessible stretch of river, you're chances of landing a few native brook trout are pretty good.

LEAVE IT TO BEAVER

Perhaps no other animal symbolizes the re-emergence of wildlife in New England better than the beaver. Before the white man's arrival, beaver ponds numbered as many as 300 to the mile and populations swelled to over 100 million in North America. But with colonization came the fur trade. The settlers persuaded the Indians to use beaver pelts as wampum in exchange for basic European goods, firearms, and alcohol. This worked well for the colonists, who William Wood noted were ineffective hunters, anyway. Wood, English traveler and author of *New England's Prospect* (published in 1633), noted that "these beasts [beavers] are too cunning for the English, who seldom or never catch any of them; therefore we leave them to those skillful hunters [Indians] whose time was not so precious." Precious or not, the fact is the Indians hunted far more efficiently than the English. Once the skins were in the hands of the settlers, they shipped the prized commodity back to Europe in exchange for a huge profit.

The decimation of beavers lasted for several hundred years, until the New England species had vanished. By the time Henry David Thoreau wrote in his journals in 1855, the long list of animals absent from the New England forest included "bear, deer, porcupines, and beaver." Fortunately, with the advent of second-growth forest, the furry critter has returned with his friends. According to wildlife experts, there are now more than 60,000 beavers in New England, and the number is increasing rapidly. The trappers are even returning, but with the purchasing of fur products at an all-time low, beavers need not worry.

On the contrary, beavers are exercising their freedom as the newest member of America's oldest colonies. They are flooding scores of public roads, backing pond water into private wells, and may even be the cause of illness. In December 1985, an outbreak of giardisis—a form of dysentery—affected 686 in Pittsfield, Massachusetts, the Berkshires' largest town. A subsequent investigation discovered that a beaver that had been trapped in a reservoir used to supply drinking water to the town was carrying the giardia parasite. So the next time your boss asks you why you were out yesterday, just tell him you had beaver fever.

—by Stephen Jermanok

Gear & Rentals

Onota Boat Livery (Pecks Road, Pittsfield; ☎ 413/442-1724) rents canoes for exploring Onota Lake near Pittsfield. **Appalachian Mountain Gear** (684 S. Main St., Great Barrington, MA 01230; ☎ 413/528-5054) and **Gaffer's Outdoors** (216 Main St., Sheffield, MA 01257; ☎ 413-229-0063) rent canoes and kayaks and provide shuttle service for those venturing out onto the Housatonic or nearby ponds and lakes.

Outfitters

Short guided trips on the Housatonic are organized by the **Pleasant Valley Wildlife Sanctuary** (472 West Mountain Rd., Lenox, MA 01240; ☎ 413/637-0320). Call for a schedule. **Gaffer's Outdoors** (see above) offers guided trips along the Housatonic.

CROSS-COUNTRY SKIING

The breadth of cross-country skiing opportunity in the Berkshires can be surprising. Large state forests (such as Beartown, October Mountain, and Savoy Mountain) remain open to skiers in winter and, for the most part, closed to vehicular traffic other than snowmobilers. Dirt roads in summer become ski, snowmobile, or snowshoe trails in winter. The terrain in these forests is not, for the most part, extremely hilly, so strenuous climbs and hairy descents are the exception rather than the rule. If you simply want to go out for a long, quiet ski in the woods—for a day or even more—the Berkshires can accommodate.

Their shortcoming is snow, or rather a lack of reliable snow. Unlike downhill skiers at lift-serviced ski areas, backcountry skiers can't count on snowmaking to make up for natural deficiencies, and there have been a couple of winters in recent years when natural snow has been pretty lean. That said, keep in mind that many of the places described here are relatively high in elevation—1,000 feet or more above the valley floors—so just because the ground is brown in Pittsfield or Williamstown doesn't mean there's no snow higher up.

Ashley Hill

Allow 2 hours. Moderate. Access: From South Egremont, take Rte. 41 south and turn right on Mt. Washington Rd. Continue for 8 miles past the entrance to Mt. Everett State Reservation until you reach the Mount Washington State Forest Headquarters. Map: Available through the Department of Environmental Management (Region 5 Headquarters, Box 1433, Pittsfield, MA 01202; ☎ 413/442-8928).

"Ashley Hill is strictly reserved for people who prefer not to see other people," Steve Jermanok wrote in the *Adventure Guide to New England*. This does not mean the place is entirely undiscovered; you might encounter evidence of snowmobilers having been here, and that may be a good thing. Snowmobiles pack down deep snow, and while their treads often leave a rough surface, a packed trail usually makes the going somewhat easier for backcountry skiers.

The terrain covered here is also described as part of the Alander Mountain day hike (see "Hiking & Backpacking," below). If you are gung-ho and bent on a long day on skis, by all means, go for it and do the full, 14-mile loop. But given the shorter days of winter and the uncertainty of snow conditions—slogging

through drifts or negotiating icy descents can be time- and energy-consuming—you're probably better off doing a shorter out-and-back.

The trail starts in an open meadow at the forest's headquarters, but soon proceeds into the forest. After crossing two bridges, the Ashley Hill Trail will be on your left. It begins as a short but invigorating climb, soon leveling out to provide a good view of the ravine cut by Ashley Hill Brook. At this point, you can continue on for a pleasant ramble through the woods for as long as you want. You'll return the same way you came, so measure out your time and stamina accordingly. If you venture far enough—about 2.5 to 3 miles into your trek—you'll be treated to the sight of several beaver dams along Ashley Brook, which parallels the trail for a while.

Beartown State Forest

Allow 2 hours. Moderate. Access: From Great Barrington, take Rte. 23 approximately 5 miles to Blue Hill Rd. Turn right. The parking lot is about 2 miles down the road. Map: Available through the Department of Environmental Management (Region 5 Headquarters, Box 1433, Pittsfield, MA 01202; ☎ 413/442-8928).

Benedict Pond sits like a small sea of tranquility in Beartown State Forest. A 2.5-mile trail loops the pond, marked by a few gentle ups and downs. Through the leafless trees of winter, the presence of the pond is a constant reference point; keep the pond in view, and you can't get lost in the wintry woods. The rolling hills of Beartown act as a backdrop for the pond, including, to the south, the imaginatively named Livermore Peak. This might conjure up the image of some lofty, jagged spire, but how can anything just 1,863 feet tall be called a peak, particularly when the pond itself sits only about 400 feet lower? Livermore Peak is one of many hills, and they are pretty hills at that.

The loop trail around Benedict Pond is just one part of a substantial trail network in Beartown devoted to cross-country skiing. If snow and temperature conditions are right, you could easily ski all day through the rolling, forested terrain. Of course you'll need snow, but why should temperature be important? Without sufficient cold, this can be wet territory, not only around the edges of the pond but also in areas that can be boggy in summer. So wait for a cold, snowy day to head for Beartown, allowing yourself a couple of hours to circumnavigate the pond at a comfortable pace, or a full day if you plan to explore deeper into the forest.

Notchview Reservation

Allow 2–3 hours. Easy to strenuous, depending on loop chosen. Access: From Pittsfield, take Rte. 9 east. Notchview is about 1 mile east of the intersection of Rte. 9 and 8A. Map: Available at the visitor center (☎ 413/684-0148).

Notchview, a 3,000-acre reservation, sits on a high plateau east of Pittsfield. By the time you have arrived at its visitor center, you will already have done most of your climbing by car during the drive from Pittsfield. So as you set out on the 30 kilometers of trail that wind through the reservation's dense forests and open meadows, you won't be facing strenuous climbs or hair-raising descents.

Elevation, of course, is a great plus when it comes to harboring snow; the slight temperature differential between Pittsfield and the much higher Notchview—where elevations range between 1,600 feet and 2,297 feet at the top of Judges Hill—can easily spell the difference between snow and precipitation of a less skiable variety. The main route at Notchview is the Circuit Trail, an old road that makes about a 2-mile loop through the woods. This is a good place to bring kids; the well-marked Circuit Trail is hard to lose, and the visitor center is never far away should the weather fail to be kid-friendly.

Trail spurs from the Circuit Trail are numerous, so go out and explore; in most cases you'll recross the ubiquitous Circuit Trail to regain your bearings. After a fresh snowfall, the sight of snow suspended on evergreen boughs, protected from the wind because of their close proximity to one another, is enough to soothe any savage heart. If you are particularly ambitious, go for the 1.5-mile jaunt up Judges Hill. Just keep in mind that if you attempt this climb—not easy on cross-country skis—you'll also have to descend via the same trail, which might be even harder.

There is an admission charge of $6 to enter the reservation, but if the snow is right, it is certainly money well spent.

October Mountain State Forest

Allow 2–6 hours. Easy to moderate. From Lenox, take Rte. 20 east past Lee to Becket Rd. Turn left and continue for about 5 minutes and make a sharp left at the two-story, white clapboard house on the left. Continue until the plowed road ends. Map: Available through the Department of Environmental Manage- ment (Region 5 Headquarters, Box 1433, Pittsfield, MA 01202; ☎ 413/442-8928).

Measuring 16,127 acres and lying on a plateau approximately 1,800 to 2,000 feet above sea level, October Mountain has both the size and the elevation to make it a superb place for an extended back-country outing. You might find the going surprisingly easy; the terrain is generally flat (the "mountains" top out at around 2,200 feet), and the trails are in fact roads that are wide and easy to negotiate. The challenge here might be orienteering. Roads are not always well marked, so it's a good idea to keep track of landmarks and intersections as you proceed. Assuming you can simply retrace your tracks in the snow is often asking for trouble, particularly on a snowy or windy day when fresh snow can quickly obliterate evidence of your journey.

County Road, your route out from the trailhead, plunges quickly into the mixed forest, which, in less than 2 miles, leads to a fork in the road. By continuing on County Road itself—the left-hand tine of the fork—you come quickly to School-house Reservoir. Bear right on Lenox-Whitney Place for a little over a mile, then left on West Branch Road, and you can explore Washington Mountain marsh (on your right) or October Mountain Reservoir by heading to your left.

While your opportunities are endless, make sure that, within this maze of trails, your journey isn't. Keep your bearings; always note where you are and where you've come from, and you'll find October Mountain is hard to beat for a full-day winter outing.

Nordic Ski Centers

Looking for groomed trails for skate skiing or classical striding? **Brodie Mountain Cross Country Touring Center** (Route 7, New Ashford, MA 01237; ☎ 413/443-4752) might be a bit of a surprise. Brodie, after all, is known among downhill skiers to be something of a party-hard place, something that would seem anathema to the aerobic cross-country crowd. Yet there is an excellent 25-kilometer network of groomed trails here, in addition to access to another 40 kilometers of unplowed roads that lead into the backcountry of Mt. Greylock Reservation.

Bucksteep Manor (885 Washington Mountain Rd., Washington, MA 01233; ☎ 413/623-5535) also combines groomed-trail skiing with backcountry opportunity. There are 25 groomed kilometers on the manor grounds, right at the edge of October Mountain State Forest.

Cranwell Resort (55 Lee Rd., Lenox, MA 01240; ☎ 413/637-1364), with 15 kilometers of groomed trails on its 380 acres, features a rarity in cross-country skiing—snowmaking. The snowmaking coverage is minimal—just 3 acres—but if you need an aerobic fix and the weather gods are uncooperative, Cranwell is the place to go. **John Drummond Kennedy**

Park (Main Street, Lenox, MA 01240; ☎ 413/637-4407) features an extensive network of groomed and ungroomed trails in Lenox on what were once the grounds of the Aspinwall Hotel, a gathering place for men of power and influence in the early 20th century.

Gear and Rentals

Ski centers with rental equipment available include **Brodie** and **Cranwell** (see "Nordic Ski Centers," above). **Berkshire Outfitters** (Route 8, Adams, MA 01221; ☎ 413/743-5900) is a good place to go if you're looking to buy equipment or accessories.

Guides and Outfitters

Stump Sprouts (West Hill Road, West Hawley, MA; ☎ 413/339-4265) offers rustic accommodations and guided backcountry skiing in nearby state forests, including Dubuque and Savoy Mountain.

DOWNHILL SKIING/ SNOWBOARDING

It is not easy being the southern neighbor of Vermont, the capital of downhill skiing in New England. Vermont's mountains are bigger, the terrain more varied, and the snowfall more abundant than what you'll find in the Berkshires. By most measures, Vermont easily one-ups the Berkshires in the world of downhill skiing.

So why bother? Quite simply, to escape the big-resort hustle and bustle. Skiing in Vermont is an industry, the driving force in what has made tourism the state's leading economic entity. In the Berkshires, a mellower atmosphere prevails. In Vermont, large resort companies have taken over skiing, building sprawling base villages and hotels. Ski areas of the Berkshires have instead held on to a ski-area-next-door character. You can essentially drive right up to the lifts, pay a modest price, and not feel self-conscious if you don't have the latest equipment or clothing. Accentuating the neighborly appeal of the Berkshires is the kind of lodging you'll find there; it's more likely to be a colonial-era inn than a functional but sterile condominium.

All of this makes Berkshire skiing best for families and less aggressive skiers who might be intimidated or turned off by the testosterone bravado that sometimes pervades the bigger, more challenging resorts. The downfall of the Berkshires is often the snow you'll find there, or lack thereof. While most ski areas have 100% snowmaking coverage (or close to it), it would be a mistake to go to the Berkshires for a winter weekend expecting plenty of light, natural fluff. And the season is certainly shorter than in the north; good skiing before Christmas or after mid-March is rare.

The Berkshires can outdo Vermont in one respect—night skiing. While night skiing is all but nonexistent in Vermont, many Berkshires resorts (among them Jiminy Peak, Brodie, Bousquet, and Berkshire East) stay open after darkness falls. And yes, they do turn on the lights.

Berkshire East

Box 727, South River Rd., Charlemont, MA 01339. ☎ **413/339-6617.** 34 trails (24% beginner, 35% intermediate, 40% expert); 1 triple chair lift, 2 doubles, 2 surface lifts; 1,180-foot vertical drop. Full-day tickets $35 weekend, $25 weekday.

A bit of a diamond in the rough, Berkshire East has some of the steepest runs in southern New England to go along with a vertical drop that also ranks in the top echelon. Expert skiers who come to northern Massachusetts tend to migrate toward better-known Jiminy Peak. In the realm of sleek resort facilities, low-key Berkshire East is no match for Jiminy. Jiminy is a ski *resort,* while Berkshire East is a ski *area.* But for sheer challenge and good snow coverage, Berkshire East is about as good as it gets south of Vermont.

Bousquet Ski Area

Dan Fox Dr., Pittsfield, MA 01201. ☎ **413/442-8316;** snow phone ☎ 413/442-2436. 21 trails (35% beginner, 35% intermediate, 30% advanced). 2 double chairs, 3 surface lifts; 750-foot vertical drop. Full-day tickets $20.

For years, Bousquet was the ski area where pretty much every kid in Pittsfield learned how to ski. In that respect, it has changed little. It is still an excellent beginner's mountain, even if the pitch does steepen somewhat toward the summit. It still bears the intimate feel of a mom-and-pop ski area, and is the kind of ski hill that used to be a staple of New England skiing, but which has largely succumbed to the emergence of the mega-resort. Bousquet is a modest-sized ski area, but it also comes at a modest-sized price—$20 for an adult lift ticket. If your measure of a ski area is runs per dollar, Bousquet can literally give bigger Berkshire ski areas a run for their money. Its shortcoming: In the age of the high-speed lift, its lifts are a bit antiquated. But that's what you should expect to find at a ski area that doesn't try to pretend to be the biggest, fastest, or fanciest.

Brodie Mountain

U.S. 7, New Ashford, MA 01237. ☎ **413/443-4752;** snow report ☎ 413/443-4751. 28 trails (30% beginner, 45% intermediate, 25% expert). 4 double chair lifts, 2 surface lifts; 1,250-foot vertical drop. Full-day tickets $39 weekend, $24 weekday.

Brodie is the unique creation of Jim Kelley, who uses an Irish ringmaster's approach to running a ski area. Traditionally, the big day of every year is St. Patrick's Day (what else would you expect from a ski area billing itself as "Kelley's Irish Alps"?), when the area throws a full-day, full-on party. In years past, St. Patty's events have included such stuff as a green-beer slalom (you must chug green-dyed beer at every gate) and slush-jumping contests. One year Kelley himself tried to jump the slush pond—on a snowmobile. (He failed.) At one time, there was also an uphill car race—all comers welcome—when the snow ran out on Brodie. Alas, that mud-fest devolved into little more than a demolition derby and had to be scrapped. Almost obscured by this wackiness is a decent ski area, catering primarily to beginners and intermediates. The vertical drop is tops in southern New England, but the runs, perhaps because of the lack of steep pitches, have a small-mountain feel to them.

Butternut

Rte. 23 East, Great Barrington, MA 01230. ☎ **413/528-2000;** snow phone ☎ 800/438-SNOW. 22 trails (20% beginner, 40% intermediate, 20% advanced). 1 triple chair lift, 5 double chairs, 2 surface lifts; 1,000-foot vertical drop. Full-day tickets $38 weekend, $26 weekday.

Mellow is the word for Butternut, making it a terrific place for families and first-time skiers. There may be a horrific-sounding run here named Lucifer's Leap, but don't be misled; there's nothing precipitous here. Butternut is not a bad choice for a romantic getaway, either. In the general neighborhood are many of the renowned inns and bed-and-breakfasts—aching with 18th- and 19th-century authenticity—that are a big part of the Berkshires' allure.

Catamount

Rte. 23, South Egremont, MA 01258. ☎ **413/528-1262;** snow phone ☎ 800/342-1840. 25 trails (35% beginner, 40% intermediate, 25% expert). 4 chairs, 2 surface lifts; 1,000-foot vertical drop. Full-day lift ticket $39 weekends, $25 weekdays.

Catamount is an oddity, a ski area partly in Massachusetts and partly in New York. To drive there from nearby South Egremont, you must briefly cross over into New York State, but by the time you're in the parking lot, you're back in Massachusetts. (One can only wonder where taxes are paid.) A solidly intermediate mountain, Catamount is a great spot for families. Its proximity to New York is also a selling point; the drive time for Big Apple skiers is less than 2½ hours.

Jiminy Peak

Corey Rd., Hancock, MA 01237. ☎ **413/738-5500;** snow phone ☎ 888/4-JIMINY. 30 trails (23% beginner, 43% intermediate, 24% expert). 1 quad chair, 2 triples, 3 doubles, 2 surface lifts; 1,140-foot vertical drop. Full-day lift ticket $42 weekends, $32 weekdays.

Imagine a larger resort in Vermont—say Killington or Stowe—in miniaturization, as if it were seen through the wrong end of a telescope. What you'd end up with would look very much like Jiminy Peak. In terms of skiing and overall amenities, Jiminy is a complete resort package. With a base-area hotel, good dining options, and modern facilities, Jiminy is one of those places resort marketers like to promote by saying that once you've parked your car upon arriving for a weekend getaway, you'll never need to use it again until you leave. But convenience isn't everything, and indeed, many Jiminy visitors may prefer staying in nearby Williamstown. What makes Jiminy particularly impressive is the skiing itself. The steeps here are legitimately steep by any standard; by Berkshires standards, they are precipitous. Yet there is also fine terrain for beginners and intermediates as well. Smaller (by a few vertical feet) than nearby Brodie, Jiminy skis like a bigger mountain, primarily because its trails follow the fall line in a more continuous manner.

FISHING

Fishing in the Berkshires is one of those good news/bad news activities. The good news is there are plenty of streams, lakes, and ponds abounding with fish. The bad news is these same streams, lakes, and ponds are also easily accessible to an abundance of fishermen. On an average summer weekend day on Onota and Pontoosuc lakes near Pittsfield, you can expect to see literally hundreds of lines in the water as fishermen go after pike, largemouth bass, and the occasional land-locked salmon. The Deerfield River, justly renowned among fly fishermen, might have dozens of hopeful anglers wading in its waters.

Fear not. Ongoing stocking pro-grams—trout, bass, salmon, and various pike species—replenish fish populations regularly, at least in more popular fishing waters. And a few smaller streams still host native brook trout, prized by anglers less interested in landing trophy-sized fish than in outfoxing a fish inherently wise to the nuances of avoiding capture in its home environment.

The best fishing probably takes place in April and May, particularly for trout-happy fly fishermen. Smaller streams, swelled with snowmelt and spring rains, are still running profusely enough to support fish populations, and the water temperature begins to climb into the mid-50s—that magic zone that seems to make trout particularly lively. And summer tourism has yet to take hold, swelling the Berkshires with both expert fishermen and wannabe hacks. Fall fishing can often be good, too. The water levels in feeder streams during fall are usually low and water temperatures high—not necessarily a good combination. But with dams on such rivers as the Deerfield releasing a regular supply of cold water, the favor-able conditions of spring can be replicat-ed in fall, and again you'll avoid the summer masses.

Keep in mind, of course, you'll need a license, available at many tackle shops or town offices. For information on licenses and stocking schedules, contact the Western Wildlife District of the Massachu-setts Division of Fisheries & Wildlife (400 Hubbard Ave., Pittsfield, MA 01201; ☎ 413/447-9789).

Deerfield River

Take Rte. 2 2 miles northwest of Charlemont and turn right at the sign for the Yankee Atomic Energy Plant onto River Rd. There are numerous pull-offs along the road.

Points North's Fred Moran, perhaps the preeminent fly-fishing guide in the northern Berkshires, says the Deerfield River "is one of the top five streams in New England in terms of frequency and size of fish. I had the longest fight of my life on that river, with a brown trout. The fish won." A boon to fishing the upper Deerfield was a decommissioning in the mid-1990s of the Yankee Atomic Energy Plant in Rowe, which used to warm the river water to temperatures trout general-ly find disagreeable. Brown, rainbow, and brook trout are plentiful in the 17 dam-free river miles from Fife Brook Dam to Buckland. There are two catch-and-release areas along this stretch of river, one just below Fife Brook and another 8.5 miles downriver. Not surprisingly, the largest fish are usually found here, since anglers are obliged to return their catch to the river. The river can be fished by wad-ing or by boat, with wading by and large the more productive method. The reason: Fishing is often easier when water levels are low (fish tend to collect in pools and migrate less); conversely, boating is usu-ally best when water levels are higher. Call the **U.S. Generating Company** (☎ **888/356-3663**) for dam-release schedules (when water is released through Fife Brook Dam, the river level is obviously higher), and plan your fishing accordingly. There is a distinct bonus in fishing the Deerfield, too; this is a scenic stretch of river, winding through a moun-tainous countryside relatively unsullied (in appearance if not in fact) by human intervention.

Hoosac River

Numerous access points to the river from Rte. 8 between Cheshire and North Adams.

The Hoosac River (sometimes spelled "Hoosic"), which flows northwest from Cheshire into Vermont before eventually emptying into the Hudson River in New York, has a reputation that is literally sullied. Despite efforts in recent years to clean up the river, decades of abuse and refuse—mills and factories being the principal offenders—have left the river chock-full of polychlorinated biphenyls (PCBs). Running through the mostly drab and industrial Adams and North Adams, the river is not surrounded by glorious scenery. None of this, however, seems to bother the fish. Pulling a 5-pound brown trout out of the Hoosac is not out of the question, an opportunity all the more enhanced by the fact that many fishermen often overlook the Hoosac. What you catch in the Hoosac might not be something you'd want to take home for dinner, given the PCB levels, but for sheer fishing thrills, the Hoosac can be surprisingly forthcoming.

Housatonic River
Accessible from Rte. 183 between Stockbridge and Housatonic and from several points off Rte. 7 between Housatonic and Sheffield.

Like the Hoosac, the Housatonic is a river with a pained history. Its passage through Pittsfield and the industrial belly of the Berkshires has made it, in years past, a receptacle for all manner of toxic effluvia. Damming has changed natural river flows and water temperatures, the sort of life changes fish do not take to happily.

Enough, then, of the bad news. Three decades of concerted cleanup efforts, stocking, and catch-and-release regulations have turned the Housatonic again into a satisfactory fish habitat. The three main branches of the river come together in Pittsfield; from here, the river passes through some mild rapids and a series of dams before flattening out south of Great Barrington. The cooler, faster-running water north of Great Barrington is the sort of environment that makes trout happy, while the slower-moving water to the

south is the kind of world pike prefer. Along Route 183 south of Stockbridge, look for pull-offs along the road, which in many places follow the river closely. Pull on your waders, find a good riffle, and go for it. Between Great Barrington and Sheffield, the river mostly runs east of Route 7, and access to the river usually means taking one of many side roads that branch off from the main thoroughfare. You're best off fishing here from a boat; the silty banks do not provide a reliable platform to stand on, particularly if you're fighting the monster fish of your dreams.

North Pond
Center Shaft Rd., Savoy State Forest. Take Rte. 2 about 4 miles east of North Adams. Turn right on Center Shaft Rd. (after two hairpin turns on Rte. 2). Follow Center Shaft Rd. 2 miles to North Pond.

On a sunny summer weekend, don't expect solitude. This pocket-sized pond, surrounded by the gentle summits of Savoy State Forest, is easily accessible, and a smooth beach allows for easy boat launching. Still, most people continue past North Pond to South Pond, where there are swimming and picnicking facilities. And on weekdays, you'll probably have the stocked pond to yourself to go after trout, pike, and perch.

Westfield River Headwaters
River Rd., West Cunningham. Take Rte. 9 3 miles west from Windsor (and the intersection with Rte. 8A). Turn left onto River Rd. at the sign for West Cunningham.

In midsummer, this peaceful stream, with forested hills tumbling steeply to the water's edge, might be no more than a trickle over sun-baked rocks. In March, with snowmelt cascading out of the mountains of surrounding Notchview Reservation and Windsor State Forest, it could be a muddy, unfishable torrent. Somewhere in between lies an opportunity to catch sizeable brown trout and smaller, native brook trout. Fish or no fish, this is, at the very least, a wonderfully tranquil place to cast a line upon the water.

Gear

Points North (Box 146, Adams, MA 01220; ☎ **413/743-4030**) features Orvis equipment and hand-tied flies. **Onota Boat Livery** (Pecks Road, Pittsfield, MA 01201; ☎ **413/442-1724**) sells tackle and bait and rents craft for fishing on Onota Lake. **Gaffer's Outdoors** (216 Main St., Sheffield, MA 01257; ☎ **413-229-0063**) sells tackle and bait and rents canoes for fishing in the southern Berkshires.

Instruction

Points North (see "Gear," above) offers fine instruction as well as instruction oriented particularly toward female anglers. **River Run** (271 Main St., Great Barrington, MA 01230; ☎ **413/528-9600**) conducts 1-day Orvis-sponsored schools in late spring and early summer.

Guides & Outfitters

Points North (see "Gear," above) provides guiding service on the Deerfield and Hoosic, as well as other smaller streams in the region.

HIKING & BACKPACKING

For hiking in southern New England, the Berkshires are unquestionably *the* region to go. The variety of terrain is enormous—mountains, lakes, streams, forests, and all the elements that make for classic hiking. Not the least of these elements, of course, is an abundance of trails. There are certainly several hundred miles of trails here, although no one seems to have attempted to make an accurate count.

Thus, the following are obviously not the only hikes possible in the Berkshires. Consider, too, some of the outings described in "Walks & Rambles," below, which can often be made longer and more strenuous if you so choose. Also, consider some of the jaunts described under "Cross-Country Skiing," as hiking possibilities as well. Just because there's no snow on the trails does not mean the trails cease to exist. Finally, some of the trails under the "Mountain Biking" section might make for fine hiking as well.

Day Hikes
Alander Mountain

Allow 3–4 hours, or up to 10 hours to make the full Alander Mountain Loop. Moderate–strenuous, depending on how far you go. Access: From South Egremont, take Rte. 41 south. Turn right on Mt. Washington Rd. just south of town, and continue for about 10 miles to forest headquarters. Map: USGS Bash Bish Falls.

This extensive trail network concentrated in the extreme southwestern corner of Massachusetts, and spilling over into Connecticut and New York, presents an array of possibilities: A 5- to 6-mile out-and-back hike to the Alander Mountain summit, featuring terrific views to the south and west; a 14-mile loop through three states and over three summits; and an abbreviated version of the loop that stays entirely—well, almost entirely—in Massachusetts. Or you can try any of the above while overnighting in a cabin near the Alander Mountain summit.

Do not be misled here by the word *summit*. Alander Mountain is just 2,250 feet high, and because the trailhead is relatively high, the elevation gain from trailhead to summit is only about 1,000 vertical feet. On your ascent you'll cross numerous feeder streams that may or may not be flowing, depending on the time of year and the weather. After a little over 2 miles, you'll reach a cabin that sits in the saddle between Alander's twin summits. Able to accommodate six, the cabin is open to overnight hikers on a first-come, first-serve basis, so if you're planning a weekend overnight, be sure to arrive early. From here, a network of trails—notably the South Taconic Trail, which reaches south to the tri-state junction of Massachusetts, Connecticut, and New York and north to the Catamount ski area—provide great opportunities for leisurely exploration. Heading south along Alander Ridge, the open views to the west of New York's Catskills are particularly impressive.

This is your moment of decision. The easy option is simply to retrace your steps. But if you want to make a grand hike of it, head south on the South Taconic Trail. Just after entering Connecticut, the trail connects with the Ashley Hill Trail, leading back to the original trailhead for a roughly 14-mile loop. But you'll probably want to make a side trip here of about 1.5 miles to the summit of 2,453-foot Mt. Frisell, passing on the trail the point where New York, Connecticut, and Massachusetts meet. How often can you step from one state into another and take your next step into a third?

The Hopper Trail, Mt. Greylock

Allow 3–4 hours one way, 6 hours round-trip. Strenuous. Access: From Williamstown, take Rte. 43 (Water St.) south about 2.5 miles. Turn left on Hopper Rd. and continue about 1.5 miles to the parking area and trailhead at road's end. Trail map available at Mt. Greylock Visitor Center.

At 3,491 feet, Mt. Greylock is not only the tallest mountain in southern New England, it is very likely the largest, spanning more than 10 miles from north to south. This considerable massif is crisscrossed with more than 50 miles of trails and roads—imagine an enormous, imaginary spider web draped over the mountain as a trail map. For that reason, the number of ways in which a hiker can take on the Greylock challenge approaches infinity. With two paved roads to the summit (the first built in 1906), one-way trips are possible; start at the bottom and have someone meet you (or leave a car) at the top, or reverse course and start at the top, hiking downward to a meeting point at the bottom.

Given this variety, it is hard to single out one hike that is the best of Mt. Greylock. Ask a gathering of local hikers to name their favorite routes, and you're apt to get as many answers as there are people. Trails that approach from the east

tend to be somewhat steeper than those that approach from the west. The eastern approaches include such famous trails as the Thunderbolt Trail, a particularly steep scramble that, as a ski trail in winter, was the site of the Massachusetts state downhill championships in an era predating lifts. Trails laid out along a north/south axis, notably the Appalachian Trail, tend to be somewhat less precipitous, but since they parallel the mountain's long ridge, they tend to be longer.

The Hopper Trail, connecting to the Overlook Trail, delivers what comes close to being a best-of-Greylock experience. This route makes the most of Greylock's unique and special features. Passing first through deep forests set on steep slopes, the route takes you past roaring brooks and across high benches strewn with wildflowers, from which panoramic views stretch out below, before eventually arriving at the summit. The trail draws its name from an area called the Hopper, a glacially carved cirque being preserved, as much as possible, in a pristine, natural state.

The trail climbs steeply along the forested periphery of the eponymous Hopper; listen for the sound of nearby Bacon Brook, which spills from March Cataract Falls. The steep ascent levels off as you reach Sperry Campground. If you're making this a one-way trip, you might want to make a side trip to March Cataract Falls, about .75 mile up a sometimes steep slope. Here, Bacon Brook tumbles over stepped ledges before plunging through the cataract, a sharply etched passageway through the mountain's granite underpinnings.

The junction with the Overlook Trail is less than a mile after you pass through Sperry Campground. You could reach the summit more directly by continuing on the Hopper Trail to the Appalachian Trail. (If you're making a round-trip hike, you might want to ascend this way and return via the Overlook Trail, just to mix things up.) But the more scenic route is the aptly named Overlook Trail, which contours along a bench above the slopes of the Hopper. Keep an eye out here for wildflowers growing in the sometimes boggy patches along the trail. After about a mile, look for a short spur to the right that leads to a clearing. Below are the steeply defined embankments of the U-shaped Hopper; far beyond to the northwest is the Taconic Range along the New York border and the mountains of southern Vermont.

After crossing the paved road, the trail doubles back to make its final ascent to the summit. On a warm, clear summer's day, the arrival at the summit after a long hike in the woods might be a shock: Cars! People! Pavement! A visitors' center, lodge, and war memorial! This may lessen the summit satisfaction and solitude you might experience elsewhere, but the views here are great. And if you don't want to, you don't have to hike back down. There's definitely something to be said for that.

Monument Mountain

Allow 1½–2 hours for the round trip. Easy–moderate. Access: From Great Barrington, take Rte. 7 north about 3.5 miles. Look for a parking lot on your left. Map: Available from the Trustees of Reservations, 572 Essex St., Beverly, MA 01915; ☎ 978/524-1858.

What first seems to interest anyone you talk to about Monument Mountain is usually not the mountain itself, but those who have spent time atop it. On August 5, 1850, Herman Melville and Nathaniel Hawthorne, having never before met, joined company with Oliver Wendell Holmes to hike up the mountain—armed with champagne, of course, to celebrate the summit moment as any proper gentleman of the time would. The Trustees of Reservations, which manages the land here, considers the meeting and the climb to have been momentous enough to merit a reenactment every year.

This is neither an exceptionally difficult hike (sometimes steep, but not long) nor an unpopular one. With a round-trip distance of about 2.5 miles, a speedy hiker from Great Barrington could complete it in an extended lunch break. But there is good reason to embark upon this hike, other than merely to walk the walk of Melville and Hawthorne. The well-maintained trail passes through forests of hemlock and laurel, climbing at a fairly steep pitch. Before breaking onto the open expanse of ledge near the summit, you'll pass what is known as Inscription Rock, a landmark honoring Rosalie Butler, who bequeathed the mountain to the Trustees in 1899. From here, scramble over exposed rock to reach the summit—not Monument Mountain, paradoxically, but Squaw Peak. In the foreground to the south is a ragged pinnacle known as Devil's Pulpit; in the background, stretching as far west as the Catskills, is as magnificent a view as you'll find in the Berkshires. Hawthorne described the mountain as "a headless sphinx wrapped in a Persian shawl." What that means is unclear; blame it on the champagne.

Race Brook, Mt. Everett

Allow 5 hours. Strenuous. Access: From South Egremont, take Rte. 41 south for about 5 miles. Look for a small parking lot on the right side of the road. Map: USGS Bash Bish Falls.

If you thought the Berkshires were just mere rolling hills, this is a trail that should change your mind. The operative word here is *steep,* but it is a steepness that comes with considerable reward. The trail more or less parallels Race Brook—hence its name—which plunges over a series of at least five waterfalls, chief among them Race Brook Falls, with a drop of close to 100 feet. When the brook is flushed with spring snowmelt, the falls are nothing short of spectacular.

In less than 2 miles, you'll reach a junction with the Appalachian Trail and a decision. North toward Mt. Everett, or south toward Mt. Race? Or both? There is no loop to return you to the trailhead, so whichever direction you go at this point, keep in mind your return route is also via the Race Brook Trail. (There is another option: Shuttle a car around Mt. Washington Road to the entrance to Mt. Everett Reservation on the west side of the mountain. From the summit of Mt. Everett, you can continue on the Appalachian Trail heading north. When the trail crosses a dirt road, turn left onto the road, which leads to the reservation entrance and your car.)

The fairly steep climb to the rocky summit of Mt. Everett affords sweeping views to the south (Mt. Frissell, Bear Mountain) and to the west (the distant Catskills). Assuming the weather and wind cooperate, you might want to have a picnic here on the rocks; the only eyesore is a rickety, defunct fire tower that for whatever reason has been left standing. From the summit, head north on the Appalachian Trail for less than 2 miles, where the views swing around 180 degrees toward the Housatonic River Valley to the east and Mt. Greylock to the north. The summit of Mt. Race is not nearly as dramatic as that of Mt. Everett, nor is the ascent as aerobically challenging. Yet south of its summit, Mt. Race becomes an extended ridge of exposed ledge, with terrific views to the north, south, and east. Before descending steeply into the woods around Race Brook, a leisurely stroll on this relatively flat, open rock provides a refreshing change of pace.

Overnight/Long-Distance Hikes

The Appalachian Trail

The famous Georgia-to-Maine trail, popularly known as AT, enters Massachusetts in the south at Sage's Ravine in Mt. Washington State Forest and exits, 85 to 90 miles later, through Clarksburg State Forest into Vermont. Much of the route passes through state forests and reservations (Mt. Washington, Beartown, October Mountain, Mt. Greylock, and others), while other portions might briefly follow roadways across more developed land. The entire Massachusetts trail can be comfortably hiked in a week, although you should expect to tack on several more miles—perhaps a day's worth of hiking—since there are no access points right on the Vermont or Connecticut borders.

In fact, for backpackers interested in just a 2- or 3-day hike, the southern and northern extremes of the trail are probably the most isolated stretches on the entire Massachusetts run. Massachusetts AT aficionados tend to prefer the southern extreme of the trail as it passes through Mt. Washington State Forest. The extended, open ridge along Mt. Race features sensational views, as does the summit of Mt. Everett (see "Race Brook, Mt. Everett" hike, above). Hiking the trail through Mt. Greylock Reservation (see below) is also an excellent overnight option.

For information and maps, contact the **Appalachian Trail Conference** (Box 807, Harper's Ferry, WV 25425; ☎ **304/535-6331**), or the Berkshire chapter of the **Appalachian Mountain Club** (see "Instruction," below). You can also try the Appalachian Trail Web site at **www.fred.net/kathy/at.html**.

Mt. Greylock Traverse

With several shelters and Bascom Lodge at its summit, Mt. Greylock Reservation is ideally suited for overnight hiking. This is an unusually big mountain, stretching at least 10 miles from north to south, with an extensive trail network, so it is easy to spend 2 days or more on the mountain without walking the same trail twice. One overnight option is to simply follow the Appalachian Trail for 14 miles starting at the trail's junction with Rte. 8 in Cheshire, and ending at the trail junction with Rte. 2 in Adams. For the most part, it's a gradual climb out of Cheshire, and then the trail follows the ridgeline of Saddle Ball Mountain on its way to the summit, about 8 miles into your hike. If camping isn't your thing, stay overnight in Bascom Lodge (be sure to make reservations), and then the next day, continue north along Greylock's ridge over the secondary summits of Mt. Fitch and Mt. Williams before making the descent into North Adams.

A LITTLE NIGHT MUSIC

After a long day of summer hiking, biking, or birding, a little Beethoven or a few words from the Bard may be just the thing to reenergize you for your next outing. If this sounds appealing, head for Lenox, where the undisputed headliners are the Boston Symphony Orchestra (BSO) and its music director, Seiji Ozawa. Their concerts are given at the famous **Tanglewood** estate, usually beginning the last weekend in June and ending the weekend before Labor Day. The estate is on West Street (actually in Stockbridge township, although it's always associated with Lenox). From Lenox, take Route 183 1.5 miles southwest of town.

While the BSO is Tanglewood's 800-pound cultural gorilla, the program features a menagerie of other performers and musical idioms. They run the gamut from popular artists (past performers have included James Taylor and Lyle Lovett) and jazz vocalists and combos (including Dave Brubeck, Chick Corea, and Sonny Rollins) to such guest soloists and conductors as Andrè Previn, Isaac Stern, Jessye Norman, and Yo-Yo Ma.

Prominent groups and individual artists of this magnitude usually appear in the Koussevitzky Music Shed, an open-ended auditorium that seats 5,000, supplemented by a surrounding lawn where an outdoor audience lounges on folding chairs and blankets. Lesser-known performers and chamber groups appear in Ozawa Hall and the separate theater. Seats in the Shed range from $14 to $76, while lawn tickets are usually $13 to $16. (Higher prices apply for some special appearances.)

For recorded **information on concert programs,** call ☎ **413/637-1666** or 617/266-1492 from September to June 10. To order tickets by mail before June, write the Tanglewood Ticket Office at Symphony Hall, Boston, MA 02115. After the first week in June, write the Tanglewood Ticket Office, Lenox, MA 01240. Tickets can be charged by phone through **SymphonyCharge** (☎ **800/274-8499** outside Boston, or 617/266-1200 in Boston). For tickets to the Popular Artists Series, call **Ticketmaster** (☎ **800/347-0808** outside Mass., 212/307-7171 in N.Y., or 617/931-2000 in Boston). Tentative programs are available after the New Year; the summer schedule is locked in by March. *Note:* Tickets, especially to the most popular performances,

Another option is to make this a west-to-east traverse, starting your trek in Williamstown along the Hopper Trail (see Hopper Trail hike, above). You can overnight at the summit or at Sperry Campground, from which you'll want to hike out to Stony Ledge, with its magnificent view of the Greylock summit, as well as points west.

For your second day of hiking, there are several options to consider for descending from the summit. The Thunderbolt Trail, the once-famous ski run, is the steepest—dropping 2,260 feet in 2 miles—and most direct option to reach Adams. It's not a route you or your knees will enjoy if you're carrying a sizeable pack. A longer but much less precipitous option is to head south along the Appalachian Trail and continue to Jones Nose—more great views here—and then loop back on the Old Adams Road Trail, ending in Adams. The total, 2-day distance for this option is roughly 14 miles. The final, total mileage you end up logging, of course, depends on how many side trips, for panoramic views or waterfalls, you decide to take.

For information and maps, contact the **Mt. Greylock Visitor Center** (Rockwell Road, Lanesboro, MA 01237; ☎ 413/499-4262).

The Taconic Skyline Trail

The Taconic Skyline Trail, a 20-mile north-south route that runs primarily through Pittsfield State Forest, was originally blazed by the Civilian Conservation Corps in the 1930s. It begins near Richmond and ends at Brodie Mountain can sell out quickly, so it's a good idea to get your tickets as far in advance as possible. If you do decide to go at the last minute, take a blanket or lawn chairs and get tickets for the lawn, which are almost always available. You can also attend open rehearsals during the week. Lawn tickets for children under 12 are free; children under 5 aren't allowed in the Shed or Ozawa Hall during concerts.

But there's even more. **Shakespeare & Company** uses buildings and outdoor amphitheaters on the grounds of The Mount to stage its late-May-to-late-October season of plays by the Bard, works by Edith Wharton, and new American playwrights. Performances by dance troupes, student actors, and even puppets flesh out the schedule. The venues are the outdoor amphitheaters, Mainstage and Oxford Court, and two indoor stages, Stables and Wharton. Staggered performances take place Tuesday to Sunday (weekends only after Labor Day), usually at 3, 5, or 8pm. Tickets range from $15 to $32 and are generally easy to get, since the theater rarely draws name actors. Call the box office at ☎ 413/637-3353; the summer's schedule is announced by February or March. Lunch and dinner picnic baskets can be purchased on site.

The estate itself (☎ 413/637-5165 June through August), with more than 500 gorgeous acres of manicured lawns, gardens, and groves of ancient trees, much of it overlooking the lake called Stockbridge Bowl, is worth a stroll. Admission to the grounds is free.

William Aspinwall Tappan first settled the estate in 1849. At the outset, the only structure on the property was a modest something referred to as the Little Red Shanty. In 1851 it was rented to Nathaniel Hawthorne and his wife Sophia. The author of *The Scarlet Letter* and *The House of the Seven Gables* stayed there long enough to write a children's book, *Tanglewood Tales,* and meet Herman Melville, who lived in nearby Dalton and became a close friend. The existing Hawthorne Cottage is a replica, now serving as practice studios. (It isn't open to the public.) On the grounds is the original Tappan mansion, with fine views.

—Herbert Bailey Livesey

in Lanesboro. Often crossing and paralleling back roads, the trail offers somewhat less of a wilderness experience than the two hikes described above. But its name is not without merit; from several viewpoints along the ridges of the Taconic Range, you're treated to superb vistas. Another feature of the trail is a neat little campsite located around the trail's halfway point at Berry Pond in Pittsfield State Forest. (Berry Pond is said to be the highest pond in Massachusetts.) This might also be the overnight hike to stimulate skiing enthusiasts. In its northern half, the trail passes over the summits of Jiminy Peak and Brodie Mountain, two popular ski areas.

For information and maps, contact the Berkshire chapter of the **Appalachian Mountain Club** (see "Instruction," below.)

Gear

Appalachian Mountain Gear (684 S. Main St., Great Barrington, MA 01230; ☎ 413/528-8811) specializes in hiking, climbing, and camping equipment. **Berkshire Outfitters** (Route 8, Adams, MA 01221; ☎ 413/743-5900) features a wide variety of hiking necessities and accessories. Before buying anything, you may want to take a look at the GearReview Web site (**http://gearreview.com/default.asp**). This site has a great collection of equipment reviews, links, and trail reviews contributed by readers and experienced outdoorsmen.

Instruction

The Berkshire chapter of the **Appalachian Mountain Club** offers instructional trips and workshops on subjects, including basic backpacking and camping, knot tying, map and compass use, and tree identification. For information, contact the Berkshire chapter through the Mt. Greylock Visitor Center (Box 1800, Lanesboro, MA 01237; ☎ 413/443-0011).

Outfitters

Appalachian Mountain Club (Berkshire Chapter, see "Instruction," above) organizes guided day hikes and overnight hikes in the region, particularly around Mt. Greylock. **New England Hiking Holidays** (Box 1648, North Conway, NH 03860; ☎ 800/869-0949) leads inn-based trips in the southern Berkshires, some along with Tanglewood concerts. **Appalachian Mountain Gear** (see "Gear," above), based in Great Barrington, also organizes group hikes on weekends.

HORSEBACK RIDING

There are many great places to ride, but few stables and outfitters. The back roads and trails in **Beartown State Forest, Dubuque State Forest, October Mountain State Forest,** and **Savoy Mountain State Forest** are perfect for a day's outing. Many of the trails are, in fact, old logging roads, lessening the chances of a horse being surprised or spooked by other trail users and mountain bikers in particular.

Unfortunately, if you don't bring your own horse, your chances of appreciating all this great riding are greatly diminished. If you're just looking for a good ride, but don't feel a need to explore all over the Berkshires, **Eastover Resort** (430 East St., Lenox, MA 01240; ☎ 800/822-2386)

offers horseback riding on its own, 10-mile trail network.

Instruction

Undermountain Farm (252 Undermountain Rd., Lenox, MA 1240; ☎ 413/637-3365) offers instruction and trail rides for all ability levels.

Outfitters

Western Riding Stables (Sawchuk Road, Millerton, NY 12456; ☎ 518/789-4848) offers guided full-day and overnight rides in Mt. Washington State Forest, as well as other guided trips.

MOUNTAIN BIKING

For mountain biking, the Berkshires must certainly rank among the best regions in the East. Sure, the mountains and the forests of northern New England might be more impressive, but they don't boast the wide variety of trails, forest roads, dirt roads, and loops that satisfy both rank beginners and aggressive experts.

What the Berkshires lack is a sense of organization. No ski areas are dedicated in summer to mountain biking (either for riding or instruction), as are several ski areas in Vermont. There are no specifically designated mountain-biking centers. Local bike shops can, and quite willingly do, offer where-to-go guidance, sometimes with hand-drawn maps. Still, the Berkshires' plenitude of riding options can become troublesome if you rely on such well-intended guidance or the often-imprecise maps. And even if you know where to go, you are apt to find trail markings unreliable. One wrong turn, and you might end up dizzyingly lost or being roundly cursed at by some private landowner not eager to see mountain bikers grinding through his back yard.

One way to get introduced to the terrain is to join organized rides that usually leave in the evening from local bike shops. The problem here can be that the rides usually take off on *weekday* evenings, not particularly convenient for weekend travelers.

What's the solution? One good strategy is to begin with out-and-back rides, rather than loops. Keep track of your outward route, and you shouldn't have much trouble finding your way back. This will help familiarize you with the lay of the land; once you've got a feel for a particular network of trails and roads, you can begin to ride connected loops. Another strategy is to buddy up with local riders; bike shops, as obvious as this sounds, are often where bikers congregate.

Of course, if you're in the mood, you can just go for it. Get a map and a ride description, and set yourself free on some of the East's best terrain. Life is short, and the mountains beckon. So what if you end up lost in the woods?

Rides

Beartown State Forest

Allow 2–3 hours. Moderate. Access: From Great Barrington, take Rte. 23 approximately 5 miles to Blue Hill Rd. Turn right. After about 2 miles, turn right onto Beartown Rd. for the parking lot at Benedict Pond. Map: Available at forest headquarters on Blue Hill Rd.

What makes Beartown a better choice than nearby October Mountain State Forest for mountain bikers? As Cliff Hague of Mean Wheels bike shop in Lenox puts it, "There are a lot more signs, and it's a little more user-friendly." Translation: It's a lot harder to get lost. Furthermore, there has been a concerted effort in recent years to improve trail conditions and signage, upping Beartown's user-friendly advantage even more.

This is, by most mountain-biking standards, relatively flat terrain, with elevations ranging between 1,500 and 2,000 feet. The most technically challenging aspects of riding here are not so much the ups and downs but the occasional bogginess, especially in spring. You can make a fairly easy, 1-hour loop on the Bridle Trail, which has been recently restored

after years of overgrowth, or you can head down paved Beartown Road to the Beebe Trail and from there make your way to the Skye Peak Trail, a fairly challenging single track.

If you're not confident of your bike-handling skills, there are many other options. You never have to leave mountain roads, but if you're looking for single track, there's plenty of that to be found. Just keep in mind that the Appalachian Trail, which passes through the forest, is off-limits to bikes.

Berlin Mountain

Allow 2–3 hours. Moderate–strenuous. Access: South of Williamstown, take Rte. 2 west for .5 mile. Turn left onto Torrey Woods Rd., then left again onto Bee Hill Rd. to the parking lot of the old Williams College Ski area. Map: Hand-drawn map available at the **Spoke** (☎ **413/458-3456**) in Williamstown.

Okay, so a good portion of this ride is in New York State, which isn't exactly southern New England. Not only is the access from Massachusetts, but it is a favorite ride of Williamstown locals, who consider it part of their home turf. So the heck with state-line technicalities. This is a Massachusetts ride.

Begin from the base of the abandoned Williams College ski area and start climbing on the Berlin Pass Trail, which was once part of the Boston–Albany Post Road. After less than a mile of moderate climbing, you'll arrive at Berlin Pass and the intersection with the Taconic Crest Trail. Turn left, and in another mile or so, you'll come to the summit of Berlin Mountain. The view from here is terrific, particularly of Mt. Greylock, which lies directly to the east.

Once you've taken in the view and fully regained your breath, retrace your path on the Taconic Crest Trail. You could simply make your way back the way you came, but far more interesting is to stay on the Taconic Trail heading north. Following a ridgeline trail with brief up-and-down spurts, you're afforded occasional views to the east and west along the way, particularly as you come to the overgrown trails of the long-closed Petersburg Pass ski area.

There are various trail options available for your descent back to your starting point, the simplest of which is to take paved Route 2. But several trails and old roads descend eastward from the Taconic Crest Trail between Berlin Pass and Petersburg Pass, and as long as you keep descending, you shouldn't get lost. Everything eventually feeds into Berlin Pass Road, which leads back to your car.

John Drummond Kennedy Park

Allow 1–2 hours. Easy–moderate. Access: The park is west of Main St. (Rte. 7A) in Lenox. Map: Available at local bike shops in Lenox.

What makes Kennedy Park such a great place to ride is that it allows you complete control of your destiny. A complex network of trails designed principally for cross-country skiing in the winter makes the number of ride and loop options here surprisingly substantial for a relatively small area. Another bonus, particularly for novice riders, is that trails are not only well marked, but are also designated by difficulty levels. Although the difficulty levels apply to cross-country skiing, they translate reasonably well for mountain biking. In short, it is pretty hard to get in over your head unless you are determined to do so.

The main trail, literally named the Main Trail, is an easy double track that operates as the main aorta from which most of the park's trails branch off and loop back. Try any trail that suits your fancy; if you feel you're overmatched, you can simply backtrack to the Main Trail. You could easily spend a morning looping around and weaving back and forth, crossing and recrossing your tracks, but never backtracking unless you chose to do so. When you've had enough, be sure to stop at the picnic area located near the start of your ride before departing. Views of the distant mountains are impressive, providing great visual stimulation after a morning of physical exertion.

Mt. Greylock Loop

Allow 4 hours. Strenuous. Access: From Adams, take West Rd. to West Mountain Rd. Turn left and continue to the parking area at the end of West Mountain Rd. Map: Available at the Mt. Greylock Visitor Center in Lanesboro.

So you think you're good? You think you're fit? Here's a ride about as tough as it gets in the Berkshires: A heavy helping of steep single track, combined with double track, dirt roads, and paved roads, make this a complete mountain-biking package. However, this is not a journey to be undertaken lightly; the total amount of elevation climbed by the end of the trip is roughly 4,000 vertical feet.

Head out from the trailhead at the end of West Mountain Road to join Old Adams Road, a double-track section, as it climbs gradually but relentlessly toward the juncture with Rockwell Road, the main paved road leading to the summit of Mt. Greylock. From here, you can follow Rockwell Road to the summit or take the CCC Dynamite Trail from Jones Nose, assuming mountain bikes are allowed on the trail. (Trail-use policies in Mt. Greylock Reservation are in constant flux, so check with the Mt. Greylock Visitor Center on mountain-bike openings.) The CCC Dynamite Trail is fairly level, but to get to it over Jones Nose requires a quick steep climb during which you'll probably want to get off and walk. The trail eventually rejoins Rockwell Road about a mile from the summit.

Phew! By the time you reach the summit, you've done a heap of climbing, so enjoy the view and start planning your return. The shortest, most direct route back is via the Cheshire Harbor Trail, which intersects Rockwell Road about .5 mile from the summit. But this is a tough go, a steep and technical downhill with sections of loose rock that is not for the faint of heart or those lacking in bike-handling skills.

The longer option is to descend via paved Notch Road from the summit, heading north. This is an easy, fast descent, but be aware you're sharing the relatively narrow road with four-wheeled vehicles. As the pitch begins to steepen and the road makes a couple of switch-backs, look for the dirt road to Notch Reservoir, the beginning of the Bellows Pipe Trail.

Time to climb again—the trail heads gradually upward, crossing a series of brooks, and after about 3 miles, reaches a shelter on your right. After a deep ravine, the Bellows Pipe Trail veers right and uphill, but for you, the climbing is over. Instead of following the trail, head straight on the forest road that descends, at a fairly steep pitch at first, to Greylock Glen. Here you can pick up paved Gould Road to West Road, turn right, and then turn right again on West Mountain Road to return to your starting point.

Pittsfield State Forest

Allow 1–3 hours. Moderate. Access: From Pittsfield, take West St. west to Churchill St. Turn right on Churchill, then left onto Cascade St., leading to the forest entrance. Map: Available at forest head-quarters at the entrance.

Pittsfield State Forest is extremely popular among local mountain bikers, and for good reason. Accessibility is one point in its favor: Leave work in Pittsfield at 5pm, and you can be riding by 5:20. The well-marked trails are numerous and, for the most part, open to bikers. A wide variety of loops, from simple to demanding, are possible.

This might suggest the forest is crowd-ed with mountain bikers, and you can probably count on having to share trails with other riders (and hikers and horse-back riders). That said, keep in mind this is a pretty big parcel of land, 10,000 acres in all, with more than a dozen trails

descending from its main ridgeline, so there's plenty of space to spread out.

So how do you make the most of all that space? The general strategy is to pick a trail to climb until you reach the Taconic Skyline Trail. Some of the climbs and descents can be pretty steep, but they are generally not super-long lungbusters; the total vertical rise is a bit over 900 feet. The Skyline Trail runs along the ridgeline as a single-track trail in some places and an old fire road in others. It's not always in the best of shape, so be prepared to do some on-foot scrambling. Ride the ridge for as long as you want until you find a descending trail to your liking, then loop back to your starting point.

Savoy Mountain State Forest

Allow 2 hours. Easy–moderate. Access: From North Adams, take Rte. 2 east to Florida (Massachusetts). Turn right on Center Shaft Rd. to reach forest head-quarters. Map: Available at forest head-quarters.

You could, if you wanted, make a long and challenging loop ride in Savoy Mountain State Forest. It is big enough and has enough trails to be full of possi-bilities. But it is also a great place for technically unskilled riders to go out into the forest on dirt roads, pass by pretty, high-mountain ponds, and finish satisfied but without the feeling lungs and legs have been sacrificed for the cause. Because most of the state forest rests on a high plateau, the amount of time spent climbing and descending is minimal, unless you go out of your way to seek out steep slopes. One thing to keep in mind: The riding here is mostly on roads open to traffic, so be prepared to encounter the occasional car.

Start at the parking area at South Pond and head south on Florida Road. After about a mile, turn right on New State Road and then left onto Tannery Road. This leads, after a mile, to Tannery Falls (see "Walks & Rambles," below), where you'll probably want to get off your bike and take the short hike down to the falls—a real spectacle when the water is running high and fast.

Hop back onboard your bike and make the quick climb up Tannery Road to its termination at paved Chapel Road. Turn right and then turn right again onto unpaved Adams Road. After a couple of miles, when the road turns to pavement, look for New State Road on your right. Turn here, and after a mile you'll come to the intersection with Florida Road, the road on which the ride started. From here you can simply go back the way you came, but for variety, you might want to continue on New State Road past Bog Pond.

Look for a trail on your left shortly after the pond; that's your route back to base camp and your chance to test your off-road riding ability. If you feel you passed the test, take a swim in South Pond and head out again to try some of Savoy's more challenging trails.

Gear, Rentals & Repairs

The Mountain Goat (130 Water St., Williamstown, MA; ☎ 413/458-8445) is your best bet for mountain-biking equipment and rental in the northern Berkshires. Also, group rides leave the shop every Tuesday, Wednesday, and Thursday evening at 5:30pm. The Tuesday rides are considered the most grueling. In the southern Berkshires, the **Arcadian Bike Shop** (91 Pittsfield Rd., Lenox, MA 01240; ☎ 413/637-3010) has rentals and gear, and is also a great spot for ride information. Another good spot for ride information and equipment in Lenox is **Mean Wheels** (57A Housatonic St., Lenox, MA 01240; ☎ 413/637-0644).

ROAD BIKING

In terms of terrain, the Berkshires approach a theoretical ideal for road riding. Rolling terrain, pretty scenery, and numerous loops are the norm. Long, grueling climbs and long, boring flats exposed to demoralizing headwinds are rarities that can be easily avoided. There

are plenty of small towns, roadside cafes, and refreshment stops that offer you the opportunity to break up a ride with a snack or allow you to replenish fluids. Ask any Berkshire cyclist to recommend a favorite route, and you're likely to get as many answers as there are cyclists.

The going here is so good you'll figure there must be a downside, and there can be. At the height of the tourist season—summer and fall weekends—the major roads can become clogged with traffic. Some solace can be found in the main drags—Routes 7 and 8—having generously wide shoulders in most places, so you don't have to worry much about wobbling out into a zone where you risk a close encounter of the vehicular kind. But even with plenty of space in which to ride, it's less than pleasant to spend a day sucking exhaust and having your ears splintered by the cacophony of hundreds of engines roaring by in unison.

There are ways to avoid all this, of course. One option is to choose a sensible time to ride, when traffic is minimal. Early in the morning—before 9am—is usually relatively car-free, particularly on weekends. And, of course, traffic lessens in the evening, too. Traffic volume diminishes considerably during the middle of the week, so if your schedule is flexible enough to allow a midweek getaway, go for it.

Another option—and the two are not mutually exclusive—is to get a good map (see below) and select a route that minimizes time on major highways. There are literally hundreds of paved back roads in the Berkshires, and what they might lack in wide shoulders and smooth pavement, they more than make up for in low traffic volume.

Rides

Dalton–Cheshire Loop

Allow 3–4 hours. Moderate; rolling, with some hills. Access: Rte. 8/Rte. 9 intersection, between Pittsfield and Dalton.

For the most part, this approximately 35-mile loop affirms that the rural Berkshires of deep forests, clear streams, and minimal human development still exists. That might not seem true at the start of this loop, where the landscape is a chilling reminder of what can happen when free enterprise is given free reign—a sprawl of fast-food restaurants, shopping malls, cheap motels, and gas stations. From the pavement of the shopping mall at the intersection of Routes 8 and 9, the bow of an embedded ship rises from the parking-lot pavement. That peculiar landmark makes as good a starting point as any for your journey.

Head east on Route 9, and once you move through Dalton (about 2 miles), the commercialism falls away quickly. The shoulder is wide, the pavement smooth, the traffic reasonable, and the forest dense and green. Climb gradually to Notchview Reservation on your left (note the tidy stone wall), and stop here for a snack or a quick hike if you're particularly energetic. In about 2 miles, after a steep descent, turn left onto River Road. (Look for the sign to West Cunningham.) The next few miles of riding climb gradually and are the highlight of the ride. The beginnings of the Westfield River flow alongside the road as a whispering stream, and as the forest crowds in near the road, you'll encounter a real feeling of wilderness-inspired serenity.

Turn left at the intersection with Route 116, and after passing through Savoy—all but a ghost town—you'll begin descending toward Adams. After a small bridge, look for a left turn onto Wells Road; if you pass Hoosac Valley High School on your right, you've gone too far. Bear right onto Wells Road (another road bears to the left), and as you pass through high farms overlooking the Hoosac River valley, you'll descend gradually into Cheshire.

You could finish the ride by taking Route 8 from Cheshire directly back to your starting point. But this traffic-laden thoroughfare is not pretty, either as an aesthetic or a recreational experience. You'll have a much more enjoyable ride by taking the back roads that wind

around the eastern side of Cheshire Reservoir. In Cheshire, take Route 8 south for just .25 mile, then bear right onto Lanesboro Road as Route 8 bears left. Very quickly, you'll find yourself off the beaten track again and back into the bucolic Berkshires. The road passes through rolling farmland, where glimpses of the reservoir are possible when the road reaches high ground.

After about 4 miles, the road comes to a T with Summer Road. Turn left, and about .25 mile later, turn right onto Partridge Road. Civilization begins to reassert itself as you pass through the tidy homes of Pittsfield suburbia. Shortly the road comes to a T at Crane Avenue. Turn left, and in less than a mile, you'll be back in the clutches of rampant free enterprise. Look for the buried ship.

Great Barrington Loop
Allow 3 hours. Moderate; 2 short climbs, otherwise rolling. Access: Information booth, downtown Great Barrington. Map: Rubel Bikemaps, Western Massachusetts.

Ask local riders where the good riding in the southern Berkshires is, and you'll find Alford is a popular answer. There are two reasons for this: the rural countryside and the absence of traffic. This 35-mile ride passes through Alford and West Stockbridge, the sort of small Berkshires towns that seem almost entirely unchanged by 20th-century civilization.

Begin in Great Barrington by heading west (from Route 7, Main Street) on Taconic Street. You'll face perhaps the hardest climbing of your ride right here. Winding under the railroad tracks, the road moves steeply upward, transforming itself in the process into Alford Road. Continue onward for about 4 miles to the village of Alford, bearing left here onto West Road. While you're winding through forests and riding past farms, don't be surprised when you're confronted by the occasional aromatic reminder that farming in this region is still a going concern.

When the road comes to a **T**, turn left onto West Center Road, which climbs gradually through farmland and then descends to join Route 102 as you make your way into West Stockbridge. Stop here for rest and refreshments to prepare yourself for a climb along Route 102 as it heads east out of town. While crossing the Mass Pike on your descent, look for the intersection with Route 183, where you'll turn right. (You can also continue on Route 102 to Stockbridge, where there is a museum honoring Norman Rockwell, reported to be a cycling enthusiast.) Route 183 will take you along the banks of the Housatonic River and through the small town of Housatonic.

After Route 183 crosses over the river, keep an eye out for Division Street, just before a large farm. Turn right here, and a mile later turn left on Route 41 to bring you back into Great Barrington. Missing the Division Street turn simply means you'll end up returning to Great Barrington on Route 7—a good lesson in why back roads are the way to go in the Berkshires on a busy summer weekend.

Washington Mountain Climb

Allow 2–3 hours. Strenuous, with one steep, extended climb. Access: Gaffer's Outdoors in Sheffield. Map: Rubel Bikemaps, Western Massachusetts.

Some riders just love a good climb that causes the sound of their heartbeat, wild in aerobic overdrive, to pound in their ears. The stiff, 2-mile climb in this 30-mile ride ought to do the trick. Beginning at the parking lot of Gaffer's Outdoors in Sheffield, head south briefly on Route 7 before turning right onto Berkshire School Road. Smooth and flat, this 3-mile stretch is an excellent warm-up. At the **T**, turn right onto Route 41. You will be surrounded by forest as the smooth road rolls north along the eastern flank of Mt. Everett.

After about 4 miles, look for signs for Mt. Washington State Forest that mark your left turn onto Mt. Washington Road. The first mile or so is flat, but be prepared; the road begins to climb gradually at first, before becoming really steep. About halfway up the climb, look for a natural spring on your right (there is a sign to mark it); this might be a good spot for a break and a water-bottle refill. After another mile or so, the climb levels off, with considerable reward. To the east is a classic Berkshires view—a sloping field surrounding a stone-walled barn in the foreground and hazy hills far in the distance.

From here, the road rolls gently up and down, passing by several neat old stone walls, on its way to the Mt. Washington State Forest Headquarters, as good a place as any to turn around. You might be tempted to make a side trip to Bash Bish Falls, but choke back temptation—the road is very steep, very narrow, and winding, and as such is hazardous. When you return to the junction with Route 41, turn left and continue into South Egremont, where there is a small general store for refreshments. In South Egremont, bear right at the triangle in the middle of town, following signs for Sheffield. This takes you onto another smooth, flat road and past open meadows that afford great views of Mt. Everett. When this road terminates at its junction with Route 7, turn right (south) and continue on for less than a mile back to your starting point.

Williamstown Loop

Allow 2–3 hours. Moderate; rolling, with one extended hill. Access: Start at the intersection of Rtes. 7 and 43, 5 miles south of Williamstown. Map: Rubel Bikemaps, Western Massachusetts.

This is the most mountainous corner of southern New England, dominated by Mt. Greylock, the region's highest peak. The assumption might be, then, that riding in this neighborhood would be uncomfortably hilly. Not so. There is one legitimate climb, between the Jiminy Peak and Brodie Mountain ski areas, but by starting the ride at the intersection of Routes 7 and 43, that climb comes about a third of the way into your ride, when you're warmed up but not tuckered out. Otherwise, the riding takes place on mostly rolling or flat terrain and even a fast but gradual downhill along Route 7.

Head south from Five Corners (the 7/43 intersection) for about 7 miles on Route 43. The smooth, rolling road passes through somnolent, rural countryside, climbing in short, gradual steps before rolling back down toward Jiminy Peak. Turn left on Brodie Mountain Road and prepare to climb; after passing the entrance to Jiminy, the mountains close in and the road tilts steadily upward. The climb isn't long—less than a mile—but there's enough here to make lungs and legs burn by the time you reach the top. Thereafter comes a swift descent to the intersection with Route 7.

Upon turning left onto Route 7, you may want to bless the road builders of Massachusetts. The shoulder here is smooth and wide, and although traffic can be heavy on this major thoroughfare, you won't be throwing yourself in front of semis to secure space to ride. There is plenty of room for everybody here. After a brief bit of climbing, the riding becomes fast and fun, descending gradually back to Five Corners.

This could be the end of your ride if you so choose. Stop at the Store at Five Corners and chow down on well-earned sandwiches or—what the heck—a bottle of wine. But you'll probably want to continue on for a second, 10-mile loop through Williamstown. Head north on Route 43, also known as River Road because—surprise—it follows the Green River closely. Farms give way to tidy homes as you near town. You'll also pass by the impressive stone portals of Mount Hope Farm, once renowned for its breakthroughs in experimental farming methods. Entering Williamstown, turn left on Route 2, passing through the heart of Williams College and its very collegiate-looking brick buildings.

Shortly, you'll come to the junction with Route 7; continue on the combined Route 2 and Route 7 south, staying on route 7 when Route 2 bears right, about 2 miles south of town. The road will climb gradually, eventually topping out with a good view of Mt. Greylock, with farm fields in the foreground. From there, it's a speedy descent back to Five Corners.

Gear, Rentals & Repairs

Arcadian Bike Shop (91 Pittsfield Rd., Lenox, MA 01240; ☎ **413/637-3010**) has bikes for rent in addition to being a full-service shop. **Mean Wheels** (57A Housatonic St., Lenox, MA 01240; ☎ **413/637-0644**) is a good place for service and ride recommendations. **The Spoke** (618 Main St., Williamstown, MA; ☎ **413/458-3456**) is the place to go in the northern Berkshires for equipment, service, and ride recommendations.

Outfitters

Easy Rider Tours (Box 228, Newburyport, MA 01950; ☎ **800/488-8332** or 978/463-6955) leads 5-day fall tours through the Berkshires. **The Bicycle Tour Company** (Box 381, Kent, CT 06757; ☎ **888/711-KENT**) leads 3-day weekend trips in summer and fall starting in New Marlborough.

ROCK & ICE CLIMBING

One-thousand-foot granite cliffs and white-knuckling 5.14s? Of course not. This is the Berkshires. Still, there are a few places to scramble around and get a feel for being suspended vertically, however briefly. Expect the difficulty levels to top out at around 5.11 and the total vertical rises to top out at around 100 feet. Exploring around in the woods, you should also keep a lookout for small rock protuberances and so-called glacial erratics, remnant boulders deposited haphazardly during the retreat of the Ice Age. Bouldering might not induce the fear and testosterone level of big-wall climbing, but for practicing moves and hand holds, it presents its own technical challenges.

So where to go? The best thing to do is to check with those in the know—the folks at **Appalachian Mountain Gear** in Great Barrington for climbing areas in the southern Berkshires, and the folks at **Zoar Outdoor** in the northern Berkshires (see "Gear," below).

Gear

Probably the best place in the Berkshires for technical gear is **Appalachian Mountain Gear** (684 S. Main St., Great Barrington, MA 01230; ☎ 413/528-5054). **Zoar Outdoor** (Mohawk Trail, Box 245, Charlemont, MA 01339; ☎ 800/532-7483) also sells some climbing equipment. Keep in mind, of course, there's not a lot of big-wall climbing in the area and hence not a lot of shops that carry a full array of ropes and high-tech gear.

Instruction

Zoar Outdoor (see "Gear," above), offers 1- and 2-day clinics for beginning and intermediate climbers.

SNOWSHOEING

The great thing about snowshoes is that as plodding as walking around on them might seem, they enable you to go almost anywhere. You can travel through forest areas that in summer are often inaccessible because of underbrush, and you can get to places that on skis would be awkward to reach. The technology of snowshoes, however, has changed in recent years, and many shoes are now designed primarily for packed trails rather than wilderness exploration. Before heading off on a deep-woods jaunt, be sure you've got the right type of shoes strapped to your feet.

Many of the trails described above under "Hiking & Backpacking" and "Cross-Country Skiing" and under "Walks & Rambles," below, are ideal for snowshoeing, too. For adventurous snowshoers, a couple of areas to consider are **Mt. Greylock Reservation** and **October Mountain State Forest.** Shelters and privies are maintained in both areas throughout the winter, so if a 2-day snowshoeing trip, with a little winter camping thrown in, is your idea of fun, Greylock and October Mountain are the places to go.

A number of inns in the Berkshires have snowshoes available for loan or rental, so if you know snowshoeing is something you'll want to try, ask first before making lodging plans and reservations.

SWIMMING

Head from Great Barrington toward South Egremont on Route 23 on a hot summer day, and you're apt to see cars parked near the bridge crossing the **Green River.** Some local environmentalists might cringe at the idea of swimming in the Green, claiming it is still not the pristine waterway it ought to be, despite clean-up efforts, but apparently it is clean enough to entice locals in for a quick cooling off.

There are small, pretty beaches at **Benedict Pond** in Beartown State Forest and **South Pond** in Savoy Mountain State Forest, complete with facilities, but don't expect to have the beaches to yourself on midsummer weekends. For bigger water, head for **Onota Lake** and **Pontoosuc Lake** near Pittsfield; although swimming beaches should be cordoned off, be alert here to a fair amount of boat traffic. Another popular, big-water swimming (and boating) spot is **Otis Reservoir,** in Tolland State Forest, east of Great Barrington.

WALKS & RAMBLES

Could there be anything more appropriate to the Berkshires—better suited to the rolling countryside, the English heritage, the evocations of Thoreau—than something called a ramble? Is there a better way to spend a summer's afternoon than a 1- to 2-hour walk through forests, around ponds, past gentle streams and waterfalls, with the songs of thrushes and warblers anointing the air?

One more question: At one point does a walk become a ramble, and a ramble a hike? Rambles and walks should, of course, be shorter and easier, but there is no clear-cut dividing point. One person's hike is another's ramble, and several of the walks and rambles described below can be extended into excursions that could legitimately be considered hikes. Similarly, some of the hikes mentioned above can be rerouted and shortened into less strenuous outings. So regardless of how ambitious you expect to be on foot, you'll probably want to look at the hikes listed under "Hiking & Backpacking," above, before making any final decisions on where to go.

Bartholemew's Cobble

Allow 2–3 hours. Easy. Access: Take Rte. 7 south from Sheffield, bearing right onto Rte. 7A south of town and then right again over the railroad tracks onto Rannapo Rd. Immediately after the road jogs left at the junction with Weatogue Rd., the entrance to the Cobble will be on your right. Maps: Available at the visitor center.

The natural diversity of this enchanting location, with an area of less than 300 acres, is truly remarkable. Numbers speak volumes: There are approximately 500 species of wildflowers, 40 species of ferns, and 100 tree species that grow here. This is also a bird-watcher's nirvana. About 240 different species have been sighted here: water fowl and eagles along the Housatonic River, songbirds in the open meadows, and still more songbirds of a different ilk around the cobble itself.

What, you might ask, is a cobble? It is an old Colonial term for an outcropping of rock. In this case, the cobble is an assortment of fists and knuckles of limestone and granite, covered with ferns, mosses, trees, wildflowers, and wild herbs. The Ledges Trail circumscribes the cobble, providing about a 30-minute walk

with interpretive stations along the way. Through the tree canopy, you can see the nearby Housatonic meandering by and cows grazing lazily on riverside pastures.

Bear left from the Ledges Trail onto the Bailey Trail, which runs along the banks of the river, and then onto the appropriately named Tulip Tree Trail. The trail climbs easily through the forest before coming to its namesake—a spectacularly enormous tulip tree that speaks volumes about why old-growth forests are worth preserving. After passing the tree, the trail breaks into open meadows and joins the Hurlburt Hill Trail. Head left up the hill; in the spring, you'll spot bobolinks nesting in the tall grasses. At the top of the hill, kick back on the two benches there and take in the views to the north and west: Mt. Everett close at hand; the broad, Housatonic Valley stretching northward; the summit of Mt. Greylock in the distance. By now the smell of wildflowers and herbs, the song of birdcalls, and the sweeping views will have overwhelmed your senses. Return to the visitor center directly via the Hurlburt Hill Trail.

Bash Bish Falls

Allow 1–2 hours. Easy–moderate. Access: Take Rte. 41 south from South Egremont. Turn right on Mt. Washington Rd. (about .5 mile out of town) and continue for 8 miles. In Mt. Washington, turn right on Cross St., and follow signs to Bash Bish Falls, about 3 miles. Parking for the falls trail is on your left.

In terms of water volume and vertical drop, Bash Bish Falls might not be the most impressive waterfall you've ever seen, but as natural sculpture it is mesmerizing. After passing through a narrow cataract set among granite cliffs, Bash Bish Brook forms two channels of water that pass, like two braids of white, around a large rock fang before tumbling into a deep, green pool. Above the falls, the forested slopes rise with breathtaking steepness; hundreds of feet almost directly above you, trees appear stapled to the sky. The short trail to the falls descends steeply from the western edge of the parking lot through a forest composed primarily of hemlock. Through the trees, the sound of rushing water can be heard, but the falls remain shy, refusing until the last moment to reveal themselves. It is only upon descending a final flight of stone stairs that the falls come fully into view.

Bring a picnic lunch and bask on the rocks that afford a full frontal view of the falls. Swimming, alas, is not permitted; the rocks and the turbulence harbor considerable hazards. Too bad—it would be a wonderful spot for a cooling dip before embarking on the stiff, 20-minute climb back to the parking lot.

Canoe Meadows Wildlife Sanctuary

Allow 1–2 hours. Easy. Access: From Lenox, head north on Rte. 7. After about 3 miles, turn right on Holmes Rd. Look for the entrance to the sanctuary on your right after about 2 miles. Map: Available at the visitor center.

Resisting the suburban encroachments of Pittsfield, this 262-acre sanctuary is just that—a haven of peace in the surrounding world of bustle and industry. As you might expect of an area managed by the Massachusetts Audubon Society, this is an ideal place for bird-watching. Trails here meander through meadows, around a pond, and through wooded swamps and wetlands. The trails' minimal elevation changes make for easy walking. There is something about this area, once considered sacred by the Housatonic tribe, that inspires visitors to move slowly and quietly and to speak in hushed tones. In fact, the trail bearing right from the parking area—a short loop passing through meadows and wetlands and along the Housatonic River—is called Sacred Way. Returning to the parking area, bear left onto Wolf Pine Trail, noteworthy for the enormous, old-growth white pine that give the trail its name. Do not rush; walk slowly and listen. The faint murmurs of industrial Pittsfield might lurk in the background, but on a typical day, the symphony of bird song will all but drown out the distant noise.

Pleasant Valley Sanctuary

Allow 2–3 hours. Moderate. Access: From Lenox, head north on Main St. (Rte. 7A) to the juncture with Rte. 7. In less than .5 mile, turn left onto West Dugway Rd. The sanctuary is less than 2 miles down West Dugway Rd. Map: Available at the visitor center.

With an exceedingly well-marked network of trails, this is a great place for an afternoon of getting lost in the woods, if only figuratively rather than literally. Go as easy or as hard as you like. The 20-minute Pike's Pond loop is as flat as the pond itself, and if your timing is right, you'll witness a group of very active beavers doing the sort of natural construction work they excel at. Or try your hand, perhaps literally, on the Trail of the Ledges; it's steep enough to require scrambling handholds to steady yourself.

What makes Pleasant Valley special? Bird life is abundant—this area is also managed by the Audubon Society—although fewer species have been sighted here than at Canoe Meadows or Bartholomew's Cobble. Should you venture to the summit of Lenox Mountain—and here is where a walk might indeed turn into a hike—the views westward toward the Taconic Range are inspiring. But perhaps the real inspiration of Pleasant Valley is its deep-forest diversity. Only minutes from the heart of Lenox or Pittsfield, the valley offers deep groves of hemlock, ponds teeming with life, and a mountain to climb—1,000 vertical feet worth—all of which can quickly rejuvenate a wilderness spirit.

Tannery Falls, Balanced Rock

Allow 1–2 hours. Easy–moderate. Access: Take Rte. 2 east from North Adams. After approximately 10 miles, turn right (following a steep descent) onto

Black Brook Rd. After 2.5 miles, turn right onto Tannery Rd. and follow it .75 mile to the parking area.

These two short walks—one to the falls, the other to the rock—render wonderful displays of the power of natural forces. Glaciers, water, and wind all combine here to define and redefine the landscape, a lesson visitors are sure to take away with them after their walk. Start by heading down through a hemlock grove for the short walk to Tannery Falls. Squeezing through a narrow sluiceway of granite, water pushes its way toward the falls. After a 5-minute walk from the parking area, the falls emerge, tumbling below you close to 100 feet over a ledge. The falls then seem to disappear, swallowed up by the tight confines of the surrounding hills and forest. It is not unlike sinkholes in Australia, where rivers descend and are swallowed up in the maw of Australia's ancient earth.

After returning to the parking area, head in the opposite direction on the multi-use trail leading to Balanced Rock. (The trail is also navigable by mountain bikes, although there are a couple of short, steep sections.) After about 20 minutes of walking, you'll find a major blow-down area, where trees have been toppled by some isolated but devastatingly violent winds. How surprising it is to see the surrounding trees entirely unaffected; the power of the wind apparently concentrated on an area less than half the size of a football field.

Continue on from here on a gradually escalating trail (with a few, steeper spurts) through a mixed forest to Balanced Rock, a rounded granite boulder about 7 feet tall and 12 feet wide, propped on the ground like some enormous petrified dinosaur egg. It is what is known as a glacial *erratic*—a glacially borne boulder left behind during the eventual melting of the ice. It is unfortunate that the rock has been turned into a canvas for thoughtless graffiti artists, but that cannot diminish the inexorable force of glacial activity that the rock conveys.

WHITEWATER RAFTING/ KAYAKING

Whitewater is essentially the result of two natural phenomena coming together—a robust flow of water and elevation change. Southern New England as a whole can be problem-prone on both counts. Most rivers that have substantial water flow are dammed, which doesn't necessarily exclude whitewater, but does change flow patterns. Dam releases—not natural influences, such as rain, snowmelt and drought—determine how hard and fast rivers run.

As for elevation changes, the mountains of the Berkshires are obviously not on the same scale as, say, the Rockies. That doesn't mean steep drops with Class V water are impossible to find, of course, but it does exclude the kind of multiday whitewater trips you might find in the West. There are plenty of thrills to fill up a half day at a time, but not much more than that.

That said, the Berkshires—the northern Berkshires, in particular—feature a number of fine, fast rivers to run. This, after all, is where the most substantial mountains of the region are found, so elevation changes can be abrupt. And if snowfall during the course of the winter has been plentiful, the spring run-off can briefly produce world-class rapids on streams that by mid-May might not amount to much more than a trickle.

In other words, whitewater can be found in the Berkshires, but it comes with two limitations. For one, timing is everything. Early spring—late March and April—is usually the prime season, when water volumes are most likely to be high and smaller rivers are at their most runnable. Rivers can also re-form in midsummer as robust torrents after a heavy or extended rainfall, but within a day after the rains subside, the rivers usually recede dramatically. Such natural cycles, of course, mean little on such dammed rivers as the Deerfield, where man rather than nature controls water levels and flow rates. If you can't time a trip in accordance with natural cycles, the Deerfield offers the closest thing you'll find in the region to a whitewater guarantee.

While in some cases dams—and dam releases—produce exciting whitewater runs, they are also a wrench in the works. Considerable damming subdivides most large rivers that run through the Berkshires, and undammed stretches exceeding 15 miles are rare. That means even if you do have dreams of a multiday trip, you'll be obliged to portage around dams, and that's not always an easy task. Power companies, for safety and security reasons, usually erect considerable fencing around dam sites. Day trips and half-day trips are the norm, and of course kayakers have been known to spend hours playing around in particularly challenging or mesmerizing rapids.

While not described in detail here, a river whitewater enthusiasts might also want to check out is the **Farmington River** above New Boston. Water levels can be iffy, but when the water is sufficiently high, a fast-paced, Class IV run is possible.

Cold River

Put in along Rte. 2, 8 miles west of Charlemont. Takeout before the river joins with the Deerfield, about 4.5 miles downstream.

What's in a name? The Cold River follows Route 2 (the Mohawk Trail) as it descends eastward from the Berkshire plateau. In March, when the river is flooded with snowmelt and at its most runnable, the Cold is often decorated with snow patches and rime ice. And coursing through a deep cut in the mountains, this is not a river that sees extended, warming stretches of sunshine. The Cold River can indeed be cold.

But it is also one of the most challenging rivers in the Berkshires, capable of summoning Class V force in high water and comfortably reaching Class IV in an average spring. It's not a river for the faint

of heart or for those at all deficient in kayaking skills. What would you expect, after all, of a run that starts at Dead Man's Curve and features a group of rapids named Pinball? In fact, Pinball, where the river races through a boulder field, may not be the most technically challenging section of the river. That honor probably goes to Cold River Falls about .5 mile before the confluence with the Deerfield; get out at the Mohawk State Forest bridge before the falls if you don't want to run it, but be sure to scout the falls regardless.

Because the river runs close by Route 2, you can scope out much of it fairly easily before running it. You might drive along the Cold in July, when it is barely moving, and wonder what the fuss is about. How could such a gentle trickle be so fearsome? It's a whole different river in March. As Bruce Lessels, owner of Zoar Outdoor in Charlemont and a former world whitewater champion, says, "This one gets very serious in high water. Don't underestimate it."

Deerfield River Dryway

Take Rte. 2 2 miles northwest of Charlemont and turn right at the sign for the Yankee Atomic Energy Plant onto River Rd. Put in at Monroe Bridge, just south of the Vermont border. Takeout 3 miles downstream at the #5 Station dam.

The Deerfield is the king of whitewater not only in the Berkshires, but arguably in all of southern New England. And that's not because its rapids are bigger, faster, and fiercer than those of the other rivers in the region; at certain times of the year, it can be out-whitewatered even by its neighbor, the Cold River (see above). What elevates the Deerfield to the throne is the regularity of its whitewater, which is maintained courtesy of the hydroelectric demands of western Massachusetts. Frequent dam releases during the course of the year ensure frequent whitewater (although when the dams close, the water subsides accordingly).

It comes with some irony to discover that the best segment of the Deerfield for whitewater enthusiasts is called the Dryway, a 3-mile section from Monroe Bridge to Bear Swamp Reservoir. On most days of the year, the Dryway is just that— a dry river bed. Water is diverted from its natural course into a canal that drives a hydroelectric turbine. It is an odd sight— a channel of grass and boulders, interrupted by the occasional puddle of water. But on approximately 30 selected days of the year, water is released in a torrent through the Dryway and suddenly it is transformed into a playground for kayakers and rafters. The rapids, bearing such names as Split Hair, the Labyrinth, and Dragon's Tooth are not inordinately complicated, but they can be big, reaching Class IV in places. Call the U.S. Generating Company's river-information number at ☎ 888/356-3663, for dam-release schedules.

Deerfield River, Zoar Gap

Take Rte. 2 two miles west of Charlemont and turn right at the sign for Yankee Atomic Energy Plant onto River Rd. Continue 5 miles to Fife Brook Dam.

On a quiet summer morning on this stretch of the Deerfield River, you are struck by the realization that true serenity has not been lost in southern New England. The hills bow down into the river, the green water whispers, and the sun filters through the forest high above the river. Numerous birds happiest in riparian environments—hawks, herons, and so on—circle, call, and wade. Even the presence of a road and railroad tracks alongside the river cannot steal from the spirit of pre-civilization that permeates the air, the feeling of nature nearing its true natural state.

However pleasant an image this is, it is nevertheless something of an illusion. The environment here has been shaped, transformed, and reconstructed in its more-or-less natural state by the railroad and the hydroelectric industry. Like the Dryway upstream, this section of the Deerfield is precisely controlled. Water is

released from Fife Brook Dam according to a predetermined schedule, and voilà— you have whitewater. But if the river and its surroundings are not purely aboriginal, your illusion shouldn't be spoiled. This is still a pretty, peaceful place and a great section of river on which to run on a raft or kayak.

The rapids of the Dryway upstream are more ferocious; below Fife Brook Dam, the rapids top out at Class III. The river drops at an average rate of 25 feet per mile, compared with the 60-feet-per-mile drop through the Dryway. That makes it a good place for intermediate kayakers or for rafters getting their first taste of whitewater. The highlight of the journey comes near the end, where the river rushes through the boulder fields of Zoar Gap. The 1993 National Slalom Championships were held here— affirmation that this is world-class kayaking country. And it's not bad for rafting, either. Call the U.S. Generating Company's river-information number (☎ 888/356-3663) for dam-release schedules.

Gear

Zoar Outdoor Adventures (Mohawk Trail, Box 245, Charlemont, MA 01339; ☎ 800/532-7483) offers a full line of kayak clothing and paraphernalia, as well boat rentals.

Instruction

Zoar Outdoor (see "Gear," above), owned by Bruce Lessels, a former whitewater kayaking champion, offers a variety of clinics and private instruction in basic kayaking technique.

Guides & Outfitters

Crab Apple Whitewater (Crab Apple Acres Inn, HC65, Box 25, The Forks, ME 04985; ☎ 800/553-7238) also leads rafting and inflatable kayak trips on the Deerfield River. **Zoar Outdoor** (see "Gear," above) is the pre-eminent rafting and kayaking guide service in the northern Berkshires, and also provides shuttle service for kayakers running sections of the Deerfield River.

Campgrounds & Other Accommodations

CAMPGROUNDS

Benedict Pond

From Great Barrington, head east on Rte. 23 to Blue Hill Rd. Forest headquarters are .5 mile north. 12 sites, no hookups, public phones and rest rooms, tables, and grills. ☎ 413/528-0904.

The campground on the edge of Benedict Pond has much to recommend it: good canoeing, a nice sandy beach, a short hiking trail looping the pond, and campsites in a hemlock grove. Expect to find the campground well used on weekends, but because the steep, winding access road discourages RVs and the campground is relatively small, a backcountry atmosphere still prevails.

Clarksburg State Park

From North Adams, take Rte. 8 north 3 miles to Middle Rd. Turn left and follow signs to campground on right. 47 sites for tents and RVs, no hookups, rest rooms with showers, tables, and grills. ☎ 413/663-8469.

If you're looking for the place to go to distance yourself from the crowds—a quiet alternative to busier Savoy Mountain State Forest to the south—Clarksburg is hard to beat. It is a particularly good place to bring the family, with pocket-sized Mauserts Pond by the campground serving as a great location for swimming, fishing, canoeing, and general exploring. Dense maple forests also make this a good spot for foliage enthusiasts in the fall.

Pittsfield State Forest

From Pittsfield, take West St. west to Churchill St. Turn right on Churchill, then left onto Cascade St., leading to the forest entrance. 31 sites for tents and RVs, no hookups, rest rooms and primitive toilets, tables, and fireplaces. ☎ 413/442-8992.

Tiny Berry Pond is the highest pond in Massachusetts, lying on the main ridgeline of Pittsfield State Forest. For backpackers trekking through the forest, it is the obvious, almost unavoidable place to overnight. Although the campground is accessible from the main, paved road that loops through the forest, it still affords a feel of remote seclusion. Bring a fishing rod and try your luck in the stocked pond.

Savoy Mountain State Forest

Take Rte. 2 east from North Adams for 5 miles to Center Shaft Rd. Turn right and follow signs to the state forest. 45 sites for tents and RVs, no hookups, phones, rest rooms with showers, tables, and grills. ☎ 413/633-8469.

This is a mostly idyllic campground, set in an old orchard at the edge of a pond, and surrounded by 11,000 acres of state forest. Yet its natural endowments coupled with easy access can make this, relatively speaking, a crowded place, heavily used by both campers and day visitors. Nevertheless, South Pond is great for swimming and fishing, and there is all that state forest to escape to should the campground scene get a bit congested. This being a popular spot, it is recommended that reservations for midsummer weekends be made several weeks in advance.

Sperry Campground

From Pittsfield, take Rte. 7 north for 5 miles to Lanesborough. Look for signs to the entrance to Mt. Greylock Reservation on your right, then follow signs to the campground. 35 sites for tents and RVs, pit toilets, tables, and fireplaces. ☎ 413/499-4262.

This isn't exactly the campground version of a room with a view, but it comes close. Nestled in the woods near Stony Ledge on the flank of Mt. Greylock, you can take the short walk from the campground to the ledge, which is, as billed, stony. This open vantage point affords sensational views of Mt. Greylock, the Hopper, and points west.

INNS & RESORTS

Bascom Lodge

Box 1800, Lanesboro, MA 01237; ☎ 413/443-0011. A bed in a bunkroom in midsummer, $27 for non-AMC members; private room, $65.

This handsome stone structure at the summit of Mt. Greylock is, at heart, a layover sanctuary for hikers along the Appalachian Trail. Managed by the Appalachian Mountain Club with hikers in mind, the lodge features inexpensive, bunkroom-style accommodations, shared baths, and group, family-style meals. There are also four private bedrooms for those disinclined to share sleeping quarters with strangers. The mountain-top setting is unrivaled in all of Massachusetts, a perfect place to spend time whether you're an Appalachian Trail through-hiker or just someone eager to head out on day hikes on the many Mt. Greylock trails that converge at the summit.

Bucksteep Manor

Washington Mountain Rd., Washington, MA 01223; ☎ 800/645-2825 or 413/623-5535. Room rates start at $80.

Who said location is everything? Bucksteep, a turn-of-the-century inn built in the style of an English country manor, lies on the periphery of October Mountain State Forest, which hosts a wealth of recreational opportunities. But you might not even make it to the state forest, given that the inn has 400 acres of its own laced with hiking trails and groomed cross-country skiing trails.

Canyon Ranch Health Resort

165 Kemble St., Lenox, MA 01240. ☎ 800/742-9000; www.canyonranch.com. Four-night packages start around $2,030 double, including meals, use of facilities, and recreation.

A ranch in the Berkshires? And a ranch without horses? These are the sort of oddities that pop up when an idea is imported from the southwest to the northeast. Canyon Ranch in Lenox is an extension of the famous health resort of the same name in Arizona. The basic concept here is to promote health through good eating and plenty of exercise, with a heavy emphasis on personal service. It all comes at a pretty healthy price tag, too, but if you can afford it, it is probably money well spent. Guided hikes, bike trips, canoe trips, and naturalist outings are all part of the program, and when the weather is dismal, head inside for fitness clinics. And yes, it's pretty posh. At this price, it ought to be.

The Country Inn at Jiminy Peak

Brodie Mountain Rd. (near Rte. 43), Hancock, MA 01237. ☎ 800/882-8859 or 413/738-5500; www.jiminypeak.com. Suites $138–$330, including breakfast.

This is one of the better lodging deals in the Berkshires if your idea of luxury is space. All units are one-bedroom suites with full kitchens and pullout sofas, great for a small group traveling together. The furniture is a bit worn, but the abundance of activities that lie almost outside your doorstep more than make up for it. A buffet breakfast is served in the restaurant during the winter and summer seasons.

Cranwell Resort

Rte. 20, Lenox, MA 01240; ☎ 800/272-6935. Rooms start around $130 in winter and spring, about twice that in summer. 3-night minimum stay July–Aug.

Mix one part resort, two parts country club, and one part outdoors adventure, shake well, and what you end up with is Cranwell. In addition to the usual clubby offerings—golf, tennis, swimming—there are hiking trails that double as cross-country skiing trails in winter. The centerpiece of the resort complex is the impressive, Tudor mansion that is a clear reminder in the world of squared-off modern hotels that they just don't make 'em like they used to.

Eastover Resort

East St., Lenox, MA 01240; ☎ **800/822-2386.** Rates from around $100 per person for dorm room to $175 for a suite, including 3 meals a day.

If Cranwell is a resort masquerading as a country club, Eastover is a resort masquerading as a summer camp for all ages. Let's see. . . there's hiking, biking, horseback riding, cross-country skiing, sleigh rides, tennis, softball, volleyball, and even a dance hall ("with live bands at night!" effuses the resort's brochure). The 1,000-acre estate, complete with a brick mansion, was once the home of millionaire Harris Fahnestock, who wanted a quiet mountain getaway for his family and staff of 75. Accommodations vary widely, from dorm rooms (true summer-camp style) to rooms and suites in the mansion.

Field Farm Guesthouse

554 Sloan Rd., Williamstown, MA 01262; ☎ **413/458-3135.** $125 double.

This pristine example of postwar modern architecture rose in 1948 in the middle of a spectacularly scenic 296-acre estate. The majority of the five guest rooms overlook meadows that stretch out to Mt. Greylock. A telescope in the living room will help wildlife viewers catch a glimpse of the beavers and waterfowl on a lake 100 yards away. The rooms here are spare, but the location is top-notch. In addition to the recreational activities that are close by, the property has its own pool, tennis court, and 4 miles of nature trails.

Race Brook Lodge

684 Undermountain Rd., Sheffield, MA 01230; ☎ **413/229-2916.** $65–$125 a room.

Race Brook Lodge, its 20 rooms located in a resorted, 18th-century barn, likes to advertise itself as being "chintz free." In other words, it's a relaxed, down-to-earth place in a relaxed, down-to-earth setting. Virtually right out the back door is the eponymous brook, which cascades down the eastern flank of Mt. Everett and Mt. Race. If you're looking for a base camp from which to attack some of the best hiking in the Berkshires in Mt. Washington State Forest, this is the place.

Chapter 3

Central Massachusetts

W hen traveling through the heart of Massachusetts, I am often overwhelmed by an impression that nature has, in almost all ways, succumbed to the will and whim of man. I am not implying that this area is roughly 3,000 square miles of paved parking lot, endless subdivisions, and urban blight sprawling to the horizon. But what I do see are rivers and streams dammed for agricultural, hydroelectric, or industrial purposes. I see orderly fields of corn, potatoes, and vegetables spread across the Connecticut River flood plains.

The mountains here—very *small* mountains—are crisscrossed with roads and trails. In hiking their summit ridges, I come across the remnant walls and foundations of restaurants and dance halls, accessible by inclined railways and popular at the turn of the century. I see small, industrial cities—Worcester, Springfield, Fitchburg, Athol— webbed together by a complex network of roadways and railways, some still active, others abandoned.

To the west, the rock and bulk of the Berkshires have resisted similar development, and while Massachusetts to the east is more densely populated, and in many ways more developed, it still abuts the grand, untamed sea. But because central Massachusetts is almost ideally suited to human settlement, with its fertile plains, abundance of water, and a relatively flat, hospitable landscape, it cannot escape the impulse to build, cultivate, dam, and pave.

This makes central Massachusetts both the state's breadbasket as well as its manufacturing base. Along the banks of the Connecticut River, around Hadley, the air is fragrant with the aromas of farming. The fields sweep back from the river's edge in a wash of green and are adorned with long, wooden barns elegant in their simplicity. To the east is Johnny Appleseed country, where the legendary planter (John Chapman by birth) got his start in the late 1700s.

Meanwhile, in pocket-sized cities like Worcester or Fitchburg, a blue-collar grit prevails—sometimes sadly, sometimes with intimations of a fierce pride. Sadness comes in seeing the dark, ghostly emptiness of the storefronts in downtown Fitchburg, a consequence of the malling of America or of time having passed Fitchburg by. Or both. Yet, the few people I know from these central Massachusetts cities seem to have ingrained within them an admirable resilience and self-reliance.

There is a softer side, too, to central Massachusetts—a Colonial gentility in tiny, all-but-forgotten crossroads such as Barre, or in the broad, tree-lined streets of South Hadley and Amherst. This is as fertile intellectual ground as it is agricultural; around Northampton and Amherst, the colleges of Smith, Mt. Holyoke, Hampshire, Amherst, and the University of Massachusetts form a concentration of higher learning unrivaled in the Northeast except, perhaps, for the college cluster of the Boston area. There is no mistaking Northampton as anything but a college town; every other storefront in the heart of the city seems to be either a bookstore or a cafe.

What intrigues me in visiting this world is that a viable kind of "great outdoors" still manages to exist, even if it has largely been shaped by human design or reconstituted from the remnants of human disregard. One of the great surprises in the region is Quabbin Reservoir, the largest man-made body of water in the northeast and the main source of drinking water for Boston. It is, of course, an unnatural phenomenon by definition. Yet to stand at the edge of the reservoir and look out on a cool summer morning, with the low hills rising above the misty shroud suspended over the water, is to behold the sort of natural vision that would surely have inspired an environmental romanticist like Henry David Thoreau. Bald eagles nest here, and I suppose it says something about the great outdoors of central Massachusetts that it has enough wildness in it to allow the great symbol of endangered American wildlife to make a healthy comeback.

One of the prime recreational hubs of the region is the Northfield Recreational and Environmental Center, a fine place for hiking, mountain biking, cross-country skiing, or just hanging around and appreciating the woods and the views. But it would not exist were it not for the efforts of Northeast Utilities, which operations a huge, underground hydroelectric pumping station under Northfield Mountain. Throughout the region, abandoned rail lines are being converted to recreational corridors for biking, in-line skating, and walking. Ponds and lakes have been created throughout the region as a result of damming; the original purpose for the damming may have been industrial or hydroelectric, but the bonus has been abundant opportunities for canoeing, swimming, and fishing.

In short, there really is something that can be called the great outdoors of central Massachusetts, even if it is almost in its entirety directly or indirectly a construct of human design. It is also almost entirely ignored by visitors to Massachusetts. Few are the people who come to this region for an extended vacation, and there are, of course, reasons for that. There are no grand, natural features like the Berkshires or the ocean that beckon irresistibly. To many people, of course, central Massachusetts is not much more than a backdrop to the Massachusetts Turnpike or Interstate 91, which cross in Springfield. Between the Berkshires and Boston, central Massachusetts is often erased in a 65-mile-an-hour blur.

Still, it has its own subtle, largely undiscovered beauty (and, to be sure, some industrial eyesores). Take a ride, for example, along the Norwottuck Rail Trail between Northampton and Amherst. The former Boston & Maine rail line passes through a heavily congested world of roadways, malls, subdivided neighborhoods, garbage dumps, and agricultural lands. Yet the path seems to exist almost magically in its own green corridor, with the tree canopy forming a kind of protective tunnel for much of the trail's 9.75-mile length.

A 9.75-mile rail trail might alone seem insufficient as a reason for an outdoor enthusiast to take notice of central Massachusetts; it is simply emblematic of how recreational opportunities can be woven easily into an otherwise well-developed landscape. For those who want bigger fish to fry in the outdoors—perhaps literally—there are further surprises. In Quabbin Reservoir, fishermen haul in lake trout as large as 20 pounds, big-league fishing by any standard. Two "long trails" cross the region from north to south—the Metacomet–Monadnock Trail and the Midstate Trail—as enticements to multiday hikers.

Man-made nature? It is a contradiction that central Massachusetts seems able to live with, and embraces comfortably.

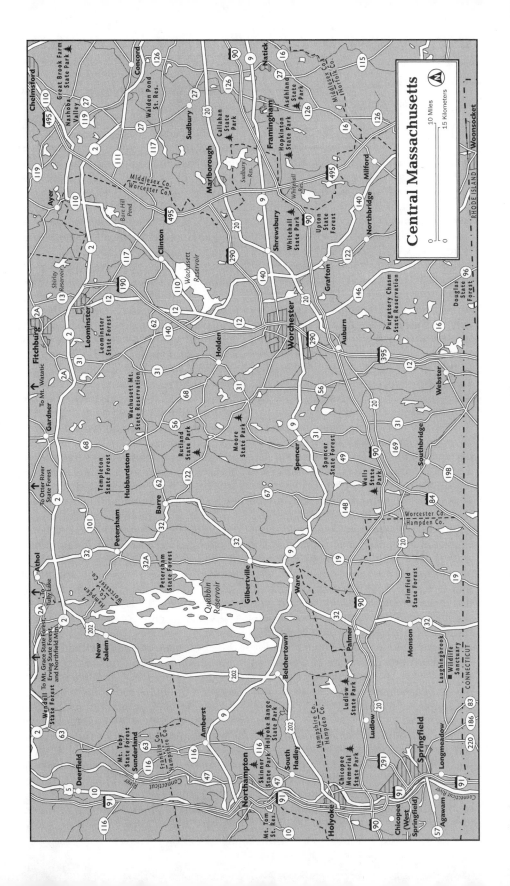

The Lay of the Land

If the Berkshires to the west are about hills, and eastern Massachusetts is about the ocean and the fingered bays that reach from it, then central Massachusetts is about water. The Connecticut River, New England's most important inland waterway, wends through the heart of Massachusetts and is the principal water source for the fertile farmlands that stretch for miles from the river's bank. And if there is a dominant feature on the central Massachusetts map, it is the giant blue bulk of man-made Quabbin Reservoir, the 412-billion-gallon source of water for Boston. The rest of the landscape is freckled with smaller bodies of water, some natural and some the result of dammed streams.

This is not a mountainous region, although there are what could marginally be (and are) called mountains, Mt. Wachusett, at 2,006 feet, standing tallest among them. Actually, it is probably more correct to call these knuckle-like protuberances the remains of mountains, the leftovers after millions of years of erosion. In some instances, their contours are abrupt, as is the case with Mt. Tom and Mount Sugarloaf, carved out of the land by the recession of the powerful glacier that once dominated what is now the Connecticut River valley. With open, rocky ledges and steep drop-offs along their summit ridges, these mountains typically afford stunning views of the valleys below—views that may be more sweeping and far-ranging that those from, say, the higher, more tree-covered summits of the Berkshires.

In fact, perhaps the more impressive natural creation of glacial origin is the valley itself, the broad and fertile floodplain that in summer is verdant (and fragrant) with agricultural activity. It is not surprising human settlement is focused here, where the soil is rich, the water plentiful, and the building easy.

Like the rest of southern New England, central Massachusetts was heavily logged in the past, and it is somewhat ironic that the only thing approaching old-growth trees are found around the towns and cities of the region. The reason should be obvious: When early settlers arrived, they left trees along village streets and around their homes for shade, while otherwise leveling the countryside for the dual purpose of producing building timber and clearing the land for agriculture.

So while mixed forests of hardwoods (primarily maple, birch, oak, and hickory) and conifers (primarily white pine, hemlock, and various species of spruce) have made a substantial recovery, the trees are relatively small. This reflects their relative youth; they are, for the most part, less than 100 years old. The forests are considered transitional—that is, they bear some of the species and characteristics of both the boreal forests to the north and the mixed deciduous forests to the south. That mixed effect means that, depending on your latitude and elevation, the variety of flora can be stunning.

Ferns and mountain laurel are the most common plants that blanket the forest floor, along with a vast array of wildflowers that bloom, depending on the variety, from early May to October. By August, blueberries along the lake and bog shores can be plentiful.

While central Massachusetts shares the same latitudes as the Berkshires, it does not share the same elevations, and the climate here is somewhat milder. The average February high in Amherst is 33°F, compared with the 30°F in Great Barrington at a similar latitude. In July, the average high is 83°F compared with Great Barrington's 80°F. The climate is also somewhat drier, with an average of 43 inches of rain falling annually in Amherst, compared with 48 in Great Barrington.

What's to be made of this difference? Winters are shorter and less snowy, obviously affecting such wintertime activities as skiing and snowshoeing. Conversely, spring comes earlier and fall lasts longer, so if you're looking for a longer hiking, biking, canoeing, or fishing season, central Massachusetts might be the place to go. But beware the ides of summer, when heat waves stew and hang over the Northeast; they can sweep through central Massachusetts with daunting oppression, feeding on the abundance of water and the moist agricultural soils to produce high humidity levels.

Orientation

Where central Massachusetts begins and ends is not necessarily a matter of precise, geographical determination. To the south, of course, is Connecticut, and to the north are Vermont and New Hampshire. To the west are the Berkshires, sloping down into what is often referred to as the **Pioneer Valley**—essentially the Connecticut River watershed and its tributaries. (The more westerly parts of what is considered the Pioneer Valley, including stretches of the Deerfield River, are covered in chapter 2, "The Berkshires.") And to the east, there is no real natural or state-border boundary. So for the purposes of this book, central Massachusetts ends approximately at **Route 495,** which makes a wide circle around Boston. Anything to the east of that is covered in chapter 4, "Greater Boston, Cape Ann & the South Shore."

Two major highways—**Interstate 91,** which runs north to south along the Connecticut River, and the **Massachusetts Turnpike** (Interstate 90), which runs west to east—crisscross the area, intersecting in Springfield. **Route 2,** running west to east through the northern quarter of the region, is the area's other major highway, intersecting Interstate 91 in Greenfield.

Small to modest-sized cities can be found throughout the region, the largest of them being **Worcester,** in the southeast, and **Springfield,** the second- and third-largest cities, respectively, in Massachusetts. Neither is a city of great architectural or cultural distinction, but are rather more functional, workaday places. If you're looking for culture, **Northampton,** the heart of Massachusetts' college country, is the region's cultural hub. For historical character, **Deerfield,** with a museum town of 17th- and 18th-century homes, is the place to go.

Parks & Other Hot Spots

Connecticut River
The river, flowing north to south, enters Massachusetts from the north near Northfield, and exits into Connecticut near Longmeadow. Various agencies manage dams, campgrounds, parks, etc. For more information and maps, the **Connecticut River Watershed Council** (☎ 413/584-0057), the **Massachusetts Department of Environmental Management** (☎ 617/727-3180), or the **Northfield Mountain Recreation & Environmental Center** (see below) may be of help.

The wide, largely slow-flowing Connecticut River bisects Massachusetts on its way south to Long Island Sound. Perhaps the most scenic sections of the river are those north of Northampton. In the south, the river passes through the more densely populated areas of Chicopee and Springfield. Dams interrupt the flow of the river, and powerboats are permitted on it, both drawbacks for canoeists or long-distance paddlers. Still, there are two pleasant 20-mile stretches between the Vermont border and Northampton, the two sections separated by Turners Falls Dam.

Erving State Forest

From Erving, take Rte. 2 east about 2 miles, bearing right onto Rte. 2A. Turn left onto Wendell Rd. at the sign for the state forest. Visitors' services are available at Laurel Lake, at the junction of Wendell Rd. and Laurel Lake Rd. Headquarters: Orange (☎ 508/544-3939).

The attraction for most visitors to Erving State Forest is the swimming beach at Laurel Lake, which on a hot summer's day can be crowded with prepubescent youth. Yet perhaps the most outstanding feature of the forest are its back roads—old logging roads and fire roads—which present some of the best mountain-biking opportunities in the region. The 4,500-acre forest is the centerpiece of several contiguous state forests—Wendell to the south and Northfield, Mt. Grace, and Warwick to the north—that form a sprawling woodland tract totaling roughly 22,000 acres. Only Quabbin Reservation, much of which is off-limits to visitors, can claim more undeveloped acreage in central Massachusetts.

Metacomet–Monadnock Trail

From Connecticut, the trail enters Massachusetts east of Southwick and exits north of Warwick, after passing through Mt. Grace State Forest, into New Hampshire. Information on the trail can be obtained through the **Appalachian Mountain Club,** 5 Joy St., Boston, MA 02108; ☎ 617/523-0636.

The Metacomet–Monadnock Trail begins in Connecticut and ends in New Hampshire at the summit of Mt. Monadnock, but it lies mostly in Massachusetts, stretching for 98 miles from the Connecticut border to the New Hampshire border. It was designed with the more famous Appalachian Trail in mind, passing over high country as much as possible. In this case, that high country includes some of central Massachusetts's noteworthy geographical features: Mt. Tom, Mt. Holyoke, and Mt. Grace. But to maintain its continuity, the trail must pass

from time to time through well-settled areas and past the occasional shopping mall, particularly in the south. So hiking the trail is not an uninterrupted wilderness experience, but established shelters and campsites along the way do provide some sense of being in the backcountry.

Midstate Trail

At the Rhode Island border, the 90-mile trail begins in Massachusetts in Douglas State Forest and terminates at the New Hampshire border in Ashburnham. For maps and information, contact the **Appalachian Mountain Club's Worcester chapter (☎ 508/797-9744).**

The eastern cousin of the Metacomet–Manadnock Trail, the Midstate Trail was originally conceived in the 1920s as a connector between Wachusett and Watatic mountains. But it was not until the mid-1980s that the trail's full length, from Rhode Island to New Hampshire, was completed. Reflecting the mottled geography of central Massachusetts, a checkerboard of settlements and forests, the trail is only sometimes a true trail; at other times it follows roads and even town streets before reentering woodlands. The trail connects in the south with Rhode Island's North–South Trail (see chapter 8, "Rhode Island & Block Island") and the Wapack Trail in New Hampshire.

Mt. Tom Reservation

From Northampton, take Rte. 5 south to Smiths Ferry Rd. Turn right and continue up Smiths Ferry Rd. about 2 miles to the Visitors Center. Headquarters: Holyoke (☎ 413/534-1186).

Jutting up abruptly from the banks of the Connecticut River, Mt. Tom has long been a recreational focal point of south-central Massachusetts. Hikers, picnickers, and motorists have for decades been coming to the long ridgeline (which technically comprises five "mountains," including, at 1,202 feet, Mt. Tom itself) to take in the sweeping views of the Connecticut River valley. At the turn of the century, a restaurant and dance hall stood on the mountain's ridgeline, accessible by inclined railway. Only the foundations remain today, but the 20 miles of hiking trails that weave through the 1,800-acre reservation are more durable links to the past. There is also a small ski area, just beyond the reservation boundary.

Northfield Mountain Recreation & Environmental Center

From Northfield, take Rte. 63 about 5 miles to the Center's entrance. Turn left and continue to the visitors center, less than .25 mile. Headquarters: Northfield (☎ 413/659-3714).

God bless utility companies, or at least bless Northeast Utilities. That's not a sentiment often heard from outdoor enthusiasts, but in the Northfield Recreation and Environmental Center, Northeast Utilities has created a gem. It was not done entirely in the spirit of altruism; located in the subterranean belly of Northfield Mountain, the main feature of the center is an enormous hydroelectric station. As part of its licensing agreement with the federal government, the utility company has created above-ground trails for hiking, mountain biking, skiing, snowshoeing, and so on, along with camping and picnicking facilities.

Quabbin Reservoir and Reservation

From Amherst, take Rte. 9 east about 12 miles to the main entrance to Quabbin Reservation. Headquarters: Belchertown (☎ 413/323-7221).

Created in the 1930s as a water supply for the metropolitan Boston area, Quabbin Reservoir is an impressive body of water. It is big—39 square miles, 18 miles long, and holding, at capacity, 412 billion gallons. And it is only a small part of the enormous Quabbin Reservation, consisting of several thousand acres in all.

The fishing in the reservoir, for lake trout and landlocked salmon, is about as good as it gets in this region. There are also some fine hiking trails, old roads abandoned when communities were displaced with the creation of the reservoir. It is important, however, to keep in mind the reservoir is a drinking-water supply, and thus many restrictions are imposed to ensure the water's cleanliness. Also, much of the surrounding lands of Quabbin Reservation are restricted to preserve wildlife habitats. Put another way, *no* is a popular word around Quabbin. Visitors are greeted at the entrance by a sign that starts STRICTLY PROHIBITED . . . and continues with a long list that includes skiing, fires, dogs, swimming, horses, excessive noise, and so on.

It is, however, an undeniably beautiful place, and perhaps because of all the restrictions, a very peaceful one, too. It's ironic that despite being man-made, this could be central Massachusetts's greatest natural asset.

Wachusett Mountain State Reservation

From Fitchburg, take Rte. 2A west to Rte. 140. Turn left on Rte. 140 south and continue 4 miles to Mile Hill Rd. Turn right at the sign for Wachusett Mountain, and continue about 2 miles to the entrance to the reservation at the crest of the hill. Headquarters: Princeton (☎ 978/464-2987).

In geologically technical terms, Wachusett Mountain is considered a monadnock. What, pray tell, is that? A monadnock is a mountain remnant, the hardest, erosion-resistant rock left after millions of years of wear and tear. To try to understand the process in fast motion, imagine the remains of a sandcastle washed over by a wave. Typically, monadnocks stand more or less alone with fairly open summits, and Wachusett Mountain is no exception. Recreationally speaking, the mountain is well developed, with roughly 20 miles of hiking trails, a lift-serviced ski area, and a paved road to the summit, from which the skyline of Boston is visible on a clear day. For local hikers, bikers, runners, skiers, and those just out for an evening stroll, Wachusett Mountain is a major hot spot.

CREATING QUABBIN

It is somewhat ironic that the most impressive "natural" feature of central Massachusetts may be the man-made Quabbin Reservoir. The 39-square-mile reservoir has achieved renown for its superb bass fishing. Hikers walk the miles of trails and old roads in the reservation surrounding the reservoir, and bird watchers come to see bald eagles nest and migrate.

But to create this special environment, something vital was lost. In the early 1900s, with growing Boston in need of a fresh water supply to satisfy the needs of an increasing population, engineers looked westward for an appropriate site for a reservoir. The Swift River valley, cutting deeply through the mountains and narrow enough to facilitate damming, appeared to be ideal.

There was just one problem: the valley was also inhabited. Dana, Enfield, Greenwich, and Prescott were well-established, economically vital communities. Local industries produced everything from hats to boxes. Passengers on the railway line connecting Athol and Springfield would stay in local inns and patronize local taverns. All that came to an end when the powers that be from Boston, exercising some sort of right of eminent domain, announced the valley would be flooded.

The 2,500 valley residents were resettled elsewhere, but not without considerable hardship, particularly as the economic forces of the Great Depression added an additional burden. Left behind were homes and factories to be demolished by crews making way for the reservoir waters. Among the necessary chores of clearing the land was the removal of 7,500 bodies from 34 cemeteries in the valley.

Construction of the reservoir began in 1927, and filling it began in 1939. So large was the reservoir that it took 7 years to fill it completely with 412 billion gallons of water. At the time, it was the largest man-made reservoir in the world solely devoted to water supply. A 117-mile system of pipelines and aqueducts located 200 feet below the earth's surface carried the water to Boston.

As an engineering feat, the creation of Quabbin was a true marvel, and the new environment that has come from it has been a windfall for outdoor enthusiasts. But left behind, too, is a trail of sadness, as voiced in "The Last Waltz of Enfield," a ballad written by Charlie Ball: "The plans have been filed and it comes down to this; four valley towns will no longer exist."

What to Do & Where to Do It

Bird-Watching

The bald eagle is alive and well at **Quabbin Reservation.** In the mid-1980s, eagles were transplanted from Canada and Michigan, and now at least six resident pairs nest on the reservation, joined by migrating eagles who pass through from the north when lakes in Canada begin to freeze in November. Thus, the best time for eagle sightings is usually in early winter, so be prepared for the cold.

At other times of year, as many as 250 species have been sighted here, included numerous raptors.

If you aren't into cold-weather birding, May and June are considered the best birding months at **Wachusett Meadow Wildlife Sanctuary.** In addition to migrating birds (migrating hawks, in particular, are often sighted from neighboring Wachusett Mountain), as many as 100 nesting species, which come alive in spring, have been recorded here. **Bolton Flats Wildlife Management Area,** southeast of Leominster and between the Still and Nashua rivers, is considered one of the best spots in the state for viewing wading birds (egrets, herons, ibis), as well as migrating waterfowl.

CANOEING

Drive the back roads of central Massachusetts, and rarely will you go more than a few miles without passing a pond, lake, or reservoir. Not all are canoe-accessible, of course, but many are, and many have boat ramps to make put-ins and takeouts that much easier. If you're the sort of person who likes roaming the countryside with a canoe or kayak lashed to the top of your car, while looking for a patch of water to explore or to fish in, central Massachusetts is a darned good place to do it.

Long-distance trips are also possible along the slow-flowing Connecticut River, although you should be prepared for logistical problems posed by dams and/or unrunnable stretches of water. For example, the 21-mile stretch from Vernon Dam to Barton Cove (see below) is a wonderful overnight trip, as is the 21-mile stretch from the confluence with the Deerfield to Northampton. Unfortunately, separating the two is Turner Falls Dam and 3 miles of river that are something less than canoe-friendly. If you can manage to make shuttle arrangements, you've got yourself a very pleasant, 42-mile canoe trip—surprisingly so, given the amount of human settlement and development not far from the river.

Barton Cove

Gill. Access: From Greenfield, take Interstate 91 north to the exit for Rte. 2 east. Follow Rte. 2 about 2 miles to Barton Cove, on your right. For camping, rental, and shuttle information, contact: **Northfield Mountain—BC**, 99 Millers Falls Rd., Northfield, MA 01360; ☎ **413/863-9300.**

Its flow constricted by dams and by the flat lay of the land, the Connecticut River for the most part runs through central Massachusetts about as fast as cold honey through a sieve. Except near the occasional confluence with feeder rivers, the river offers up about as far from a whitewater experience as river paddling can

get. It is particularly slow-moving as it eddies back into Barton Cove, making canoeing here ideal for novices.

If you want, you can simply paddle around Barton Cove itself, where bald eagles are occasionally spotted. Picnic on the grounds, spend a few more hours paddling around in the afternoon, and then call it a day—a very pleasant day. But if you're unwilling to make this an overnight trip by shuttling 21 miles up the river to Vernon Dam (just across the border in Vermont) and paddling downstream, you'll be missing out on a grand opportunity.

You might encounter some faster-flowing water just below the dam, but the current slackens quickly as you make your way over the 6 miles to the Massachusetts border. On weekends, you might have to put up with a bit of power-boat traffic, but on weekdays you can be pretty much assured of a peaceful ride through the low hills and farmland just off the river's banks.

After 13 miles, you'll come to the Munns Ferry campground on the left bank. It is a rarity in central Massachusetts or anywhere else, for that matter—a campground accessible only by boat. Do not take this to mean it is a particularly primitive campground; maintained by Northeast Utilities, the campground features such backcountry luxuries as drinking water, shelters, and firewood. (For reservations, call ☎ **413/659-4465**).

After an overnight at Munn's Cove, continue on a leisurely 8-mile trip to Barton Cove, passing through French King Gorge, where the hills along the river's edge rise steeply as the Millers River joins the Connecticut from the east. The going, depending on the water level, can be choppy here, so an alternative is to take out here rather than to continue the last couple of miles to Barton Cove. (Route 2 crosses the Connecticut at this point, so it's possible, if you plan ahead, to leave a shuttle car here.) But in most cases, canoeists will find the going here manageable, and soon you'll be gliding back into the peaceful waters around Barton Cove.

If you want to continue onward, you'll need to make arrangements for portaging around Turners Falls Dam (contact Northeast Utilities; ☎ 413/774-2221, ext. 4451). Once past the dam, you'll face roughly 20 miles of peaceful, slow-motion paddling to Northampton.

Lake Denison

Winchendon. Access: From Gardner, take Rte. 68 north to Baldwinville. Turn north on Rte. 202 and continue about 2 miles to the entrance to the Lake Denison Recreation area, on your right.

There might be better lakes and ponds to explore in central Massachusetts, but perhaps none is better than Lake Denison for introducing kids to paddling. The main reason may be that there are things to do here other than canoeing—swimming off a pleasant, sandy beach; camping and picnicking in pine groves; and cavorting in open fields.

The latter may have much to do with Lake Denison's recent history as something of a natural and not-so-natural amusement park. Back in the '30s, a dance hall and a steamer ship that roamed the lake were among the attractions aimed at luring summer visitors. Such concessions are long gone; Lake Denison now is a much mellower place—unless you choose to visit on a hot, summer weekend, when beach activity is in full gear.

The lake also has an interesting geological history. It is considered a kettle hole, an isolated remnant of receding glacial ice. This could explain the lake's sandy bottom, composed of settled silt that was once glacier borne.

There isn't much here in the way of nifty coves to explore, or beds of lily pads, or natural shoreline curiosities. But for a quiet, easy paddle (motorboats are prohibited here) amid a quiet, undeveloped landscape, Lake Denison on a weekday is first-rate.

Pottapaug Pond

Hardwick. Access: From Ware, take Rte. 9-32 east, bearing left on 32 east of town. Continue on Rte. 32 to Gilbertville, and bear onto Rte. 32A toward Petersham. In Hardwick, turn left onto Greenwich Rd., at the sign for Gate 43 to Quabbin Reservoir. Continue to the boat-mooring area, through Gate 43.

Canoes are prohibited on Quabbin Reservoir itself, and that's not necessarily a bad thing. The reservoir is exposed to winds, the shoreline lacks exciting features to explore, and powerboats are permitted (albeit with a 20-horsepower restriction). Canoes are, however, permitted on Pottapaug Pond, a 3- to 4-mile finger extending from the main reservoir, and that is a good thing, too. Here the entirely undeveloped shoreline is deeply indented with small bays filled with waterlilies. The water has the crystalline clearness you'd expect of a carefully protected drinking-water source. If you can block out this being a man-made body of water—or the interruption of the occasional motorboat (the horsepower limit in the pond drops to 5)—you might capture the feeling of what it would have been like to have been a scout in this region in the early 18th century.

Make a day of exploring around the pond; the farther you venture from the boat-mooring area, the more complete your wilderness experience. Few boaters venture into the far northeastern recesses of the pond, so the chances of having it to yourself, if you go that far, are excellent.

The downside is that, this being Quabbin Reservation, there are a number of restrictions. You are not permitted to leave your canoe, to either swim or venture on shore, and camping is not allowed. But fishing is permitted, and since at least one person in every boat that ventures onto Pottapaug is required to get a fishing license for the day, you might as well make the most of it. Your chances of catching smallmouth bass or perch are excellent.

Tully Lake

Athol. Access: From Athol, take Rte. 32 north. Continue about 3 miles to the lake access, on your right.

As you approach Tully Lake, imperious signs of the Army Corps of Engineers, taking credit for the creation of the lake, greet you. It is an intimidating start. Yet after an hour or two—or a day or two—of paddling, you'll probably find yourself heaping praise on the Corps. Surrounded by tall, white pines in an undeveloped patch of land north of Athol, the lake is in many ways a canoeist's dream. Once you've paddled about the clear waters of the lake proper and perhaps slipped in for a swim (not permitted by the Corps in Tully Lake, so don't go bragging about it), you can head up the Tully River to explore Long Pond.

It is about a 1.5-mile paddle up the gentle, small, and slow-moving river, with more pond life (such as waterlilies) than you'll find in the main lake. If you're lucky, you might spot a great blue heron or a beaver. Returning to Tully Lake, you can overnight at a campground on the north shore of the lake. While the 24 campsites are just off Doane Hill Road, which skirts the lake's northern perimeter, they are accessible only by a short hike, so you'll be treated to a reasonable amount of backcountry quietude. For information, contact the park ranger, Tully Lake, RFD #2, Athol, MA 01331; ☎ 508/249-9150.

Outfitters

Adventure In, Adventure Out (Box 474, Monson, MA 01057; ☎ 413/283-2857), an organization that focuses on environmental education as well as recreation, leads day trips (and sometimes moonlight trips) for flatwater canoeists and kayakers on the Quaboag and other rivers.

CROSS-COUNTRY SKIING

When it comes to cross-country skiing in central Massachusetts, **Northfield Mountain Recreation & Environmental Center** (see "Parks & Other Hot Spots," above; snow phone: ☎ 413/659-3713) must surely top the list. An extensive network of both groomed and ungroomed trails wind around Northfield Mountain. So bring whatever gear suits your fancy—skate skis, classical skis, backcountry touring skis—and you'll find some terrain for getting your yayas out.

Relatively warm winters in recent years have made snow an iffy proposition. Finding the best snow is usually a matter of going north in latitude or up in elevation, or both. Hence, the best backcountry conditions are usually found in state forests in the northern part of the region: **Mt. Grace, Warwick, Northfield, Otter River,** and **Erving.** Of course, the conditions that make for good skiing usually make for good snowmobiling as well, so don't be surprised to encounter a group of motorists flying by you in the woods. But before cursing what might seem an intrusion, you might want to shout a word of thanks in their wake. Snowmobilers, far more than backcountry skiers, are responsible for clearing and maintaining trails.

DOWNHILL SKIING/ SNOWBOARDING

If you're looking for big mountains, big snows, and big steeps, central Massachusetts is not the place for you. Still, there are at least two ski areas, Nashoba Valley and Wachusett Mountain, that can render a decent day of skiing, thanks to snowmaking. Keep in mind, however, that both are within about an hour's drive of Boston, meaning that the slopes on weekends can be pretty crowded. But if you can manage to get away on a weekday, you'll not only have much of the mountain to yourself, you'll save a few bucks on cheaper weekday lift tickets.

Nashoba Valley

Powers Rd., Westford, MA 01886; ☎ 800/400-SNOW or 978/692-3033. 17 trails (20% beginner, 50% intermediate, 30% advanced). 3 triple chairs, 1 double, 5 surface lifts; 240-foot vertical drop. Full-day tickets $29 weekends, $20 weekdays, $18 night.

Big, no. Popular, yes. Nashoba Valley, just beyond the Boston-area perimeter defined by Interstate 495, is where Boston learns to ski and snowboard. The vertical drop might be a tenth of what you'd find in major resorts in northern new England, but Nashoba Valley, with 100% snowmaking coverage, makes the most of what it's got. Special events, such as professional ski races, are regular weekend occurrences, adding liveliness to the modest skiing scene. And although it might not be big or steep, Nashoba still managed to produce a world-class ski racer in Pam Fletcher, a 1988 Olympian.

Wachusett Mountain

499 Mountain Rd., Princeton, MA 01541; ☎ 978/464-2300. 18 trails (25% beginner, 35% intermediate, 40% advanced or expert). 1 high-speed quad chair, 1 triple, 1 double, 2 surface lifts; 1,000-foot vertical drop. Full-day lift tickets $37; $26 night.

Topping out at 2,006 feet, Wachusett Mountain is the big kahuna among the mountains of central Massachusetts. That means skiing here very nearly approaches the kind of big-mountain skiing you'll find in Vermont or New Hampshire. The runs here are certainly longer, and in many cases steeper, than those at nearby Nashoba Valley, so experienced Boston-area skiers are more likely to be satisfied here. Another advantage of the mountain's elevation (the base is also above 1,000 feet) is that precipitation falling as rain in the lower valleys is often snow at Wachusett Mountain. The slightly cooler temperatures of the higher elevation also help in the production of man-made snow when nature is uncooperative.

FISHING

Fishing in central Massachusetts can be something of a mathematical exercise.

While fishermen are many, so are there many bodies of water. And, thanks largely to the state's Division of Fisheries and Wildlife, fish are plentiful as well. In the spring of '99, for example, more than 250,000 trout, some as large as 4 pounds, were stocked in the central and Connecticut valley districts. Solving the fishing equation is, therefore, a straightforward exercise: Find among those many bodies of water a place with few fishermen and lots of fish, and the results should be productive.

In **Quabbin Reservoir,** lake trout are known to run as large as 20 pounds, with 4- and 5-pound fish being common. While Quabbin might seem an obvious attraction to fishermen, the number of anglers here is kept down somewhat by the fact that a boat is essentially a necessity and boat-launch areas are relatively few. And, although a large part of the reservoir is entirely off-limits to humans, there is a lot of territory that spreads out the fishermen and fish.

A number of central Massachusetts rivers are stocked with trout in the spring and fall, but the **Millers River** is a local favorite, even if the scenery along its shores is often less pristine than many wilderness-minded anglers might like. Also popular and well stocked is the **Swift River** below Quabbin Reservoir around Belchertown. The Swift was the principal river to be dammed in the making of Quabbin, and outflow from the reservoir generally guarantees the steady stream of cool water that makes trout happy.

If you prefer fishing for trout from a boat in still water, some of the best bets for trout are **Wallum Lake** in Douglas State Forest and **Lake Denison** (see "Canoeing," above). If it's bass you're after, try **Wachusett Reservoir** for smallmouth or **Quaboag Pond** for largemouth. These, however, are only two of many possibilities. Bass thrive in the ponds, lakes, and reservoirs that are so plentiful in central Massachusetts, so consider almost any body of still water, particularly those with grassy or reedy shorelines, to be good bass habitat.

Gear, Outfitters, & Instruction

In addition to stocking a full line of fly-fishing gear, **Flagg's Flies & Tackle** (207 Daniel Shays Hwy., Orange, MA 01364; ☎ 508/544-0034) provides guide service for the Millers River and Quabbin Reservoir. **The Lower Forty** (134 Madison St., Worcester, MA 01605; ☎ 508/752-4004) features an excellent selection of fly-fishing gear and conducts clinics in fly-tying as well as fly-casting technique at various locations throughout the state.

HIKING & BACKPACKING

This is not an area conducive to long wilderness excursions or bold ventures to high mountain summits. At the same time, many areas have well-developed and well-marked trail networks. Opportunities for short hikes are abundant, and the nature of the mountains in this area, with their rocky crests and ridges, rewards most hikers with the kind of expansive views harder to come by in the tree-covered Berkshires or the mountains of northern New England. These are small mountains indeed—barely mountains at all, really—but standing atop one, with the low-slung valleys of central Massachusetts spread out below, can make you feel as though you are standing on top of the world.

Day Hikes

Holyoke Range
Allow 3–4 hours. Moderate–strenuous. Access: From South Hadley, take Rte. 47 north 3.5 miles to Mountain Rd. and turn right. After .5 mile, bear right into Skinner State Park and continue another 1.5 miles to the Summit House. (*Note:* The road is open May–Nov.) Map: Available at the Summit House.

The section of the Metacomet–Monadnock Trail that runs for nearly 10 miles over the Holyoke Range is a roller coaster of a hike, crossing over seven mountains (although the highest among them is Mt. Norwottuck, at just 1,106 feet). It is a bit of a surprise, too, in that much of the landscape is relatively unspoiled—surprising because surrounding the range is a good deal of human development. Ultimately, this is a hike mostly about views, or rather a succession of views, that come along the range's bare ledges and summits.

This hike works best as a one-way trip; if you can arrange to have a car awaiting you where the trail crosses Route 116 (an approximate halfway point) or at Harris Road at the end, you'll make the most of it. Otherwise, you'll have to double back, most likely upon reaching the Route 116 intersection. That's not a terrible option, of course, but you'll miss out on some of the neat features of the second half of the hike, including Horse Caves, where Daniel Shays was said to have harbored horses during Shays Rebellion, the famed farmers' uprising of 1786.

Climb onto rocky outlooks, descend into deep hemlock forests, and then climb again to rocky outlooks—that's the basic theme of this hike. Starting from the Summit House, you're treated to great views right off the bat from the grassy picnic grounds surrounding the house. After descending into Taylor Notch, a brief, steep climb leads to the summit of Bare Mountain, with more terrific views in all directions. Then it's down again to the junction with Route 116 and the Holyoke State Park Visitors Center, a good place to refresh water bottles.

Move onward, then, to the rocky summit of Mt. Norwottuck for more good views, particularly to the north, and then down to the Horse Caves—they're overhanging ledges, really, rather than caves penetrating deep into the earth, but a cool (literally) spot nonetheless. Then it's upward again to the wonderfully named Rattlesnake Knob and another saddle before Long Mountain and its rock ledges give way to a steep descent to Harris Road and the finish line.

With no mountain here topping 1,106 feet, you could easily assume this is a tame hike, but don't be deceived. For every bit of elevation gained, there is usually a corresponding descent, and the total amount of climbing done over the 10-mile stretch adds up.

Mt. Tom

Allow 2 hours. Easy–moderate. Access: From Northampton, take Rte. 5 south to Smiths Ferry Rd. Turn right and continue up Smiths Ferry Rd. about 2 miles to the Visitors Center. Map: Available at the Visitors Center.

Mt. Tom is only a small part of Mt. Tom Reservation, which essentially is a long (roughly 6-mile) ridgeline that runs from 1,202-foot Mt. Tom to 827-foot Mt. Nonotuck and includes at least three other "peaks" in between. Now one might fairly ask: Can you really call a series of bumps on the face of the earth, none rising higher than 1,202 feet, mountains? The answer is a matter of opinion, of course. But with its steep ridgeline rising to overlooks that provide sweeping views of the Connecticut River valley, Mt. Tom can engender a legitimate feeling of standing on ground tall enough to be considered mountainous.

Many hiking trails wind in and out of the reservation's forests, principal among them being a 7-mile stretch of the Metacomet–Monadnock Trail (the M-M Trail, in local parlance), the transstate long trail. You can use this as your main reference point as you explore the ridgeline and branch off on side hikes from it.

Starting at the visitors' center, head north toward Mt. Nonotuck. Views are the main features of this trail segment; after less than a mile, you'll come to a short side trail that leads to a lookout tower on the top of Goat Peak. By all means, take it. The 360-degree panorama from the three-story tower is one of the highlights of the hike, although you might find it disconcerting to be able to hear, from this lofty perch, the sound of traffic on Interstate 91 far below.

From here, you can continue on to Dry Knoll and its fine view of a large oxbow in the Connecticut River, and then go on to the ruins of what was once Eyrie House, a mountaintop restaurant at the turn of the century. Tread politely through the old walls and archways, being careful not to disturb the young lovers who seem to frequent the ruins.

Retracing your steps, you can head south from the Visitors Center on the M-M Trail. Views to the west come frequently along this stretch, particularly from the craggy cliff of Whiting Peak, from which nearby Mt. Tom, to the south, stands out. In fact, one of the most impressive things about this stretch of ridgeline is the rock—a jumble of boulders, scree, and cliffs that suggest a once-mighty mountain in its final stages of collapse. A group of radio towers graces Mt. Tom itself—not exactly the most scenic natural wonder, but views from here to the south, and even over the ridge to the east, can be impressive.

Return again to the Visitors Center, check your stamina, and decide if you want to explore the network of trails that descend through the mixed forest down Mt. Tom's eastern flank. (The western flank is far too steep for any reasonable hiking.) You can wend your way down through the woods to tiny Lake Bray, but keep in mind that the key word here is "down." The elevation difference between the Visitors Center and the lake is about 500 vertical feet, and you might feel disinclined to hoof it back uphill to complete a full morning or afternoon of hiking.

Mt. Watatic

Allow 3 hours. Moderate. Access: From Ashburnham, take Rte. 101 north 4 miles to Rte. 119. Turn left and continue 1.5 miles to the trailhead parking, on your right. Map: Available from Friends of the Wapack, Box 115, West Peterborough, NH 03468.

When is a mountain not a mountain? This hike may offer some clarification. It reaches the top of Nutting Hill at an elevation of 1,620 feet, after passing over Mt. Watatic, which rises to 1,832 feet. Apparently in north-central Massachusetts, mountainhood is gained somewhere within that 212-foot difference.

This loop combines two noteworthy trails of the region—the Midstate Trail, which reaches southward to the Rhode Island border, and the Wapack Trail, which continues northward to Mt. Monadnock in New Hampshire. Don't be surprised during your hike if you encounter "through" hikers, those making the trek of 120 miles or so from Rhode Island to New Hampshire.

The first part of this 4-mile hike, a scramble along the Wapack trail up the sometimes steep southern slopes of Mt. Watatic, is probably the most strenuous. (You could also do this hike in the opposite direction, but ending with a descent down this section of the trail when you're presumably a bit tired will increase the likelihood of sustaining a twisted ankle or a profoundly stubbed toe.) The climb doesn't last long; in about a mile, you'll reach the rock top of Mt. Watatic and the view that comes with it. The stony protuberance of Mt. Monadnock in New Hampshire is to the north, Wachusett Mountain is to the south, and, with favorable weather, you should be able to make out the Boston skyline to the east and the Berkshires to the west. In other words, you'll be looking at most of Massachusetts, with a little bit of New Hampshire and Vermont thrown in.

From the summit, look for signs to New Hampshire. From here, the trail makes its way past the abandoned trails of the erstwhile Mt. Watatic ski area. The trail then rises again to the summit of

Nutting Hill before descending to the New Hampshire border, marked by a stone wall. Follow the stone wall west about .125 mile until you reach the Midstate Trail at its northern terminus. From here, it is a pleasant 1.5-mile walk in the woods back to your starting point.

Northfield Mountain Recreation & Environmental Center

Allow 2 hours. Moderate. Access: From Northfield, take Rte. 63 about 5 miles to the Center's entrance. Turn left and continue to the visitors center, less than .25 mile. Map: Available at the visitor center.

There is something vaguely unsettling about entering the Northfield Mountain Recreation & Environmental Center. Here is something forbiddingly called a "center" (rather than something more inviting, like a sanctuary or a forest) run by a utility company and housing all sorts of hydroelectric machinery. The possibility that this center might turn out to be a prime hiking area seems at first dubious.

But a prime hiking area it is. Northeast Utilities, the company that manages the place, has created a 25-mile trail network that includes both wide grassy roads and narrower trails. An all but infinite number of loops are possible, so the idea here is simply to bite off as large a chunk of trail as you think you can chew. There are, however, a couple of highlights you'll want to work into whatever hike you choose to undertake.

You'll probably want to make your way to the summit overlooking Northfield Mountain Reservoir to the east and the mountains of southern Vermont. Just be aware that there is also a road to the summit, the route by which non-hikers come on regularly scheduled buses from the visitors' center. To conquer a mountaintop and be surrounded by others who have achieved the same result by much easier means can sometimes be disheartening.

You'll also want to include on any hike the Rose Ledge Trail that passes by

> *Hiking Alert!:* Northfield Mountain is a popular mountain-biking area. Although many trails, including the Rose Ledge Trail, are closed to bikers, many others are considered multi-use. Stay alert.

the 80-foot cliffs that give the trail its name. Marked with vertical and horizontal cracks and schisms, the ledges look like squared-off boxes of granite piled upon one another.

Overnight/Long-Distance Hikes

How surprising it is to discover in a region so thoroughly worked over by human intervention—subdivided by cities, farms, roads, dammed reservoirs, etc.—that there are two fine long-distance trails and a third trail of moderate length. On any of the three trails, of course, you won't find yourself immersed in the wilderness for days on end. There are road crossings and stretches of trail that run through busy state parks. From the trails' ridgetops, the sights and sounds of nearby civilization might still be perceivable. These trails are not quite as removed or isolated as, say, the Appalachian Trail, the big daddy of long-distance trails in the East. Still, they offer more backcountry isolation than you might imagine and are vigilantly maintained by local groups that don't want to see their environment swept up entirely in the encroachments of industry, transportation, and commerce.

The **Metacomet–Monadnock Trail,** referred to by those in the know simply as the **M-M,** does not belong exclusively to Massachusetts. It begins in Connecticut, passes due north through the heart of Massachusetts, and technically terminates at the summit of Mt. Monadnock in southern New Hampshire. However, another trail, the Monadnock–Sunapee Greenway reaches onward to Mt. Sunapee, making a continuous hike of more than 200 miles possible.

The vast number of hikers walk only short portions of the trail, particularly those sections that pass over Mt. Tom and the Holyoke Range in southern Massachusetts. But the trail, originally conceived in the early 1950s by Professor Walter Banfield of the University of Massachusetts, is designed to accommodate long-distance hikers. There are four shelters and several designated campsites along the way, and, because the trail does weave in and out of settled areas, inns and B&Bs are also possible overnight stopovers.

That such a trail exists at all is remarkable in that it passes through a complex patchwork of private and public lands—state forests, wildlife sanctuaries, municipal districts, and others—calling for extensive permitting and cooperation. This patchwork also reflects the character of the trail: At one point, you might be on a mountaintop ledge surrounded by dense forest; a few miles later, you might be walking down Main Street in some mid-Massachusetts town.

The trail is managed by the Berkshire chapter of the **Appalachian Mountain Club** (5 Joy St., Boston, MA 02108; ☎ **617/523-0636**).

A stepchild of the Metacomet–Monadnock Trail, the **Robert Frost Trail** is much shorter, covering a 33-mile stretch from Holyoke Range State Park to Mt. Toby State Forest. In fact, the Robert Frost Trail and the M-M are one and the same in several spots, particularly in the Holyoke range.

While shorter, it is in some ways a more complicated trail than the M-M. It follows numerous twists and turns, on and off of roads, in and out of forests, over hills, and through flatlands. Overnight hikers will have a harder time finding suitable campsites; for anyone interested in hiking the full trail, the best way to accomplish this is a couple of long day trips. Arrange for a pickup at an approximate halfway point along the trail (the parking lot of the Amethyst Brook Conservation Area is a good choice). For information and maps, ask at local outdoor stores for the "Guide to the Robert Frost Trail," published by the Kestrel Trust.

The **Midstate Trail** lies to the east of the M-M, making its due-north run from the Rhode Island state line to the New Hampshire border. While technically it lies in Massachusetts, it also joins with other trails—the North–South Trail in Rhode Island and the Wampack Trail in New Hampshire—to form a trail much longer than its 90-mile distance.

The trail passes over the two most prominent peaks in eastern Massachusetts, Wachusett Mountain and Mt. Watatic. In fact, the trail was initially formed in the 1920s as a link between the two mountains, and only later—more than 50 years later—did the full trail come into being. It passes in and out of settled areas, as any long-distance trail through this part of Massachusetts must, but the extent to which it is a walk in the woods, or a walk through meadows, bucolic countryside, and woods, is quite remarkable and a testament to ingenious trail planning. There are some shelters and campsites along the way, thanks largely to the maintenance efforts of the Worcester chapter of the Appalachian Mountain Club and the Midstate Trail Committee. For maps and information, contact the **Appalachian Mountain Club's Worcester chapter** (☎ 508/797-9744).

Gear

Eastern Mountain Sports (7 Neponset St., Worcester, MA 01606; ☎ **508/856-9606**), in Greendale Mall, is a member of the large outdoor-retailing chain. From time to time, EMS stores also conduct clinics on such stuff as backcountry cooking and knot tying.

Outfitters

North Country Adventures (1385 Bernardstown Rd., Greenfield, MA; ☎ **413-775-0080**) leads overnight trips on the Metacomet–Monadnock Trail. **Mountain Lynx** (Box 902, Ashburnham, MA 01430; ☎ **800/307-0426**) leads day hikes in central Massachusetts as well as the Berkshires and New Hampshire.

HORSEBACK RIDING

The state forests—**Douglas State Forest, Erving State Forest,** and **Otter River State Forest** in particular—provide some terrific riding opportunities, mostly on old logging and fire roads. But for the most part, if you want to ride, you'll need to bring your own horse. Stables that organize guided rides are a rare find in central Massachusetts. If you need a riding fix and you happen to be horseless, try **Grafton Riding Stables** (137 Upton Rd., Grafton, MA; ☎ **508/839-6367**), south of Worcester.

MOUNTAIN BIKING

The relatively lowland nature of central Massachusetts takes some of the "mountain" out of mountain biking. You can find climbs or single-track descents if you're looking for them; they're sometimes plenty steep but rarely very long. If there is one type of trail that characterizes mountain biking in the region, it would probably be the double-track forest road, a common (and welcome) find, primarily in state forests. This makes central Massachusetts a particularly good riding area for less technically skilled riders and families.

That doesn't mean the riding is wimpy; you can find great long loops that take you deep into the forest, and technical challenges are there if you seek them out. But if you want killer steeps, you're better off going west to the Berkshires.

Douglas State Forest

Allow 2 hours. Easy–moderate. Access: From Worcester, take Interstate 395 south to the exit for Rte. 16. Turn east on Rte. 16 and continue 6 miles to Cedar Street, and turn right at the sign for the state forest. Continue to the forest entrance and headquarters, about 1 mile, on your right. Map: Available at the forest entrance.

What a scene . . . on a hot, summer day on the shores of Wallum Lake, it seems that half the junior-high population of southern Massachusetts and northern Rhode Island is there to greet you upon arrival. The coconut aroma of suntan lotion hangs in the air, as do squeals of laughter and the chimes of ice-cream trucks. You might initially think this is not the sort of place to find woodsy solitude on a bike, but your first impression would be incorrect. There are about 30 miles of trails that wind through this 4,500-acre forest, and it takes very little riding to escape the sights and sounds of the beach scene.

If you're looking for a warm-up ride, start with the smooth, straight rail trail (the Southern New England Trunkline Trail) that runs through the heart of the forest. There's nothing technically or aerobically demanding about it; it's just a pleasant, easy ride. After that, try one of several old forest roads that run primarily north and south through the forest, occasionally crossing a main thoroughfare, such as Route 16.

Head north through the forest for several miles on Center Trail to quiet Wallis Pond, quite a contrast to the bustle around Wallum Lake. The going is mostly double track, with an occasional single track, and while you may encounter a few tricky obstacles—rocks, mud, etc.—you won't encounter any grunt-worthy steeps or scary descents. Return the way you came, and you might find the beach scene newly inviting. After all, a swim after a long ride is about as good as mountain biking gets.

Erving State Forest

Allow 1–2 hours. Moderate. Access: From Erving, take Rte. 2 east about 2 miles, bearing right onto Rte. 2A. Turn left onto Wendell Rd. at the sign for the state forest. Map: Available at the visitors center at Laurel Lake.

Navigable forest roads, easy access, loops of varying difficulty, a pond at trail's end for swimming—Erving State Forest has all the ingredients for first-time mountain bikers to get a feel for the thrills that experienced riders wax rhapsodic about. There are enough ups and downs here to allow you to get a taste for both the challenge of climbing and the rush of descending. But there's nothing gruelingly long or particularly treacherous here (unless you intentionally go out of your way). At the same time, there is enough tough stuff here to keep even the most experienced rider satisfied. A few short but steep single-track runs can be found in the forest, and you can also take off on a few long-distance rides that stretch into neighboring Wendell, Northfield, and Warwick State forests.

One other nice thing for the novice mountain-biker—if you don't stray too far afield, there's almost always an out, with paved Laurel Lake Road more or less bisecting the forest. So when you feel you've had enough, or if you feel you're in over your head, just keep track of where you are in relation to central Laurel Lake Road, the way back to the trailhead and parking. And also the way back to the swimming, of course, in Laurel Lake. There is a fine, sandy beach here that can draw crowds, but it's still a great place to make a splash after working up a sweat on your bike.

Erving State Forest comes with one other bonus—an abundant variety of trees. It lies where the boreal forests of northern New England meet the primarily deciduous forests of southern New England. So when you've had enough of riding, disembark, sit down, and just appreciate all those trees.

Otter River State Forest

Allow 2–3 hours. Easy–moderate. Access: From Gardner, take Rte. 68 north to Baldwinville. Turn north on Rte. 202 and continue about 2 miles to the forest entrance, on your right. Just after the forest entrance is the entrance to the Lake Denison parking area. Map: Available at forest headquarters or at Lake Denison.

Exactly where Otter River State Forest, Birch Hill Wildlife Management Area, and Lake Denison State Park begin and end is not entirely clear. The three continuous areas abut one another seamlessly, and for mountain bikers that is a decidedly good thing. You can spend hours exploring old dirt roads and the occasional easy single track, and once you've decided you've had your fill, jump into Lake Denison for a cooling swim.

With its public beach and campground, Lake Denison is the most populated area here, so if you want to steer clear of anything resembling a crowd, steer clear of the lake. You can make a variety of loops—long, short, or interlocking, depending on your stamina and interest. Almost all the riding is on dirt roads, so if you're a single-track enthusiast, you're largely out of luck here. Elevation changes are minimal, with the entire area lying between 800 and 950 feet, so your cardiovascular workout will depend on how far and fast you want to ride, not how hard you want to pound up a hill.

Use Lake Denison as your base of operations; should you get disoriented in the maze of roads, you can always ask the other bikers or hikers you're likely to encounter how to get back to the lake.

ROAD BIKING

Central Massachusetts certainly does not lack for roads to ride. What it does lack are plenty of extended loops that avoid major, heavily trafficked thoroughfares. Typically, you'll find yourself riding 15 to 20 miles on a pleasant back road only to find that completing your loop back to your starting point (without backtracking) requires several miles on Route 2A, 9, or 202. If you want to do loop rides, you might have to resign yourself to a few less-than-pleasant miles for the reward of an otherwise fine ride.

There are a couple of short, out-and-back rides worth noting. The **Norwottuck Trail,** between Amherst and Northampton, is a 9.75-mile rail trail, converted from what was once a railway line. In-line skaters (not always in full control) may be more prevalent here than cyclists, but it is still a nice ride. At least one highlight is the .5-mile, wood-planked bridge crossing the Connecticut River, a nice place to take a break and watch fishermen in their boats trolling the water.

The 5-mile road through **Quabbin Park** may be short, but traffic is all but nonexistent, and there are several good vantage points, particularly the fire tower at the top of Quabbin Hill. It is possible to make this a loop ride, but that means riding a couple of miles on busy Route 9.

Finally, if you like climbing, you can also ride the 2.5-mile road to the summit of **Wachusett Mountain,** where the annual Fitchburg-Longsjo bike race, one of the most distinguished races in the country, finishes. It's a hard but not brutal climb, popular with local riders. Ride here in the early evening, and you're almost certain to encounter other cyclists who may be able to pass along a few tips on good riding spots in the area.

Athol–Warwick Loop

Allow 2 hours. Easy–moderate. Access: Start at Laurel Lake in Erving State Forest. Turn north from Rte. 2A onto Wendell Rd., about 2 miles east of Erving and continue to Laurel Lake, on your left. Map: Rubel Bikemaps Central Massachusetts.

Try this peaceful, 27-mile ride along backcountry roads with overhanging trees providing an abundance of shade—it is about as good a ride as you'll find in central Massachusetts on a hot summer's day. To complete the route, you'll have to ride for a while on Route 2A, a main thoroughfare, but given how nice the rest of the ride is, this drawback is worth putting up with.

Start at the parking area for Laurel Lake in Erving State Forest, and turn left onto Wendell Road. The road seems almost to burrow into the forest, so dense are the trees that line and overhang it. There are a few small cabins around pretty little Moore's Pond, but for the most part, signs of civilization are minimal. After the pond, the road climbs gradually into the town of Warwick, a quiet little crossroads if ever there was one.

Cross Route 78 in Warwick and continue on to Athol Road, following signs to Athol. Some of the endearingly anachronistic signs feature painted hands with fingers pointing out directions. Athol Road eventually turns into Tully Road, a name change you won't notice at all, but do be sure to bear left when Creamery Hill Road bears right.

After approximately a mile, you'll reach Royalston Road, which crosses Tully Road along the north shore of Tully Pond. You could simply continue on Tully Road into Athol, turning right onto Exchange Street before making another right onto 2A. But a better option is to turn left on Royalston Road, which leads to a T at Route 32 and Tully Lake.

Turn right, and you'll see a small picnic area and boat launch on your left; it's an ideal place for lunch or a snack. After that, you'll be fortified enough to take on the increased stress of riding on Route 2A, which you'll encounter after heading south for 3 miles on Route 32 into Athol.

The roughly 6-mile stretch of Route 2A between Athol and Erving can be busy. But the shoulders are, for the most part, generous, and most of the heavy traffic opts for high-speed Route 2 rather than local 2A. So the likelihood of your being blown off the road by muscular trucks is relatively small. The 2A riding is

not painfully unpleasant; it seems like drudgery only because the rest of the ride is so agreeable. But the serene atmosphere does reappear for the last mile or so on Wendell Road, and at Laurel Lake, a nice, refreshing swim awaits you.

Hardwick–Petersham Loop

Allow 3–4 hours. Moderate. Access: The ride begins in Ware, on Rte. 9. Find an appropriate place to park your car for 3 hours. Map: Rubel Bikemaps, Central Massachusetts.

Most interesting about this rolling ride of roughly 40 miles is how civilization, in progressive stages, is first stripped away and then renewed. You can shorten this ride and start in Gilbertville, where Routes 32 and 32A diverge, but parking and shopping (for water, snacks, and other things to bring along for the ride) are somewhat more convenient in Ware.

Ware is the quintessential central Massachusetts city; it's small, as cities go, with streets lined with factories and churches, and possesses a vague aura that time has passed it by. Head east on Route 32 (Route 9 splits off from 32 just east of town), and then in Gilbertville, a couple of miles later, branch up a hill on Route 32A. You'll soon pass through Hardwick, a pretty town of 18th- and 19th-century clapboard homes, a soulful contrast to blue-collar Ware. From here, the road begins to edge along the periphery of Quabbin Reservation, and you suddenly feel like you are truly out in the wild. The forest closes in and, for several miles, no man-made structures or settlements stand out to remind you that you are in the heart of well-developed central Massachusetts.

Approaching Petersham, turn right onto Route 122/32, which leads to Barre, another pretty, clapboard town with a look that will transport you back a century or more. Make sure to stay on Route 32, for the most part a smooth road with a wide shoulder and minimal traffic, although you can expect traffic to increase as you near your starting point in Ware. You are, after all, reentering civilization.

Gear & Rentals

Valley Bicycles (319 Main St., Amherst, MA; ☎ 413/256-0880) has two locations: one in Amherst and one on the Norwottuck Trail in Hadley. It is a good choice for rentals, but for a better selection of equipment and bikes for sale, check out **Northampton Bicycle** (319 Pleasant St., Northampton, MA 01060; ☎ 800/464-3810 or 413/586-3810).

Outfitters

While no major outfitters lead tours in the region, you are welcome to join rides organized by **Bicycles Unlimited** (322 High St., Greenfield, MA; ☎ 413/772-2700). Daily loops vary in length and difficulty, and there is also a family ride every Sunday during warm-weather months.

ROCK & ICE CLIMBING

Big-wall climbing? Of course not. A 100-foot wall is about as big as you'll find in central Massachusetts, with climbs topping out at a difficulty rating of about 5.11. All can be done with secure toproping, enhancing safety. Because of their modest size and difficulty, climbs in the region are a great way for novices and kids to learn the basics without getting in over their heads.

Prime climbing spots include **Rose Ledges** in Northfield Mountain Recreation & Environmental Center (see above), **Chapel Ledge** in Chapelbrook Reservation west of Deerfield, and **Purgatory Chasm** (see "Walks & Rambles," below), south of Worcester. The rock varies from granite at Purgatory Chasm to white quartzite at Chapel Ledge. If you're looking for views upon summiting, Chapel Ledge is your best bet; the cliffs of Purgatory Chasm are enveloped deep in the woods. Keep in mind that climbing permits are usually required. The idea

behind the permits is not to discourage or restrict climbing but rather to make sure all climbers have the appropriate gear and safety devices. Ask for information at the appropriate visitors center.

Gear

Adventure Outfitters (451 Russell St., Hadley, MA 01035; ☎ 413/253-5500) features an excellent selection of climbing equipment.

Instruction

Zoar Outdoor Adventures (Mohawk Trail, Box 245, Charlemont, MA 01339; ☎ 800/532-7483) offers private and group clinics at Rose and Chapel Ledges.

SNOWSHOEING

Two things are necessary for a good snowpack: northern latitude and high elevation. Central Massachusetts, of course, is not greatly blessed with either, but you'll probably find that **Northfield Mountain Recreation & Environmental Center** features about the best combination of the two in the region. It also has a good trail network and is, in general, pretty snowshoe-friendly. The back roads of **Otter River State Forest** (see "Mountain Biking," above) are great for winter exploring, too, although your forest solitude might be interrupted by the occasional snowmobiler, particularly on weekends. You might also want to check out **Mt. Grace** and **Northfield State Forests;** neither one is heavily visited, although neither has as well developed a trail network as Northfield Mountain or Otter River does.

SWIMMING

Wallum Lake in Douglas State Forest, **Laurel Lake** in Erving State Forest, and **Lake Denison** all have the twin essentials—clear, cool water and fine, sandy beaches. They might also have a few things you may or may not be looking for, the stuff you'll find at your typical public beach. There are concession trucks selling ice cream and sodas, life guards, rest rooms, and, on a hot summer day, many, many kids. So don't expect privacy or backcountry solitude on those hot summer days when you and just about everyone else is looking for a place to cool off. The experience is nothing like stumbling across a secluded pond in the woods after a long hike. But if you just want to go for a swim and don't mind sharing the water with others, these are about the best swimming holes you'll find in the region.

WALKS & RAMBLES

Thanks largely to the Massachusetts Audubon Society and the Trustees of Reservations, it is hard to go very far in central Massachusetts without finding a plot of land good enough for a short stroll. Central Massachusetts is in many ways a transitional zone—between the mountains to the west and the maritime environment to the east, between northern forests and the mixed deciduous forests to the south, etc. Thus, in a short walk you might encounter an unusual variety of flora and avian life.

Laughing Brook Wildlife Sanctuary

Allow 1–2 hours. Easy. Access: From East Longmeadow, take Rte. 83 south 1.5 miles to Hampden Rd. Turn left and continue 2.5 miles to Somers Rd. (look for the sign for Laughing Brook). Turn right, then left onto Main St. Look for the entrance to the Sanctuary in about 2 miles, on your left.

You've got to figure that any wildlife sanctuary that also calls itself an education center is going to be a great place to take kids, and so it is at Laughing Brook. In fact, the sanctuary's history is rooted in childhood fantasy, having once been the home of children's author Thornton W. Burgess, creator of such memorable characters as Peter Cottontail and Old Mr. Toad.

There are pens with deer and geese, dinosaur tracks, trails with ample signage

explaining facts about the environment and wildlife of the area, and other attractions that will hold the interest of kids. But this can be a captivating place for adults, too, in that the sanctuary encapsulates the transitional nature of central Massachusetts. Its 340 acres include a complex mix of habitats: woodlands, wetlands, open meadows, and riparian environments along the banks of Laughing Brook and the Scantic River. This habitat mix also attracts an unusual wildlife mix, from songbirds and migrating butterflies to bobcats and flying squirrels.

The longest trail here is about 1.5 miles and the going is almost entirely flat, so great fitness, endurance, or athleticism is not required. The idea here is to go gently, to keep your eyes and ears open, to relax in a gazebo along the edge of a pond. Guided tours are also offered, a bonus for students of the environment both young and old.

Purgatory Chasm

Allow 1 hour. Easy. Access: From Worcester, take Rte. 146 south about 10 miles to the exit for Purgatory Rd. Bear right onto Purgatory Rd. Continue less than a mile to the chasm, on your left, or the visitors center, on your right.

Purgatory Chasm can't quite be called a miniaturized Yosemite Valley of Massachusetts. But its 70-foot granite walls come as such a surprise—who would expect to find such a geological feature in the low hills of southeastern Massachusetts?—that it can create an almost Yosemite-sized impression. Put another way, Purgatory Chasm is very cool, both in a figurative and literal sense. Scrambling down into the chasm over granite boulders, you pass by small caves that may be as much as 40 or 50° cooler than the surrounding air temperature.

The chasm walls seem almost to close in overhead, and more often than not, rock climbers are ascending and rappelling, supported by ropes anchored to trees at the top of the gorge. The walk from one end of the chasm to the other is not long—less than .5 mile—and it takes you past such wonderfully named rock formations as Lover's Leap, Devil's Pulpit, and Fat Man's Misery. You can make a loop by returning along the upper rim of the chasm for a different perspective— being careful, of course, not to make that fateful last step.

Quabbin Park

Allow 1–2 hours. Moderate. Access: From Amherst, take Rte. 9 east about 12 miles to the main entrance to Quabbin Reservation. Maps are available at the visitors center, about .5 mile on your right.

This is a terrific place for a short morning or sunset walk. You'll walk through a mixed hardwood forest of maple, birch, oak, and cherry, with ferns covering the forest floor like a mist of green. While Quabbin Reservation is enormous, exceeding 100,000 acres, the park, at the southern end of the reservation is fairly small, and no hiking loop here much exceeds 3 miles.

The trails here wind over and around Quabbin Hill, marked by a stone tower from which views of the reservoir and the surrounding countryside are spectacular. Go for a relaxed stroll through the woods; you're likely to encounter deer, whose numbers on the reservation are considerable. If you are very lucky, you might even spot a black bear or a moose; sprawling, undeveloped Quabbin is the obvious place that larger mammals of the wild choose to hang out in central Massachusetts.

Also, be sure to bring along binoculars. Hawks are common sights over the reservoir, and bald eagles are sometimes seen as well. This is particularly true if you start your hike at the Enfield Lookout, a turn-off from the one paved road that loops through the park. Enfield Lookout is considered the prime spot for eagle sightings, and even if you don't see the great birds, you'll likely be treated to a terrific sunset over the reservoir if you're out for an evening walk.

Wachusett Meadow

Allow 2 hours. Moderate. Access: From Princeton, take Rte. 62 west about .5 mile to Goodnow Rd. Turn right and continue 1 mile to the parking area, on your left.

Wachusett Meadow Wildlife Sanctuary is, at 1,000 acres, one of Massachusetts's largest wildlife sanctuaries. It is another fine example of a state in environmental transition—part mountain, part wetland, part meadow (as the name should imply), and part woodland. Depending on the season, nature's palette is amply displayed, with an abundance of wildflowers in summer and the radiantly changing colors of the leaves in the fall.

Much of the hiking here is through open meadows, often along stone walls that are reminders this was once working pastureland. If you want to work up a sweat, you can take the Summit Trail to the top of Brown Hill, an elevation gain of about 800 vertical feet, from which the open views spread out in all directions. Otherwise, the walking is fairly easy going, with a couple of noteworthy features to take in along the way.

A number of trees here can be considered old growth, some dating back to the Revolutionary period. Most distinguished among them is the Crocker Maple, which is at least 250 years old and said to be the oldest sugar maple in the country. You might also want to venture up the Glacier Boulder Trail to see— surprise—a glacier boulder. Technically, this large, isolated chunk of rock is a glacial erratic, deposited here when the last Ice Age retreated more than 10,000 years ago.

WHITEWATER RAFTING & KAYAKING

As in other northeastern regions, whitewater is mostly a spring phenomenon in central Massachusetts. Snow melts, rivers swell, and the whitewater builds. Otherwise, whitewater enthusiasts must wait for the occasional heavy rain or the occasional dam release, and taking advantage of the latter can be a tricky business. Because dams are constructed for different purposes (hydroelectric power, flood control, water supply), they are managed by different agencies, and the release schedules can be changed with little notice.

Finding out who to call for release schedules (which vary) is probably more of a challenge than simply tapping into the local whitewater pipeline. Both Hampshire College and the University of Massachusetts have active outing clubs, and a local outdoor store such as Adventure Outfitters (see "Gear," below) is usually a good source of river information.

Millers River

Put in just east of Erving off Rte. 2. Look for a sign for the Erving Paper Company and turn right to a railroad underpass and a bridge crossing the river. Takeout 7 miles downstream, where the Millers joins the Connecticut River.

Rafting or kayaking the Millers, an east-to-west flowing river, can't exactly be called a pristine wilderness experience. There are certainly some very pleasant stretches that pass peacefully through low-slung, forested hillsides, but paper mills, railroad tracks, and nearby Route 2 are more common sights. This is a river with an industrial past, and while clean-up efforts have made progress toward restoring its pre-industrial purity, this is not a river you would feel inclined to dive into or to drink from freely. The dark color of the water is reputedly natural, caused by resident minerals or some such, but this might simply be wishful thinking by those touting the natural darkness.

Regardless, the last 7 miles of the Millers, before it empties into the Connecticut River, offer perhaps the best whitewater experience in central Massachusetts. This section is known locally as the Lower Millers, differentiating it, among kayakers, from the Upper Millers, another 7-mile run between Royalston and Athol—also a fine though less challenging ride.

The highlight of the trip comes at about the halfway point, when the river drops quickly and squeezes through a section known as the Funnel. It is a Class IV run when the river is churning at mid-spring levels, with big haystacks and fast-moving water that can steer you into a nasty rock called the Piton if you're not on your best paddling game. Make sure to scout it before running it—there's no honor lost in portaging if you think you're going to take a pounding. After this, the river mellows back down to mainly Class II water, with only the broken dam at Millers Falls, complicated by industrial debris, demanding caution.

Yes, that's industrial debris, as in old pieces of dam and other discards from the nearby Millers Falls Paper Company. But there is also, in this last stretch, some pretty scenery along the river's banks. That, in a nutshell, is the Millers: industry, scenery, whitewater, and the need for caution all wrapped together in one fun whitewater run.

Quaboag River

Put in just north of Warren, in Lucy Stone Park. In Warren, turn north from Rte. 67 onto River Rd. and continue for a .5 mile to the park. The usual takeout is 5.5 miles downstream, at one of several roadside turnouts on Rte. 67 after Devil's Gorge.

Native Americans used the Quaboag in the 17th century as a transportation route. The prime reason: The river's watershed includes several lakes and ponds that help maintain a fairly high water level, even in the normally low-water summer months. This, of course, can also be a boon to whitewater kayakers.

It is possible to make this an extended, full-day trip, if you start in Quaboag Pond, east of Brookfield, and continue 20-some miles to Three Rivers. But the middle section of the river is what gets the juices of whitewater diehards going. The first and last 6 miles or so are essentially flatwater (or Class I quickwater) rides. The middle 5 or 6 miles, however, pass through Devil's Gorge—an impressively ominous name and a challenging section of river to run—and it is just one of several sections of whitewater that range from Class II to Class IV.

From the put-in at Lucy Stone Park, the river begins with a series of Class II rapids, leading to an old dam just before West Warren. Don't even think about trying to run the dam; the risks far exceed the potential thrills. Portage and continue on to the next set of rapids, beneath a railroad bridge. (You should use extreme caution when surveying the rapids from the bridge, which is not much wider than the trains that pass over it.) While this can be a fast, technically difficult run, there is a good pool at the end that allows you to regain your equilibrium.

After another portage around a dam, you pass through Angel Fields Rapids and into Devil's Gorge, a succession of three increasingly difficult rapids. The water runs fast, and the waves can build to as tall as 4 feet, but the faster water at the higher levels is a better bargain than the rocky run you'll face if the water is low.

In an average year, you can run this section of the Quaboag well into May. As for riverside scenery, well . . . the industrial underbelly of central Massachusetts reappears in the form of old dams, factories, and railroad bridges. Keep your eyes on the water, however, and it won't make much difference.

Gear

Adventure Outfitters (451 Russell St., Hadley, MA 01035; ☎ **413/253-5500**) features an excellent selection of kayaks and river supplies.

Outfitters

Crab Apple Whitewater (HC 63, Box 25, The Forks, ME 04985; ☎ **800/553-7238**) and **Zoar Outdoor Adventures** (Mohawk Trail, Box 245, Charlemont, MA 01339; ☎ **800/532-7483**) guide spring rafting trips on the Millers River.

Campgrounds & Other Accommodations

CAMPGROUNDS

Barton Cove

From Greenfield, take Interstate 91 north to the exit for Rte. 2 east. Follow Rte. 2 about 2 miles to Barton Cove, on your right. 23 sites, tent camping only, showers, fireplaces, canoe rentals. ☎ **413/863-9300.**

A tiny, wooded peninsula juts out into the Connecticut River to form a surprisingly idyllic campground. Northfield Utilities, which manages the campground with Connecticut River canoeists in mind, has taken pains to ensure a relatively pristine river experience. Hence, RVs are not allowed, and the campsites, well secluded in an evergreen grove, further enhance the natural ambience. Kudos to Northeast Utilities.

Federated Women's Club State Forest

From South Athol, take Rte. 202 south to Rte. 122. Turn left and go east about 3 miles to the campground, on your right. 6 sites, no facilities. ☎ **508/939-8962.**

So you really want to get away from it all? Here's your chance—a "primitive" campground set in the woods on the edge of Quabbin Reservation. The concept is simple; sites have been cleared to set up tents, nothing more or less. That's anathema, of course, to the RV crowd, but for the backcountry diehards, this is about as close to the backcountry as a drive-in campground gets in central Massachusetts.

Lake Denison

From Gardner, take Rte. 68 north to Baldwinville. Turn north on Rte. 202 and continue about 2 miles to the entrance for the Lake Denison Recreation area, on your right. 151 sites for tents and RVs (no hookups), toilets, showers, tables, fireplaces. ☎ **508/939-8962.**

This pretty spot lies in a pine-tree forest that slopes gently to the shore of the lake. The campground, with 151 sites, is fairly large, but it is a fairly quiet place, too. There are no hookups for RVs—a discouragement to the oversized noisemakers—and because motorized boats aren't permitted on the lake, noise reduction is taken a step further. But don't expect solitude; this is a popular place on summer weekends.

INNS & RESORTS

Bullard Farm

89 Elm St., North New Salem, MA 01364; ☎ **508/544-6959.** $75 per person double occupancy, includes full breakfast.

This 18th-century home has been converted to a B&B and conference center (as odd as that combination might sound) and was redone with outdoor enthusiasts in mind. There are cross-country skiing and hiking trails on the farm's own 300 acres, as well as an extensive network of hiking trails on nearby Quabbin Reservation. This is a very cyclist-friendly place; the proprietors can provide maps and recommendations for nearby rides ranging from 10 to 40 miles.

Wildwood Inn

121 Church St., Ware, MA 01082; ☎ **800/860-8098** or 413/967-7798. Room rates $50–$90, with breakfast included.

This 1880 Victorian inn is located in the heart of Ware, one of those small cities so characteristic of central Massachusetts. Ware is a good place to establish a base camp for some of the best road cycling in central Massachusetts. The inn is also well located for canoeing, fishing, and hiking in Quabbin Reservation.

Chapter 4

Greater Boston, Cape Ann & the South Shore

It might be a stretch to call Boston the birthplace of American environmental consciousness, but historical evidence would definitely support the city's claim to that title. Ralph Waldo Emerson and Henry David Thoreau penned their seminal works in this region in the middle of the 19th century. The country's first Audubon Society was born here. The country's first regional park commission (the Metropolitan District Commission) was established here more than a century ago. The Trustees of Reservations, the world's oldest private land trust, was founded in the Boston area and now protects more than 21,000 acres of Massachusetts land. The Appalachian Mountain Club, quite possibly the country's foremost outdoor-recreation organization, is headquartered in Boston.

An environmental conscience still exists in this city. It is a conscience borne out by a surprisingly large number of tracts of undeveloped and protected land. And it is a conscience that engages in proactive expression: The recent clean-up of Boston Harbor, little more than a sludge pool not long ago, ranks as one of the great environmental triumphs in the eastern United States during the waning years of the 20th century.

Of course, if all of greater Boston were under the governance of some great, unspoken environmental manifesto, its five million residents would all be living Thoreau-style, in tiny cabins, austerely respectful of nature. Needless to say, that isn't so. Boston and its environs form a well-developed urban entity, a fact that has its obvious ecological shortcomings. The jumble of cities and towns that form Boston's outskirts have grown together haphazardly in what appears to be an almost total absence of urban planning. Greater Boston looks, from a land-management perspective, like a paisley design—a loop of roadway here, a whirl of development there, a splash of parkland, spots of water, and so on. There is no orderly grid that characterizes, say, New York City, or even the hub-and-spoke design imposed by Pierre L'Enfant on Washington, DC.

But the parks, forests, preserves, and sanctuaries of this area are integral parts of this apparently haphazard mix. Greater Boston lacks a single, enormous patch of undeveloped countryside, like Philadelphia's Fairmount Park, and it has no defining greensward like New York City's Central Park. As you travel around greater Boston, however, you rarely seem to travel far without passing by some patch of land or body of water that has been preserved as a natural and/or recreational enclave.

Part of the reason for greater Boston's crazy-quilt layout arises from its rich history, which predates any modern concepts of urban planning. When European settlers arrived in the 1600s to clear land and build towns, open spaces were abundant, and anyone back then who might have envisioned urban sprawl would have been either insane or a visionary. But more than 3 centuries is plenty of time for small towns to grow into larger ones and then into small cities, one overlapping the other.

There is a bonus to this, of course. Boston is the epicenter of early American history, reaching from one era into the next. In 1620, the Pilgrims established their colony at Plymouth, south of Boston. The Boston Tea Party, Paul Revere, Bunker Hill, the Minutemen—the aura of the American Revolution still hangs in the air. A literary tradition emerged in the 19th century due to the likes of Hawthorne, Longfellow, Emerson, and Thoreau. And there still remains the ongoing saga of the sea, of the fishing and whaling life that has captivated writers from Herman Melville to Sebastian Junger.

All of this contributes to Greater Boston's appeal to outdoor-minded people. Not only is there the experience of the outdoors itself, but there is also the lure of the city's historical aura. You can ride a bike along the same route that Paul Revere rode, or take a whale-watching trip to the same offshore reefs that whalers from Gloucester went to almost 3 centuries ago. A little outdoors and a lot of history make for an enticing mix.

The Lay of the Land

Look at a map of the greater Boston coastline, and you'll see a contorted facial profile. The brow, extending from New Hampshire, is a soft land—marshland, estuaries, tidal basins, dunes, and broad, sandy beaches. The upturned nose is Cape Ann, a feisty concentration of bedrock refusing to crumble against the incessant pounding of the ocean. Cape Ann's reliably immobile underpinnings, as opposed to the shifting sands in the

north, are one reason Gloucester developed as a commercial fishing port centuries ago.

The gaping mouth is Boston Harbor, including Quincy and Hingham bays, which appears to be swallowing up the harbor's many small islands. And the drooping chin forms around Cohasset, as the coastline makes its gradual turn southward toward Cape Cod.

There is nothing in the region that could be called a mountain, and barely anything that could be called a hill. Among the small hills that do crop up, many are geologically classified as *drumlins,* the remnants of the last ice age. Imagine rivers of ice and melting ice pouring out of the north and into the sea. Left behind by these rivers were little more than piles of glacial rubble, some of which, as islands immediately off the coast, have subsequently succumbed to the power of the ocean. Those farther inland stand as not much more than enlarged, tree-covered blisters on an otherwise flat landscape, at most a couple of hundred feet high and a mile across.

Drumlins are not the only glacial leftovers. *Kettle ponds,* originally formed by freshwater deposits of glacial ice, are now fed primarily by rainwater and/or the subterranean water table (rather than by streams) and number in the hundreds in the greater Boston area. Most famous among them is Walden Pond, the inspiration for Henry David Thoreau. Among bodies of water, major rivers are less prevalent. The largest is the Merrimack, winding out of New Hampshire in an easterly flow; the best known is the Charles, particularly as it flows through Cambridge and Boston, where world-class rowing regattas are held regularly.

For agricultural purposes, the soils of eastern Massachusetts are not particularly distinguished, except perhaps for commercial berry cultivation. For this reason—along, of course, with pervasive urban and suburban development—there are few large farms. The influence of the nearby ocean, most notably toward the

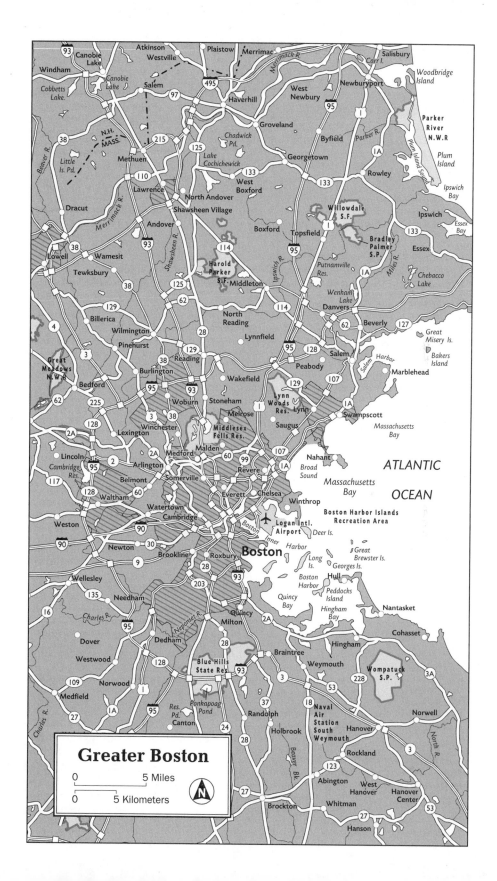

Greater Boston

0   5 Miles

0   5 Kilometers

southeast and Cape Cod, has left soil in most places characterized more by sand than fertile loam, and the forest growth reflects that character. Pines and scrub oak are abundant, as are berries late in the summer. It is worth noting that as you travel south of Boston toward the Cape, you are entering the heart of cranberry-bog country.

Boston's maritime climate means it is milder in winter than western Massachusetts and naturally cooled, at least immediately along the coast, by the sea breezes of summer. (This is not to say, of course, that greater Boston is immune to the kind of brutal heat wave that gripped the Northeast in the summer of 1999.) But its close proximity to the ocean also exposes eastern Massachusetts to ocean-bred storms that are typically most frequent in the fall. While hurricanes commonly lose a good deal of their ferocity as they boil up from the tropics and pass over the cooler waters of the northern Atlantic, nor'easters, a coastal New England specialty, can be particularly devastating.

Orientation

Among the Northeast's major metropolitan areas, Boston is probably the most decentralized. According to recent U.S. census figures, the population of Boston itself ranked below the populations of New York, Philadelphia, Baltimore, and Washington. But taken as a metropolitan area, greater Boston was outranked in the east only by New York and Philadelphia. The city is only the 20th largest in the country; the metropolitan area is the 7th largest.

This might suggest a kind of urban sprawl, which is partly the case, but to a large degree, it is also a reflection of Boston's early roots. Independent communities—Cambridge, Concord, Newton,

Quincy, Lawrence, and many others—have, over 3 centuries or more, gradually melded together. Residents in these communities would be indignant if one were to suggest they are all part of one great urban complex. But as you explore the area that lies approximately within the perimeter of Interstate 495, you'd be hard-pressed to determine precisely where one community ends and another begins. In short, greater Boston's growth over the centuries has been more of an implosion rather than an expansion.

Interstate 495, which forms a crescent around Boston for a radius of about 20 to 25 miles, can be considered the rough dividing line between greater Boston and the rest of Massachusetts. Closer in, **Route 128** also loops around the city, lined by the malls and business complexes that are the hallmarks of American life in the latter third of the 20th century.

To the north of Boston, **Cape Ann** reaches out into Massachusetts Bay and the Atlantic Ocean as a curled fist of rocky shoreline. Its principal community, **Rockport,** is a tourist hub during the summer months, while **Gloucester,** to the west, remains an active commercial-fishing port. Farther north, where the Merrimack River flows from New Hampshire into the Atlantic, is **Newburyport,** where elegant, old homes surround an attractively revitalized city center, well worth a visit. In between are **Essex** and **Ipswich** and vast, estuarial marshlands that make for some of the finest sea kayaking and canoeing in southern New England.

To the northwest, **Lawrence** and **Lowell** are the largest cities at the edge of the greater Boston boundary, but the towns of **Concord** and **Lincoln,** with their famous historical backgrounds, are better known in the realm of tourism. Closer in, within the Route 128 perimeter, the cities of **Arlington, Belmont, Medford, Malden, Chelsea,** and others, run together inseparably as tidy

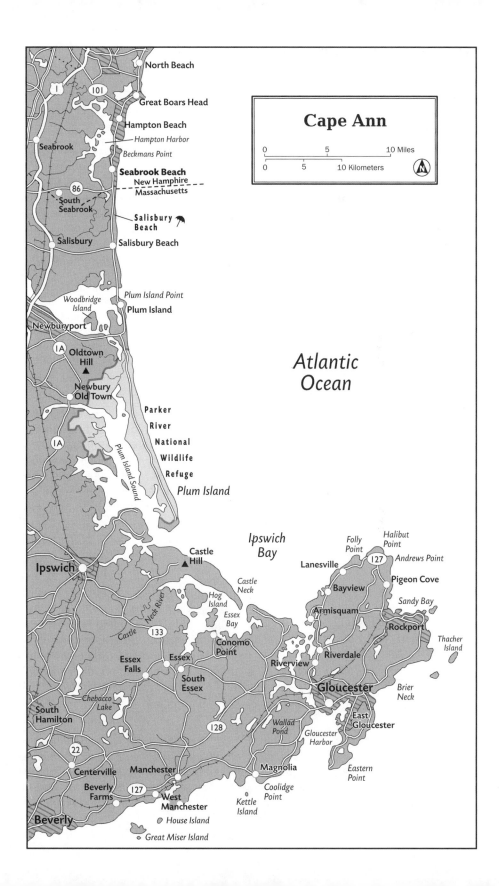

North Beach

Great Boars Head

Hampton Beach

Hampton Harbor

Beckmans Point

Seabrook

Seabrook Beach
New Hamphire
Massachusetts

South
Seabrook

Salisbury
Beach

Salisbury

Salisbury Beach

Woodbridge Island

Plum Island Point

Plum Island

Newburyport

Oldtown
Hill ▲

Newbury
Old Town

Parker

River

National

Wildlife

Refuge

Plum Island Sound

Plum Island

Cape Ann

0   5   10 Miles

0   5   10 Kilometers

*Atlantic
Ocean*

*Ipswich
Bay*

Castle
Hill ▲

*Castle
Neck*

*Hog
Island*

*Essex
Bay*

Neck River

Castle

133

Essex

Essex
Falls

South
Essex

Conomo
Point

Riverview

Ipswich

*Chebacco
Lake*

South
Hamilton

128

22

Centerville

Manchester

Beverly
Farms

127

West
Manchester

Beverly

○ House Island

○ Great Miser Island

*Kettle
Island*

Magnolia

*Coolidge
Point*

*Wallad
Pond*

*Gloucester
Harbor*

Gloucester

East
Gloucester

*Eastern
Point*

Riverdale

Armisquam

Sandy Bay

Rockport

*Thacher
Island*

*Brier
Neck*

Bayview

Lanesville

*Folly
Point*

*Halibut
Point*

127

Andrews Point

Pigeon Cove

middle- and working-class communities. They form the last barrier to the urban nexus of **Boston** and its sister city, **Cambridge,** best known as the home of such academic institutions as Harvard and MIT.

Along the south shore, **Quincy, Weymouth,** and **Hingham** cluster around shipyards with their massive construction frames and derricks. Hingham is a principal departure point for people venturing out into **Boston Harbor,** by commercial tour boat, private vessel, or sea kayak, to explore the harbor's many islands. To the east are the towns of **Cohasset** and **Scituate,** with pocket-sized harbors full of handsome sailboats and shorelines adorned with stately, high-end homes.

From here, **Route 3** is the principal thoroughfare reaching southeastward to Cape Cod. The urban complex gradually gives way to scattered small towns, **Duxbury** and **Plymouth**—where the Pilgrims landed, of course—being most notable among them. Also noteworthy is **Myles Standish State Forest,** the largest tract of state land in Eastern Massachusetts, which is popular among mountain bikers, horseback riders, and fishermen.

Parks & Other Hot Spots

Blue Hills Reservation

From Exit 2 off Interstate 93, take Rte. 138 north about .25 mile. Turn right onto Hillside St. at the sign for the entrance to the reservation. Reservation headquarters are Hillside St., about 2 miles from the entrance. ☎ 617/698-1802.

Just a few miles south of downtown Boston, this 6,500-acre reservation is Boston's favorite outdoor playground. It is under the aegis of the Metropolitan District Commission, the country's first regional park commission, which was established in 1893. The MDC's early commissioning allowed it to acquire such a large parcel of land before metropolitan real-estate values skyrocketed.

Blue Hills is laced with hiking trails—reportedly totaling more than 200 miles—that double as cross-country skiing trails in winter. This is also a popular spot for mountain biking and horseback riding. Canoeing (on Ponkapoag Pond and the Neponset River), fishing (on several ponds on the reservation), and swimming (in Houghton Pond) are also possible. So too are rock climbing and downhill skiing, although the challenge in both cases is relatively tame. And give the MDC credit—it has done a good job of marking trails and maintaining a reservation that for the most part is clean and well managed, despite heavy use.

Boston Harbor Islands

Island ferries depart from Long Wharf in Boston and from Hewitt's Cove in Hingham. For Long Wharf, take Exit 24 off Interstate 93 (for the Callahan Tunnel) and follow signs to Long Wharf. The Hewitt's Cove terminal is located off Rte. 3A in Hingham. Water taxis also leave from Hingham and from George's Island to smaller islands. ☎ 617/223-8666.

Thirty islands are now included in a National Recreation Area, so designated in 1996 as a response to the impressive clean-up efforts in Boston Harbor. George's Island, home to Fort Warren, which served as both a pre–Civil War training ground as well as a Civil War prison, is the hub from which water taxis ferry visitors to the outer islands. Shell-covered beaches, rocky bluffs, flowering meadows, historic structures, hiking trails, camping areas, and spectacular views of Massachusetts Bay and the Boston skyline are among the islands' attractions. Sea kayakers—taking care to avoid channels for large vessels—can have a field day exploring the islands and beaches that those relying on public transportation have more difficulty reaching.

Crane Wildlife Refuge & Reservation

From Exit 14 off Rte. 128, take Rte. 133 toward Essex. About 3 miles along, look for the Woodman's Restaurant on your left. Access to the river is across the road. Contact the **Trustees of Reservations,** Northeast Regional Office (Box 563, Ipswich, MA 01938; ☎ **508/356-4351**), for more information.

This is one impressive expanse of marshland and estuary, with 2,100 acres under management of the Trustees of Reservations, but far more acreage than that open to sea kayaking, canoeing, birding, and general exploring. With a good chart and a keen awareness of the tides, you could wend your way by boat from Essex to Plum Island to the north. But wandering so far afield isn't necessary. The marshlands of the Essex River basin are expansive enough and teem with bird life. Choate's Island (formerly Hog Island) is a popular half-day sea-kayaking destination, as is Crane's Beach, a sandy spit where the river meets the sea.

Great Meadows National Wildlife Refuge

From Concord, take Rte. 62 east 1.8 miles to Monsen Rd. Turn left and continue to the entrance to the refuge, along a dirt road that goes straight when Monsen Rd. makes a sharp right. ☎ **508/443-4661.**

If Henry David Thoreau (or someone possessing Thoreau's romantic sensibilities) were to arrive in the greater Concord area at the start of the 21st century, he'd more likely be drawn to Great Meadows than to Walden Pond. Marsh grasses, cattails, wildflowers, a nonstop symphony of bird song, and a prevailing aura of serenity are nature's gifts here. It is a place ideally suited for a leisurely stroll, for bird-watching, or simply for nodding off on a bench in the shade.

Halibut Point State Park

From Rockport, take Rte. 127 north through Pigeon Cove to Gott Ave. and a State Park sign. Turn right; the parking area will be on your right. ☎ **508/546-2997.**

A quarry at the edge of the ocean is something of an oddity. This small park on Cape Ann is a great place for a stroll around the quarry, as well as a scramble down the rocky shoreline to the ocean's edge.

Maudslay State Park

From Newburyport, take Rte. 113 west and turn right on Noble St. at a State Park sign. Turn left on Ferry Rd. and continue about 2 miles to the parking area, on your right. ☎ **508/465-7223.**

The property of the Moseley family in the mid-1800s, this was a spot renowned for its "literary festivals," which attracted the likes of Ralph Waldo Emerson and John Greenleaf Whittier. A showcase in spring for blooming dogwoods and azaleas, the park along the banks of the Merrimack River is also a place to come throughout the warm weather for hiking and biking.

Myles Standish State Forest

From I-495, take exit 2 to Rte. 58 north. Continue 3 miles to South Carver, then follow signs to the forest. ☎ **508/866-2526.**

At 14,651 acres, this is the second largest tract of state land in Massachusetts. The state's largest campground, 475 sites strong, is a major attraction, ensuring the presence of plenty of people on summer weekends. Many miles of trails and roads weave through the park, although since motorized recreational vehicles (ORVs and motorcycles) are permitted on most roads, this is not necessarily a place to find woodsy solitude and serenity. Just 3 miles of trails are reserved for hikers only. Horseback riders and mountain bikers will fare better here.

Parker River National Wildlife Refuge

From the center of Newburyport, take Water St. east, following signs to Plum Island. After crossing the Plum Island causeway, turn right to the refuge's entrance. ☎ **508/465-5753.**

When they say wildlife refuge, they mean it. The beaches here are often closed during midsummer to protect the nesting habitat of piping plovers, an endangered species. When the summer heat builds, some might find that hard news to swallow, for here are 7 miles of spectacularly undeveloped beach, a snapshot of what the New England coast might have looked like when settlers first arrived centuries ago. However, at least some of the beach is usually open by July and almost all of it is by September. Regardless, the beach is only part of the attraction here. The marshland that is protected by the barrier-island beach is home to a wide variety of birds, particularly such wading birds as egrets and herons.

Walden Pond State Reservation

From Concord, take Rte. 126 south through the intersection with Rte. 2. The parking area for the pond is on your right. ☎ 978/369-3254.

If you go for the solitude of the divine wilderness that Henry David Thoreau wrote about, you go in vain. Walden, a 300-acre reservation surrounding the pond, is a popular spot, heavily used in the summer for swimming, short walks, and canoeing. It is still a pretty little body of water, with trees overhanging the shoreline. But on a hot summer weekend, you would probably find more solitude in Fenway Park.

What to Do & Where to Do It

BIRD-WATCHING

If you have a great appreciation for shorebirds and wading birds, this is the place for you. The estuarial marshlands that reach inland from the sandy barrier islands north of Boston provide the habitat for a stunning array of birds. **Parker River National Wildlife Refuge** is often reported as closed in an effort to protect the nesting activity of the endangered piping plover. But it is really only the beaches, where the plovers do their thing, that end up being closed, and these closures take place only during the midsummer months. Furthermore, beaches are only a small part of the Parker River refuge. Inland, along the marshes, you'll see wading ibises, egrets, hawks, plovers, migrating waterfowl, and many other species. And don't expect a big crowd— the beach closures tend to discourage all but dedicated birders.

The freshwater wetlands of **Great Meadows National Wildlife Refuge** are another great spot to see wading birds, including herons, ibises, and egrets. If you've got a boat, floating down the Ipswich River through the **Ipswich River Sanctuary** can be another birder's bonanza. The sighting list for the sanctuary includes 221 species, 98 of which are reported to nest here.

BOARDSAILING

Duxbury Bay, on the South Shore, is probably the area's prime spot for boardsailing, given its combination of generally reliable winds and waters protected from large, ocean swells. The absence of big-boat traffic coming in and out of the bay also helps keep unpleasant chop to a minimum. If you're more interested in open-water sailing, head north for the beaches of **Plum Island. Nahant Beach** near Lynn is a popular place among some boardsailers, especially since it is relatively close to downtown Boston. But that can also be its shortcoming; boat traffic in this area can get heavy, particularly on weekends.

CANOEING

So many are the small lakes and ponds within the radius of greater Boston that you're never too far from a launch site to head out for a short paddle. But *small* is the key word here. Don't expect day trips

WALDEN REVISITED

It is no longer the pristine site that in 1845 lured Henry David Thoreau to the woods to seek wilderness solitude and inspiration. These days, Walden Pond is part local swimming hole, part tourist attraction, part park, but certainly not wilderness.

Commuter trains charge by noisily on one edge of Walden Pond Reservation. On a hot summer day, the swimming beach is packed. There is a souvenir shop that, to its credit, sells mostly the literate works of Thoreau, Emerson, and others. But it also features a healthy supply of T-shirts and cutesy stuffed animals. Not far away, busy Route 2 roars with commuter traffic.

At the same time, there is an aura about Walden Pond that may come simply from its enduring image in the American consciousness as an ideological sanctuary. When the sunlight is just right, or the wind just light enough to ruffle the water's surface, or perhaps in winter when there is a dusting of snow on the bare trees, pocket-sized Walden Pond still possesses a kind of ethereal magic.

Thoreau is often thought of as an environmentalist, perhaps even the granddaddy of environmentalism. This is not quite true, although certainly his oft-quoted works seem inspired by some unwritten environmentalist manifesto. But Thoreau was, more accurately, a transcendentalist.

Transcendentalism (based on the works of Plato and the German philosopher Immanuel Kant) began in Boston in 1836, with the creation of the Transcendental Club, headed by the likes of Ralph Waldo Emerson and Margaret Fuller. The transcendentalists held that an ideal spiritual reality exists beyond the day-to-day, observable reality of the world. They believed that this spiritual reality found one of its purest expressions in nature, and so it was nature about which they wrote with great fervency and romance.

Thoreau's 2-year stint in a cabin in the woods near Walden Pond, from 1845 to 1847, was thus a search for some transcendental ideal, a spiritual rediscovery of himself through self-reliance in a natural world. In the mid-1800s, 2 miles from Concord, such a pursuit was more or less possible.

"I go and come with a strange liberty in Nature, a part of herself," he wrote. "As I walk along the stony shore of the pond in my shirt-sleeves, though it is cool as well as cloudy and windy, and I see nothing special to attract me, all the elements are unusually congenial to me. The bullfrogs trump to usher in the night, and the note of the whip-poor-will is borne on the rippling wind from over the water. Sympathy with the fluttering alder and poplar leaves almost takes away my breath; yet, like the lake, my serenity is rippled but not ruffled."

He would be unlikely to experience such a transcendent moment at Walden Pond today. But for all the encroachments of civilization, the world of Walden remains imbued with Thoreau's spirituality. Go at dawn, when the light is right and the shores unpeopled, and you may come closer to the Walden that Thoreau knew.

of exploration along extended, deeply indented shores, and don't expect long stretches of undeveloped shorelines.

For a quick cruise, **Walden Pond** is a popular spot, although you could easily paddle from one end of the pond to the other in 20 minutes. Don't be surprised to encounter many other canoeists or kayakers learning their craft; this is a good spot for beginning kayakers to learn how to roll.

If you're looking to escape the company of other canoeists, you'll probably have your best luck heading south from the city. **Aaron River Reservoir** in Wompatuck State Park is a relatively secluded spot, although the shoreline scenery, including such fixtures as chain-link fences, leaves something to be desired. **East Head Pond** in Myles Standish State Forest is another good place to escape crowds, at least on weekdays.

Rivers, of course, are another option. The broad, deep **Merrimack River** is lined with docks and marinas, so expect to share the water with powerboats and, as you near the mouth of the river in Newburyport, with sailboats. On the South Shore, the **North River** meanders for roughly 20 miles from Hanson into the ocean south of Scituate. And of course there is the **Charles River,** famous as a rowing mecca as it enters Boston and Cambridge. Just be prepared to be intimidated by finely chiseled, world-class oarsmen who train and compete on the river.

Ipswich River

Allow 3–4 hours. Access: Take Rte. 1 north past the Topsfield Fairgrounds and turn right at the second light onto Ipswich Rd. **Foote Brothers Canoe Rentals** (☎ 978/356-9771) is on Ipswich Rd., 3 miles east of Rte. 1.

Trees crowd in over the slow-moving, green water of the Ipswich River, and for a moment you'll feel as though you have been transported to England, to the setting of some Brontë novel. The river wends its way through the Ipswich River Sanctuary, a one-time estate that now is the largest sanctuary under the aegis of the Massachusetts Audubon Society.

Park at Foote Brothers Canoe Rentals in Topsfield and arrange a shuttle across Route 1 to Salem Road (a service Foote Brothers will provide). The first stretch of river is outside the sanctuary, but as you work downstream, this Brontë-like world begins to envelop you. According to Audubon Society records, 221 different bird species have been sighted here, and 98 species nest here. So your trip will almost certainly be in the company of a host of ducks and birds of prey—and on very rare occasions, bald eagles.

Outfitters

Guided trips on the Charles River are arranged through **Broadmoor Wildlife Sanctuary** (☎ 508/655-2296 or 781/235-3929).

Rentals & Instruction

Charles River Canoe & Kayak (2401 Commonwealth Ave., Newton, MA 02466; ☎ 617/965-5110) offers clinics on the Charles River, as well as other locations throughout the area.

CROSS-COUNTRY SKIING

Cross-country skiing is the sort of sport that, for whatever reason, seems to appeal to a broad mindset within the greater Boston community. Snow might be an irregular and unreliable visitor to Boston, but when it appears, almost every Bostonian with a pair of cross-country skis in his or her closet seems to head out to find some patch of the white stuff to slide around on.

The **Weston Ski Track** (200 Park Rd., Weston; ☎ 781/891-6575), with 15 kilometers of groomed trails, may be the top spot in the region for track skiing, largely because snowmaking fills in where nature falls short. Snowmaking is also featured at **Great Brook Farm Ski Touring Center** (1018 Lowell St., Carlisle; ☎ 508/369-7486), with 15 kilometers of trails west of Boston.

If you don't need grooming and you're willing to wait for natural snow to fall, try **Blue Hills Reservation** south of the city for a long, backcountry jaunt or **Bradley Palmer State Park,** north of the city in Topsfield, for a more leisurely cruise.

DOWNHILL SKIING

If you want dependable conditions, you'll probably want to head west to either **Nashoba Valley** or **Wachusett Mountain** (see chapter 2, "The Berkshires"). But if you need a quick fix and don't feel like driving an hour to go skiing, **Blue Hills** (4001 Washington St., Canton; ☎ **617/828-5090**) has a 350-foot vertical rise, seven trails, and one double chair, along with night skiing. **Bradford Ski Area** (South Cross Road, Haverhill, MA; ☎ **508/373-0071**) has two triple chair lifts, and 10 trails for day and night skiing. The vertical rise is just 250 feet, so expect to get in plenty of runs for your money.

FISHING

The fish around Boston are living the good life again. In the past, the long-term pollution of Boston Harbor chased all sensible fish out to sea or to other bodies of water, and a fisherman with any hope of catching anything had to venture far away from the immediate Boston area. But the Boston Harbor clean-up has played itself out in stages. Cleaner water has attracted smaller bait-style fish back to the harbor, and where smaller fish go, the bigger fish that feed on them follow.

So now **Boston Harbor** has become an excellent fishing ground, particularly for striped bass. When the bluefish run, the harbor can also be a hot spot, but then so can just about anywhere else from Plymouth to Duxbury.

For those with a deep-sea interest, **Gloucester** is a good place to start out, a fact that should not surprise, given that Gloucester is the oldest fishing port in the country. Deep-sea fishermen out of Gloucester generally head about 35 miles to the east to Stellwagen Bank, a major feeding ground for a wide variety of species. Halibut and cod fishing may not be the most exciting of sports—hauling in a halibut is like hauling in an old boot full of water—but the trip out to sea and the freezer full of fresh steaks you'll return with make it all worthwhile.

If you prefer shore-bound fishing, probably the best place for surfcasting is **Plum Island,** particularly **Parker River National Wildlife Refuge** when its beaches are open. These beaches are less populated than most of the others in the greater Boston area, so your chances of catching a fish, rather than a swimmer, are much better. On the south shore, the place to head is **Humarock Beach,** where fishermen head for the mouths of the North and South rivers.

Gear & Instruction

Firefly Outfitters (One Federal St., Boston; ☎ **617/423-FISH**) specializes in fly-fishing equipment and clothing, both for saltwater and freshwater fishing. The store also conducts clinics in fly-tying and casting techniques.

Charters

Reel Dream Charters (59 Greenfield Lane, Scituate; ☎ **781/545-6263**) specializes in small parties (of up to three fishermen) for saltwater fly-fishing and spin fishing in Boston Harbor. **Essex Downriver Fishing Charters** (85 Western Ave., Essex; ☎ **978/468-1285**) takes small groups fly-fishing for stripers in the estuarial waters of the Essex River Basin. **The Yankee Fleet** (75 Essex St., Gloucester; ☎ **800/942-5464**) offers halfday to overnight deep-sea fishing expeditions for fishermen going for cod, halibut, and tuna.

HIKING & BACKPACKING

Backpacking? You'd have to use considerable imagination to invent a backpacking trip in the greater Boston area, although something called the Bay Circuit Trail, a 200-mile route connecting Newburyport to the north of Boston and Duxbury to the south, is a work in progress. But even this is a route that primarily connects existing trails through what urban planner Charles Eliot once referred to as "the emerald necklace" of parks and open spaces that surround Boston. This might be a long route, but it is not a wilderness route.

That said, hiking opportunities are more plentiful than might be imagined. **Bradley Palmer State Park,** the former estate of the eponymous philanthropist, is a great spot to lose yourself in the woods for an afternoon. The 720-acre park in Ipswich features 20 miles of well-maintained trails, winding through a forest that in some places is so dense it seems subtropical. If that's not enough to satisfy you, you can cross Ipswich Road into **Willowdale State Forest,** 2,400 acres of forest, meadow, and swampland. **World's End** in Hingham (see "Walks & Rambles," below) and **Maudslay State Park** in Newbury (see "Mountain Biking," below) are also great places for a leisurely hike. When does a ramble turn into a hike? That's for you to decide.

Blue Hills Reservation

Allow 3 hours. Moderate–strenuous. Access: From Exit 2 off Interstate 93, take Rte. 138 north about .25 mile. Turn right onto Hillside St. at the sign for the entrance to the reservation. Reservation headquarters are Hillside St., about 2 miles from the entrance. Map: Available at reservation headquarters.

That Blue Hills, at 6,500 acres, exists at all is a remarkable thing. The Metropolitan District Commission, the country's first regional park authority, pounced on Blue Hills early, before the turn of the century and the sprawling of metropolitan Boston. A land acquisition of such enormity would certainly not be possible today; open spaces like this just don't exist anymore, and if they did, the land would be far too expensive.

The heart of the city is just 10 miles away, yet once you commit yourself to a walk in the woods here, every trace of city life vanishes; you might as well be in the Berkshires. Well, almost. The trails of Blue Hills are well traveled, particularly if you stick relatively close to the park's headquarters or Houghton Pond, the popular swimming spot. So don't expect to have a trail to yourself here as you might in some secluded Berkshires nook. But hey—how secluded can you expect a trail to be when there are close to five million people living within 45 minutes of it?

Blue Hills' signature hike is along the Skyline Trail, which at 9 miles is the reservation's longest, and it does indeed feature great views of the Boston skyline. The trail traverses the complete length of the reservation, and you can do it as a one-way trip if you make car-shuttle arrangements. But because of the reservation's large trail network, you might prefer doing a loop hike, walking along a section (or sections) of the Skyline Trail, then using another trail to make your way back to your starting point.

Reservation headquarters, which sits approximately in the center of the reservation, is a good place to start. From here, a popular 3-mile loop, starting on the North Skyline Trail and returning on the South Skyline Trail, leads to Great Blue Hill, at 635 feet the reservation's high point. There are no long climbs along the way, of course, but the ups and downs are considerable as the trail passes over Hancock, Hemenway, and Wolcott hills on its way to the highest hill of them all.

The reservation literature proudly boasts that Great Blue Hill is "the highest peak on the Atlantic Coast south of Maine!" It's not much of a "peak," of course, but from the Eliot Tower at its summit, the panorama of Boston to the north and Wachusett to the northwest can, on a clear day, make you feel like you're on top of the world. Returning via the South Skyline Trail, you'll also pass over stone ledges before reaching the summit, from which the views to the south are equally impressive. The trail also passes over Houghton Hill before descending to Hillside Avenue, about 200 feet from the reservation headquarters.

Want more? Then cross the road to continue eastward as the Skyline Trail passes over another series of low hills—Boyce, Buck, Tucker, and Chicatawbut—for a 6-mile out-and-back from reservation headquarters. The climbing might be minimal—Chicatawbut Hill, at 517 feet, is the highest of the lot—but the grades in places are steep and rocky, so this is certainly not just an easygoing stroll in some grassy, suburban park.

Parker River National Wildlife Refuge

Allow 2–5 hours. Easy–moderate. Access: From the center of Newburyport, take Water St. east, following signs to Plum Island. After crossing the Plum Island causeway, turn right to the refuge's entrance. Map: Unnecessary.

Is there a more soulful and romantic thing a person can do than walk along a deserted beach while the mists come off the ocean and the surf rolls in? Walking along the 7-mile stretch of beach at Parker River National Wildlife Refuge is as fine a beach walk as you'll ever find. Here is a barrier island entirely undeveloped; the only evidence of human intervention is the occasional sign indicating off-limits areas for the protection of wildlife habitats. Otherwise, there is nothing here but surf and sand, dunes and dune grasses, and birds and shells.

You may encounter the occasional wanderer, but the refuge beach attracts a relatively small crowd, and for good reason—it isn't always open. For much of the summer, the beach—or most of it—is closed to allow piping plovers, an endangered species, to nest in peace. So the beach crowds of greater Boston assume, by and large, that Parker River is always closed, or closed so often that it might as well be closed all the time.

But you can be fairly certain that in September and October, great beach-walking months, that the beach will be open. By then the plovers have done their thing and have moved on, leaving the beach to gulls, terns, and shell collectors.

This is the sort of hike in which you bite off as much as you feel like chewing. Start at the first parking lot after the entry gate, or start 7 miles down the road at the last lot near Sandy Point. The entire, 14-mile round-trip is a healthy bit of walking, particularly in soft sand, but it is possible to do in a day. Keep three things in mind: Bring plenty of water (there's no fresh water source along the beach), bring plenty of sunblock, and be cautious about swimming in the absence of lifeguards. Nasty currents and riptides may lurk within the surf during the fall, the prime hurricane season.

HORSEBACK RIDING

Probably the best riding in the Boston area is in **Blue Hills Reservation,** which has not only the terrain, but also the services to keep riders happy. There are several stables in the area that rent horses, offer instruction, and lead organized rides. Contact reservation headquarters (☎ 617/698-1802) for a stable listing.

In the South Shore area, the **Briggs Riding Stables** (☎ 617/826-3191) in Hanover offers lessons and trail rides. If you want to go riding north of Boston, check out **Bobby's Ranch** (☎ 508/263-7165), in Acton, which offers group rides.

MOUNTAIN BIKING

"Mountain biking" in a region without mountains is probably a misnomer—"off-road riding" would probably be more accurate. But this, too, might not be quite correct. Much of the best mountain biking in greater Boston takes place on roads or reasonable facsimiles. Bashing through trees and streams on single-track trails is not a common activity around Boston. You're more likely to find yourself on an old forest road or fire road, with only the occasional run on something more technical. Perhaps the biggest challenge on some roads and trails is the sandy soil, in which tires tend to swim and lose traction.

This might disappoint aggressive jocks seeking bike-handling challenges, but it's great for novice riders and families interested primarily in a good ride in the woods. There is some decent single-track riding in **Ames Nowell State Park** in Abington and at **Gilbert Hills State Forest** in Foxboro. But for the most part, aggressive riders should head west to the Berkshires or north to New Hampshire.

Maudslay State Park

Allow 1–2 hours. Easy. Access: From Newburyport, take Rte. 113 west and turn right on Noble St. at a State Park sign. Turn left on Ferry Rd. and continue about 2 miles to the parking area, on your right. Map: Available at the parking area.

My, how the times have changed. More than a century ago on the grounds of Maudslay State Park, such luminary writers as Ralph Waldo Emerson and John Greenleaf Whittier strolled and discussed the more profound issues of literature. They did so at the behest of the Moseley family, the former owners of the land, who enjoyed the idea of staging what they called "literary festivals." Today, mountain bikers pedal around the carriage roads that wind through this 480-acre park.

This is one of those places that is perfect for family riding. The roads are well maintained, and while you can ride loops of up to 6 miles, you're never far from your starting point. Explore the gardens of the former Moseley estate, which the state has been making an effort to restore. This is a particularly inviting place in the spring, when azaleas, dogwoods, and rhododendrons bloom. Ride along the banks of the Merrimack River, keeping an eye out for waterfowl and, if you are exceedingly lucky, the very rare bald eagle.

This is no ride to rush, and no one who comes to ride here really has any intention of doing so. Hiking trails, which in another place might double as challenging single track, are off-limits to bikes; hence, serious high-speed riders tend to go elsewhere. So bring the family, take it slow, breathe in the floral fragrances, and imagine what the literary legends might have thought upon seeing a mountain bike whiz by.

Wompatuck State Park

Allow 2 hours. Moderate. Access: From Hingham, take Rte. 228 south. Turn right on Main St. (look for a sign for the park), which turns into Union St. before the park entrance, on your left. Map: Available at park headquarters.

Covering 3,500 acres, Wompatuck State Park is exceeded in size only by Blue Hills Reservation among parklands close to Boston. It is something of a hub for Boston-area cyclists: Informal road races are held on its paved roads, and organized group mountain-bike rides are regular occurrences on its unpaved roads and trails.

The riding here is easy, on mostly dirt roads and double track, with the occasional paved stretch or single track thrown in. With numerous roads and trails crisscrossing the park, your options here are plentiful, and since nothing in the park is too far from anything else, you should have no problems finding your way back to wherever you started from. What's more, you'll encounter plenty of other riders using the trail—not enough to create crowds, but enough to give you guidance should you lose your way. The going is reasonably flat, with only a few small rolls to elevate your heart rate. So do what many who come to Wompatuck do—bring along the kids and take it easy as you explore the largest tract of forest land within a few minutes of downtown Boston.

Gear & Rentals

There are dozens of fine bike stores in the greater Boston area. One store that is centrally located is **Back Bay Bicycles** (336 Newbury St., Boston, MA 02115; ☎ 617/247-2336). **Fat Dog Pro Bicycle Shop** (940 High St., Westwood, MA 02090; ☎ 781/251-9447) specializes in high-end bikes and equipment.

ROAD BIKING

First, the drawbacks. Atop the list is traffic, which should be no surprise. You don't want to spend much time on such major roads as Route 2 or 3A; riding these highways at rush hour is something akin to a death wish. Even secondary routes can get clogged, and shoulders, generous in many other parts of Massachusetts, are often slender to nonexistent around Boston.

There is a way of avoiding all this—by riding loops almost exclusively on side roads and back streets, of which there are many in the region. But the avoidance strategy also has its drawback—you face the proposition of getting hopelessly lost.

Finally, the ocean is nearby, and with it comes the wind. Riding along the ocean's edge has its undeniable appeal, but if it means pounding into a stiff headwind, the appeal can lose much of its luster.

So what do you do to minimize the drawbacks and get the most out of riding in the greater Boston area? First, get a good, detailed roadmap. It is not only the best and simplest guide to the intricate web of the area's secondary and tertiary roads, it is also your best source for getting unlost if (or when) you do get disoriented.

Second, play smart with the wind. Winds are usually calmest in the early morning—also, coincidentally, when rush-hour traffic is still light. But rising at dawn to ride is not everyone's cup of tea. So check local weather reports regarding wind direction, and plan on riding any loop that includes a seaside stretch in a direction that puts the wind at your back when you're nearest the ocean. The wind even a mile inland can be much lighter, so ride inland stretches into the prevailing wind direction.

Two good loops are described below, but for short, easy riding—particularly for family riding—there are a couple of other good places you might want to check out. The 6-mile road through **Parker River National Wildlife Refuge** is paved for half its length and has gravel on the rest. It is almost water-level flat, sees very little

traffic (which is strictly kept to 25 m.p.h. by park rangers), and passes by marshland on one side and dunes on the other. The whole area teems with birds. It's a great starter ride for kids. Also, the roads in **Wompatuck State Park** (some of which are paved, others not) can make for a leisurely, traffic-free afternoon of pedaling.

Cape Ann Loop

Allow 2–3 hours. Easy–moderate. Access: Take Rte. 128 toward Gloucester, looking for signs to Stage Fort Park. Turn right onto Washington St. (Rte. 127) into Gloucester center, looking for Stage Fort Park, on the left. There is a parking lot a short way up the hill. Map: Rubel Bikemaps, Cape Cod & North Shore.

Greater Boston or the Maine coast? Cape Ann is where the two meet, with the dense settlement of Boston and the rocky shoreline of Maine. This ride starts as you descend from the parking area to perhaps the North Shore's most recognizable landmark—"The Man at the Wheel" statue, a memorial to the many fishermen who have lost their lives at sea. Gloucester, of course, is vitally linked to 3 centuries of seafaring history and the tragedy that comes with it. It is from Gloucester that fishermen sailed into disaster in *The Perfect Storm,* Sebastian Junger's wrenching, bestselling tale.

Turn right at the statue onto Route 127 as it wends around Gloucester Harbor. Then turn right again at a stoplight onto East Main Street, moving through the village of East Gloucester and onto Rocky Neck, a spur that extends southward from Cape Ann into Massachusetts Bay. The Neck is home to the country's oldest working artists' colony, a refuge for the likes of Winslow Homer and John Frederick Kensett. So it should be no surprise that as you loop around Rocky Neck, galleries featuring the works of artists past and present are a common sight.

Continue on East Main Street past Niles Beach and onto Eastern Point, where grand summer homes line the shore. At the end of the road is Eastern Point Lighthouse, the guiding light into Gloucester Harbor. A .5-mile-long jetty extends into the mouth of the harbor; if you happen to have fishing gear strapped to your bike frame, join the other fishermen casting their lines out from the jetty.

Returning to Rocky Neck, turn right on Farrington Avenue, which turns into Atlantic Road as it hugs the eastern shore. At the junction with Route 127A (Thatcher Road), turn right, passing the popular beaches of Cape Ann's southern shore as you make your way toward Rockport.

Make of Rockport what you will—it is part artist colony, part tourist trap, part fishing village, part summer enclave. The numerous galleries may carry anything from truly fine art to absolute schlock, so buyer beware. There is a similarly broad range of restaurants, so if you don't trust your buying instincts, at least you'll find a good place to stop for a snack or lunch.

From Rockport, join Route 127 as it heads north toward Pigeon Cove and Halibut Point State Park; it's worth a short side trip and a stroll around (see "Walks & Rambles," below) to stretch your legs, or perhaps to work off your Rockport lunch. From this point, Route 127 wends along Cape Ann's northern shore, offering occasional bay views as you begin to loop southward again toward Gloucester. The small village of Annisquam, where the Annisquam River enters Ipswich Bay, is worth another side trip. It encapsulates the character of Cape Ann, where fishing, art, and tourism join together.

Route 127 eventually reaches a rotary at its junction with Route 128. This can be a nasty clog of traffic to negotiate, but as you work around the rotary, look for Route 127 (Washington Street), which leads back to the "Man at the Wheel."

In summer, traffic can be heavy, particularly around Gloucester, and riding early in the morning is probably the best traffic-avoidance strategy. On the plus side, the speed limits are low and drivers seem not to be in a hurry anyway. Most, after all, are doing the same thing you are—going for a leisurely tour and taking in the sights.

Cohasset Loop

Allow 2–3 hours. Easy–moderate. Access: Headquarters, Wompatuck State Forest. From Hingham, take Main St. south to Union St. The park entrance is on the left. Map: Rubel Bikemaps, Eastern Massachusetts.

Here's a 30-plus-mile ride that features a little bit of just about everything that greater Boston has to offer: seaside arcades, grand mansions overlooking the ocean, quiet back roads, a state forest, and, yes, a little bit of traffic thrown in. Start in Wompatuck State Park, a popular biking spot, primarily for mountain bikers. Head out of the park and turn right onto Union Street, which in quick succession becomes Middle Street and then Main Street as you enter Hingham proper. After crossing busy Route 228, turn right onto North Street, and then right onto Route 3A. From here until Hull, you'll have to deal with a fair amount of traffic, but at least the roads are wide, so there should be plenty of room for cars to get by safely.

After going around a rotary, follow signs to Hull and Nantasket. Soon you'll turn left onto George Washington Boulevard, which leads to Nantasket Beach. This is a beach that resonates with the joys of childhood, including amusement-park rides, game arcades, and young teenagers and preteens just getting into the heady experience of being out from under the wing of parental supervision. Turn right onto Nantasket Boulevard, which runs along the beach, and after crossing a bridge, turn left onto Atlantic Avenue.

Stay on Atlantic Avenue as it winds along the shore, passing through an enclave of magnificent seaside homes before arriving at Cohasset. Things get tricky here, so if you get a little lost, simply ask for Border Road south. To get there, you'll veer left from the harbor onto Elm Street, then quickly left onto Border Street, crossing a bridge. Essentially what you are doing is jogging around pretty Cohasset Harbor, so if you feel you are getting far from the sea, you're probably getting lost.

For the next couple of miles, you'll be riding on a quiet, tree-lined road. When you come to a **T**, turn right, then turn right again after .75 mile onto Hatherly Road. You can take Hatherly all the way into Scituate, but you'll probably want to turn left at the light at Turner Road to make a side trip to Old Scituate Lighthouse, overlooking the impressive collection of yachts in Scituate Harbor.

Upon entering Scituate, take Front Street around the harbor. Front Street turns into Kent Street, New Kent, and Driftway as the road proceeds out of town and away from the shore. In a couple of miles, you'll come to the intersection with Route 3A. Cross it with care and continue onto Old Oaken Buck Road, marked by the sign OLD SATUIT TRAIL. This is a wonderfully quiet little road through sparsely populated woods, and you might find your attention drifting into peaceful bliss. But stay alert after 2.5 miles for Mt. Blue Road on your right. Turn here, and in another 2.5 miles, the road comes to an end at a closed gate, the back entrance to Wompatuck State Park. Work your way around the gate and continue on for another mile or two to your starting point.

Yes, there are lots of turns to make things complicated. But get yourself a good map, and you'll probably be able to stay on track. And you'll probably be pleasantly surprised to discover that riding around Boston doesn't have to be all honking horns and sucking exhaust.

Gear & Rentals

See "Gear & Rentals" under "Mountain Biking," above. Also, **Seaside Cycle** in Manchester (23 Elm St.; ☎ **508/526-1200**) rents bikes for the Cape Ann loop.

SAILING

Boston lies in the heart of perhaps the greatest cruising waters in America. The heavily indented shoreline of the Northeast from Maine to Connecticut, the many natural harbors, the generally reliable winds, and the inspiring, rugged coastal scenery is more or less the ideal atmosphere for recreational sailing.

Of course, Boston itself is a busy commercial port, but even **Boston Harbor,** with its many islands, is a terrific place to explore. As you head north and south, harbors and bays become smaller and less commercial, and thus even more attractive to cruising vessels. Along the North Shore, **Marblehead** and **Manchester** are famous among yachtsmen and have been breeding grounds for some of the country's most talented competitive sailors.

The pocket harbors of **Cohasset** and **Scituate** along the South Shore are almost postcard perfect—handsome yachts, with their halyards clanging in the wind, set against the backdrop of pretty New England villages. Cohasset Harbor, however, does have its menacing side; the rocky entrance can be a hazard in high winds or low water if you don't proceed cautiously. Farther to the south, **Duxbury Bay** is another competitive sailing hotbed where, on summer weekends, large racing regattas are the order of the day.

Boat rentals and charters are available at numerous marinas in the region, for day sailing or for extended cruising. In fact, if you're planning an extended cruise along the New England coast—north to Maine or south to Cape Cod or Rhode Island—the Boston area is probably the best place to charter a boat. Charter services are concentrated here, whereas elsewhere along the coast, the pickings are slimmer. Sailing schools are also an easy find. In short, you need neither the boat nor the know-how to experience one of the great pleasures of Boston's great outdoors.

Gear

The **Marine Exchange** (202 Newbury St., Peabody, MA 01960; ☎ **800/888-8699**) offers a broad selection of both new and used equipment. **C.G. Edwards** (272 Dorcester Ave., Box 358, Boston, MA 02127; ☎ **617/268-4111**) is an excellent source for charts as well as marine supplies.

Rentals & Charters

There are too many charter companies in the Boston area to list them all, but here are a couple to get you started. On the South Shore, **Plymouth Bristol Charters** (Box 903, Plymouth, MA 02362; ☎ **508/746-3688**) rents a 41-foot yacht for day or overnight trips. On the North Shore, check out **Atlantic Charters** (13 Drumlin Rd., Marblehead, MA 01945; ☎ **781/639-0055**), which has a fleet of boats from 23 to 36 feet available for day rentals or extended charters.

Instruction

The **Boston Sailing Center** (The Riverboat at Lewis Wharf, Boston, MA 02110; ☎ **617/227-4198**) offers courses that range in length from 4 days to 5 weeks, for everyone from beginners to advanced offshore sailors. Also in the Boston Harbor area is the **Piers Park Sailing Center** (95 Marginal St., East Boston, MA 02128; ☎ **617/561-0564**), which offers 2- to 3-hour learn-to-sail courses on smaller boats. On the North Shore, **Atlantic Charters** (see "Rentals & Charters," above) offers an excellent instructional program.

SCULLING

For years, the Ivy League has represented perhaps the highest order of competitive rowing in America, and Harvard perhaps the highest order of competitive rowing in the Ivy League. The epicenter of all of this oarsmanship is the **Charles River,** the Yankee Stadium of American rowing (even if proper Bostonian sports fans cringe at the analogy). The Head of the Charles Regatta, held every fall, is something akin to the World Series of American rowing, attracting more than 5,000 athletes in 20 events.

On an average day, the Charles, particularly from the Science Museum to the B.U. Bridge, teems with boats. Many of these boats are piloted by former or future Olympians, but there are many other oarsmen out there simply looking for a good time and some exercise—and perhaps hoping that some of the championship legacy will drift their way.

Gear, Rentals & Instruction

Charles River Canoe & Kayak (2401 Commonwealth Ave., Newton, MA 02466; ☎ **617/965-5110**) is as good a starting point as any for a sculler who has come to dip his or her oars in the Charles for the first time.

SEA KAYAKING

Sea kayaking around Boston basically boils down to two choices: inland (rivers and estuaries) or open water (bays, harbors, islands, the ocean itself). Each has its own rewards and drawbacks.

The inland waterways are great for bird-watching and easy paddling, and are well protected from strong ocean winds. But tides can be tricky; if you err in your planning, you might discover that what was a body of water on your outgoing trip has turned into a bed of low-tide mud on your return trip. Also, the green flies in the marshes, in the absence of any breeze, can be almost unbearable in July.

There is a great thrill to boating in open water, particular in exploring islands or deserted beaches unreachable by car. But wind and current are constant considerations, and battling either for any length of time is nobody's idea of fun. In addition to the two trips described below, you might want to look into kayaking along the southern coast of **Cape Ann,** and from there westward toward

BOSTON HARBOR REBORN

Those with a political memory will recall that when Michael Dukakis campaigned for president in 1988, he declared himself an environmentalist candidate. This pronouncement, however, turned into an invitation for ridicule; opponents pounced, gleefully revealing that Boston Harbor, right in Dukakis's backyard, was one of the most polluted bodies of water in the country.

Indeed, for more than 200 years, Boston Harbor waters were awash with sewage. Water-treatment efforts were grossly inadequate—a 1968 treatment plant on Deer Island that was supposed to speed waste out to sea on the wings of the outgoing tide instead dumped 50 tons of sludge a day into the harbor from 1968 to 1991. At the same time, Boston sewers, with inadequate drainage, were jettisoning 10 billion gallons of raw sewage into the harbor annually. According to one report, a "gray, mayonnaise-like substance coated the harbor floor."

The result: closed beaches, disappearing wildlife, abominable water, and, of course, lawsuits. Not to mention the collapse of Michael Dukakis's political career.

That was then, this is now. Dukakis has descended far beyond the political horizon, and Boston Harbor has risen like a phoenix. A new treatment plant on Deer Island and sewer projects, implemented by the Massachusetts Water Resources Authority and the Boston Water and Sewer Commission, have had a major impact on Boston Harbor's water quality.

A screening process, implemented in 1989 at treatment plants on Deer Island and Nut Island, halted the discharge into Boston Harbor of more than 10,000 gallons per day of the floating pollution indelicately known as scum. Sludge from the 43 communities served by the MWRA sewer system, instead of ending up in the water, is now pelletized in a plant in Quincy and recycled as fertilizer.

The results of this clean-up are abundantly evident. Beach closings, while still an occasional occurrence, have been reduced by more than 50%. Harbor seals and porpoises have made a dramatic comeback, largely due to a return of forage fish, which have returned because of improved water quality. Fishermen are reeling in healthy striped bass, and sea kayakers are island hopping. The harbor islands have become recreational hot spots, and harbor cruises are in vogue. As something of an official reward, in 1996 the National Park Service designated the Boston Harbor islands collectively as a national recreation area.

The pollution has not disappeared entirely, but Boston Harbor is no longer the environmental and political nightmare it was in 1988.

Manchester and **Marblehead.** Milk Island is an easy paddle from Long Beach on Cape Ann, while Great Misery Island is a popular trip from Manchester, where Longfellow was inspired to write his famous poem "The Wreck of the Hesperus."

Boston Harbor

Access: The best launching area is Hingham Cove off Rte. 3A on the South Shore. Nautical charts are available from **C.G. Edwards Marine,** 272 Dorchester Ave., Boston, MA 02127; ☎ **617/268-4111.**

A smattering of small islands with shell-strewn beaches, wildlife, wild berries, Colonial ruins, hiking trails, secluded campgrounds . . . all this just a couple of miles from Boston? Indeed, Boston Harbor (including contiguous Quincy and Hingham bays) is a special place, perhaps surprisingly so. The harbor, after all, was little more than a cesspool a decade or so ago, a waste basin for Boston's sewage. But clean-up efforts have been remarkable (see "Boston Harbor Reborn," above), and the Boston Harbor islands are now officially a National Recreation Area.

So sea kayaking in Boston Harbor, an unimaginable concept even 10 years ago, is now a very cool thing to do. Harbor tours and water taxis may take you to a few of the islands, but a sea kayak expands your possibilities considerably. There are at least 30 islands here—depending on what you consider an island—ranging in size from a single acre to the 241 acres of Long Island. Most are accessible only by private boat.

You might, for example, want to visit Slate Island, where trails wind around quarries that date back to the mid-1600s. Or Ransford Island, with its gravel beaches, which was home to a smallpox quarantine in the 1700s. Or Calf Island, the site of a great mansion built in 1902 by Benjamin Cheney and his wife, the noted actress Julia Arthur. To paddle in Boston Harbor among the porpoises and seals returning in considerable numbers can be not just a paddle to remote islands, but something of a journey back into history.

There are campgrounds on some of the more developed islands, most notably Bumpkin Island in Hingham Bay. The campgrounds are small—10 sites or so—so reservations are necessary. And the state of Massachusetts and the National Park Service are continuing to develop more trails and recreational opportunities, so what is good now may be even better in a couple of years. Regardless, an evening paddle in the harbor, with the sun setting behind the Boston skyline, is alone worth the trip.

One note of caution: Motorized boat traffic, particularly in the major channels, can be a hazard. Get a good chart and be vigilant, and you shouldn't have any problem.

Essex River Basin

Access: From Gloucester, take Rte. 133 toward Essex. As you enter Essex, look for the ERBA (Eastern River Basin Adventures) sign on your right. You can launch here into the Essex River Harbor, or ask the ERBA folks about other launching sites. Parking is available across Rte. 133, in a roadside park behind the Woodman's Restaurant. Charts are available from **Waterproof Charts, Inc.,** 320 Cross St., Punta Gorda, FL 33950; ☎ **800/423-9026.**

The Essex River area is something close to a sea kayakers' dream: marshlands teeming with bird life, islands to explore, sandy beaches and dunes along the ocean, and miles of estuaries and rivers offering almost limitless exploration. As Ozzie Osborn, who heads up Essex River Basin Adventures, says, "This is one of the most pristine areas of coastal land and open marshland anywhere." Indeed it is. Within the greater Boston perimeter, this is about as pure as the great outdoors gets.

The decision about where to go here is limited only by your own imagination and energy—and, to some degree, tidal activity. A typical day or half-day trip would almost certainly include a visit to Choate's Island, formerly known (and still known by most locals) as Hog Island. There is a landing area on the north shore of this drumlin, which in the 18th century was the private dominion of Thomas Choate. A trail leads to the original house, which has been restored, and its grounds, one of Osborn's favorite spots for a picnic lunch.

Depending on the strength of the wind, a paddle out to Castle Neck and Crane's Beach should also be high on your to-do list. Here, where Essex Bay meets the ocean, dunes and sand form an idyllic beach. Winds and currents can be tricky here, however, so this isn't something you'd want to do on a rough day.

This might be all you want to take on in one day, but other possibilities still beckon. Passing through a man-made channel, originally cut in the 1800s for shipbuilders transporting spars, you can connect with the Ipswich River and wend your way up into Plum Island Sound and the marshlands of the Parker and Rowley rivers. This involves a hefty amount of paddling, and you'll probably want to arrange some kind of shuttle service to get you back to your starting point. But if you can pull it off, you'll have experienced sea kayaking as good as it gets in the Northeast.

One drawback here is an absence of campgrounds, since wildlife refuges cover much of the territory. That might change in the future, but for the time being, multiday trips are, sadly, not a reasonable option.

Gear

Charles River Canoe & Kayak (2401 Commonwealth Ave., Newton, MA 02466; ☎ **617/965-5110**) stocks a full line of boats and accessories.

Outfitters

Essex River Basin Adventures (66R Main St., Box 270, Essex, MA 01929; ☎ **800/KAYAK-04** or 978/768-3722) leads half-day and full-day trips in the Essex River area, as well as off the coast of Cape Ann. **Charles River Canoe & Kayak** (2401 Commonwealth Ave., Newton, MA 02466; ☎ **617/965-5110**) leads trips through Boston Harbor and other bodies of water in the area. **Adventure Learning** (67 Bear Hill, Merrimack, MA 01860; (☎ **800/649-9728** or 508/346-9728), transports kayakers on a large boat to Stellwagen Bank (see "Whale Watching," below), where they can paddle among the whales.

Instruction

Essex River Basin Adventures, Charles River Canoe & Kayak, and **Adventure Learning** all offer sea-kayaking clinics, some for first-timers and sometimes with guided trips.

SURFING

If the swell is coming from the right direction, **Long Beach** on the southern shore of Cape Ann is a good surfing spot, although a storm surge is usually required. **Plum Island** to the north and **Nantasket Beach** to the south are classic Atlantic beaches, meaning they have constantly shifting sands. This, in turn, means constantly changing surf conditions, and the drop-off to the water is often too steep for an ideal break. But when conditions are right, these are probably the best surfing spots in the area. Bring a wet suit; the ocean water here is too cold for drifting on a board for more than a few minutes at a time.

SWIMMING

As the Gulf Stream and its warm waters veer eastward from the coast of the Northeast, the ocean water along beaches from Massachusetts to Maine is literally left in the cold. The exceptions to this are Martha's Vineyard and Nantucket, which are farther out to sea, but the beaches around Boston adhere to the cold-water rule. Temperatures in the 70s are essentially unheard of, temperatures in the 50s common, and temperatures in the 60s are pretty much the midsummer norm.

So if you plan to step into the ocean, expect the water to introduce itself with a brisk hello. That said, there are some exceptionally fine beaches within a 45-minute drive of downtown Boston. One of the nicest is **Crane's Beach,** east of Ipswich on the North Shore. The beach is essentially unspoiled and undeveloped, and its great dunes and relatively shallow surf make it a good deal for families.

For those looking for a little more action to go along with their swimming—arcades, rides, ice-cream stands, etc.—the place to go is **Nantasket Beach,** near Hull on the South Shore. For those looking for absolutely no action at all, except for the rolling drama of the surf, head for the beaches of **Parker River National Wildlife Refuge** on Plum Island on the North Shore. The refuge is often closed to protect nesting birds, so call ahead (☎ **508/465-5753**). However, the beaches on Plum Island north of the refuge are also relatively unpopulated, perhaps

THE FREEDOM TRAIL

You won't find a whole lot of natural scenery on this walk, but this easy 3-mile trail—blazed with either red paint or red brick—is steeped in history and conveniently situated in the heart of Boston. The hard-core history fiend can spend 4 hours or more peering at every artifact and reading every plaque along the trail, and will wind up at Bunker Hill feeling weary but rewarded. Others, especially those with kids tagging along, will probably appreciate the enforced efficiency of a 90-minute ranger-led tour.

The Freedom Trail (**http://thefreedomtrail.org**) actually begins at the **Boston Common Information Center** (146 Tremont St., on the Common), but if you want to take a free 90-minute guided tour with a park ranger, you'll need to start at the **Boston National Historic Park Visitor Center,** 15 State St. (☎ **617/242-5642**). To get there, take the "T" to the State Street station; the visitor center is across the street from the Old State House. An audiovisual show about the trail provides basic information on the trail. It's open daily from 9am to 5pm except January 1, Thanksgiving, and December 25. Pamphlets are available if you want to walk the trail by yourself. The recent installation of prominent markers and plaques makes the trail's 16 historical sites even easier to identify.

Here are a couple of the trail's highlights:

- **Boston Common.** In 1634, when their settlement was just 4 years old, the town fathers paid the Rev. William Blackstone £30 for this property. In 1640, it was set aside as common land. Be sure to stop at Beacon and Park streets to visit the memorial designed by **Augustus Saint-Gaudens** to celebrate the deeds of Col. Robert Gould Shaw and the Union Army's **54th Massachusetts Colored Regiment,** who fought in the Civil War. You may remember the story of the first American army unit made up of free black soldiers from the movie *Glory.*

- **Massachusetts State House** (☎ **617/727-3676**). **Charles Bulfinch** designed the "new" State House, and **Gov. Samuel Adams** laid the cornerstone of the state capitol in 1795. Tours (free, both guided and self-guided) leave from the second floor.

- **Old Granary Burying Ground.** This cemetery, established in 1660, contains the graves of—among other notables—**Samuel Adams, Paul Revere, John Hancock,** and the wife of Isaac Vergoose, better known as **"Mother Goose"** from the nursery rhymes of the same name. It's open daily from 8am to 4pm.

- **King's Chapel,** 58 Tremont St. (☎ **617/523-1749**). Completed in 1754, this church was built by erecting the granite edifice around the existing wooden chapel. The **burying ground** (1630), facing Tremont Street, is the oldest in Boston.

- **Site of the First Public School.** Founded in 1634, the school is commemorated with a colorful mosaic in the sidewalk on (of course) School Street. Inside the fence is the 1856 statue of **Benjamin Franklin,** the first portrait statue erected in Boston.

- **3 School St.** This is the former Old Corner Bookstore. Built in 1712, it's on a plot of land that was once home to the religious reformer **Anne Hutchinson.**

because parking is limited and expensive. On the South Shore, the beaches of **Duxbury** and **Plymouth** are healthily populated when summer's heat rolls in.

Swimming doesn't have to be exclusively a saltwater deal around Boston. **Walden Pond** near Concord is a favorite hangout of west-of-Boston locals. Wander around the pond from the main beach and you'll find a secluded flight of stone stairs that reach down to the water's edge; it's like having your own private swimming hole. Almost.

- **Old South Meeting House,** 310 Washington St. (☎ **617/482-6439**). Originally built in 1670 and replaced by the current structure in 1729, it was the starting point of the Boston Tea Party. It's open daily April through October from 9am to 5:30pm, November through March weekdays from 10am to 4pm, weekends from 10am to 5pm. Admission is $3 for adults, $2.50 for seniors, $1 for children 6 to 12, and free for children under 6.

- **Old State House,** 206 Washington St. (☎ **617/720-3290**). Built in 1713, it served as the seat of Massachusetts's colonial government before the Revolution and as the state's capitol until 1797. It now houses the Bostonian Society's museum of the city's history.

- **Boston Massacre Site.** On a traffic island in State Street, across from the "T" station under the Old State House, a ring of cobblestones marks the location of the skirmish of March 5, 1770.

- **Faneuil Hall.** Built in 1742 (and enlarged using a Charles Bulfinch design in 1805), it was given to the city by the merchant **Peter Faneuil.** National Park Service rangers give **free 20-minute talks** every half hour from 9am to 5pm in the second-floor auditorium.

- The **Paul Revere House,** 19 North Square (☎ **617/523-2338**). The oldest house in downtown Boston (built around 1680) presents history on a human scale. Revere bought it in 1770, and it became a museum in the early 20th century. It's open November 1 to April 14 from 9:30am to 4:15pm, and April 15 to October 31 from 9:30am to 5:15pm; closed Mondays January through March, January 1, Thanksgiving, and December 25. Admission is $2.50 for adults, $2 for seniors and students, $1 for children 5 to 17, and free for children under 5.

- The **Old North Church,** 193 Salem St. (☎ **617/523-6676;** www.oldnorth.com). Paul Revere saw a signal in the steeple when he set out on his "midnight ride." Officially known as Christ Church, this is the oldest church building in Boston; it dates to 1723. It's open daily from 9am to 5pm; Sunday services (Episcopal) are at 9 and 11am and 4pm. The quirky gift shop and museum, in a former chapel, is open daily from 9am to 5pm; all proceeds go to support the church. Donations are appreciated.

- **Copp's Hill Burying Ground,** off Hull Street. The second-oldest cemetery (1659) in the city, it contains the graves of **Cotton Mather** and his family and of **Prince Hall,** who established the first black Masonic lodge. It's open daily from 9am to 5pm.

- **USS** *Constitution* (☎ **617/242-5670**), Charlestown Navy Yard. Active-duty sailors in 1812 dress uniforms give free tours of "Old Ironsides" daily between 9:30am and 3:50pm.

- **Bunker Hill Monument** (☎ **617/242-5644**), Breed's Hill, Charlestown. The 221-foot granite obelisk honors the memory of the men who died in the Battle of Bunker Hill (actually fought on Breed's Hill) on June 17, 1775. If you're feeling energetic, climb the 295 stairs to the top. National Park Service rangers staff the monument, which is open daily from 9am to 4:30pm. Admission is free.

—by Marie Morris

WALKS & RAMBLES

Halibut Point State Park

From Rockport, take Rte. 127 north through Pigeon Cove to Gott Avenue and a State Park sign. Turn right; the parking area will be on your right.

What goes into a perfect seaside ramble? Well, you'd probably want a rocky shore to scramble around on, so you can search for seaborne knickknacks washed up with the tide. You'd probably want a lighthouse, because lighthouses have a way of confirming that you have come to some final point where land and sea meet.

You get both at Halibut Point, but you get a couple of bonuses in the deal, too. This walk starts with a short stroll through an almost arbor-like passage through the low-slung seaside trees on a path of soft wood chips. It is a neat way to approach the sea, as if emerging from a tunnel into a sudden, bursting expanse of bright sea and sky.

And quarry. As you emerge from the arborway, what confronts you first is not the ocean, but an enormous quarry, long ago abandoned by the Rockport Granite Company and now filled over the years with rainwater. Gulls drift lazily over the quarry's waters and rest on its stone ledges.

Take the trail to your left and wend through the brush until you reach the rocky shore. (Nearby Rockport was given its name for good reason.) If you're into exploring, you won't be alone; the rocks here are a popular hangout for cormorants and other shore birds.

Head back to the main trail and veer right to complete a loop of the quarry. You'll notice on your right a sign indicating the trail to the park headquarters, which happen to be housed in an old lighthouse. It is impressive in its simplicity—neither large nor small, new nor achingly old. Instead, it is what a New England lighthouse should be—a plain, functional clapboard structure rising to the light tower, solitary on a promontory overlooking the ocean.

Great Meadows Wildlife Refuge

From the Concord, take Rte. 62 east 1.8 miles to Monsen Rd. Turn left and continue to the entrance to the refuge, a dirt road that goes straight when Monsen Rd. makes a sharp right. ☎ **508/443-4661.**

Once you've experienced the hubbub of Walden Pond (see below), take a trip to nearby Great Meadow, just for the contrast. The pace of the fast-spinning world slows, and with each step you take, a greater peace seems to settle in. Cattails bow in the gentle breezes, the marsh grasses shimmer as if polished, the bloom of wildflowers (if you come at the correct time of year) is right out of a Monet painting.

Well, maybe Great Meadow isn't that glorious. There are problems even in this idyllic world. One of the most handsome among the wildflowers, purple loosestrife, is a non-native invader that refuge managers say is out of control, choking out native species. If this, however, is the most serious problem you must face each day, life must be pretty good.

The great "meadow" isn't really that at all; rather, it is a large wetland along the Concord River. The principal hiking path, the Dike Trail, is, however, quite properly named—a dike traversing the heart of the wetlands. It is short, less than 2 miles long as it crosses the wetlands and then circles back around the perimeter. Tread slowly and softly; this is popular birdwatching territory, and you wouldn't want to disturb the binoculars crowd. And Great Meadow is also as much about what you can hear as what you can see, with songbirds in abundance. If you do not spot a blue heron, consider yourself exceedingly unlucky, for this is their kind of country.

And it is proper to walk softly and slowly here because, simply, there is an aura of hallowed ground about Great Meadow. It is a special place.

Walden Pond Reservation

From Concord, take Rte. 126 south through the intersection with Rte. 2. The parking area for the pond is on your right. ☎ **978/369-3254.**

What was once the epicenter of naturalist spirituality has evolved into a hub of recreational activity. There is no retreating to the woods here to find inspiration or solitude, particularly on a hot summer day. The pond abounds with swimmers, canoeists, and kayakers, and none, it is probably fair to say, come with the same spiritual sensibilities that brought Henry

David Thoreau here. There is another drawback—a metal fence, constructed as part of an effort to restore pondside vegetation and habitat, lines the trail that loops the pond. The fence may be well meant, but it certainly detracts from the experience of walking in the footsteps of Thoreau.

Still, this is a pretty place; the walking is easy, and as you loop the pond, there are many breaks in the fence, and at the stone stairs leading to the water's edge, you can head to the water for a quick dip. You can take a trail that leads through the woods to the site of Thoreau's cabin. And if you come early in the morning or in the off-season, you might get at least a taste of the serenity that inspired Thoreau.

World's End
Allow 2 hours. Access: Take exit 14 from Rte. 3 and follow Rte. 228 north to the intersection with Rte. 3A. Turn left onto 3A for a mile, then right onto Summer St. for .3 miles. Cross Rockland St. to Martin's Lane and continue to the end. Map: Available at the tollhouse.

All around is the bustling seaport world: ferries to points all over Boston Harbor, busy marinas with private yachts and fishing charters, and the boatyards of Quincy and Hingham. In the midst of this is a tranquil patch of earth—a 250-acre peninsula jutting out into Hingham Bay. The main geographical feature of the peninsula is a kind of double drumlin that forms a sort of figure-eight connected by a neck of land.

Frederick Law Olmsted, the man who laid out New York's Central Park, originally (and literally) had designs on this place, but his elaborate scheme, including a planned community of 150 homes, was never realized. Instead, the land was left as farmland until the Trustees of Reservations acquired it in 1967.

The walk here is pretty straightforward (if such a thing can be said of a circular route). A 4-mile trail loops around the perimeter of the peninsula through thick trees and past rocky shores and sand beaches. From atop Planter's Hill, a

view of Boston Harbor with the city skyline as a backdrop unfolds. This alone might make World's End a neat place to spend an hour or two, but the real draw is that this retreat in the heart of a busily urbanized and industrialized world is here at all.

WHALE WATCHING
Stellwagen Bank, about 25 miles east of Boston, is a major feeding ground for whales. The 18-mile long bank, similar in appearance to a deep-water reef, attracts a wide variety of fish, as well as whales. Whale-watching tour operators boast that visitors have virtually a 100% chance of seeing whales on a 4- to 5-hour tour. Tours depart from Boston Harbor and Cape Ann from spring through fall. Among the reputable whale-watching operators, the **New England Aquarium** (Central Wharf, Boston, MA 02110; ☎ **617/973-5281** for reservations) runs tours from Rowe's Wharf near Logan Airport. **Captain Bill's Whale Watch** (30 Harbor Loop, Gloucester, MA 01930; ☎ **800/33WHALE** or 978/283-6995) runs tours out of Gloucester.

Campgrounds & Other Accommodations

CAMPGROUNDS
Boston Harbor Islands National Recreation Area
Island ferries leave from Hingham at 349 Lincoln St. (Rte. 3A). Ferries also leave from Long Wharf in Boston. ☎ **617/740-1605.** 41 sites on 4 islands. Primitive toilets, no fresh water.

Not so long ago, camping on the islands of Boston Harbor might have seemed less than a pleasant prospect. But with the impressive clean-up of the harbor and the ongoing effort to upgrade recreational opportunities on the islands, this has suddenly become a cool place to camp. Or places to camp—the sites are located on four islands: Bumpkin, Lovell, Grape, and Peddocks. Beaches, old ruins, and hiking through copses of wild berries are some of the campground's attractions.

Harold Parker State Forest

From the junction of I-95 and Rte. 114, take 114 northwest about 10 miles and look for signs to the forest. ☎ **508/686-3391.** 125 sites, no hookups. Fireplaces, tables, rest rooms, showers.

Relatively close to Boston, this campground within the hardwood forest feels more in-country than suburban. There are good mountain-biking and hiking trails within the forest, as well as a few small stocked ponds to keep fishermen entertained.

Myles Standish State Forest

From Rte. 3, take exit 5 and head west on Long Pond Rd. Look for signs to the forest entrance. ☎ **508/866-2526.** 475 sites in several campgrounds, no hookups. Handicapped rest rooms, showers, tables, fireplaces.

When you're talking 475 sites, you're usually not talking much privacy. But at least there is not one, massive campground; instead, camping areas are separated throughout the forest. The forest is heavily used by recreational enthusiasts, many of whom travel by off-road vehicles. But there is also room to roam here for horseback riders and mountain bikers. Plymouth, with its beaches and historic sites, is just a few minutes away.

Salisbury Beach State Reservation

From Salisbury, head 2 miles east on Rte. 1A. ☎ **508/462-4481.** 483 sites, 324 with full hookups. Handicapped rest room facilities, tables, grills.

On Salisbury Beach, a popular surf-and-sun spot north of Boston, this campground sees plenty of business in the summer. It is also a popular spot for people with boats. From here, it's a 7-mile sail to the Isles of Shoals, a string of small, rocky offshore islands.

Winter Island Park

From the junction of Derby St. and Fort Ave. in Salem, head northeast on Winter Island Rd. ☎ **508/745-9430.** 41 sites, 8 with hookups. Handicapped rest rooms, tables, grills, snack bar, boat launch.

This is a good base camp for sea kayakers interested in exploring the coves and harbors of the north shore from Salem to Marblehead. A fairly long open-water jaunt (about 6 miles) will also take you to Great Misery Island. For swimmers and surf-casters, the ocean beach is close.

INNS & RESORTS

Atlantis Oceanfront Motor Inn

125 Atlantic Rd., Gloucester, MA 01930; ☎ **978/283-0014.** Rooms in low season start at $80; in high season, at $120. 3-night minimum during high season. Closed Nov to mid-Apr.

The stunning views from every window of this motor inn across the street from the water on Cape Ann would be enough to recommend it, so the heated outdoor pool is icing on the cake. The good-sized guest rooms are comfortable and every one of them has a terrace or balcony.

Emerson Inn by the Sea

Phillips Ave., Pigeon Cove, MA 01966; ☎ **508/546-6321.** Double rooms start at $95, with breakfast included.

This is the archetypal summer hotel of the pre-World-War-II era. Large porches overlook manicured lawns that reach down to the rocky shore. It is easy to imagine it as the setting for a movie of the thirties, with men dressed in seersucker suits wandering through the spacious, airy lobby. A highlight of the inn is a small saltwater pool, elevated enough to afford a sweeping view of the sea.

Governor Bradford on the Harbour

98 Water St., Plymouth, MA 02360; ☎ **800/332-1620** or 508/746-6200; www.governorbradford.com. Double rooms start around $100 during summer.

Life for the Pilgrims would have been much easier if this inn had been around when they landed on Plymouth Rock in 1620; the inn is just a block from the rock. Accommodations are in fairly standard motel-style rooms, but they're clean and pleasant, and if the Plymouth area is the focus of your travels, it's hard to beat the location.

Clark Currier Inn

45 Green St., Newburyport, MA 01950; ☎ **800/360-6582** or 978/465-8363. Double rooms start at $75.

Newburyport is a neat place. Once a thriving seaport, it lost its way in the early part of the 20th century, falling into disrepair. But in recent years it has made a remarkable showcase of restoration. The heart of downtown Newburyport is almost movie-set perfect, with its 18th- and 19th-century brick buildings and cobblestone streets reaching toward the harbor on the Merrimack River. Surrounding the downtown core are elegant clapboard homes in which Newburyport's wealthy elite once lived during the city's heyday. The Clark Currier Inn is just such a home, built in 1803, and recently renovated as a bed-and-breakfast. In it you'll find all the ingredients of a fine New England inn—canopy beds, antique furnishings, rocking chairs, and beautifully crafted fireplaces that alas, because of strict city codes prohibiting fires, must go unused. Explore the city from the inn, then head out to nearby attractions—the beaches of Plum Island, Parker River National Wildlife Refuge, Maudslay State Park, and the Merrimack River.

Chapter 5

Cape Cod, Martha's Vineyard & Nantucket

What person who has grown up anywhere near the water does not have an enduring childhood memory of the beach? My own memory is of being 5 years old on the rocky shores of the Cape along Buzzards Bay. Waves pushed in by the prevailing summer winds from the southwest would wash up treasures on the rocks—opaque, colored shards of sea glass, shells, and trinkets lost or discarded overboard from boats at sea. All were great discoveries in a 5-year-old's world, and to me that image of the beach remains a vital vision of what the Cape is all about.

But it is only my personal take, only one of the Cape's many personalities squeezed together on one very small patch of sandy turf—or three patches, if you include the outlying islands of Martha's Vineyard and Nantucket. The dunes of Truro and Provincetown may be the Cape's most exotic physical feature, but there is much more to the Cape and the islands than that. There are the many kettle ponds—some say they number 365, or one for every day of the year, although more than 500 is a better estimate—that are the freshwater remnants of glacial recession. There are the inland forests of scrub oak and pine, all gnarled and wind-battered, with a distinctive aroma that can summarily bring me back to being young again.

There are the islands of Monomoy National Wildlife Refuge, spectacular strips of desolate barrier-island beach that probably constitute the last, true wilderness in southern New England. Then there are the many harbors and inlets that pock the shoreline—Hyannis Harbor, Edgartown Harbor, Hadley's Harbor, Wings Neck Harbor, and the Bass River, all well traveled by everything from Boston Whalers to great sailing yachts cruising up and down the New England coast.

It is an ever-changing landscape, both in geographic terms and in terms of human settlement. The sands shift and the shoreline erodes, and the Cape and the islands a few hundred years hence will likely leave a different print on the map than they do today. Small islands and beaches have already been swallowed up, while others have emerged. As I walk the southern beaches of Martha's Vineyard, for example, I can readily imagine how easy it would be for a heavy storm to crash through the sandy barrier of the beach to join the fragile, protected coastal ponds with the sea.

The changes brought on by human settlement, however, are more immediate and in some ways more alarming. The Cape and the islands are becoming more populated, not only by year-round residents, but by summer visitors as well. The combined factors of retirement, increased leisure time, and the decentralization of some industries (thanks largely to computers and mobile communications) have enabled more people to set up more-or-less permanent shop on the Cape. A drive from Falmouth to Hyannis on Route 28 tells the story: outlet-store clusters, retirement communities, restaurants with names like the Skipper's Table and the Sea Shanty (decorated with the obligatory fishing nets and buoys), car repair shops, and malls. It is very built up, and, depending on your tastes regarding such matters, it is probably not a pretty sight.

Meanwhile, the Cape and the islands remain as hot as ever as vacation spots. The year-round population of Edgartown, for example, is less than 4,000, while the summer population exceeds 35,000. One of those 35,000-plus in recent years, of course, has been Bill Clinton, whose presence helped to focus the national spotlight on Martha's Vineyard as a vacation destination.

It probably goes without saying, then, that this can make the Cape and the islands extremely crowded places from May through September. And so they are. Yet there are many ways in which the crowds end up becoming dispersed. Mile after mile of broad, sandy beach provides plenty of space for humanity to spread out. Beyond that is the allure of the sea; it is impossible to make any fair estimate on the number of boats of all manner of propulsion—sail, motor, oar, paddle—at sea on the waters of Cape Cod and Buzzard's bays and on Vineyard and Nantucket sounds. A great many is a reasonable if imprecise guess.

In addition, there may be no region in the country where dedicated bike paths have been given such high priority and been so fully developed. The bicycle, both as a means of transportation and recreation—and thus as a means of escaping traffic-congested roadways—is an honored and respected device on the Cape and the islands. When traffic is bumper-to-bumper on major routes—6, 6A, 28—the opportunity to escape the congestion is omnipresent.

The quick-and-easy motel is a Cape staple, as it is in many seaside regions. But given that settlers made their way here well over 300 years ago, this is one of the great regions in America to get lost in the mist of history at some centuries-old inn. The world of crowded highways and modern amenities can be almost instantaneously displaced by old whaling stories and talk of ghosts, amid architectural details imbued with the spirit of an era long gone.

Finally, there is Cape Cod National Seashore, the only tract of land in southern New England graced with national park status. Actually, *tracts* of land would be more accurate. The national seashore designation came in 1961, more than 300 years after human settlers set up shop, so the national seashore lands are interspersed with privately held property. Still, given the way development has boomed elsewhere on the Cape in the past 25 years, it is sobering to imagine what the landscape might have looked like had the federal government not stepped in. As it is, the dunes, the beaches, the low-slung forests, the ponds, the marshlands, the drumlins, and the small islands are all evidence of what a stunning natural environment the Cape can be.

It is the sort of environment that awed the likes of Henry David Thoreau, who wrote in his treatise, *Cape Cod*: "We were traversing a desert, with the view of an autumnal landscape of extraordinary brilliancy, a sort of Promised Land, on the one hand, and the ocean on the other . . . The solitude was that of the ocean and the desert combined. A thousand men could not have seriously interrupted it, but would have been lost in the vastness of the scenery as their footsteps in the sand."

His memory of the beach is quite different, of course, from my own childhood memories. But what is inspiring to me, after the many years that have passed since both Thoreau's writing and my experience on Buzzard's Bay, is that both Thoreau's Cape and mine can still be found.

Another memory of mine worth dredging up comes from the early '70s. I had arrived by boat on Cuttyhunk, the tiny island at the end of the Elizabeth chain extending southwestward from the

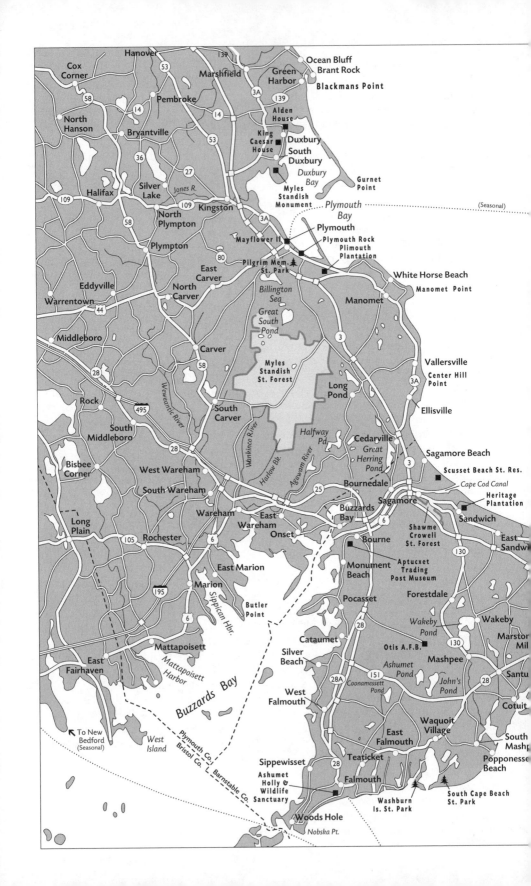

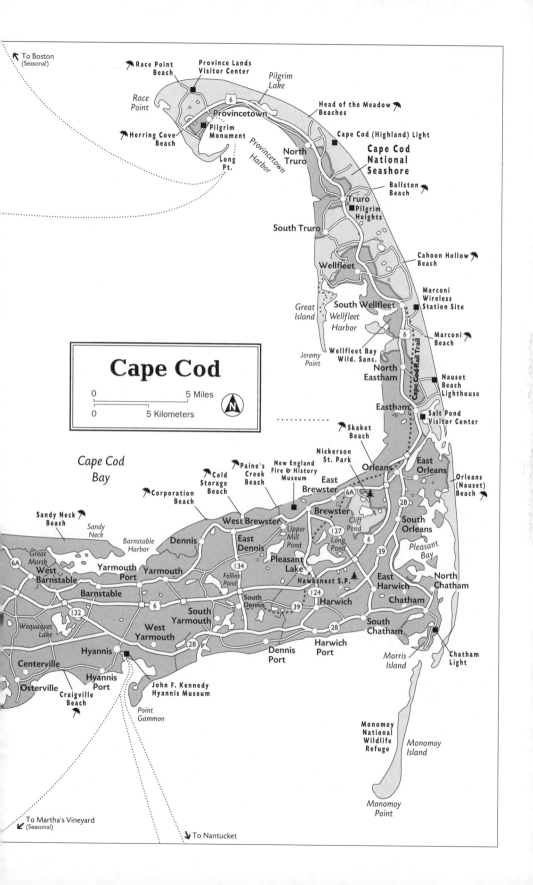

Cape. There was barely a town—only a few houses—and just a few lobstermen and their boats populating the harbor. It was early May and still cold on the water. On a hand-cranked phone, I called home to learn that I had been accepted in college. Today the hand-cranked phone is gone, but I'm happy to report that in most other ways, Cuttyhunk has hardly changed. The lesson I learned: Development might continue and the summer throngs might come, but a wild, rugged, and untouched Cape still remains to be discovered.

The Lay of the Land

Sand, sand, and more sand, eventually giving way to the sea—that, in a nutshell, is what the landscape of the Cape and the islands is all about. Sand and sea are the fundamental constituents of the environment even where that might not seem to be so. The inland forests, for example, are almost entirely scrub oak and pine, and the trees rarely reach heights of greater than 50 feet. There are two reasons for this. First, given the sandy, acidic nature of the soil, these are the only kind of trees that can thrive. Second, the harsh, saline air that blows in off the water discourages trees from growing very large.

Dunes are often thought of as the most recognizable physical feature of the Cape and the islands, and rightfully so. Dunes that reach heights of up to 100 feet are the defining elements of the landscape from Wellfleet north to Provincetown, on Sandy Neck north of Barnstable, on the Monomoy islands, and on the southern and eastern shorelines of Martha's Vineyard and Nantucket.

Of course, there is more to the Cape and the islands than this Saharan environment. Typically the dunes form a barrier protecting inland marshes and coastal ponds—most with a high saline content—

from the sea. Aesthetically and ecologically, these marshes are every bit as spectacular as the dunes that protect them. Bring your camera to Nauset Marsh in Eastham, the Great Marshes in Barnstable, or Poca Pond on Martha's Vineyard, and you will be sure to be rewarded. The morning mist hanging over the marsh grasses and illuminated by the rising sun is certainly one of the great sights to see on the Cape and the islands.

From an ecological perspective, the marshes and ponds are also great incubators of life. Shellfish, crabs, herring, eels, and turtles all breed in the marsh water and muck, attracting in the process an extraordinary array of bird life. Ospreys, herons, egrets, cormorants (and in late fall and winter, the rare bald eagle)—all the great fishing birds of the east—congregate on the marshes like patrons packing a popular restaurant.

Like almost all of New England's geographical features, the Cape and the islands were carved out about 12,000 years ago by the last great glacial recession. In essence, the Cape forms what geologists would call a *terminal moraine,* a final deposition of rock, silt, sand, and soil. The grinding of glacial movement and the battering effects of the sea are primarily responsible for the sandy soil, although rocky, boulder-strewn terrain, most notably on the southwestern shores (such as Buzzard's Bay), can also be found.

As the glacier receded, it left behind a pockmarked landscape in which fresh water settled. The Cape's hundreds of "kettle" ponds are the result, and now act, in effect, like giant cisterns in gathering rainwater. While not unique to the Cape, these ponds add an inland ecological diversity that is, in terms of flora and fauna, quite different from that found in and around the brackish ponds close to the coast.

The glacier is of course long gone, but storms and the ocean continue to reshape the land. The soft soils are easily eroded,

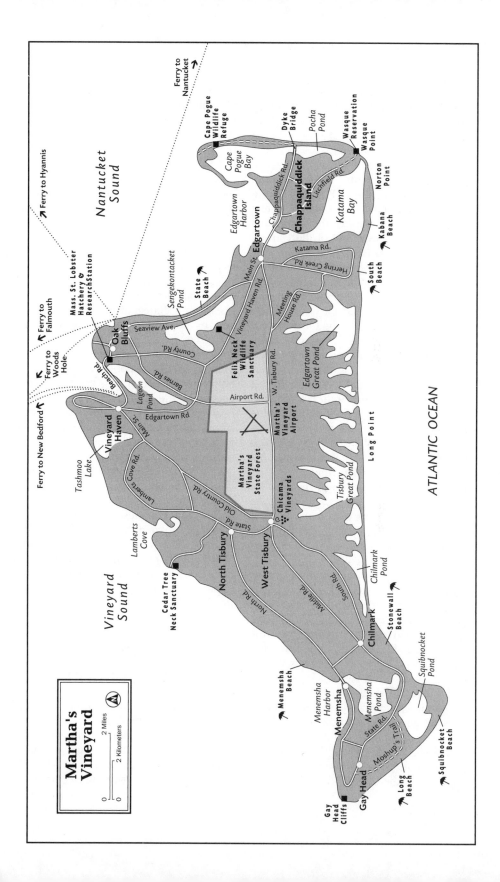

sometimes spectacularly so. The cliffs of Gay Head on Martha's Vineyard, and similar cliffs that rise over Nauset Beach on the Cape, are dramatic examples of an eroding shoreline, as clay and soft soils continue to be pared away. And while some land is lost to the sea by erosion, other land is reclaimed. For example, a narrow neck of land now connects Great Island near Wellfleet to the mainland, closing off the direct flow of the Herring River to Cape Cod Bay.

As the early settlers discovered, this is not a great place to attempt to farm. For the most part, the soil is too acidic and the air too saline. This is what the settlers who came to the north end of the Cape—to the Province Lands near Provincetown—in the 1600s discovered. Encountering dense forests, they proceeded to do what settlers did in those days; they immediately set about clearing the land for their homes and farms. Unfortunately, this proved not to be the kind of environment that would succumb to the will of these people. Crops wouldn't grow, and the land would not recover. The sandy soil in which the forests had somehow managed, over many years, to take root, asserted itself, urged on by the harsh weather blowing in from the sea. The settlers moved on, leaving behind land that would redefine itself as a world of windswept dunes.

What does grow well in this kind of environment are heaths—low-lying bushy plants that can adapt to the acidic soil conditions and remain, while close to the ground, relatively protected from the wind. Wild blueberries, huckleberries, beach roses, bayberry bushes, dune grasses, and wildflowers decorate the land where the sandy dunes give way to more solid ground. And settlers did eventually hit upon one crop that could thrive in this environment. Cranberries, which flourish in boggy areas, have over the years become perhaps the most important cash crop of the Cape and the islands.

Warm summers cooled by sea breezes and mild winters characterize the climate of the region. The mean temperature in July is 70°F, while the mean January temperature is 32°F. The more southerly parts of the region, particularly Martha's Vineyard and Nantucket, are affected by the relative proximity of the Gulf Stream, which brings warm winds and ocean waters up from the south. As a result, the air and water temperature, even in September and early October, can be fairly pleasant. Not so to the north, which is shielded from the Gulf Stream. Even in midsummer, water temperatures in the ocean off Wellfleet, Truro, Provincetown, and in Cape Cod Bay struggle to get above 60°.

The wildlife of the region is fairly modest—foxes, raccoons, and deer are at home in the forests, but don't expect to encounter the larger mammals (such as bear and moose) that you might come across elsewhere in New England. If you're looking for big mammals, head offshore; whale watching is a major activity during the summer months, and of course whaling played a vital part in the history of the region. Birds, however, find the ponds, salt marshes, and moors of the area much to their liking. Close to 300 different species have been sighted on the Monomoy islands alone. If you are a bird or a human lover of sand and sea, the Cape and the islands are something near to a paradise.

Orientation

Most people who come to the Cape traverse the Cape Cod Canal via one of two bridges. **Bourne Bridge** to the west connects with Route 28, which continues southward to **Falmouth** and **Woods Hole.** Those who plan to continue on

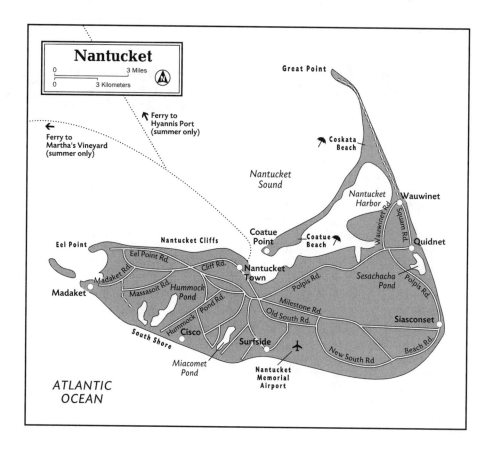

Nantucket

0   3 Miles
0   3 Kilometers

Great Point

Ferry to
Hyannis Port
(summer only)

Ferry to
Martha's Vineyard
(summer only)

Coskata
Beach

Nantucket
Sound

Nantucket
Harbor

Wauwinet

Eel Point

Nantucket Cliffs

Coatue
Point

Coatue
Beach

Wauwinet Rd.

Squam Rd.

Quidnet

Eel Point Rd.

Cliff Rd.

Nantucket
Town

Madaket Rd.

Polpis Rd.

Sesachacha
Pond

Polpis Rd.

Madaket

Massasoit Rd.

Hummock
Pond

Pond Rd.

Milestone Rd.

Old South Rd.

Siasconset

South Shore

Hummock Pond Rd.

Cisco

Surfside

New South Rd

Beach Rd.

Miacomet
Pond

Nantucket
Memorial
Airport

ATLANTIC
OCEAN

to **Martha's Vineyard** or **Nantucket** usually opt for this bridge. To the east is Sagamore Bridge, the connector between Route 3 from Boston and Route 6, the Cape's main drag. This is the bridge most people use if they're planning to head eastward to the heart of the Cape and onward to **Chatham, Wellfleet,** and **Provincetown.** If you happen to have time in your travels, you might want to make a quick side trip to **Sandwich,** with its handsome historic district, just across the Sagamore Bridge.

Whichever bridge makes more sense for your travels, expect to encounter a traffic jam if you arrive late Friday afternoon or evening. The traffic scenario over the bridges is comparable to sands squeezing through the neck of an hourglass. At other times, however—and any time between October and May—traffic flows relatively smoothly over the bridges. If you're headed for

Provincetown and want to avoid the bridges, there is an option. **Bay State Cruises (☎ 617/723-7800)** runs a ferry between Boston and Provincetown during the summer months.

Local references to the subregions of the Cape can be a bit confusing. The "lower Cape" refers to the forearm, or the Cape extending from Chatham to Provincetown. Meanwhile, the "upper Cape" refers to the Cape west of Chatham, even if the upper Cape appears to be lower than the lower Cape. Fortunately, references to the mid-Cape, meaning the region approximately surrounding **Hyannis,** are relatively unambiguous. Also somewhat less confusing are the terms "inner" and "outer" Cape, the former referring to the Cape west of Chatham, the latter referring to the Cape north of Brewster.

The Cape's commercial and transportation hub is Hyannis; its airport is the

RESERVATIONS POLICY FOR CAR PASSAGE TO MARTHA'S VINEYARD

Vehicle reservations are required to bring your car to Martha's Vineyard on Friday, Saturday, Sunday, and Monday from mid-June to mid-September. During these times, standby is in effect only on Tuesday, Wednesday, and Thursday. Vehicle reservations are required to bring your car to Martha's Vineyard on Memorial Day weekend, too. There is no standby service available during these dates. Although, technically, reservations can be made up to 1 hour in advance of ferry departure, ferries in season are almost always full, and you cannot depend on a cancellation during the summer months. Also be aware that your space could be forfeited if you have not checked into the ferry terminal 30 minutes before sailing time. Reservations can be changed to another date and time with at least 24 hours' notice; otherwise, you have to pay for an additional ticket for your vehicle.

If you arrive without a reservation on a day that allows standby, come early and be prepared to wait in the standby line for hours. The Steamship Authority guarantees your passage if you're in line by 2pm on designated standby days only. For up-to-date **Steamship Authority** information, check out its Web site (**www.islandferry.com**).

only one on the Cape open to commercial flights. Don't come to Hyannis expecting a quaint or quiet Cape getaway; even during the off-season, Hyannis is a focal point of Cape activity. But venture not too far from Hyannis—to **Hyannisport,** made famous by the Kennedys, or eastward to **Dennis,** or north to **Sandwich**—and you'll find a more relaxed Cape that evokes much of the region's history, character, and traditions.

After the bend in the elbow, you pass first through **Orleans** as you head northward toward Provincetown. After Orleans, the presence of **Cape Cod National Seashore** begins to assert itself. Signs of commercialism dwindle as Route 6 passes through **Eastham, Wellfleet, Truro,** and finally **Provincetown.** There is still the occasional clam shack, drive-in movie theater, or budget motel, but the national seashore designation has helped to prevent the kind of developmental sprawl that characterizes Hyannis and Falmouth. That said, there may be no community in Massachusetts more devoted to attracting the tourist dollar than Provincetown, with its restaurants, galleries, saltwater-taffy shops, and souvenir stands.

It is possible to fly to Martha's Vineyard or Nantucket, and for a quick weekend getaway, that's probably not a bad, if expensive, way to go. Yet most people make their way to the islands via ferry. The **Woods Hole Steamship Authority** (☎ 508/477-8600) runs ferries throughout the year to and from **Vineyard Haven** and **Nantucket Town,** and is the ferry service most people use. However, ferries also run from Hyannis and New Bedford. The ride from Woods Hole to Vineyard Haven takes about 45 minutes; from Woods Hole to Nantucket is about a 2¹/₂-hour ride.

Both the Vineyard and Nantucket are small enough that a car, for the most part, is not only unnecessary, but is in some cases a possible inconvenience. Taxis, buses, and rental bikes make getting around the relatively small islands easy, and you'll save the considerable cost of ferrying your car back and forth. If you do need to bring the car, make sure you've got a ferry reservation (see "Reservations Policy for Car Passage to Martha's Vineyard," above for more information).

On the Vineyard, the first point of entry is usually Vineyard Haven, where most ferries arrive, or nearby **Oak Bluffs,** famous for its tiny and colorful gingerbread cottages, the leftovers from a religious-revival period of the previous century. However, Edgartown, on the east end of the island, is where many visitors prefer to set up camp. With its many inns, restaurants, and shops, and with its historical roots exposed and its harbor resplendently filled with great sailing yachts, Edgartown is quintessential Martha's Vineyard. To the west, toward **Gay Head,** the island becomes increasingly rural, typified by the small fishing village of **Menemsha.**

Nantucket is about half the size of the Vineyard and, being somewhat harder to reach, is less developed. Nantucket Town, where ferries arrive, is the only settlement of any significant size on the island. Otherwise, Nantucket is occupied mostly by beaches, dunes, and scattered summer homes.

Parks & Other Hot Spots

CAPE COD

Cape Cod National Seashore

The Salt Pond Visitors' Center (☎ 508/255-3421) is located at the intersection of Rte. 6 and Nauset Rd., north of Eastham. There is also a visitors' center for the Province Lands in Provincetown (☎ 508/487-1256). Headquarters: Box 250, South Wellfleet, MA 02663; ☎ 508/349-3785.

The total acreage of this protected area is approximately 43,000, although with the shifting tides and shorelines, that figure is a guess at best. The actual seashore—the eastern shore along the ocean—extends for roughly 40 miles, from Provincetown southward to Chatham. Dunes, sand, and clay bluffs as high as 175 feet and broad, flat beaches are the national seashore's principal features. Between Truro and

Eastham, there are 11 officially designated beaches monitored by lifeguards during the summer months, with the most popular being **Coast Guard Beach, Nauset Light Beach,** and **Nauset Beach.** (Many of the beaches are managed by local towns rather than the National Park Service.)

For beachgoers seeking a true getaway, there are the roughly 8 miles of Nauset Beach that extending southward from Orleans Beach to Chatham. Seclusion might seem an unlikely prospect upon arrival. Where Beach Road out of Orleans meets the beach is one of the livelier sun-and-surf scenes on the Cape. But start walking south and the crowds dwindle, and pretty soon you'll have the beach pretty much to yourself.

Those seeking the dunes for which the Cape is so famous should head north to the **Province Lands** near Provincetown. There is so much sand here it is not uncommon for drifts to form across Route 6 on particularly windy days. Miles of hiking and biking trails wind through the dunes, and if you want to scramble off-trail, be prepared for a workout; the soft sand does not make for easy going. At the northern end of the Province Lands is **Race Point Beach** at the Cape's northernmost point.

The national seashore, however, is about more than just the seashore in the strict sense of the word. **Great Island,** extending southward between Cape Cod Bay and Wellfleet Harbor, features perhaps the best hiking trails on the Cape. To the south in Eastham, **Salt Pond** and **Nauset Marsh** are features of a large wetland area that is a prime location for bird-watching.

Cape Cod Rail Trail

The southern terminus of the trail is off Rte. 134, .5 mile south of Rte. 6 in South Dennis. The northern terminus is off Rte. 6 at Lecount Hollow Rd. in Wellfleet. There are numerous other access points in between. Information: ☎ 508/896-3491.

The 25-mile trail, which follows a rail line abandoned in 1965, is the king of bike paths in a region well endowed with them. It is, however, more than just a bike path. Passing inland through Dennis, Brewster, Orleans, Eastham, and Wellfleet, the trail in summer is popular with all sorts of non-motorized travelers—cyclists, in-line skaters, horseback riders, and walkers. The trail also connects with bike paths in Nickerson State Park and Cape Cod National Seashore.

Monomoy National Wildlife Refuge

Accessible only by boat. Monomoy is made up of two islands and a small portion of the mainland, south of Chatham. Headquarters: Morris Island (☎ 508/945-0594).

Two islands, combining for roughly 2,700 acres, form perhaps the last true wilderness in southern New England. In fact, the refuge was officially designated a wilderness area in 1970, the only one of its kind in the region. The wilderness character of the islands is ensured by their limited accessibility. The islands can be reached only by private and chartered boats, meaning that even on a busy day, only a handful of visitors actually come ashore. The refuge is truly a birders' paradise, where as many as 60 species nest during the summer. Harbor seals also frequent the waters offshore. If you don't have your own boat, trips to the island can be arranged through the Wellfleet Bay Wildlife Sanctuary or the Cape Cod Museum of Natural History.

Nickerson State Park

From Brewster, take Rte. 6A east and look for the entrance to the park on your right. Or take exit 12 from Rte. 6 and head west on Rte. 6A to the park entrance. Headquarters: Brewster (☎ 508/896-3491).

At 1,900 acres, Nickerson State Park is a fairly large tract of undeveloped public land on the Cape, where undeveloped public land (outside the boundaries of Cape Cod National Seashore) is a hard find. Undeveloped, however, does not mean unused. The park includes 420 campsites, and if you are able to secure one on a summer weekend, it will likely be a hard-won prize. For campers, this is *the* place to stay on the Cape. Within the park boundaries are eight kettle ponds for canoeing, fishing, and swimming. There are also trails for biking and hiking that connect with the Cape Cod Rail Trail.

Sandy Neck & the Great Marshes

From Barnstable, take Rte. 6A west to Sandy Neck Rd., on your right. Look for the sign to Sandy Neck Beach. Boat access is also possible from Barnstable Harbor. Information: ☎ 508/790-6200.

Sandy Neck is an appropriately named 6-mile strip of sand that extends eastward between Barnstable Harbor and Cape Cod Bay. If you thought dunes on Cape Cod were found exclusively around Truro and Provincetown, you're in for a surprise here. The dunes of Sandy Neck, which can reach heights of 100 feet, are a worthy rival of their counterparts at the end of the Cape. Sandy Neck Beach is a popular place in summer for swimming and surf-casting, and shell-hunters willing to wander along the water's edge are likely to be rewarded.

This is a good place for hiking along the beach and through the dunes, but be forewarned on two counts. First, there is the lack of shade and fresh water; in summer, the heat reflected from the abundance of sand can be oppressive and dehydrating. Second is the fact that the neck is open to off-road vehicles, which can disrupt what might otherwise be a relatively placid seaside stroll.

The Great Marshes protected by Sandy Neck combine for about 4,000 acres, making it the largest living salt marsh in New England. The marsh is an active habitat for a rich variety of species, including birds (herons, marsh hawks, warblers, and others), mammals (foxes, raccoons), and shellfish (hermit crabs and fiddler crabs). Come in fall, when the neck and marsh swarm with migrating monarch butterflies.

Wellfleet Bay Wildlife Sanctuary

The sanctuary entrance is off Rte. 6 at the junction with West Rd. in Wellfleet. Headquarters: South Wellfleet (☎ 508/349-2615).

This 1,000-acre sanctuary is a microcosm of the inland Cape environment. Salt marsh covers more than 430 acres; otherwise, pine forests that have an undergrowth of bayberry, beach plum, honeysuckle, and huckleberry are the predominant feature, along with meadows, freshwater ponds, and tidal pools. This is a magnificent setting for birdwatching, and about 250 species have been sighted here. There are about 5 miles of hiking trails, and in summer, guided walks and canoe outings are offered.

MARTHA'S VINEYARD

Chappaquiddick Island

In Edgartown, follow signs to the Chappaquiddick (or "Chappy") ferry, which leaves from the end of Kelly St. The ferry ride takes about 2 minutes. Cape Poge Wildlife Refuge, Wasque Reservation, and Mytoi Garden are all managed by the Trustees of Reservations (☎ 508/921-1944).

Poor Chappaquiddick. The mere mention of its name raises the specter of Ted Kennedy's tragic episode in 1969, and the memory of that watershed event in American political life is likely to be a burden Chappaquiddick will bear forever. The famous bridge that led to the death of Mary Jo Kopechne—and Ted Kennedy's presidential aspirations—is almost invariably the sight first-time visitors want to see. Overshadowed by such nonsense are Chappaquiddick's real treasures: the Cape Poge Wildlife Refuge, Wasque Reservation, and Mytoi Garden. This is the wild side of the Vineyard, despite its proximity to bustling Edgartown; most beachgoers

head to South Beach rather than bother with the extra time and expense of riding the ferry to get to Chappaquiddick's East Beach.

The Cape Poge Wildlife Refuge is a 6-mile barrier strip protecting Cape Poge Bay from the sea. Beach, dunes, tidal flats—this is everything a barrier beach is supposed to be. To the south, Wasque Reservation is a mass of wild marshland, beach, tidal pools, and low sandy cliffs. Mytoi is a 14-acre cultivated Japanese garden—not wild, of course, as are Cape Poge or Wasque, but a special place nonetheless. Birding, canoeing on Pocha Pond, swimming, and just walking along the beach are all highlights of a visit to the place local folk simply call "Chappy."

Gay Head Cliffs

From Vineyard Haven, take State Rd. to West Tisbury, then take Middle Rd. to State Rd. in Chilmark, following signs to Gay Head all the way.

Also known as Aquinnah, a Native American word for "land beneath the hill," Gay Head is Martha's Vineyard's most famous natural feature, and rightfully so. The cliffs of Gay Head on the Vineyard's westernmost extremity tumble to the beach and the sea in layers of multicolored limestone. The cliffs are a popular tourist attraction; if you time your visit incorrectly, the parking area is inundated with tour buses, and the sale of T-shirts and shell trinkets from the souvenir shops near the top of the cliffs is extraordinarily brisk. There are two ways to avoid the tourist crush. Walk down to the beach, from which the view of the cliffs is better anyway, and the crowds disappear quickly. Or come early in the morning or late in the evening, the preferred time for photographers seeking to capture the low sunlight illuminating the cliffs' subtle gradation of colors.

Martha's Vineyard State Forest

From Vineyard Haven, take Edgartown Rd. south and turn right at the blinking light onto Airport Rd. Forest headquarters are located on the left side. Headquarters: Edgartown (☎ **508/693-2540**).

Also known as Manuel F. Correllus State Forest, this 4,300-acre forest is the largest tract of undeveloped land on the island. Or almost undeveloped, given that the island's main airport sits in the heart of the woods. Mountain biking and horse-back riding, on the roads and trails that crisscross the forest in a grid pattern, are the most popular activities here. Pine woods, sandy soil, and open meadows are its main physical features. You come here not necessarily to be wowed by spectacular countryside, but instead to appreciate the sort of woodsy solitude that is otherwise hard to come by on the island.

NANTUCKET

Coatue and Coskata-Coatue Wildlife Refuges

From Nantucket Town, take Milestone Rd. and turn left onto Polpis Rd., then left again onto Wauwinet Rd. to the Wauwinet gatehouse. For information, contact the **Nantucket Conservation Foundation** (118 Cliff Rd., Nantucket; ☎ **508/228-2884**).

These barrier beaches, attached to the northeastern edge of the island like two giant, swept-back wings, constitute Nantucket in its wildest form. The charac-teristic features of barrier lands are all here: dunes, salt marshes, trees stunted by the salt air and wind, and over 20 miles of beaches. Exploring this area is not easy. You must do so on foot, which can be hot and cumbersome in the shifting sands, or with a four-wheel-drive vehicle, properly prepared (with tires deflated) to drive in soft sand. If you want to get away from it all on Nantucket—to walk the beach, to surf-cast, to watch for birds—this is the place to come.

Sanford Farm, Ram Pasture, and the Woods

From Nantucket Town, take Madaket Rd. 2 miles west. For information, contact

the **Nantucket Conservation Foundation** (118 Cliff Rd., Nantucket; ☎ **508/228-2884**).

Sanford Farm was the site of Nantucket's original Colonial settlement, while Ram Pasture and the Woods were used for grazing livestock. If you're looking to do any kind of hiking on Nantucket—other than walking on the beach—this is the place to come. Over 6 miles of trails wind through forest, swamp, and, of course, former pastureland, all reaching to the edge of the ocean. Look for pheasants, hawks, and osprey as you wander about the well-marked trail system.

What to Do & Where to Do It

BIRD-WATCHING

Any time you enter a region blessed with such a variety of microenvironments, you can count on a great wealth of birding opportunities. Shore birds—terns, gulls, pipers, etc.—are attracted to the many miles of shoreline that grace the Cape and the islands. Marshes and tidal wetlands attract fishing birds, such as ospreys and marsh hawks. Songbirds congregate in inland forests, moors, and meadows. Wild berry bushes and beach roses attract birds of all sorts. Large ponds, both freshwater and brackish, attract migrating waterfowl. And so on. A Cape bird listing would include roughly 300 species, from tiny hummingbirds to bald eagles, and the actual number might exceed that. There are many reasons to visit the Cape and the islands, but bird-watching ought to be foremost among them.

Another bonus for Cape bird watchers is the substantial tidal change that for part of the day can turn complete bays and harbors into muddy flats that are the equivalent of a set table for birds, who come and feed on stranded fish, crabs, and other organisms. Wandering around on such tidal flats, of course, calls for caution. When the tide moves back in, it can do so with surprising speed. If you're fixated on spotting some rare species through your binoculars and aren't watching the tides, you might find yourself swimming back to shore.

So in this realm of great abundance, where to go? There are multiple answers to that question, and the suggestions here are no more than that—suggestions. **Wellfleet Audubon Sanctuary,** with its mix of forest and wetlands, is a great place to spot shorebirds and waterfowl as well as songbirds. **Nauset Marsh,** just inland from Nauset Beach, is another good place to watch for shorebirds and waterfowl. This can be particularly rewarding on windy days, when birds like to hunker down in the marsh grasses. The same goes for the **Great Marshes,** which are also popular among herons and egrets.

Brewster Flats, north of Route 6A, can be a great place for spotting droves of sandpipers and oystercatchers, feeding off the exposed tidal flats. The same goes for parts of **Wellfleet Harbor.**

On Martha's Vineyard, head inland to **Cedar Tree Neck Sanctuary,** facing Vineyard Sound in North Tisbury, if you're interested in woodland species. Or head toward the shore, to **Long Point Refuge** off West Tisbury Road, if shorebirds are your prime interest. But perhaps the best places for bird-watching on the Vineyard are **Cape Poge** and **Wasque Reservation** on Chappaquiddick Island. Several species, in particular terns and plovers, use the east-facing dunes and beaches of Chappaquiddick for nesting in the summer.

Coatue and Coskata-Coatue Wildlife Refuges on Nantucket are also good places to spot nesting shorebirds, but you should be prepared to work for the opportunity. If you don't have a sand-ready four-wheel-drive vehicle, the walk from the refuge gateway to Great Point is about 6 miles. There are osprey poles at Ram Pasture to provide those most athletic

of fishing birds a perch from which to spot their prey. If you want to check out ospreys in action, this is probably the best place to go on Nantucket. Windswept Cranberry Bog, off Polpis Road on the way to Quidnet, is a good place to go look for waterfowl.

Monomoy National Wildlife Refuge

Accessible only by private or chartered boat. Headquarters: Morris Island (☎ 508/945-0594). Island tours are arranged by the **Wellfleet Bay Wildlife Sanctuary** (☎ 508/349-2615), or the **Cape Cod Museum of Natural History** in Brewster (☎ 508/896-3867).

If you were a bird flying around the neighborhood, you'd have a hard time passing up the Monomoy islands. There are tidal flats rich in food, dunes for nesting, sufficient woods for shelter from inclement weather—it's an avian dreamland. On top of that, there are almost no human beings to bother you. If you were a bird, you would definitely want to spend time on the Monomoy islands.

And indeed, this is one of the great spots along the East Coast of the United States to come to see shorebirds, as well as migrant waterfowl and raptors. Brave the cold of the off-season, and you stand a reasonable chance of spotting bald eagles making their way south for the winter. Yet, certainly the time when most people come—and when both the Cape Cod Museum of Natural History and the Wellfleet Bay Wildlife Sanctuary lead trips to the islands—is in the summertime. You might not see bald eagles, but you will not be disappointed.

As islands go, North and South Monomoy are barely adolescents. It was not long ago that they were fully attached to the mainland of the Cape. But in 1958, a powerful storm steamrolled through a narrow barrier beach, cutting off Monomoy from the mainland. Twenty years later, rough weather carved out a second channel, and a single island become two.

None of this seems to make a great deal of difference to the many birds that come here, except that humans, who cannot walk on water, are unable to come here other than by boat. For such a relatively small bit of land—2,700 acres, give or take a few acres depending on the tides and beach erosion—the variety of bird life is quite remarkable. The last count listed 285 species that had been spotted on the islands, and something on the order of 60 species nest here.

So rich, in fact, is the birdlife of Monomoy that people began coming here in the 1800s to appreciate it. Not all came with gentle intention; there were hunters among them in those days. But there were well-meaning naturalists too, whose records now provide century-old details of the comings and goings of various species on the islands. One well-known ornithologist, Ludlow Griscom, made over 300 trips to Monomoy.

The bird life of the two islands can be quite different. North Monomoy is favored by nesting birds in summer, among them plovers, terns, skinners, gulls, and herons. As fall migrations begin, activity on South Monomoy tends to pick up, as waterfowl of all sorts pass through the area. Yet both islands throughout the year teem with bird life, with species nesting, migrating, or just hanging out.

Gear

The Bird Watcher's General Store (36 Rte. 6A, Orleans; ☎ **800/562-1512** or 508/255-6974) is a rarity—a store devoted to bird-watching. Of course, this being the Cape, there are also T-shirts and souvenirs in the merchandise mix, but if you're looking for binoculars, field guides, or other birding paraphernalia, this is the place.

Guides

The **Wellfleet Bay Wildlife Sanctuary** (West Road, South Wellfleet; ☎ **508/ 349-2615**), under the auspices of the Massachusetts Audubon Society, conducts guided trips in various locations around the Cape, including Monomoy Island, Nauset Marsh, and the sanctuary itself.

BOARDSAILING

What conditions make for first-rate boardsailing? The first answer most experienced boardsailers give would be steady, reliable winds. And for those who get their kicks using waves to ramp up and go airborne, a steady diet of waves would probably be the second answer.

Buzzard's Bay and Nantucket Sound in the summer are well known for both. On a typical summer day, with a big Bermuda high settling in off the East Coast, strong, steady winds tend to kick up late in the morning and maintain their steam throughout the afternoon. Wind speeds exceeding 20 knots are more the norm than the exception. In addition, both the bay and the sound are relatively shallow bodies of water, so that when the winds begin to blow, waves mount quickly.

As a result, the bay and the sound are renowned among the boardsailing communities for some of the best sailing on the East Coast. It is not necessarily easy sailing; there may be more mellow places along the coast for learning the sport. Light morning winds are often flukey, and afternoon conditions may be too rough for first-timers.

For hard-core boardsailing jocks, **Chappaquoit Beach** in West Falmouth is one of the best places on the Cape for wave riding, particularly when the prevailing summer wind is from the southwest. The beach is oriented almost due southwest, so when the wind blows, the waves pound in big, choppy swells.

Consistent winds make **Kalmus Beach** south of Hyannis what one local boardsailing enthusiast calls "maybe the most famous beach in all of Massachusetts." It too has a southwestern orientation. Its downfall is its popularity; known as *the* boardsailing mecca on the Cape, it attracts a considerable crowd on summer weekends. For a less crowded alternative, head east to **West Dennis Beach,** where very similar wind patterns prevail. One reason West Dennis Beach sees fewer sailors than Kalmus is that setup is not quite as convenient; a short walk through the dunes is required to get to the water's edge.

If the winds and tides are right, one of the coolest things to do is sail to Monomoy National Wildlife Refuge. If a quick run to Monomoy grabs your fancy, **Forest Beach** or neighboring **Red River Beach,** both south of Harwich, are probably the best staging areas. It's about a 4-mile run over open water from either beach to either of the two Monomoy Islands, and if the wind is out of the southwest, you'll have a fast reach going in both directions.

There are few classic boardsailing areas on Martha's Vineyard and Nantucket, although those learning the sport might have better luck on the islands. The sheltered waters of **Edgartown Harbor** on the Vineyard and **Nantucket Harbor** are more accommodating to first-timers, but some caution should be exercised. These are active harbors, so steer clear of busy channels.

Gear

Sound Sailboards (223 Barnstable Rd., Hyannis; ☎ 508/771-3388), for equipment and repairs, is less than 2 miles from Kalmus Beach.

Rentals & Instruction

Nauset Sports (Route 6A, Orleans; ☎ 508/255-4742) offers rentals and instruction on the Cape. On Martha's Vineyard, the place for rentals and instruction is **Wind's Up** (199 Beach Rd., Vineyard Haven; ☎ 508/693-4252). On Nantucket, head to **Force 5** (☎ 508/228-0700), on Jetties Beach.

CANOEING/FLATWATER KAYAKING

With all of those kettle ponds—between 300 and 600, depending on who is doing the counting—canoeing opportunities are obviously plentiful on the Cape. Yet most of the kettle ponds are small, and while the paddling can be pleasant, these ponds are hardly enough to sustain a day's outing. Some of the best kettle-pond paddling—and some of the most easily accessible, given the amount of private-property frontage on the Cape—is in **Nickerson State Park.**

The real bounty for flatwater paddling on the Cape and the Islands are the many salt marshes, coastal ponds, bays, tidal inlets, and rich estuaries—the many places where fresh water and the sea come together. Just be prepared for tidal changes and the occasional strong wind.

Cape Cod

Herring River

Allow 2 hours. Access: There is a boat launch off Rte. 28 in West Harwich, about 2 miles east of the intersection with Rte. 134.

There is a reason for the Herring River's name; it is a breeding ground for the eponymous fish. In fact, in the spot where the river meets the West Reservoir, you can watch herring swim from pool to pool during the spawning season.

After putting in at Route 28, head north as the river winds through salt marshes and through low forest where the trees crowd down to the river's edge. Technically, you are heading upriver, but don't be too concerned about the current. Most of the river is estuarial, and when the tide is coming in, you'll probably get a gentle push upriver from the tide. Of course, the farther upriver you go, the less saline the water becomes. It is probably best to time your trip to coincide with high tide; this simply leaves more inlets and nooks to explore that might otherwise be dry at low tide.

If there is a compelling reason to paddle the Herring River, other than the sense of immediacy rendered in traveling through marshland so close you can brush it with your paddle as you pass by, it is the abundant wildlife. Cormorants and herons congregate here to feed on—what else?—the herring, and flocks of migrating ducks often touch down here in fall. Upon entering West Reservoir (you'll have to portage your canoe over the dike separating the reservoir and the river), you'll also discover that this is a place where turtles gather. Keep careful watch from your boat; what appears to be a cluster of rocks on the shore may well be a family of painted turtles.

Waquoit Bay

Allow a day or 2 days for an overnight trip. Headquarters for the **Waquoit Bay National Estuarine Research Reserve** (149 Waquoit Highway, Waquoit Bay; ☎ 508/457-0495) is 3.5 miles west of the Mashpee rotary on Rte. 28. Ask at the headquarters for maps, various put-in locations, and camping permits.

Waquoit Bay itself, about 2 miles long and a mile wide, is just the main feature of this complex 2,500-acre ecosystem. The reserve, established in 1988, includes Washburn Island, several saltwater ponds, great marshland expanses, and freshwater rivers. Given the way Falmouth and Mashpee have grown in recent years, there is plenty of reason to be thankful that steps have been taken to protect this special place.

These are shallow waters; traveling around in an average water depth of 3 feet, you could almost pole your way around rather than paddle. It is a perfect environment for the engine of nature to set itself in motion. Eels, herring, and shellfish flourish here, attracting birds to feed off this bounty. This being an estuary, the environmental complexity is compounded by the meeting of saltwater and freshwater ecosystems. Most of the fresh water enters from the Childs and Quashnet rivers on the north boundary of the reserve; saltwater, of course, arrives thanks to the tidal push from the south.

You could easily spend a half day or more exploring here, poking up the rivers, meandering through the marshes, or turning south to South Cape Beach, the barrier beach separating the bay from Vineyard Sound. Or you could spend more than a day. There are 11 primitive campsites on Washburn Island, and this is a rare opportunity on the Cape to experience something close to a wilderness camping experience. You'll need a permit from the reserve headquarters, and it's worth it.

Martha's Vineyard

Edgartown Great Pond

Allow 3–4 hours. Access: From Edgartown, take the Edgartown–Tisbury Rd. to Meeting House Way. Turn left and continue 1.5 miles on the dirt road, then turn sharply right on another unpaved road. You'll come to the boat-launch area in less than a mile.

Edgartown Great Pond is one of three "great" ponds on Martha's Vineyard's south shore, Tisbury Great Pond to the west and Katama Bay to the east being the others. The three earn their greatness simply by being the largest of a series of ponds along the Vineyard's southern coast that are protected from the ocean by fragile barrier beaches.

Or partially protected, that is. The barrier beaches are no match for full-blown hurricanes such as Bob, which in 1991 cut a swath directly over the Vineyard and the Cape. Ocean water rushed in to join the pond water, raising the salinity level of the water significantly in just a few hours. As a result, Edgartown Great Pond is a curious patchwork of both saltwater and freshwater environments. Paddle inland, deep into the fingered coves that reach away from the sea, and you can still find small freshwater pockets.

For the most part, however, the pond is saline. Salt-marsh grasses, crabs, oysters, plovers, terns—all in their element around saltwater—are at home here. So too are ospreys and herons, the great fishing birds that populate any body of water rich in marine life.

Edgartown Great Pond is a terrific body of water to explore, to roam in and out of its many coves, to watch for bird life, to keep an eye out for schools of herring that spawn in the pond's waters. If there is a drawback, it is that almost all the shoreline is privately owned, so pulling ashore for a picnic lunch is unfortunately not an option. To enjoy the pond to its fullest, come early in the morning, when the sun is shimmering off the water and rising out of the vastness of the ocean beyond the barrier beach. The experience can summon up the strange illusion of paddling at the edge of a flat Earth, with the barrier beach demarcating the absolute end of the world and beyond it nothing but golden sky.

Pocha Pond and Cape Poge Bay

Allow 3–4 hours. Access: From Edgartown, take the ferry to Chappaquiddick Island. Continue on Chappaquiddick Rd. Where the paved road turns sharply left (becoming School Rd.), continue straight on Dyke Rd., following the Trustees of Reservations signs. Park on either side of the road when you come to the water's edge.

It probably goes without saying that the more difficult a place is to get to, the fewer people go there. Such is the case with Poca Pond and its northern neighbor, Cape Poge Bay. It isn't that access is especially difficult; you ride the Chappaquiddick ferry for a couple of minutes, then drive along Chappaquiddick Road till you branch off onto a dirt road that leads to the pond. But the ferry seems to limit the number of visitors, and by the time you arrive at the put-in area, the crowds of Edgartown and South Beach have been left far behind.

From the put-in, head south into the heart of Pocha Pond, its tide-fed marshes rich with shellfish. Paddle around here for a while, sharing the peacefulness of the place with cormorants, herons, and terns, and then head north, through a narrow channel that connects the pond with Cape Poge Bay. The bay is certainly the larger of the two bodies of water and can be exposed to wind, so be cautious here on a windy day.

At all times to your east is the ocean beach, and this is probably the highlight of paddling through the pond and the bay. Find an appropriate spot to pull up your craft (mindful of tidal movements that might carry your boat away), cross over the dunes, and you'll find yourself on an almost entirely secluded beach, more so as you travel farther from the put-in area at Dyke Road. Take a walk or take a swim. (See Wasque Reservation & Cape Poge Wildlife Refuge under "Hiking," below.) You might come across a handful of other beachcombers, but you'll encounter nothing like the crowds that come to the Vineyard's more popular (that is, more accessible) beaches.

If the winds are low and favorable and you want to make a full day's outing of it, you can continue on through Cape Poge Gut and into Edgartown Harbor. From the far end of Pocha Pond to the piers of the harbor is about 5 miles, although with all the meandering and exploring you'll want to do, you'll end up traveling much farther. This is probably not a good idea, however, if the winds are blowing freshly out of the northern quadrant. You'll find yourself banging around through wind-blown chop in the harbor—a rough finish to an otherwise easy-going ride.

Gear & Rentals

Waquoit Kayak Company (at Edwards Boatyard, East Falmouth; ☎ 508/548-9722) sells and rents kayaks and canoes for exploring Waquoit Bay and its contiguous rivers and ponds. **Goose Hummock** (Town Cove, Orleans; ☎ 508/255-2620) also rents canoes.

Rentals & Instruction

Kayaks of Martha's Vineyard (Box 840, Martha's Vineyard, MA 02575; ☎ 508/693-3885) offers kayaking instruction at Lambert's Cove on the Vineyard. Kayak rentals are also available.

THIS LAND IS MY LAND, THIS LAND IS YOUR LAND

In most coastal states in the United States, the beach area between low tide and high tide is considered public land. It is irrelevant who owns the land immediately inland. If you want to go for a walk along the beach and you're on the sea-side of the mean high-water line, nobody can stop you.

Unfortunately, that's not the law of the land in Massachusetts, only one of two states in the country (Maine being the other) where private property legally extends to the water's edge, regardless of tide. In a state where roughly three quarters of the coastline is privately held land, that law can often lead to uncomfortable confrontations. Landowners assert their right to privacy, while beachgoers insist they should have a right to walk on the beach.

The Massachusetts law has its roots in the 1600s, when the colony, as a way of boosting economic growth, extended coastal landowners' property rights to the water's edge to promote the construction of piers and wharves. At the same time, the law also gave the public the right to fish and "navigate" in the intertidal area, which in some places on the Cape and the islands might extend several hundred yards out to sea.

So far, an amendment to the law, passed in 1991 by the state legislature, has failed to have the desired effect—to allow people to walk on beaches in the intertidal area. The law's ineffectiveness stems from a statute that requires the state to compensate landowners if a change in the law affects the value of their property. If the state were to compensate the thousands of coast landowners, of course, the cost would be enormous. So with the state unlikely to dig deeply into its pockets, the terms of the old law remain in effect.

Some clever opponents have sought to sidestep the law by contending that "navigate" has broad meaning. Isn't walking, they say, a form of navigation? You might want to think so, but Massachusetts's courts do not agree.

So welcome to the beachfront battle zone. Local officials report that on Martha's Vineyard and Cape Cod, confrontations between private landowners and the public have been on the rise in recent years. And the problem is not simply between individual landowners and beachgoing passers-by. Large stretches of beach are often owned by private beach associations and open only to dues-paying members. It might look to you like a public beach, but when you stroll by in front of people who have paid their dues, you might find a difference of opinion.

So beach walkers, beware. Many landowners, of course, are good sports who don't mind the rare walker passing by at the water's edge. But they are technically within their rights to press trespassing charges, and there have been recent cases on the Vineyard and the Cape of landowners doing just that. Tread carefully then, and carry a fishing rod. At least if you can convince the court that you were fishing (not just navigating by foot), you might be considered within your rights according to the centuries-old law.

Guides

Cape Cod Canoe & Kayak (☎ 888/CANOE93 or 508/564-4051) leads day trips in various locations around the Cape, including Pleasant Bay in Orleans and Waquoit Bay in Mashpee. Some tours are offered along with the Cape Cod Museum of Natural History. **Trustees of Reservations** (☎ 508/627-3599) leads 2-hour naturalist tours of Cape Poge and Pocha Pond on Martha's Vineyard.

Reservations are a must. **Great Expeditions** (Box 2091, Nantucket; ☎ 508/825-2555), a Nantucket-based, multisport tour operator, leads day trips to Coatue Wildlife Refuge and Hummock Pond.

CROSS-COUNTRY SKIING

No one would ever make his or her way to Cape Cod just to go cross-country skiing. But if it does happen to snow on the

Cape—not a frequent occurrence, but not an entirely rare one, either—and if you happen to need a cross-country fix, head for **Nickerson State Park.** You can also make your way along the **Cape Cod Rail Trail,** which because of its smooth, paved surface requires relatively little snow to be skiable. Of course, as the pavement warms, the snow disappears quickly, so at some point you might be forced to dismount and walk. But then what do you expect in a region not exactly famous for high-quality skiing?

FISHING

If you want to be a very cool person these days, become a saltwater fly fisherman. Saltwater fly-fishing is *the* hot sport in the angling world these days. Freshwater fly-fishing is a spiritual exercise—standing waist-deep in a mountain stream and drifting a tiny fly over the water's surface in pursuit of some mystery trout. Saltwater fly-fishing, on the other hand, takes on the character of big-game hunting with small weaponry. You're out there on the savanna of the sea, chasing after seriously big bluefish, striped bass, and albacore with lightweight tackle that might seem more suited to fishing for a more modest-sized trout. When that 40-pound striper strikes, you'll think you've caught Moby Dick himself.

The waters off the Cape and the islands are the hallowed grounds of striped-bass and bluefish fishing. One reason is that the waters are relatively shallow, and fish don't have the option of diving several hundred feet deep and out of fishing range. Also, the waters of **Buzzard's Bay, Vineyard Sound,** and **Nantucket Sound** are rich in the sort of small fish and nutrients that big fish feed on. And feed they do. Should you come across a school of bluefish in a feeding frenzy, you're almost guaranteed a strike with every cast.

Just where are the hot spots? It all depends, of course, on whom you ask. **Monomoy,** as the last barrier between Nantucket Sound and the open sea,

seems to be a place where fish congregate. On the north side of the Cape, **Barnstable Harbor** is a place where knowledgeable fishermen tend to congregate. The waters off **Great Point,** the northeastern tip of Nantucket, are said to be filled with trophy-sized stripers. But these are just suggestions; ask any three Cape fishermen where the fish are, and you're apt to get three different answers. Or no answers at all. Fishermen, after all, are notoriously tight-lipped about revealing the location of their secret spots.

Actually, the real problem might not be in finding out where the fish are, but in getting to them if you don't have your own sturdy vessel. For most people who come to the Cape and the islands for fishing, chartering a boat or hiring a guide is the way to go. A few recommended charter boats are listed below, but head for any of the major harbors in the region—particularly **Falmouth, Hyannis, Barnstable, Chatham,** and **Edgartown** harbors—and you're almost sure to find a reliable charter boat, fully licensed and geared up with all the necessary tackle to take you out on the water. It's worth spending the extra money to go out on a small boat that carries six people or fewer. Hanging over the railing of some larger vessel with dozens of other fishermen is more production-line fishing than it is a sport.

Of course, you don't have to fish from a boat. There are plenty of good surf-casting spots on the Cape and the islands. Head south on **Nauset Beach** to escape the crowds. To the north, big fish have been known to come close to shore near **Race Point,** the northernmost part of the Cape. On Martha's Vineyard, surf-casters tend to head east to **Cape Poge** and **Wasque Reservation;** if you can score a sand-ready four-wheel-drive vehicle, which are permitted from Dyke Road to Cape Poge, your mobility—and your chance to find hot spots—will be greatly improved. (Over sand vehicles—OSVs, for short—can be rented from various auto-rental locations on the island.) On

Nantucket, there is good surf-casting near **Great Point** and **Eel Point.**

Incidentally, don't think that just because summer comes to an end, the good fishing does as well. In fact, the annual Martha's Vineyard fishing derby runs from mid-September to mid-October, and the fish reeled in at that time of year aren't exactly small fry. Striped bass weighing in at over 40 pounds and blue-fish weighing over 15 pounds are not uncommon catches during the derby. The albacore fishing in **Buzzard's Bay,** where the water stays relatively warm well into the fall months, often reaches its peak in late September.

Charters

Pleasant Bay Charters (Box 146, West Chatham; ☎ **508/430-2277**) takes light-tackle fishermen to the waters of Chatham and Monomoy in pursuit of striped bass, bluefish, and bonito. **Cape Cod Charter Fishing** (Box 894, South Orleans; ☎ **508/240-7896** or 508/246-6691) takes anglers into the waters of Nantucket Sound for bluefish and stripers or into deeper water for cod and blue-fin tuna. **Big Eye Charters** (Box 1822, Edgartown; ☎ **508/627-3649**) fishes the waters both close to shore and offshore near Martha's Vineyard. Captain Leslie Smith of **Backlash Charters** (Main Street, Edgar-town; ☎ **508/627-5894** or 508/627-0148) takes anglers aboard his 26-foot Regulator for light-tackle fishing off the shores of Martha's Vineyard.

Gear & Guides

The place to go for saltwater fly-fishing gear, instruction, and guide service on Nantucket is **Cross Rip Outfitters** (24 Easy St., Nantucket; ☎ **508/228-4900**). On the Vineyard, **Coop's Bait & Tackle** (147 W. Tisbury Rd., Edgartown; ☎ **508/627-3909**) has gear for sale or for rent, and can also provide on-shore and offshore guide service.

Instruction

Fishing the Cape (Harwich Commons, East Harwich; ☎ **508/432-1200,** or 800/235-9763 for Orvis Fishing School reservations) conducts 2½-day saltwater fly-fishing courses on the Cape under the Orvis aegis.

HIKING

There is little long-distance hiking (and no overnight backpacking) on the Cape and the islands, unless you're someone who likes walking for miles along the beach. In that case, you could walk the length of **Cape Cod National Seashore,** from the southern tip of Nauset Beach north to Race Point, a distance of some-thing like 40 miles. Now *that* would be some kind of walk on the beach. But because camping is not permitted within the national seashore boundaries, it is an inconceivable outing, unless you are able to walk 40 miles in a day.

Most hikes, then, are relatively short (see "Walks & Rambles," below), topping out at around 2 miles. There are, howev-er, exceptions, although the three hikes described below still enter into the terri-tory that almost any extended hike on the Cape and the islands must—the walk on the beach. If you want to take a hike inland, a couple of places you should consider are **Punkhorn Parklands** near Brewster and **Martha's Vineyard State Forest** on the Vineyard. Both areas are described under "Mountain Biking," below.

Cape Cod

Great Island

Allow 3–4 hours. Moderate. Access: From Rte. 6, take the exit for Wellfleet Center. Turn left on East Commercial St., then right onto Chequessett Neck Rd. Look for the parking area for Great Island several miles down the road on your left. Map: Available at the Salt Pond Visitors' Center (☎ **508/255-3421**), for Cape Cod

FISHING OFF CUTTYHUNK ISLAND

Like a misplaced Greek Island, tiny Cuttyhunk—just south of Cape Cod—sits at the tip of the mostly private and uninhabited Elizabeth Islands. On the eastern side of the island, homes are tightly clustered on the hill overlooking the sheltered harbor. Most of the remainder of the island, which measures about 2.5 by .75 miles, is conservation land and pristine beaches popular with bird watchers and solitude-seekers. Accessible from Martha's Vineyard and New Bedford, Cuttyhunk offers an unusual off-the-beaten-track island experience.

In the late 19th century, an exclusive group of millionaires from New York, Boston, and Philadelphia convened at the Bass Fishing Club, a one-story, shingled bunkhouse on Cuttyhunk, for the ultimate anglers' vacation. The names of several U.S. presidents are scrawled in the guest book alongside railroad and oil magnates. For club members, days were spent perched on the edge of fishing stands jutting out over the rocky shores, while hired "chummers" baited the hooks and gaffed the prized catches. Evenings, over sumptuous five-course meals, relaxed industry titans would discuss the stock market, politics, and the best place to catch striped bass. Over cognac and cigars, they'd decide who would be president.

In 1906, William Madison Wood, head of the American Woolen Company and one of the richest men in America at the time, joined the club. Wood, an Horatio Alger poster boy, was born to an impoverished Portuguese family on Martha's Vineyard; by virtue of hard work, good sense, and a timely marriage to the boss's daughter, Wood rose to be head of the American Woolen Company. His passion for Cuttyhunk manifested itself in a keen acquisitive nature; by 1912, he had bought the club and most of the island. Although the Cuttyhunk Club disbanded in 1921 and the building is now a B&B, Cuttyhunk itself hasn't changed much in the ensuing 85 years. Wood's descendants are still prominent landowners on the island, and devoted anglers can still ply these waters for striped bass with some of the most skilled fishing guides on the East Coast. The fishing guides are **Capt. George Isabel (☎ 508/991-7352,** or off-season 508/679-5675), **Capt. Duane Lynch (☎ 508/522-4351), Capt. Jim Nunes (☎ 508/993-7427),** and **Capt. Charlie Tilton (☎ 508/992-8181**).

A word of warning: Cuttyhunk is a seasonal destination—mid-June to mid-September. Some years, the winter population dips to the single digits. The island has one road and few cars. Those who don't walk use golf carts. Dining and lodging options are quite limited.

How to get there: *By ferry:* The **M/V** *Alert II* ferry (☎ **508/992-1432;** www.cuttyhunk.com; e-mail: alert2@cuttyhunk.com) departs New Bedford Pier 3. Reservations are highly recommended. Round-trip tickets are $16 for adults and $11 for children. Call for times. *By seaplane:* **Bayside Air Service,** New Bedford (☎ **508/636-3762**), charges $80 to charter the plane, which holds three passengers. To sail on the Catamaran S/V *Arabella* from Menemsha on Martha's Vineyard to Cuttyhunk, call **Hugh Taylor** at ☎ **508/645-3511.**

Where to stay: The **Cuttyhunk Fishing Club** (☎ **508/992-5585**) has nightly rates (including continental breakfast) of $75 to $275; **Cuttyhunk Bed and Breakfast** (☎ **508/993-6490**) has two rooms at $70 to $100 per night.

Where to eat in season: **Bart's Place** is open for lunch and dinner and serves hamburgers, hot dogs, fish-and-chips, and even petit filet mignon. Cuttyhunk Shellfish Farms's **Floating Harbor Raw Bar** (☎ **508/971-1120**) offers lunch and dinner to go at the dock.

—Laura M. Reckford

National Seashore, at the intersection of Rte. 6 and Nauset Rd., north of Eastham.

"Island" is actually a misnomer. Great Island is, in fact, a peninsula jutting southward to separate Wellfleet Harbor from Cape Cod Bay. But it has earned the right to be called an island because that is what it once was, until drift and erosion connected the island with the mainland in the mid 19th century. Such is the way it is with the shifting sands of the Cape—land comes, and land goes.

The 7-mile Great Island Trail is the longest trail within the boundaries of Cape Cod National Seashore. The walk has a little bit of everything germane to the Cape; it is a walk through the forest, along the beach, through dunes, around marshland, and even to what remains (in spirit, anyway) of an old tavern frequented by whalers. From the parking area, the trail descends through the woods to the edge of a marsh fed by the Herring River. From here, the trail loops to the right, heading around the marsh as it makes its way toward the Cape Cod Bay shore.

The narrow throat of land you come to before bearing left along the dunes and the beach is called the Gut. At one time, the Herring River cut through here, and Great Island was indeed an island. No more. When you arrive at a fork in the trail at the southern end of the Gut, bear left, continuing to skirt around the edge of the marsh, bearing left again to visit the site of the old tavern on a nose of land extending into Wellfleet Harbor.

Or was it the site of an old tavern? So legend has it. Supposedly whalers came to this spot to drink and carouse—activities that were not favorably regarded by the prim folk of Wellfleet. It is a likely story, except that no one has been able to verify it, and no identifiable remains of the tavern have been left behind. So go with the legend and your imagination, since there's no harm in believing a good old story.

From the tavern spot, the trail loops back to rejoin the main trail to Great Beach Hill. The short climb up the hill can be a bit taxing because of the soft sand, but if you have an aversion to walking in sand, you're in the wrong place. Once over the hill, you come to another marsh,

beyond which is Jeremy Point and the end of the island. If the tide is out, it is possible to walk well out to Jeremy Point, looking for whatever crabs and shellfish the tide has left behind. If the tide is in, Jeremy Point will be submerged.

To make your way back, return via the beach rather than the main trail. It is a pretty and isolated strip of beach and dunes, and while it might be hard to do so, watch where you are walking. This can be a real treasure trove if you are someone who collects seashells. After a couple of miles, look for a boardwalk to climb back over the dunes at the Gut. This leads to the beginning of the trail on which you started. Turn left to make your way back.

Sandy Neck & the Great Marshes

Allow 4–5 hours for the 9-mile hike. Easy–moderate; be sure to bring plenty of water on a sunny day. Access: From Barnstable, take Rte. 6A west to Sandy Neck Rd., on your right. Look for the sign to Sandy Neck Beach. A parking fee is charged. Map: Ask for a trail map at the gatehouse, although a map is really not necessary.

How far do you want to go? That's the question to ask yourself as you head off on a hike on Sandy Neck. The theme of the hike is fairly simple. Walk along the beach, cross over the dunes, and walk back along the marsh. The big question is when should you cross the dunes? If you decide to go all the way to the end of the neck, you're in for a hike of roughly 14 miles. That's a pretty long hoof, even on flat ground, given that much of the walking is on sand. Along the way, however, are various crossovers—the prosaically named Trails 1, 2, and 4. By crossing over at Trail 2, you're in for a 5-mile hike; crossing over at Trail 4 turns it into a 9-mile hike.

The dunes of Sandy Neck might not get all the attention that the dunes farther out on the Cape do, but they are nearly as impressive, rising in some places to heights of 100 feet. In fact, during World War II, the U.S. military trained on Sandy Neck in preparation for doing battle in the Sahara. Closer to the beach, the dunes are more rugged and seemingly sandier; as you move inland, they seem more established, covered with dune grasses, wildflowers, and wild cranberries. They can also yield unexpected treasures as you venture away from the water's edge. Native Americans were known to set up summer camps on the neck, and if you're lucky, you might come across an arrowhead, a broken tool, or a shard of pottery. When the wind blows and the sands shift, surprise finds can be uncovered.

After crossing over the dunes on Trail 4 (or Trail 2, if you opt for the shorter hike), turn right on the Marsh Trail to make the return trip. The trail runs between the dunes and the marshes, a remarkable contrast in habitats. Expect to see herons, egrets, and cormorants working the marsh waters, and you'll probably see turtles as well. If you visit at the right time in fall, you may be treated to the monarch butterfly migration. Whatever season you come, bring a pair of binoculars. Like any marsh, this is a vibrantly active natural world, and you don't want to miss the show.

Martha's Vineyard

Wasque Reservation & Cape Poge Wildlife Refuge

Allow 4–8 hours, depending on how far you want to go. Easy–moderate; be sure to bring plenty of water on a sunny day. Access: From the Chappaquiddick ferry, take Chappaquiddick Rd., which in 2.5 miles turns into School Rd. after making a sharp right turn. Look for Wasque Rd. on your left and turn here for Wasque Reservation. A small fee is charged during the summer months. Map: Unnecessary. It would take a wild imagination to get lost here.

A walk on the beach doesn't get much better than this. Here you'll find more than 6 miles of barrier beach and dunes

fronting the ocean, shielding inland salt marshes and salt ponds, all of it pristine and undeveloped. One of the major reasons, of course, that this area remains undeveloped is that it is a constantly shifting, unstable environment. Anything built here would stand little chance of lasting very long. The ocean, rendered surly by hard-hitting north-Atlantic storms, has breached the barrier beach often enough, and the beach and dunes are regularly reconfigured by less severe weather events. In other words, this is a great place to visit, but you wouldn't want to live here.

Wasque is a Native American word for "the ending," appropriately so in that this is the easternmost extreme of Martha's Vineyard. Perhaps it is somewhat ironic to begin a hike at the ending, but so be it. From the Wasque Reservation parking area, take the boardwalk that leads to the beach. Turn north, and from here, it's up to you how far you'll go. The lighthouse at the end of Cape Poge is 6 miles away, a distance that might not seem especially daunting given that the land is absolutely flat. Keep in mind, however, that walking on sand is not as mechanically efficient as walking on firm ground, and each step requires a little more effort.

For as long as you decide to go northward, of course, the Atlantic Ocean will be on your right side. On your left will at first be Pocha Pond, a classic salt pond surrounded by marsh grasses. North of Pocha Pond you'll come to East Beach, where swimmers and sunbathers from Edgartown congregate near the area where Dyke Bridge makes the beach easily accessible. North of East Beach is popular surf-casting territory, since sand-ready vehicles are permitted here. Surf-casting involves a great deal of standing around and waiting, so you'll probably find fishermen eager to strike up a conversation as you pass by.

About a mile north of Dyke Bridge is The Cedars, a cluster of low red cedars, whose growth has been stunted by the incessant battering of the wind and saline air. This marks an approximate halfway point, and is a good spot to set up a picnic lunch and then turn back if you opt for a shorter hike. From here to the lighthouse, windswept dunes separate the beach from Cape Poge Sound, and you might want to take a walk among the dunes via one of several boardwalks that lead from the beach. The recent history of the lighthouse itself is a testament to just how unsuitable this area is to development. When the lighthouse was originally built in 1802, it sat several hundred feet from the shoreline. But by 1987, erosion had narrowed the distance to 20 feet, forcing the Coast Guard to lift the lighthouse by helicopter and move it back to safer ground.

Gear

Eastern Mountain Sports (233 Stevens St., Hyannis; ☎ **508/775-1072**) has a good selection of hiking gear and clothing.

Guides

Wellfleet Bay Wildlife Sanctuary (Route 6, South Wellfleet; ☎ **508/349-2615**) has a summer outing program of guided hikes at various locations on the outer Cape. **Goose Hummock** (Town Cove, Orleans; ☎ **508/255-2620**) offers organized hikes at various locations between Harwich and Provincetown.

HORSEBACK RIDING

On the Cape, **Punkhorn Parklands** near Brewster and **Great Island** in Wellfleet are a good places to ride (see "Hiking," above), as is **Martha's Vineyard State Forest** on the Vineyard. Finding somewhere to ride is probably easier than finding a horse to ride, if you don't have your own. **Deer Meadow Riding Stable** (Route 137, East Harwich; ☎ **508/432-6580**) offers 7-mile rides as well as lessons and pony rides for kids. For a ride in the dunes, try **Nelson Riding Stable** (43

Race Point Rd., Provincetown; ☎ **508/487-1112**), which offers 2-hour rides on National Seashore lands.

MOUNTAIN BIKING

Mountain biking is obviously a misnomer in a region where the land's high point is below 200 feet above sea level. That said, the Cape and the islands offer their own unique challenges to off-road riders. Soft sand is a hard surface to ride on, and sand covers many of the area's back roads and trails. Two things are required to ride effectively in sand. First, you need to reduce tire pressure to improve traction. Second, stay balanced on your bike and don't force the action. Aggressive pedal strokes usually cause wheels to spin out, so relax and apply soft but firm pressure, and don't be shy about getting off your bike and walking. There is some sand too soft even for the most skilled bike handlers to negotiate.

Long backwoods loops are hard to find on the Cape and the islands, primarily because large tracts of public land are hard to come by. For single-track enthusiasts, there are a few places on the Cape to get your ya-yas out. But for the most part, the riding is on dirt and sand roads, and the occasional foray onto pavement is certainly not out of the question. Be willing to explore, but also be mindful of private property, which there is plenty of on the Cape and the islands.

In addition to the rides described below, **Nickerson State Park** has a network of paved trails and dirt roads that meander among the eight kettle ponds within the park. You can come up with something close to a 10-mile loop by linking together dirt roads and paved roads between **Lagoon Pond** and **Lake Tashmoo** near Vineyard Haven on Martha's Vineyard. Probably your best bet for off-road riding on Nantucket are the dirt roads around **Madaket** and **Eel Point** on the western end of the island.

The rental bikes offered at most shops on the Cape and the islands are what are considered hybrids, bikes that fall halfway between being road bikes and mountain bikes. For much of the riding you encounter on dirt roads, these bikes are perfectly adequate. But if you plan to do much legitimate off-road riding, particularly on soft sand, you'll want a more maneuverable mountain bike with the appropriate tires and treads.

Cape Cod

Mashpee River Woodlands

Allow 1 hour. Easy–moderate; rolling hills. Access: From Falmouth, take Rte. 28 toward Hyannis. Continue through the Mashpee rotary, and 1.5 miles later, make a sharp right onto Quinaquisset Ave. Continue past the sign for MASHPEE RIVER WOODLANDS/NORTH PARKING LOT until you reach Mashpee Neck Rd. Turn right and look for another sign for MASHPEE RIVER WOODLANDS and a smaller parking lot.

If you're a mountain biker who is just beginning to get into the thrills of single-track riding, Mashpee River Woodlands is a great place for you. There are about 5 miles of single track here, most of it through flat or gently rolling woodlands, making this a good place for novice single trackers on two counts. One, it's hard to get lost in this fairly compact area, and two, you're not going to encounter steep climbs and hair-raising descents calling for skilled bike handling. In short, it's pretty hard to get in over your head here.

The trail system here consists of essentially three trails. The main drag is a trail running along the Mashpee River, and don't be surprised to encounter a hiker or two out for an afternoon stroll. But because this is a relatively hidden spot in the heartland of the Upper Cape, you're apt to have the place more or less to yourself. Two short loops diverge from the main trail—the Chickadee Loop on the southern end and the Partridge Loop on the northern end. By riding the entire trail system, you'll have logged about 5 miles, so if you've still got energy, go ahead and do it again. And if you feel you've got the hang of single-track riding, you might be ready to head off to the nearby Trail of Tears (see below) for a more serious challenge.

Punkhorn Parklands

Allow 1–2 hours. Easy–moderate; mostly flat with a few low hills. Access: From Brewster, take Rte. 6A east toward Dennis. Turn left at Stony Brook Rd. (at a blinking light) and make another left onto Run Hill Rd. The sign for the parklands, and room for parking, are on the left side of the road. Map: Should be available in the box at the trailhead.

This 800-acre tract of conservation lands owned by the town of Brewster has a complex system of dirt roads and trails that total about 45 miles. The trails are not always well marked, so getting lost might seem a reasonable prospect. But the area is reasonably well defined by Westgate Road (the continuation of Run Hill Road, by which you enter the area) and Eastgate Road.

The landscape here is classic inland Cape. Woodlands give way to marshes and bogs, which in turn give way to kettle ponds. There is also a little bit of history tossed in here and there. Some of this land was used for agricultural purposes in the 19th century, and evidence of the clearing of the land remains. Also, the Deep Punkhorn Path, which runs through the parklands, is said to have been an important route traveled by Native Americans before European settlers arrived.

So grab a map at the trailhead and go exploring. There is nothing extremely challenging here, certainly no steep, scary single track to put the fear of God in you. If you do embark on any of the single-track trails, just be alert to other trail users, horseback riders in particular. Otherwise, go for it. At some point you're bound to find your way to the edge of Seymour Pond, a good place for a rest and a snack (being respectful, of course, of the private property here). And when you feel you've had enough, simply make tracks for Westgate Road, which is never far from any spot in the parklands. Turn north on Westgate, and you'll be headed back toward your starting point.

Trail of Tears, Barnstable

Allow 1–2 hours. Strenuous, with short but steep hills. Take exit 5 from Rte. 6 and take Rte. 149 south before taking a quick right onto the service road. There is space for parking on the left under the power lines.

If you're looking for something close to "mountain" biking, as opposed to off-road biking, the Trail of Tears on the Barnstable Conservation Lands is the place for you. This hellish trail was devised by motorcross motorcyclists before they were booted off the grounds. Go for it! Start riding under the power lines and then take your second left. Within moments, you're huffing and puffing up a steep hill before cruising down single tracks with very little room to maneuver. You're looking at another hill as soon as you touch bottom, and before you know it, you're coasting down again. The cycle is unrelenting—up, down, up, down, until you make it out of this area 30 to 45 minutes later, sweating like a sprinkler system.

If your legs feel like Jell-O, take a right on the double-track path and head back to the parking lot. If you still want more, take a left and cross under the power lines twice before ending up back where you started. If you get lost, simply follow the power lines back to the parking lot.

Martha's Vineyard

Martha's Vineyard State Forest

Allow 2–3 hours. Easy–moderate; mostly flat, dirt-road riding, with the difficulty determined mainly by the distance you ride. Access: From Vineyard Haven, take Edgartown Rd. south and turn right onto Airport Rd. at the blinking light. Forest headquarters are on the right. Map: Ask at forest headquarters.

This is something of an odd place. It goes by two names—Martha's Vineyard State Forest and Manuel Correllus State Forest, although most people refer to it as the former. In its midst is the main airport for the island. It is full of dirt roads to ride, most of which form an almost perfect grid. Looking at a map of the forest is like looking at a tennis net close up.

Yet the forest is certainly the best place for mountain biking on the island, encompassing more than 4,300 acres of pine and oak forests, scrub growth, and open meadow. It is both easy and hard to get lost here. Because of the similarity of the grid-pattern roads, you may quickly get a sense of déjà vu; you'll think you've ridden a road you haven't, just because its route through the forest is much like a road you already have ridden. Don't become too alarmed. There are some useful references to keep you oriented, particularly if you stick to the western half of the forest. One is the airport, which occupies the south-central part of the park.

Paved bike paths, which form a border around the western part of the forest (and a portion of the eastern part), are also good reference points. If you come to a bike path, you know you've arrived at either the edge of the forest or the path that leads back to your starting point near the airport. If you feel lost even on the paved paths, just ask passers-by for directions; in summer, the paths see plenty of use.

A few single-track trails wind through the grid, so give them a go if you want to. One of the biggest challenges in riding here is the sandy soil, so keep a lookout for pockets of deep sand as you ride along. Nothing can throw off your balance more abruptly than hitting deep sand at high speed. It's a good way to execute the classic, over-the-handlebars maneuver—the bike stops, you keep going. So take it easy, and watch out.

Gear & Rentals

See "Gear & Rentals" under "Road Biking," below.

ROAD BIKING

So many things might suggest that the Cape and the islands are a less than ideal area for cycling. Traffic congestion can be considerable on summer weekends, and few roads have generously wide shoulders to accommodate cyclists comfortably. There are few big hills, of course, but winds can be considerable, particularly close to the water.

And yet this region is one of the best for riding in New England, largely because such an incredible effort has been made to make cyclists feel welcome. Not only are there miles upon miles of bike paths and trails—the 25-mile Cape Cod Trail, as well as the trails that cross the dunes in the **Province Lands,** being the most noteworthy among them—but several bike routes have also been mapped out and clearly marked with signs. By following the bike-route signs, you can for the most part steer clear of major roadways and traffic congestion, experiencing the back roads of the Cape and the islands at their scenic best.

Most motorists—not all, but most—seem to be willing to give cyclists a break. Blaring horns and angry curses are rarely heard, and there are probably two reasons for this. One is that most people, whether in motorized vehicles or not, have come to the Cape seeking a slower pace of life, and having to wait a few seconds to get by a cyclist seems to fit right into the program. Second, cyclists are much more prevalent on the Cape and the islands than in most other parts of New England. Familiarity seems to have bred détente; motorists and cyclists have apparently learned that it is possible to coexist.

Finally, the popularity of cycling on the Cape and the islands has led to the development of a widespread support system. Shops renting, selling, and repairing bikes are far too numerous to list here. On Martha's Vineyard alone, there are more than a dozen places to rent bikes, and many inns on the island have their own bike fleets for guests to use.

In addition to the rides described below, try riding the trail along the **Cape Cod Canal.** If you're looking for something of a competitive challenge along the 7-mile trail, try keeping up with ships as they pass through the canal. There is more great riding to be had on the paved trails in the **Province Lands,** east of Provincetown. There are just a little over 5 miles of trails here, but because the quick ups and downs are considerable—and sometimes steep—as you pass over the dunes, you can get a reasonably good workout in a relatively short ride. This is one of the best ways to immerse yourself in the dunes (and realize that the dune world is not just about sand); there are few roads through the dunes, and walking through the sand and low brush can be cumbersome. Finally, there is the **Shining Sea Bike Path** in Falmouth. It might not be the most exciting ride on the Cape, but something in the name makes you think you ought to be delivered into the hands of God.

Cape Cod

Cape Cod Trail

25 miles long. Allow 5–6 hours to ride a complete round-trip of the trail. Access: In the northeast, the trail begins in South Wellfleet at Lecount Hollow Rd., just east of Rte. 6. In the southwest, the trail begins in South Dennis, about a mile south of Rte. 6 off Rte. 134. The trail is also accessible from several points in between. Map: Rubel Bikemaps' *Cape Cod & the North Shore.*

While train-era romantics might rue the gradual dwindling of railroads in the latter half of the 20th century, bicyclists have much to be thankful for. The conversion of abandoned rail lines has been a boon to cycling, and nowhere has it been more of a boon than on Cape Cod.

The Cape Cod Rail Trail stretches for 25 miles from South Dennis to Wellfleet, following a rail line abandoned in 1965. For the most part it is easy riding, not only because on the Cape there is nothing that could fairly be called a hill, but also because rail lines feature gentle railroad grades. Anything that a big, burly train can climb ought to pose little challenge to a svelte, relatively lightweight human rider.

Thus, while 50 miles might seem to the average recreational cyclist to be a long way to go, the rail trail is, if such a thing is possible, an easy 50-mile ride. Also, because it is inland and mostly within the shelter of trees, it is not exposed to the kind of winds that can sweep over roadways closer to the water. But if 50 miles strikes you as too much, it is easy enough to make the ride shorter. The rail trail is an out-and-back ride no matter how far you go, so simply turn around and reverse directions when you feel you've gone far enough.

Starting from the south, the trail winds through cranberry bogs in Harwich, makes a neat passage between Long Pond and Seymour Pond between Harwich and Brewster, and then enters the pine forests of Nickerson State Park, a good spot for a picnic lunch. For the supplies for that picnic, you might want to stop at the Pleasant Lake General Store in Harwich, a favorite oasis for rail-trail travelers. But if you choose not to make the stop, fear not—there is no shortage of stores, ice-cream shops, and restaurants along the trail to assuage your appetite or quench your thirst.

In Orleans, the trail ends briefly and you must ride local roads for a mile or so, passing Rock Harbor with its many boats at anchor. Simply follow the bike-route signs to rejoin the trail as it makes a straight run due north to Wellfleet. If you've got the energy, you might want to make a side trip along the way, taking the bike trail from the Salt Pond Visitors Center—the main visitors' center for Cape Cod National Seashore—to Coast Guard Beach. Lock your bike, head down to the beach, and (if you dare) take a swim in the often frigid waters of the Atlantic.

If there is a drawback to the Cape Cod Rail Trail, it is its popularity. In-line skaters, walkers, families with dogs and baby carriages—all make their way onto the trail. If you're someone looking to hammer hard, testing your aerobic threshold, the trail is not for you. But if you're happy ambling along at a leisurely pace, enjoying the inland Cape scenery, this is a hard ride to beat.

Martha's Vineyard
East Island Loop
Allow 3–4 hours. Easy. Access: Begin in Vineyard Haven. It is also possible to pick up the loop in Oak Bluffs or Edgartown. Map: The Martha's Vineyard Commission's free *Biking in Martha's Vineyard* should be available at the ferry terminal and bike-rental outlets.

When you disembark from the ferry in Vineyard Haven, you may at first wonder why people say cycling on Martha's Vineyard is an enjoyable experience. The scene is bustling, to put it kindly, and you are almost immediately thrust into a crazy, five-way intersection where no one seems to know who has the right of way. Stick with it; the situation improves quickly.

Look for signs to Oak Bluffs that will lead you onto Beach Road and over a causeway separating Vineyard Haven Harbor and Lagoon Pond. Crossing a drawbridge (and being careful of the slippery grating on the bridge), you'll enter Oak Bluffs. Turn left after the causeway and hug the shore, following signs to East Chop and the lighthouse that, with its partner across the way on West Chop, marks the entry into Vineyard Haven Harbor. The road winds back along bluffs overlooking Nantucket Sound before depositing you onto New York Avenue. Turn left here to enter the heart of Oak Bluffs, with the harbor on your left.

You'll want to spend a little time in Oak Bluffs exploring the cluster of famous gingerbread houses. Tiny, brightly painted, and adorned with flowers, these houses, tracing their origins to the days when Oak Bluffs was a religious-revival center in the 1830s, possess a quaintness that is almost storybook. You'll almost expect Little Red Riding Hood to be skipping around somewhere in the neighborhood.

From Oak Bluffs, continue on Beach Road, where a bike path parallels the road just outside of town. For a while, the path runs between the beach on Nantucket Sound and Sengekontacket Pond, a classic example of why Cathy Cover, a guide for Vermont Bicycle Tours, says, "The best thing about riding on the Vineyard is riding along the sea. There's nothing quite like it."

As you approach Edgartown and the bike path comes to an end, the route gets complicated. Follow the bike-route signs and eventually you'll find your way into the town's center, but don't be surprised if you find yourself making a few wrong turns along the way. With its old clapboard and shingle homes, its picket fences, its narrow streets, and its harbor filled with boats, Edgartown is the epitome of the New England seaside town. Of course, you won't be the first person to discover this; in the middle of summer, the place is packed, and the town's many shops, selling everything from T-shirts to the works of world-renowned artists, do a brisk business.

Grab a bite to eat here, then if you've got the time and energy, ride the Chappaquiddick Island ferry for a short side trip. Chappaquiddick Road is paved, but unfortunately Dyke Road, which leads to secluded East Beach, is not, and its soft, sandy surface can make for hard going for most bikes. If you want to hit the beach for a swim, it's easier to take the 2-mile ride from Edgartown to South Beach on the bike path that parallels Katama Road.

From Edgartown, head back toward Vineyard Haven, picking up the inland bike path that runs along Edgartown-Vineyard Haven Road. If you want to make an aerobic push, this is the place to do it; the bike path continues more or less uninterrupted for several miles before you approach Vineyard Haven. You'll have ridden a total of 20-some miles, depending on how many side excursions you choose to take.

Vineyard Haven–Gay Head Loop

Allow 5–6 hours. Moderate; rolling terrain with a few very short but steep hills. Access: Begin the ride at the ferry terminal in Vineyard Haven. Map: The Martha's Vineyard Commission's free *Biking in Martha's Vineyard* should be available at the ferry terminal and bike-rental outlets.

The western half of Martha's Vineyard is about as rural an area as you'll find on the Cape and the islands. Deep forests give way to rolling pasturelands where sheep graze, with the ocean far in the distance. Small country stores and the occasional small gallery or antiques shop are reminiscent of rural Vermont. But then you arrive at Gay Head, with its magnificent, oft-photographed cliffs overlooking Vineyard Sound, and it becomes very clear that you are not in Vermont anymore.

While this ride shouldn't be considered hilly, it certainly isn't flat, as the roads roll up and over the many undulations in the land. You won't be required to face any long, arduous climbs, but then again don't expect the kind of leisurely roll you typically encounter elsewhere on the Cape and the islands.

Battle your way out of Vineyard Haven (Center Street to West Spring Street is probably the best way of avoiding most of busy State Road), looking for signs to Gay Head when in doubt. You'll have to spend at least a little bit of time on State Road, but almost immediately after leaving town, look for signs to Lambert's

Cove. Turn right where the narrow road winds through the woods into a parking area for the cove, located on your right. Lock your bike here and take the short walk through the dunes to the beach, a great place for beachcombing for shells and stones made round and smooth by the movements of the ebb and flow of the water.

Returning to your bike, continue on Lambert's Cove Road as it loops back to State Road. Look soon for a right turn onto North Road, looking for signs to Menemsha, the small fishing village known as a hang-out for the likes of James Taylor and Carly Simon. In fact, it is Taylor's brother Hugh who runs the bike ferry you ride to cross the inlet into Menemsha Pond. Once across the ferry, continue on West Basin Road, turning right at the T, and right again on Lighthouse Road, leading to Gay Head.

Don't be surprised when you arrive at Gay Head, after the gradual climb up Lighthouse Road, to encounter a sizable cluster of tourists. Be patient—big groups come and go as the tour buses come and go. Settle in for a picnic lunch, wander down to the beach, and wait a while. The crowds usually disappear, at least until the next bus comes along.

Leaving Gay Head, turn right onto Moshup Trail, through the low seaside growth and views of Vineyard Sound on your right. In a couple of miles, you'll come to State Road, which rises up over a knoll as it passes between Menemsha Pond and Squibnocket Pond before turning inland. At the next major junction, turn right onto South Road, which rolls for 5 miles through farmland on its way to West Tisbury. Here you might want to stop in at Alley's General Store, the kind of old-fashioned country store that seems barely to have acknowledged the coming of tourism.

From here, turn right briefly onto Edgartown West Tisbury Road, then left onto Old County Road, which soon joins busy State Road for the ride back to Vineyard Haven. The total distance covered is roughly 40 miles. But if you take your time, soak in the scenery, and stick your feet in the sand at Lambert's Cove or Gay Head, you'll probably feel fresh enough to do it all over again. Or perhaps combine it with the ride described above to Edgartown. Who says you can't ride 60 miles in a day?

Nantucket
Island Loop
Allow 3–5 hours. Easy–moderate; strong winds rather than hills are apt to provide the toughest challenge. Start at the Steamship Wharf in Nantucket Town.

Covering just 54 square miles, Nantucket is almost the ideal island for bicycling. It is small enough so that you can easily ride from one end of the island to the other in less than 2 hours, yet it is large enough to get an aerobic workout if that's what you're after. There are essentially no hills, and while you might find yourself battling a stiff headwind from time to time, it is always good to remind yourself that a headwind becomes a tailwind upon reversing direction.

As is the case throughout this region, Nantucket is decidedly bicycle-friendly. There are four main bike paths that radiate from Nantucket Town—east along Milestone Road to Sciasconset, east again along Polpis Road toward Sciasconset, south along Surfside Road to Surfside Beach, and west to Madaket and Long Pond. That means you can ride around Nantucket and will barely have to deal with motorized traffic. So if you're coming for just a short visit, you might as well leave the car back at Wood's Hole or Hyannis and use a two-wheeler as your main mode of transportation.

For an easy, 3-hour tour of the island, head east from Nantucket Town on the Milestone Road bike path toward Sciasconset, generally known in more abbreviated form as Sconset. You'll have to do a little maneuvering to get out of town; some of the streets are paved with cobblestones that don't make for easy riding. Make your way southeast to the rotary at which essentially all roads on Nantucket converge; from here you can pick up the bike path.

The path passes by cranberry bogs on its way to Sconset, a picturesque old fishing village, where tiny fishermen's shacks have been converted into tiny summer homes. These modest digs are a marked contrast from some of the elegant homes built by the rich and famous who summer on Nantucket.

After the bike path ends, continue on to the rotary, where you can turn right onto Ocean Beach Road for a swim at the beach. Or take Sankaty Road north to connect with the Polpis Road bike path that begins to make a loop back toward Nantucket Town. Look for the turn onto Wauwinet Road on your right, and make a detour to splurge for lunch at the Wauwinet (see "Inns & Resorts," below). You'll drop a few bucks here—maybe as much as $25 a person—but to spend an hour or so in this special setting, with its manicured lawns and gardens sloping to the water, is worth every penny.

Leaving Wauwinet, turn right again onto the Polpis Road bike path and, in about 5 miles, make a right on Milestone to return to the central rotary. Take Orange Street back into town and call it a day if your energy level is low. But if you're up for more riding, head west on Main Street to pick up the bike path along Madaket Road. It's about a 12-mile round-trip to Madaket, through sandy grasslands that, if the time of year is right, are strewn with wildflowers. When you return to Nantucket Town, you'll have earned a meal at one of several great restaurants that are an excellent reason to come to Nantucket in the first place.

Gear & Rentals

To list all the places that rent bikes on the Cape and the islands would take up an entire chapter of this book. Suffice it to say there are many rental outlets, particularly near the ferry terminals on Martha's Vineyard and Nantucket. Here are just a few recommendations to get you started, but if you don't get what you're looking for, don't hesitate to go elsewhere. There is plenty of competition. For riding the Cape Cod Rail Trail, **Rail Trail Bike Shop** (302 Underpass Rd., Brewster; ☎ **508/896-8200**) is, as the name implies, conveniently located. **Martha's Bike Rentals** (4 Lagoon Pond Rd., Vineyard Haven; ☎ **508/693-6593**) rents both hybrids for road riding and mountain bikes and will deliver to any location on the island. **Young's Bicycle Rentals** (Steamship Wharf, Nantucket; ☎ **508/228-1151**) rents both hybrids and full-suspension mountain bikes by the day or week and is conveniently located on Steamship Wharf in Nantucket.

Outfitters

Vermont Bicycle Touring (Box 711, Bristol, VT 05443; ☎ **800/245-3868** or 802/453-4811), leads popular 5-day tours of Martha's Vineyard and Nantucket throughout the summer and fall.

SAILING

Can sailing possibly get much better than this? Here you'll find steady winds; bays, harbors, and inlets to explore; islands to visit; and the open sea. There are regattas for larger boats, and weekend races for smaller boats are held weekly from Buzzard's Bay to Nantucket. So many are the sails you can see in looking across Nantucket Sound on a Saturday in summer that you might think you were looking at a blue Broadway littered with confetti after a ticker-tape parade.

The prevailing summer winds are from the southwest, averaging more than 15 knots by the time they pick up steam in the afternoon. And pick up steam they do, quite literally. Drawing moisture off the water, the summer winds are locally known as smoky sou'westers because of the haze associated with them. They can also quickly churn up swells of 3 feet and higher, in larger part because Buzzard's Bay, Vineyard Sound, and Nantucket Sound are shallow bodies of water, rarely more than 40 feet deep.

Because of these sizeable swells, even many smaller boats are keel-bottomed (rather than centerboard-equipped) for added stability in big seas. For many years, one of the most popular boats for day sailors and racers in the waters off the Cape was the Herreshoff 12, a tubby but unsinkable 12-footer with more than 800 pounds of ballast to keep it upright. The boat came from the drawing board of the famous Herreshoff family, who designed and built many of the early America's Cup yachts. More than 80 years after being introduced, sturdy Herreshoff 12s are still bobbing around the waters of Buzzard's Bay and Nantucket Sound.

You can expect literally smoother sailing in **Cape Cod Bay,** although the winds are not necessarily as steady or as reliable. That's because the Cape itself shields the bay from those smoky prevailing winds. Small-boat sailors piloting shallow-draft boats, such as Lightnings, Penguins, and Lasers, frequent the bay.

But if you are into overnight cruising—chartering a boat and poking around from harbor to harbor—you'll want to spend your time in **Buzzard's Bay, Vineyard Sound,** and **Nantucket Sound.** Working your way southward from the head of Buzzard's Bay to the Elizabeth Islands and then east through Nantucket Sound, here are some of the popular anchorages for cruising yachtsmen:

Well-sheltered **Wing's Neck Harbor** near Pocasset is a great getaway spot. There are no services or dockside stores or restaurants to intrude on the serenity of this small private harbor. **Hadley's Harbor** on the northeastern edge of Naushon Island, the largest of the Elizabeths, is a little more active, but if you're looking to go ashore for a lively time, you're better off pulling in across the channel in **Wood's Hole.**

A great spot for a lunch break and a swim on Naushon Island is **Tarpaulin Cove,** on the island's south side. The smooth, sandy beaches of this crescent-shaped cove and the undeveloped shores of the privately owned island create the illusion of what it might have been like to have arrived here in the 17th century, when the place was all but deserted and still uncharted. At the end of the Elizabeth chain is **Cuttyhunk,** a windswept, picturesque island with a year-round population of less than 30.

One of the great social scenes in yachting is the **Edgartown Regatta,** held every year in July on Martha's Vineyard. There is racing, of course, including a Herreshoff 12 competition, but generally the idea is for yachtsmen in spectacular vessels to come together and do what yachtsmen do—visit one another's boats for cocktails. At other times of year, **Edgartown Harbor** is still the perfect place to visit when you're ready to go ashore for a meal at a fine restaurant and, perhaps, a high-end shopping session.

Along the southern Cape Cod coast, there are a number of small harbors to explore, from **Cotuit** to **Hyannis** to **Chatham.** Some harbor channels, however, can be narrow and/or shallow, so be sure you read your tide charts carefully and there's enough water in which to navigate safely. Finally, on the east end of Nantucket Sound is **Monomoy National Wildlife Refuge.** The refuge isn't a great place for anchoring offshore overnight, but as a spot to go ashore for a picnic lunch on the beach, it's hard to beat.

Rentals & Charters

Flyer's (131A Commercial St., Provincetown; ☎ 800/750-0898 or 508/487-0898) rents a wide variety of boats, from Sunfishes to a 27-foot sloop for overnight excursion on Cape Cod Bay. For small-boat rentals on Martha's Vineyard, **Wind's Up** (199 Beach Rd., Vineyard Haven; ☎ 508/693-4252) has a fleet of single-hulled boats and catamarans for a day of sailing. *Note:* Charter boats are available at many marinas in the area, but for extended yacht charters, you'll find a better selection in the Boston area and Rhode Island, both an easy day's sail from the Cape. See the Boston and Rhode Island chapters (chapter 4, "Greater Boston, Cape Ann & the South Shore," and chapter 8, "Rhode Island & Block Island") for recommended charter operators.

Instruction

Island Sailing Schools (Box 3126, Edgartown, MA 02539; ☎ **508/627-5720**) offers sailing classes for both adults and children, ranging from half-day clinics to 8-day programs.

SCUBA DIVING

Given the seafaring history of the area, there are plenty of wrecks to visit beneath the waters off Cape Cod and the islands in addition to natural phenomena. Just one caveat: Beware the cold water. A good wetsuit is a must.

Adventure Diving Services of Cape Cod (Locust Road, Eastham; ☎ **508/255-5953**) conducts certification courses for beginners, as well as courses for advanced divers. Once you're certified (or if you already are certified), the Adventure Diving folks can take you to wreck sites in Provincetown Harbor, as well as other saltwater and freshwater sites.

SEA KAYAKING

When it comes to sea kayaking, life doesn't get much better than this. In fact, when it comes to experiencing the complete ecological complexity of the Cape and the islands, there is probably no means of transportation more versatile than the sea kayak. Its draft is shallow enough to enable you to explore tidal marshes, while at the same time it is sturdy enough to venture into open water (unless of course the wind is howling).

In short, the sea kayak is an ideal exploratory vessel, and there is much to explore. All the trips described above in "Canoeing/Flatwater Kayaking" are possible in a sea kayak. The only limitation might be that if you are paddling in a larger, double boat, your ability to maneuver in some of the tightest spaces might be a bit restricted. The many harbors of the Cape and the islands are great for paddling around among the handsome yachts that come and go during the summer, if just to experience vicariously how the other half lives. If you're into checking out multimillion-dollar yachts, take a trip around **Hyannis Harbor, Edgartown Harbor,** or **Chatham Harbor.**

Pleasant Bay near Chatham and Orleans, **Barnstable Harbor,** and the **great ponds** of Martha's Vineyard are large bodies of relatively wind-protected water that are good places to go if the wind is up on the open water. Just be sure to keep an eye on the tides, which can leave the careless kayaker stranded until higher water returns. And the ambitious kayaker, with a little planning, could put together a multiday trip starting in **Woods Hole,** possibly venturing across open water to **Vineyard Haven,** then return to explore the southern coast of Cape Cod, from **Waquoit Bay** eastward to **Chatham** and **Monomoy National Wildlife Refuge.** The main limitation here is the absence of harbor-side camping facilities (although there is a small, primitive camping area on **Washburn Island** in Waquoit Bay). Thus, any multiday trip would have to be primarily an inn-based trip.

If you do venture out into open water, plan wisely and be prepared to modify your plans. Tidal currents in some areas can be powerful—particularly through Woods Hole—and to cross against the current can be a hazardous undertaking. Either plan to hit the tides at the right moment, or be willing to wait for the current to turn or slacken. Also, the steady winds and big seas that boardsailers love can be a menace to sea kayakers. If the forecast is for strong winds, particularly from the southwest, think about postponing your trip for another day.

Sea kayaking opportunities around Martha's Vineyard and Nantucket are somewhat more limited than around the Cape. There are plenty of protected bodies of water to explore, most notably the **great ponds** of Martha's Vineyard, and **Nantucket Harbor,** particularly Head of the Harbor and Coskata-Coatue Wildlife Refuge. But the opportunities to travel back and forth between open water to harbors, bays, and inlets are fewer on the islands. For the best sea kayaking, stick to the Cape.

Bassetts Island

Access: Take Rte. 28 south from the Bourne Bridge rotary and, after about 3 miles, turn right at the sign for Pocasset, Barlow's Landing, and Wing's Neck. This is Barlow's Landing Rd. Continue on this road till it ends at Barlow's Landing. Chart: Cape Cod Canal & approaches (NOAA Chart #13236).

Look at a map of Bassetts Island, and it looks like a giant gull in flight. This is an off-the-beaten-path part of the Cape, where few visitors, other than those who own private summer homes here, ever venture. In fact, the island itself is privately owned.

You can loop the island in either direction, but check the wind before setting out. If the wind is from the southwest, as it usually is in summer, going clockwise around the island is more sensible to avoid bashing into the wind-driven waves on the more exposed western side of the island.

Heading south from Barlow's Landing, bear left through the channel between the northern edge of the island and the mainland into a world of quiet marshes and tiny coves and harbors. Marsh grasses grow along the shore, waiting to be immersed in the waters of the incoming tide. The south wing of the island is a narrow, sandy strip, a beautiful place to come ashore for a stretch—being mindful, of course, that this is private property. Across the way, small boats come and go from Cataumet Harbor.

Circling around this northern spit of land, you'll enter the more open waters of Buzzard's Bay, although Scraggy Neck to your south acts as a shield against prevailing southwest winds. However, as you continue around the island into the channel that leads into Wing's Neck harbor, be prepared for a brief wild ride if the wind is indeed from the southwest. Wind-blown waves in the channel can be surprisingly large, and if you time your entry right, you can get a nice little push from the surf as you make your entry into the harbor.

Pull up to the small, sandy beach in Wing's Neck Harbor for a picnic lunch. Then continue on through all the moored sailboats back to Barlow's Landing, riding what should now be the gentle push of the wind.

Monomoy National Wildlife Refuge

Access: The most direct departure point from the Cape is from Stage Harbor in Chatham. Other possible departure points include the beaches of south Chatham, among them Cockle Cove Beach, Ridgevale Beach, and Hardings Beach. Chart: Chatham and Monomoy (NOAA Charts #13244 and 13248).

What is there left to be said about Monomoy National Wildlife Refuge that hasn't already been said under "Bird-watching," above? Perhaps that it is also a terrific and relatively easy destination for sea kayakers. To do a complete circumnavigation of the islands would require experience and strong kayaking skills and would certainly be a full-day trip. But such a long outing is hardly necessary to appreciate the islands.

The journey from Chatham to North Monomoy Island is no more than a couple of miles, and to make a loop of the island is a relatively easy half-day trip. You'll pass through the break between the two islands—a passage that has existed only since the late 1970s, when storm seas cut through the delicate barrier of sand. Then, if your energy level is high and the weather is agreeable, you can turn south to explore the ocean beaches of south Monomoy Island, a great place to come ashore for a picnic. Keep your eyes open not only for birds, but also for the harbor seals that are often spotted on the island's beaches.

Naushon Island

Access: The best spot to launch from is Eel Pond in the center of Woods Hole. Chart: Woods Hole and the Elizabeth Islands (NOAA Charts #13235 and 13229).

What might the Cape and the islands have been like 100 years ago? In some ways, this excursion is a trip back in time, to an era that predates development. That's because Naushon Island, which extends like a long, southwest-reaching tail from Woods Hole and is the largest in the Elizabeth Island chain, is privately owned. Thus, the island is all but undeveloped, with just a few private homes here and there. It is easy to imagine that the Cape and Martha's Vineyard, before turning into such popular summer vacation spots, might have looked like Naushon many years ago.

This full-day journey of close to 20 miles starts in Woods Hole. Start early in the morning when the wind (usually) is low, and make the circumnavigation in a counterclockwise direction. By doing so, you'll be passing along the northwestern, more exposed shore of the island before the wind typically picks up. Nevertheless, expect to face some kind of wind—and current—during the course of a fairly long day of paddling.

From Woods Hole, head directly across Woods Hole Passage to Hadley's Harbor at the northeastern end of Naushon Island. This can be a tricky crossing if the tidal currents are unfavorable (and even treacherous), so you'll really do well if you manage to plan for a day when the early-morning tide is reasonably slack.

Hadley's Harbor is a very popular stopover point for people cruising up and down the New England coast. So if you indeed make an early-morning departure from Woods Hole, expect, as you pass all the handsome yachts, to see disheveled skippers and crew emerging on deck after a night's sleep. Continue through the main harbor into the inner harbor, passing small Bull Island on your right. Continue around Bull Island, looking for the small channel that separates Uncanteena and Naushon. At low tide, you might find yourself having to portage a short distance here, but at most times you ought to be able to scrape through.

Soon you'll break out into the open water of Buzzard's Bay and bear southwest along Naushon's shore, keeping tiny Weepecket Island on your right. Explore the shoreline, but be mindful that the island is private. The owners generously allow visitors to stop along some shore areas and beaches, but hiking inland is not permitted. A good place to stop along the north shore for a break and a snack is Kettle Cove. This will give you a chance to rest up and prepare for what can be a tricky passage through Robinson's Hole.

As in Wood's Hole, tidal currents in Robinson's Hole can be powerful. You'll have a few things in your favor through Robinson's Hole, however. For one, even if the current is against you, it will generally be directly against you—not easy going, certainly, but not as troublesome as a crosscurrent. Also, Robinson's Hole is smaller. Once you make it through the narrow throat, it's easy going the rest of the way. And finally, you won't encounter any of the big boats (for example, the Vineyard and Nantucket ferries) that pass in and out of Wood's Hole.

As you turn northeastward to make the return trip, make sure to leave time for a trip into Tarpaulin Cove, one of the prettiest spots anywhere on the Cape and the islands. A perfectly crescent-shaped cove, with bright sand beaches and an undeveloped shoreline, it has views across Vineyard Sound to the cliffs of Gay Head. Take a swim and enjoy the view— just the right tonic to reinvigorate you for the last 5 to 6 miles back to Woods Hole.

Travel Tip

Watch out for the greenhead flies at North Shore beaches in late July and early August. They don't sting—they take little bites of flesh. Make sure you bring or buy insect repellent before hitting the beach.

Unfortunately, there is no camping allowed on Naushon, but a variation on this trip is possible if you're up for a 2-day adventure. Continue on to the end of the Elizabeth Island chain to Cuttyhunk, another 5 or 6 miles beyond Robinson's Hole. A tiny island with a one-room schoolhouse and fewer than 30 year-round residents, Cuttyhunk looks like it could have been plucked from the coast of Scotland. There are a couple of bed-and-breakfasts on the island, and after a few days on this remote place, you may find you never want to leave.

Gear & Rentals

Cape Cod Kayak (Box 1273, North Falmouth, MA 02556; ☎ **508/540-9377**) rents single and double sea kayaks. Delivery is included in the rental charge. **Eastern Mountain Sports** (233 Stevens St., Hyannis; ☎ **508/775-1072**) has a wide variety of kayak equipment for sale and kayaks for rent. Instructional clinics and guided tours are also offered through the store.

Outfitters

Cape Cod Kayak (☎ **508/540-9377**) leads day tours of the bays, rivers, and harbors around Falmouth and Mashpee. **Off the Coast Kayak** (3 Freeman St., Provincetown; ☎ **877/PTKAYAK**) guides half-day tours on the Cape Cod Bay side of Provincetown, Truro, and Wellfleet.

SURFING

Wherever ocean and beach come together, surfing is a possibility. The Cape and the islands are not known for big-wave beaches; for some reason, Rhode Island has a more widespread reputation in the surfing community as a hot spot. Nevertheless, if a storm is brewing in the Atlantic—more likely during the late summer and fall—10-foot waves are not out of the question.

On the Cape, **Nauset Beach** near Orleans is usually the place where surfers go, although **Ballston Beach** in Truro has also been known to produce a good break. On the Vineyard, check out **Squibnocket Beach** on the far southwestern corner of the island. On Nantucket, while **Surfside** might sound like it's the place to go, most surfers head west to **Cisco** and **Madaket** beaches.

Rentals

Nauset Sports rents boards from two locations on the Cape: in Eastham (on Route 6; ☎ **508/255-2219**), and in Orleans (on Route 6A; ☎ **508/255-4742**). On Martha's Vineyard, rental boards are available from **Wind's Up** (199 Beach Rd., Vineyard Haven; ☎ **508/693-4252**).

SWIMMING

There is obviously no shortage of beaches on the Cape and the islands. One reliable map lists 140 public beaches, a number that doesn't really tell the whole story. Most are simply beaches that have lifeguards during the summer months; if you're willing to go swimming without a lifeguard's supervision, the beach count increases dramatically. Some of those public beaches are also large enough to be several beaches rolled into one. For example, **Nauset Beach,** which stretches southward from Orleans to Chatham, is itself about 8 miles long. And if you throw in private beaches—some hotels and resort complexes have their own beaches reserved exclusively for their guests—the beach count goes up even more.

Three main factors (other than the simple proximity to where you happen to be) will affect your choice of beach on the Cape and the islands. The first is water temperature. The ocean waters off the Cape and the waters of Cape Cod Bay are cold with a capital C. Even in the heat of summer, the water temperature usually remains in the 50s. For some, the numbing effect is refreshing, something like a reverse sauna; for others, it can be downright painful. But when those hot and hazy summer days arrive, a dip in frigid water can be just the right tonic to wash away the heat.

The water temperature along the beaches of Nantucket Sound on the southern coast of the Cape tends to be warmer, since it is influenced by the Gulf Stream. So too is the ocean water off Martha's Vineyard and Nantucket, where swimming can be relatively pleasant even into the fall months.

The second factor to take into consideration is surf. If you're into body surfing, the ocean beaches are the place to go, unless the usual summer winds from the southwest blow powerfully enough to create a wind swell on the beaches of the southern Cape coast and Buzzard's Bay. If ocean swells are what you want, head for the beaches of the outer Cape and the southern shores of Martha's Vineyard and Nantucket. Conversely, if you want protected water—if you've got young children, for example—the Cape Cod Bay beaches, the harbor beaches along the southern coast, or even the inland pond beaches are the way to go. In Nantucket harbor, in fact, there is **Children's Beach,** specifically geared toward small fry.

The third factor in choosing a beach is the type of water—saltwater or fresh water. Those hundreds of kettle ponds are often an overlooked asset, and that can be a good thing. If you want to escape the crowds (and also the seacoast

winds), heading inland to a freshwater beach is one way to go.

All right, then—so where are the best places to go swimming? Weeding out the stars from the also-rans in a world of 140 beaches is no easy task, but here's a go at it. The most popular beaches along the outer Cape are **Marconi, Nauset,** and **Coast Guard** beaches. This probably has as much to do with ample (or usually ample) parking available—for a fee, of course—as it does with the inherent qualities of the beaches themselves. The great features of the beaches here are the looming sandstone cliffs that form a dramatic backdrop to the ocean.

If you're looking for an active beach scene—guys checking out girls and vice versa, kids building sandcastles, beach chairs, parasols in the sand, and so on—Nauset is the place to go. If you're looking for an ocean beach scene that's a little lower key, try **Race Point,** on the northern tip of the Cape. Probably the biggest beach scene along the southern Cape shore is at **Craigville Beach,** just a few miles from Hyannis.

Probably the most popular ocean beach on the Vineyard is **South Beach** (also known as Katama Beach) south of Edgartown. The main reason: It's easy to get to. For more seclusion, head to **East Beach** on Chappaquiddick Island or to **Long Point Beach,** which is part of Long Point National Wildlife Refuge. **Moshup Beach,** with the cliffs of Gay Head as its backdrop, can be a scenic place to flop down in the sand with a towel; don't expect to have the beach to yourself, however, and if the wind is out of the southwest, don't expect the water to be pond-water smooth. A pretty getaway spot on the north shore of the island is **Lambert's Cove,** although you might want to bring along a pair of flip-flops for wading in through the pebbles.

Surfside, on the southern shore of Nantucket, is appropriately named. If a storm at sea has roiled up the ocean waters, this can be a great place for body surfing. It is also the closest ocean beach to Nantucket Town, and so attracts a crowd, at least by the relatively small crowd standards of Nantucket. To get away from it all, head for **Madaket Beach,** on the east side of the island and popular among surfers, or to **Sconset Beach** on the east side.

As far as the freshwater scene goes, look for anything named Great Pond—there must be at least two dozen Great Ponds on the Cape. Long Pond is another popular name. In fact, **Long Pond** between Harwich and Brewster is a good place to go if you like your ponds big; it's one of the biggest on the Cape. There are other good ponds for swimming in this general area, including **Seymour Pond** (right off the Cape Cod Rail Trail) and **Slough Pond.** Near Wellfleet, check out tiny **Gull Pond,** near **Newcomb Hollow Beach.** As the crowds rush to the ocean side, Gull Pond gets the cold shoulder. It's also not a bad place to take a freshwater dip to wash off the salt after swimming in the ocean.

WALKS & RAMBLES

While there may be few areas on the Cape and the islands to embark on a long aerobic hike, there are plenty of places to throttle down and take a leisurely stroll. Simply head for the closest beach, and you can hardly go wrong. Some notable beaches for short walks and beachcombing are **Morris Island Point,** part of Monomoy National Wildlife Refuge in Chatham, **Lambert's Cove** near Vineyard Haven on Martha's Vineyard, and **Eel Point** near Madaket on Nantucket.

Regardless of where you go for a stroll, you're apt to find yourself birdwatching. So if you've got a pair of binoculars, don't leave home without them.

Cape Cod

Indian Lands Conservation Area

Allow 1–1½ hours. Easy. Access: Take exit 9 on Rte. 6. Drive south on Rte. 134 to the third traffic light and turn right onto Upper County Rd. Make the next right on Main St. and look for the Dennis town offices. Park here.

This area along the Bass River was once used as wintering ground by the Nobscusset tribe, who fished the river and hunted in the surrounding forests. The river, a tidal flow rich in marine life, also attracted European explorers and settlers—quite obviously, the Nobscussets had come upon a very good thing. In recent years, the area has been the site of archeological digs that have turned up all sorts of Native American tools and implements. Today it is something of a small, hidden gem, largely because few people other than Dennis-area locals know about it.

From the parking area, head north on Main Street and turn left on the dirt road along the power lines. Train tracks also run along the road, an abandoned route that very likely will become a paved bike path if recent trends on the Cape continue. Shortly you will come to a sign indicating the Indian Lands trailhead on your left. Make a left here, and then go left again at the next fork.

From here the trail leads into a broad marsh and the Bass River. As the trail divides, stay to your left along the banks of the river for a wonderful .5-mile loop through a predominantly pine forest. Along the way, you'll come to a bench with a nice view across the river to the homes and docks that line the edge of the river's other side. Take a seat, breathe in deeply, and take in this classic, postcard-Cape view. After passing more marsh (keep an eye out for ducks and herons), the loop is complete. Turn left at the junction, retracing your steps back to the power-line trail and back to your starting point.

John Wing Trail

Allow 1 hour. Easy. Access: From Brewster, take Rte. 6A east toward Dennis. Look for the Cape Cod Museum of Natural History on your right, and park in the museum parking lot. Map: Available from the museum.

If you're seeking the unusual experience of walking through tidal flats, this is the place to come. Tiny Wing Island along the Cape Cod Bay shore is named for John Wing, the first European settler to come to this area in the mid-1600s. When Wing arrived, the island was indeed an island, but today, the sands have shifted, and island and mainland are now one.

The trail departs from the Cape Cod Museum of Natural History, and it is an easy, flat walk to Wing Island, first through the forest and then through marsh grasses before arriving on the island. Here the trail loops the small island; note along the way a plaque that marks the site where Wing first built his home.

If you come at low tide—the best time to come—you can leave the island and walk far out onto the tidal flats of Cape Cod Bay. It can be an odd sensation to walk here, the geographic features adding to the illusion that you're walking on water. In fact, if you're not vigilant or aware of the tides, you may literally end up walking on water since the tide moves in quickly. Tidal charts are available at the museum. Return to the island and pass through beach-plum bushes on your way back to the museum. If you do not purchase beach-plum jam or jelly during your visit to the Cape, you are depriving yourself of one of nature's great treats.

Salt Pond & Nauset Marsh

Allow 1–1^1/$_2$ hours. Easy–moderate. Access: From the Eastham rotary, take Rte. 6 north to the Salt Pond Visitors Center of the Cape Cod National Seashore, about 4 miles along on your right. Park in the visitors center lot. Map: Available at the visitors center.

This is an easy, 2-mile walk and a popular one, primarily because the trail begins at the Salt Pond Visitors Center, a hive of activity in summer. Still, given all the people who come and go at the center, only a small percentage of them venture too far from the cars. So although you're sure to see other people on the trail, don't expect to have to elbow your way through a crowd.

Salt Pond is an unusual phenomenon on the Cape because that is just what it is—a salt pond. Almost all of the Cape's kettle ponds contain fresh water, but at some time in the past, the ocean managed to burst through and infiltrate Salt Pond, causing its salinity. As a result, the kinds of grasses and flowers that grow around the pond are unlike those you might find in a freshwater environment.

After skirting the edge of the pond, the trail crosses a dike to Nauset Marsh. If the inherent serenity of a saltwater marsh is the sort of thing that captivates you, it doesn't get much better than this. It's one of the prettiest marshes on the Cape, with Nauset Beach and the ocean as a backdrop. Be sure to have your binoculars along, because the bird-watching here can be extraordinary. Also, depending on the tide, look for shell fishermen working the tidal flats.

After reaching the marsh, the trail turns back inland, through the oak and pine forest, before merging with the Buttonbush Trail. There is a very short interpretive loop here, and you'll pass a tiny kettle pond before returning to the visitors center.

Wellfleet Bay Wildlife Sanctuary

Allow 1–2 hours. Easy. Access: From Wellfleet, head south on Rte. 6 about 4 miles and look for the entrance to the sanctuary on your right. Map: Available at the sanctuary headquarters.

The sanctuary has a distinguished history as a place for bird-watching. Before being acquired by the Massachusetts Audubon Society in 1958, the area was a well-regarded ornithological research station. That ought to tell you something: Birds love this place. A wide variety of over 250 different species have been sighted here, so you can feel fairly certain your walk here will be accompanied by birds actively announcing their presence.

The main loop here is the Goose Pond Trail, an easy, 1.5-mile trail past tiny Goose Pond, through a pine and oak forest, and to the edge of a salt marsh. The pond itself is actually man-made, created to add more habitat diversity to the sanctuary (as if there weren't already enough!).

In fact, if you're looking for real habitat diversity, make a point of timing your visit with low tide. When the tides recede, it is possible to make a short walk out to Try Island (itself usually accessible in all but the highest tides) and beyond to the tidal flats of Cape Cod Bay. The oak and hickory forest of the island is said to be one of the last of its kind on the outer Cape, although such forests were common when the early European settlers arrived in the 1600s. Make sure you wear water-resistant shoes if you plan to wander out onto the tidal flats, where you'll join the many shorebirds who come to feed on whatever morsels the tide has left stranded. And like those shorebirds, keep an eye on the tide. It can come in quickly.

Martha's Vineyard

Cedar Tree Neck Sanctuary
Allow 1–2 hours. Easy. Access: From Vineyard Haven, take State Rd. south toward West Tisbury. Turn right at Indian Hill Rd. and follow signs to the sanctuary. Map: Available at the trailhead.

Cedar Tree Neck is a place where land and sea connect. That might seem a common concept around the Cape and the islands, but in most cases, the sea and the inland forests are separated by a seascape of dunes, marshes, and salt ponds. Not so on this neck of land that juts out into Vineyard Sound.

There are about 4 miles of interconnected trails passing through this 300-acre sanctuary. For the longest loop, start on the White Trail, which leads through an oak and sassafras forest to tiny Ames Pond, where a pondside bench allows you a moment's rest to contemplate the true meaning of the kettle pond. If the concept is meant to imply a natural kettle full of water, then Ames Pond is exactly what a kettle pond ought to look like.

Continue on the White Trail around the pond and down to a bog, where another bench enables you to contemplate just what bogs are all about. From here, the trail leads to the edge of the sound for a short walk along the beach. Be alert for some small treasure that might have washed ashore, since this is fine beachcombing territory. Soon you'll turn back inland, through beach rose and bayberry shrubs, to join the Red Trail, where you'll turn left.

Make a point of taking the short spur trail on your left that leads to a fine viewpoint above sandy bluffs overlooking the sound, the Cape, and the Elizabeth Islands in the distance. Go back to the Red Trail to loop around Cedar Tree Neck Pond, the heart of what once was a working cranberry bog. The red cedars in the forest here are what give the neck its name, and yes—there is a bench at the pond's edge, so take a few minutes for more pondside contemplation before returning to the trailhead.

Long Point Wildlife Refuge
Allow 1–1$^1/_2$ hours. Easy. Access: From Edgartown, take West Tisbury Rd. west. Shortly after the entrance to the airport (on your right), look for Waldrons Bottom Rd. on your left. Turn here and continue about 3 miles to the parking area. A parking fee is charged.

This is a great place to come in summer to swim and simply hang at the beach; it's relatively removed from the crowds that frequent South Beach to the east. So if you do nothing else, come here on a sunny day, flop down on a towel, and enjoy the oceanside solitude. But if you're motivated to get up and move around, head for the refuge trail that runs inland for about a mile between Tisbury Great Pond to the west and Long Cove to the east.

The layout is pretty simple—two trails, the Orange and the Yellow, that more or less parallel one another. Walk inland on one path, then return to the sea on the other. If you happen to be a painter of seascapes, this is the sort of place that would likely draw you back again and again, with its dunes, windswept grasses, and the sun shimmering on the salt-pond water. If you were a birding enthusiast, you'd certainly make this a regular hangout, particularly if you are a fan of hawks and ospreys. And you don't need to be a painter or a birder to enjoy the rare opportunity to roll together a day at the beach and a walk through a unique seaside environment.

Gay Head Cliffs

Allow 2–3 hours. Easy–moderate. Access: From Vineyard Haven, take State Rd. south toward West Tisbury and continue to follow signs to Gay Head. The most direct route is via Middle Rd. (which mysteriously turns into State Rd. again) through Chilmark. Park in the lot between State Rd. and the Moshup Trail. A parking fee is charged in the summer. Map: Unnecessary.

Gay Head is one of those great examples of the odd way that tourism in America sometimes works. Busloads of visitors come to the cliffs in the summertime to take a quick snapshot, buy a few souvenirs and T-shirts, and then move on, barely noticing the scenery they came to see. Only a handful venture beyond the tourist enclave at the top of the cliffs. So what might seem like a crowd when you arrive will quickly dissipate within minutes after hitting the trail.

To further distance yourself from the crowds, come here near sunset, when all the tour buses are gone and the cliffs capture the flaming light of the lowering sun. The cliffs have often been photographed—posters and postcards in shops throughout the island attest to that—and most of the really dramatic photos have been taken late in the day.

It's about a 10-minute walk to the beach from the parking area along a sandy trail through the low seascape brush. The beach is Moshup Beach, named for a Native American of Bunyonesque legend. According to legend, Moshup could eat a whale by himself in one sitting. When you reach the beach, turn right to walk beneath the cliffs. In the late-afternoon sun, the striated colors in the cliffs can be especially striking from this vantage. Look also for holes in the cliffs, where swallows nest.

How far you go may depend on the tides. The farther north you go, the more the beach dwindles and the cliffs dive directly into the sea. If the tide is low, however—the best time for beachcombing—there is a little more room to maneuver along the north side of the cliffs. Once you've gone far enough, simply return the way you came.

Nantucket

Sanford Farm, Ram Pasture, and the Woods

Allow 2–3 hours. Easy–moderate. Access: From Nantucket Town, take Madaket Rd. west for 2 miles. Look for the parking area on the left side of the road. Map: Available at the trailhead or from the **Nantucket Conservation Foundation (☎ 508/228-2884)**.

Sanford Farm is the site of the first European settlement on Nantucket, and Ram Pasture and the Woods were originally used as grazing land. Today, nearly 1,000 acres in all, they are protected under the aegis of the Nantucket Conservation Foundation, and that is a very good thing. As second-home construction grows at a steady pace on the island, this is one of the last large tracts of undeveloped land left. As such, it is about the best place for a walk on the island, other than a long walk on the beach, of course. If you've got the energy, you can embark on a hike of nearly 7 miles, although shorter loops are possible.

The trail begins as a dirt road, after you pass through a turnstile, and from there leads through open, grassy fields where, depending on the season, wildflowers bloom abundantly. After passing a marsh and traveling over gentle ups and downs, the trail rises to an abandoned barn in a clearing. The views from here are terrific—Hummock Pond in the foreground, the town of Madaket in the distance in another direction, and finally the ocean.

From here, the trail descends through Ram Pasture to the ocean, running between the two separate sections of Hummock Pond. At one time, these two sections were connected as a single pond, but this kind of seascape is forever changing. A storm in 1978 reconfigured the sand and soil, and one pond became two. After reaching the beach, take a break before returning the way you came, for a walk of about 4 miles in all. Along the way, be sure to keep your eyes open for ospreys; osprey poles have been set up on both sections of the pond to assist the birds in their hunt for fish.

Guides

See "Guides" under "Hiking," above.

WHALE WATCHING

At one time, of course, whaling was one of the major industries of the region, and Nantucket in particular remains imbedded in whaling lore. Now the only sort of whaling going on is of the sightseeing variety, and that, in its own way, is becoming a significant industry as well. In direct ticket sales alone, whale watching off the New England coast reportedly brings in more than $25 million a year. Whale-watching trips depart regularly during the summer months from Provincetown, Hyannis, Chatham, and Nantucket.

Most tour operators guarantee you'll see whales, and with good reason—there are plenty of them in the waters off the Cape and the islands. From Provincetown, most boats head northeast to Stellwagen Bank, almost due east of Boston. This bank was once an offshore island that gradually became submerged with the retreat of the last Ice Age. The bank is now in essence an underwater reef, ranging from 80 to 500 feet below the surface, and fish and whales of all sorts congregate here by the thousands. The basics of the food chain take over; tiny fish attract larger fish, and larger fish attract even larger fish. And so on. In the past 25 years, the Center for Coastal Studies has identified and named more than 700 humpback whales in the Stellwagen Bank area.

As far as fish (and whales) are concerned, Stellwagen is the equivalent of a giant, underwater fast-food restaurant. The U.S. government sees it somewhat differently. In 1993, Stellwagen Bank was designated a National Marine Sanctuary, the first of its kind in New England.

From Nantucket, boats head to the same nearby feeding grounds that attracted whalers 2 centuries ago. Most boats head for the Great South Channel along the Nantucket shoals, offshore Nantucket's version of Stellwagen Bank. Summer is the prime whale-watching season—in colder weather, the whales migrate elsewhere—but many whale-watching operations run trips from April to November.

Trips with **The Dolphin Fleet** (Box 243, Provincetown; ☎ 800/826-9300) depart from Provincetown for Stellwagen Bank with a naturalist from the Center for Coastal Studies on board. The ticket office is in the Chamber of Commerce Building in Provincetown. **Hyannis Whale Watcher Cruises** (☎ 800/287/0374 or 508/362-6088) is actually misnamed. Trips leave from Barnstable Harbor on the north shore of the Cape, making for a much quicker ride (than from Hyannis) to Stellwagen Bank. The **Yankee Fleet** (☎ 800/942-5464), a Gloucester-based operation, also offers whale-watching

TURNING ON THE OFF-SEASON

It wasn't so long ago that the Cape and the islands pretty much closed up shop the day after Labor Day. Hotels and restaurants boarded up their windows right along with all the summer-home owners in a mass evacuation. Only a hardy few would stick around for an off-season that extended until Memorial Day of the next year.

No more. To be sure, you're not going to encounter big crowds if you decide to take a drive to Provincetown in the middle of February. But recent statistics indicate that year-round residency on the Cape is an exploding phenomenon, and tourism during what was once considered the shoulder months—May and September—is also on the rise.

According to figures published in the *Boston Globe,* the number of residential building permits issued on Cape Cod rose more than 40% between 1996 and 1998. Where people go, businesses follow; commercial development, particularly in the Hyannis area, has grown at a similarly brisk pace. Meanwhile, in the supposedly slow month of September, Cape Cod National Seashore now sees more than 20,000 visitors a day.

So if you think a trip to the Cape in May or September will mean having the place to yourself—or the place to yourself at vastly discounted rates—guess again. As people are discovering in rapidly increasing numbers, there is more to life on the Cape than the dog days of summer.

trips that depart from the Hy-Line docks on Straight Wharf in Nantucket.

Incidentally, whales are not the only marine mammals you might come across. Seals also frequent the beaches of the Monomoy islands. If you want to go on a seal watch, several boat services lead tours to Monomoy from Chatham Harbor.

Campgrounds & Other Accommodations

CAMPGROUNDS

Dunes' Edge Campground
From Rte. 6 going north to Provincetown, turn right at mile marker 116. The campground is on the right. 100 sites, 22 with hookups. Showers, tables, grocery store. ☎ 508/487-9815.

Perhaps the name says it all. The campground is indeed at the edge of the dunes that are Provincetown's featured attraction. Sites are nestled into the tree-

covered dunes, offering privacy and a good degree of shelter from the weather. Most of the sites are for tent camping only, so this is a fairly low-key place. Hiking trails leave directly from the campground to the National Seashore and Race Point, and the center of Provincetown is an easy bike ride away.

Hosteling International
Hosteling International/American Youth Hostels maintains hostels in 4 locations in the region—Eastham and Truro on the Cape, West Tisbury on Martha's Vineyard, and in Nantucket Town. For information, contact the organization's **Eastern New England Council** (1020 Commonwealth Ave., Boston, MA 02215; ☎ **617/731-6692**).

No, staying in a hostel isn't quite like staying in a campground. But then again, it's not quite like staying in a resort, either. The four hostels in the region are all well located, particularly for cyclists on an extended tour. The Eastham hostel (75 Goody Hallet Drive; ☎ **508/255-2785**) is close to the Salt Pond Visitors Center for Cape Cod National Seashore, the Wellfleet Bay Wildlife Sanctuary, and the Cape Cod

Trail. The Truro hostel (North Pamet Road; ☎ 508/349-3889) is housed in a former Coast Guard station with terrific views of the beach and dunes. The Martha's Vineyard hostel (Edgartown Road, West Tisbury; ☎ 508/693-2665) is located in almost the exact geographical center of the island, at the edge of Martha's Vineyard State Forest. The Nantucket hostel (31 Western Ave., Nantucket; ☎ 508/228-0433) is in an 1874 life-saving station. The accommodations are in hostel-style large dormitories, but if you don't mind sharing a room with several of your best friends, the locations and the price are hard to beat.

Nickerson State Park

From Brewster, take Rte. 6A east and look for the entrance to the park on your right. Or take exit 12 from Rte. 6 and head west on Rte. 6A to the park entrance. 420 sites, no hookups, handicapped rest rooms, tables, grills. Headquarters: 3488 Main St., Brewster (☎ 508/896-3491).

With 420 sites in seven camping areas, you might think that in Nickerson State Park you'll have plenty to choose from. Guess again. Nickerson fills up early, to put it mildly. By mid-May, most of the sites have likely been reserved for the summer, so call well ahead to make a reservation. Without a reservation, you might get lucky, particularly on a weekday, and will arrive when the park isn't completely booked or a reservation has been canceled. But don't count on it. With hiking and bike trails and ponds to explore, the 1,900-acre park is much more than just a campground; its popularity is well deserved.

Shawme Crowell State Forest

Take exit 1 from Rte. 6 near Sagamore and turn right at the traffic light onto Rte. 6A. Turn right again on Rte. 130 and follow signs to the forest. ☎ 508/888-0351. 280 sites, no hookups, tables, grills.

If Nickerson State Park is all booked up, this is your next best bet. It is on the Cape but barely so, just a couple of miles over the Sagamore Bridge. There are walking and biking trails in the 742-acre state forest, and the historic village of Sandwich is nearby.

INNS & RESORTS

Cape Cod

Beechwood Inn

2839 Main St. (Rte. 6A), Barnstable, MA 02630. ☎ 800/609-6618 or 508/362-0298. Off-season, rates start at $90; summer, rates start at $135. Rates include full breakfast.

This small 1853 inn, restored and furnished in a Victorian style, is on the Cape's quiet side, only a few miles north of Hyannis but well removed from Hyannis's commercial bustle. The inn is well situated for those wanting to explore Sandy Neck and the Great Marshes, just north of Barnstable, or for bicycling along Route 6A to explore the many antiques shops between Barnstable and Dennis.

Old Sea Pines Inn

2553 Main St., Brewster, MA 02631. ☎ 508/896-6114; www.oldseapinesinn. com. Rates during high season $70–$125 double, including breakfast and afternoon tea.

This grand 1907 shingle-style mansion once housed a charm school for women. A great deal of the charm is still there, and best of all, a number of the inn's 23 rooms are available at bargain rates. This is one of the few spots on Cape Cod where solo travelers can find a single room and pay no surcharge. These rooms have shared bathrooms and no air-conditioning, but the price is right; if you want something more upscale than a campground without busting your budget, you won't do any better than this.

Ship's Bell Inn

586 Commercial St., Provincetown, MA 02657. ☎ **508/487-1674.** Motel room rates start at $85.

There's nothing especially fancy here—just a comfortable, well-kept, and simply furnished cluster of motel rooms, suites, and apartments. The modest room rates and lack of pretension are particularly attractive for families. The inn's great location allows guests to take advantage of the best Provincetown has to offer. Explore the nearby dunes of the Province Lands by bike, or join a whale-watching cruise departing from Provincetown.

Wequassett Inn

178 Rte. 28 (Pleasant Bay), Chatham, MA 02633. ☎ **800/225-7125** or 508/432-5400. Rooms with breakfast $280–$515 in summer. Closed Nov–Mar.

Staying at the Wequassett Inn is like spending time at a luxurious summer camp for grown-ups. The inn is in fact not really an inn, but a complex—a camp-like cluster of guest cottages and other buildings, some dating back 200 years. Situated along the shores of Pleasant Bay, it's a hotbed of sporting activity. Sailboats and canoes are available for inn guests to explore the bay, and tennis buffs can practice their swings on the property's five tennis courts. The inn provides a boat-shuttle service across the bay to the secluded southern end of Nauset Beach, far from the madding crowds to the north. Golf packages are available. There is also a small fitness center to keep people occupied on inclement-weather days. Get the picture?

Martha's Vineyard

Daggett House

59 Water St., Edgartown, MA 02359. ☎ **508/627-4600.** Off-season, rates start at $90; in-season, rates start at $150.

Vermont Bicycle Touring uses the Daggett House as its base camp for tours of the Vineyard, and with good reason. The inn combines the feel of a centuries-old inn—the main inn itself dates back to 1750—with a relaxed atmosphere that doesn't make you feel out-of-place among stuffy antiques when you walk in from a day's ride in your sweaty biking clothes. The cottage rooms, located right on the harbor, are the nicest. Watch your head as you walk down to the inn's excellent restaurant on the lower level—the low ceilings and narrow stairway attest to the inn's age. Ghosts are also said to reside here, but then what inn that is 250 years old doesn't have a good ghost story attached to it? Situated in the heart of Edgartown, the inn is just a block away from the Chappaquiddick Island ferry.

The Oak House

Box 299, Seaview Ave., Oak Bluffs, MA 02557. ☎ **800/245-5979** or 508/693-4187. Room rates, including breakfast and afternoon tea, start at $150. Closed Nov to mid-May.

Built in 1872 as a summer home, the Oak House reflects the unpretentious lifestyle of Oak Bluffs. While the sleek and famous head eastward to Edgartown, those who prefer simply to kick back and avoid the trappings of fancy society stay in Oak Bluffs or Vineyard Haven. The brightly painted or wood-paneled rooms are imbued with the character of a classic summer cottage. Sliding into the wicker furniture on the inn's sun porch, with views of Vineyard Sound, is a great way to finish off a day of cycling around the island.

Nantucket

Jared Coffin House

29 Broad St., Nantucket, MA 02554. ☎ **800/248-2405** or 508/228-2400. Double, including a full breakfast, starts at $95, off-season; $160, summer.

If you want to stay in the heart of Nantucket Town, this is the place. The 1845 house, a Nantucket landmark built of red brick, evokes an aura more of the Colonial South than of Nantucket, with its preponderance of weathered shingles. The brick construction proved a godsend in 1846, when a fire destroyed much of the town but left the solid Jared House more or less unaffected. The house has since been restored to period authenticity by the Nantucket Historical Trust. The public areas on the ground floor, with Oriental carpets and Chippendale furnishings, are a center of Nantucket Town's comings and goings. If you want to steer clear of the activity, ask for a room in one of three outlying houses.

The Wauwinet

120 Wauwinet Rd., Nantucket, MA 02554. ☎ **800/426-8718** or 508/228-0145; www.wauwinet.com. Room rates, including full breakfast and afternoon port, $330–$790, summer. Closed Nov to mid-Apr.

What is a seaside inn on Nantucket supposed to look like? The answer is The Wauwinet. Located on a spit of land between Nantucket Harbor and the Atlantic Ocean, the inn has an ideal setting. Lawns yield to dunes, dune grasses, beach roses, and the other characteristic flora of a seaside location. The inn itself has all the appropriate features: weathered-shingle siding, open porches with wicker chairs and views of the sea, ceiling fans humming, beds adorned with a multitude of overstuffed pillows. All of that would be enough to recommend the place. But when you throw in all the recreational opportunities—the tennis courts, the sailboats and bikes available to guests, the private beaches (on the harbor and the ocean) for swimming and surfcasting, the neighboring wildlife refuges for long walks on the beach—staying at The Wauwinet becomes a no-brainer. A no-brainer, that is, if you can afford it. These are not cheap digs (room rates start at around $330 a night, escalate rapidly, and don't include any meals), but if you can stretch your budget, it is worth it.

Chapter 6

The Litchfield Hills &
Western Connecticut

W hen last I was in western Connecticut, the big news circulating around the neighborhood was a bear sighting. Actually, it was the second of two bear sightings. A mother and three cubs were on the loose in West Hartford, this just a month after a 285-pound black bear had been captured by state conservation officers in Goshen before being tagged and released.

I presume these reports were intended in large part to be a public alert. Bears, after all, are big, wild, and potentially dangerous. They do not coexist happily with humans, and they aren't the sort of creatures you ought to have wandering around in your backyard. Yet the public reaction, it seemed to me, was not so much one of alarm but rather of unspoken, almost celebratory pride. The bear sightings were confirmation that the structured and civilized lifestyle of one of the most populous states in the country hadn't completely squelched the natural world. In some deeply satisfying way, I think, people felt that the bear sightings had put them back in touch with a seemingly lost spirit of the wild.

Of course, western Connecticut is not true wilderness, the presence of a bear or two notwithstanding. It is basically a civilized and structured place, a very human-oriented environment. When I look at a map of the entire state, I see something like a milk carton turned on its side, with the spout pointing to the southwest. If you're able to imagine the state's population as a fluidic substance, you could probably envision a steady flow of people—literally millions—collecting in the southwest and then pouring into the great megalopolis of New York City. Essentially, that's exactly what happens every weekday morning between 7 and 9am. New Haven, Milford, Bridgeport, Fairfield, Norwalk, Stamford—each city follows one another on an essentially continuous urban/suburban string.

There's no wilderness here, that's for sure. Yet I am always surprised how quickly all the cities, malls and suburbs fall away as you move away from the shore and from the Route 91 corridor that stretches north from New Haven through Hartford. Those bears, after all, were sighted less than 10 miles from Hartford, so what does that tell you? And by the time you reach the state's northwestern corner, the milk carton is almost entirely empty—except, of course, in summer and fall, when tourists and weekenders come to tap into the area's aura of rural, sylvan bliss.

The northwest isn't wilderness either, but in places it comes pretty darned close. In an area roughly 40 miles by 30 miles, there are at least 40 parks, state forests, and wildlife sanctuaries totaling more than 50,000 acres. And this represents only a fraction of the region's undeveloped land. There are enough woods in these parts to get thoroughly lost, and I know because I've done it.

At the same time, there is something supremely civilized about northwestern Connecticut. It is virtually impossible to travel more than 4 or 5 miles without passing through some small town, with its clapboard homes, antiques stores, steepled churches, and, depending on the season, array of farm stands. As far as I can make out, there is no smokestack industry at all; the region seems to survive entirely on tourism and agriculture. The towns—Salisbury, Kent, Cornwall, Goshen, Lakeville, Litchfield, Canaan, Washington, Riverton, and many others—are small nodes of commerce and habitation within a patchwork of forest and farm land.

I doubt any comprehensive plan contributed to this design. Settlement in western Connecticut has been more than 3 centuries in the making, a lot of time to allow for changes in vision and values. I have to assume that any conscientious planning or zoning has also been matched over time by haphazardness, accident, or luck. Yet, by whatever process (or lack of it), a balance between the civilized and natural worlds has been achieved in northwestern Connecticut, and it is incredibly satisfying. Some things just work out.

In fact, northwestern Connecticut is perfectly set up for those who want to get in touch, physically and spiritually, with the New England outdoors, but who at the same time don't want to dedicate themselves to wilderness survival. A typical day in the life of a western-Connecticut visitor looks something like this: breakfast at some small cafe; a day of hiking in the woods, canoeing or fishing on the Farmington or Housatonic River, or cycling back roads; and a well-appointed meal and a good night's sleep in some elegantly refurbished, 18th-century inn.

In enumerating the virtues of the northwest, I don't mean to disparage the southwestern coast. Yes, it is well developed and congested. At the same time, however, you can board a sailboat or sea kayak, head out into Long Island Sound,

and quickly be removed from the commotion of the I-95 corridor. In fact, western Connecticut is the only region in southern New England with both mountains and sea, or at least some semblance of both. It is possible, then, to go for a morning's sail and follow it up with a hike through the woods to a mountaintop vista in the afternoon. I know; I've done just that. And no, of course I'm not talking about an unspoiled seascape or towering peaks. I'm just saying it's possible, and surprisingly so, given the millions of people living in this area.

The Lay of the Land

If you can understand the basic concept that water runs downhill to the sea, you can understand the basic geography of western Connecticut. The farther north you go, and the farther away you get from Long Island Sound, the larger the hills are. The highest elevations here are modest, generally topping off at around 2,000 feet, with the highest point in Connecticut being a 2,380-foot shoulder of Mt. Frissel, a mountain that straddles the Massachusetts–Connecticut line, but peaks in Massachusetts at 2,683 feet. It is a geographical oddity of Connecticut that its highest mountain—Bear Mountain, at 2,316 feet—is not the highest point in the state.

While there are no high peaks in western Connecticut, it is nonetheless a hilly place, particularly in the northwestern quadrant. It is a hilly place with fairly solid underpinnings, too. The cliffs of Ragged Mountain, Sleeping Giant, West Rock Ridge, and Orenaug Park all show that not far beneath the surface soil lies a base of solid igneous rock, also known as traprock.

Two major river systems drain the region—the Housatonic to the west and the Connecticut to the east. In between

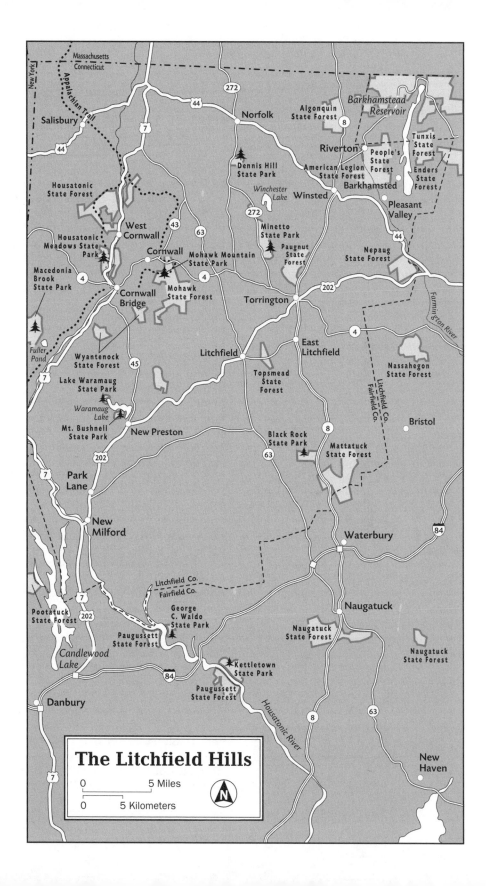

The Litchfield Hills

0   5 Miles

0   5 Kilometers

are countless smaller rivers and streams, all of which eventually feed into either the Housatonic or the Connecticut, or directly into Long Island Sound. Also trapped within the natural pockets created by the hilly terrain are numerous ponds and lakes, as well as man-made reservoirs.

Mixed forests of maple, oak, ash, balsam, spruce, and pine cover the hills, and beneath the canopy, mountain laurel—Connecticut's state flower—grows in abundance. Despite heavy logging in the past, second-growth forests have recovered well and are thriving in places. In Cornwall, for example, the 200-year-old cathedral pines, standing 150 feet tall, indicate that given the opportunity, the forests can regenerate with gusto.

Wildlife is making a pretty good go of things, too—at least as you move inland from the densely populated corridor along the Long Island Sound coast. As mentioned, bears are making a comeback in the area, and white-tailed deer are numerous enough for many local residents to consider them pests rather than admirable denizens of the wild. The same goes for coyotes. Bald eagles have also begun to return in small numbers to the Housatonic River and Farmington River watersheds.

The climate of the region can vary considerably, given the variations in latitude and elevation. In the north, snow usually covers the mountains from late November until early March. Proximity to the ocean in the south causes milder winters; an occasional snowfall usually disappears within a few days. The average high temperature in Hartford in July is 84°, while the average in January is 35°. Head north and west of Hartford, and those temperatures generally average a couple of degrees cooler; head south and west, and the averages are slightly warmer.

Orientation

In the natural world, Connecticut is divided in two parts by the Connecticut River, which cuts through the heart of the state. For the purposes of this book, however, it is a man-made artifice—**Interstate 91**—that separates western and eastern Connecticut. To the south, the **Long Island Sound** coast is the region's boundary. It is also the region's main population center, with a string of cities stretching from **Stamford** in the west to **New Haven** in the east along the **Interstate 95** corridor. To the west lies New York; to the north, Massachusetts.

In addition to the interstate highways, **Route 8,** reaching northward from **Bridgeport** through **Waterbury** to **Winsted,** forms an important commercial corridor. **Route 7,** however, is probably the more significant north-south route in the region as far as vacationing or weekending visitors are concerned. North of **Danbury,** Route 7 passes through the heart and soul of rural western Connecticut. Towns such as **Kent, Cornwall, Falls Village,** and **Canaan,** strung like charms along the Route 7 bracelet, are emblematic of the weather-worn, Colonial roots of the region. The **Housatonic River,** which flows alongside Route 7, is perhaps the essential recreational feature of western Connecticut. Knowledgeable fly fishermen insist that the Housatonic offers up some of the best fishing in New England, and the river is a popular spot for kayakers and canoeists as well.

The principal east-west route through the region is **Interstate 84,** which runs from **Danbury** to **Hartford** as it angles toward the northeast. It can be considered an approximate boundary line between urbanized western Connecticut to the south and rural western Connecticut to the north. **Route 44,** which runs westward from Hartford through **Winsted** and **Canaan,** is the approximate east-west counterpart to Route 7. Before entering New York State, Route 44 passes through **Salisbury,** a classic, clapboard, southern New England town.

Actually, there is probably no town in the region that is more of a New England classic than **Litchfield.** In 1790, it was one of the five largest towns in America, with a population of 20,000 residents. Its population today is less than half that, but it has held on to its Colonial past. With its broad streets lined by regal shade trees, and with grand, mansion-sized homes set back behind manicured lawns, Litchfield is exactly what a New England town ought to look like. These well-kept homes, with late-model Mercedes and BMWs parked out front, provide a rare display of the second-home wealth that has migrated into the region from the New York area. For the most part, you'd hardly know it; the sort of ostentation you might encounter in the Hamptons of Long Island is exactly what people who move here, or spend their summers here, are trying to escape.

Parks & Other Hot Spots

Appalachian Trail
From the south, the trail enters Connecticut by crossing the New York border just north of Bull's Bridge. In the north, the trail continues into Massachusetts after crossing over Bear Mountain in the northwestern corner of the state. For trail information, contact the Berkshire chapter of the **Appalachian Mountain Club** (☎ 413/443-0011).

The famous trail, stretching from Georgia to Maine, makes a short run through the northwestern corner of Connecticut. The trail covers just a little over 50 miles in Connecticut, and it parallels the Housatonic River for most of its length. There is one public campground along the Connecticut section of the trail in Housatonic Meadows State Park, roughly halfway between the New York and Massachusetts borders.

Housatonic River
Accessible for fishing from various pull-offs along Rte. 7. The section of the river between Falls Village and West Cornwall is a "trout management area," with a catch-and-release restriction. The best sections of the river for canoeing, rafting, and kayaking are north of Bull's Bridge. For area information, contact either the **Department of Environmental Protection** (Office of Parks and Recreation, 79 Elm St., Hartford, CT 06106; ☎ **860/424-3200**) or **Housatonic Meadows State Park** (Cornwall Bridge, CT 06754; ☎ **860/927-3238**).

The river enters Connecticut from the north, near Canaan, and empties into Long Island Sound in the south, near Stratford. Recreational activity—canoeing, kayaking, rafting, and fishing—is generally best on sections of the river north of New Milford. Whitewater kayaking and rafting are best in the spring, when water is released from dams to relieve the build-up from spring snowmelt. Fishing is usually best in late spring and fall, when the river level is low, and the water temperature cools to a level that makes trout more active feeders.

Lake Waramaug
For the state park, head north from New Preston on Rte. 45 for about a mile, then turn left on Lake Waramaug Rd. Headquarters: 30 Waramaug Lake Rd., New Preston, CT 06777; ☎ **860/868-0220.**

In summer, 680-acre Lake Waramaug, arguably the most scenic lake in Litchfield County, is a hub of recreational activity. Country inns and elegant summer homes line the shore, and vineyards cling to the surrounding hillsides. This is a particularly good place for large-lake canoeing, with motorized boat traffic kept to a minimum. In the fall, the Women's National Rowing Regatta is held on the lake. There is a 77-site campground on the lake's northwestern shore.

Macedonia Brook State Park

From Kent, take Rte. 341 west to Macedonia. Turn right onto Macedonia Brook Rd. to enter the park. Headquarters: 156 Macedonia Brook Rd., Kent, CT 06757; ☎ **860/927-3238.**

For hiking in northwestern Connecticut, it doesn't get much better than this 2,300-acre state park. The terrain is fairly rugged, as western Connecticut goes, with lots of steep ups and downs, but the summit ridges offer great views of the Catskills and Taconic Mountains to the west in New York. There is also a campground with 80 sites.

McKinney National Wildlife Refuge

Eight separate units, including stretches of coastal beach and wetlands as well as offshore islands, stretch from Norwalk in the west to Westbrook in the east. Headquarters: Box 1030, Westbrook, CT 06498; ☎ **860/399-2513.**

Some of this widely scattered refuge is technically in eastern Connecticut, or east of New Haven. However, important refuge units in western Connecticut included the Norwalk Islands, Milford Point, and Great Meadows in Stratford. This is Connecticut's original national wildlife refuge, established in 1971, and it seems to be an ever-changing entity. New tracts have been added to the refuge as recently as 1994. In the interest of wildlife preservation, access to some units is limited at various times of the season. However, taken as a whole, the refuge provides some of the best bird-watching opportunities in the state.

Peoples State Forest

From Pleasant Valley, take Rte. 318 east across the Farmington River Bridge. Turn left shortly after the bridge onto East River Rd., which leads into the state forest. Headquarters: Department of Environmental Protection, Office of Parks and Recreation, 79 Elm St., Hartford, CT 06106; ☎ **860/424-3200.**

Peoples is, in fact, just one of four state forests (the others being Tunxis, American Legion, and Algonquin) that surround Barkhamsted Reservoir, just south of the Massachusetts border. Together, the four state forests total roughly 15,000 acres of undeveloped land. Opportunities for hiking are superb, particularly in Peoples and Tunxis state forests. The Farmington River, running through the heart of the area, is considered one of the best rivers for trout fishing in southern New England. There is a campground with 30 sites in American Legion State Forest. By contrast, Algonquin is the least developed of the four state forests, lacking both facilities and a well-developed trail system.

Sleeping Giant State Park

From Hamden, take Rte. 10 north about 3 miles. Turn right on Mt. Carmel Ave. The entrance to the park is on the left. Headquarters: Department of Environmental Protection, Office of Parks and Recreation, 79 Elm St., Hartford, CT 06106; ☎ **860/424-3200.**

At almost 1,500 acres and with 30 miles of trails winding through it, this is perhaps the best area for hiking in the southwest. A 2-mile ridge that, from a distance, looks vaguely like a giant lying on its back gives the park its name. The high point in the park is 739-foot Mt. Carmel.

What to Do & Where to Do It

BALLOONING

Hot-air ballooning is a pretty big deal in western Connecticut. A number of companies will take you up for a classic, early-morning flight—with the obligatory champagne served after the flight, of course. If the weather is right (that is, the wind is low, the thermal energy high), you might want to try a sunset flight instead—a certifiably romantic way to experience the Connecticut countryside, particularly when the leaves are changing color in the fall. If you really want to immerse yourself in the culture of ballooning, you ought to check out the Northwest Connecticut Balloon Festival, held every June in Goshen. Who knows? You might manage to talk one of the participating balloonists into taking you up for a free ride.

Otherwise, you'll have to pay to play. **Berkshire Balloons** (Box 706, Southington, CT 06489; ☎ 203/250-8441) not only offers morning flights of an hour or more throughout the year, but also has a high-end, overnight package in conjunction with stylish Chimney Crest Manor in Bristol. **Watershed Balloons** (☎ 203/274-2010), in Watertown, and **Livingston Balloon Company** (☎ 860/651-1110) are just two of more than a dozen commercial balloon companies that operate in the western half of the state.

BIRD-WATCHING

Bird-watching in western Connecticut is a diverse affair. Head south to the shore, and of course you'll find shorebirds, although heavy shoreline development in this area has wiped out many wetland areas where birds normally congregate. Head north to the forests for songbirds, to the interior lakes and ponds for waterfowl, and to the Housatonic River in early winter for bald-eagle sightings. Approximately 400 species have been sighted in the state, according to the Connecticut Audubon Society.

Probably the best bird areas along the shore are those protected under the aegis of the **Stewart B. McKinney National Wildlife Refuge,** most notably the Norwalk Islands and Milford Point. The **Connecticut Audubon Coastal Center** (1 Milford Point Rd., Milford; ☎ 860/878-7440) has a full schedule of walks and workshops throughout the year. Of particular interest are walks in the spring and fall, when annual migrations are in full gear.

In the northwest, the **Holbrook Bird Observatory** at the White Memorial Foundation, south of Litchfield, has stations set up specifically for bird-watching and photography. The mix of habitats here—pond, meadow, forest, and marsh—attracts a wide variety of birds. **River Road** in **Kent,** along the Housatonic River, is renowned as a spot to look for spring migrants, most notably warblers and vultures.

The **Connecticut Audubon Society** maintains several sanctuaries throughout the state, conducts various birding programs, and is an otherwise excellent resource for general birding information in the state. The best way to contact the society is through the Coastal Center at Milford Point (see above).

BOARDSAILING

The western half of Long Island Sound is less than ideal for boardsailing. Winds can be shifty and unreliable, public beaches for launching are relatively few, and there is enough powerboat traffic to be a nuisance. Less than ideal, however, doesn't mean out of the question. There are a few good places where you can rip along on a long, fast reach when strong winds blow, particularly out of the southern and western quadrants.

Weed Beach in Darien is, despite its unprepossessing name, a good place to launch into Wescott Bay. **Shippan Point** in Stamford isn't the easiest place to launch from—no smooth beach on which to ease into the water. Yet the point juts well out into the sound, so you'll get away from land in a hurry to where the breezes are steadier and more reliable.

One of the best places for boardsailing in the area is **Calf Pasture Beach** in Norwalk. Your best bet here is to hook up with the **Gone with the Wind Surf Club** (☎ 203/852-1857), which is based at the beach.

CANOEING/FLATWATER KAYAKING

If your preferences run toward stillwater or what canoeists call "quickwater"—the stuff that moves, but isn't ferocious enough to be called whitewater—your options in western Connecticut are excellent. There are more than enough ponds and lakes with public boat launches in the northwest to keep flatwater explorers entertained for an entire summer's worth of weekends without paddling the same body of water twice. And for quickwater, with rapids up to a Class II level at times, sections of the **Housatonic** and the **Farmington** rivers are negotiable by paddlers of almost any ability, except when dam releases have raised the water level and quickened the pace of the flow.

For relatively big, open water, try **Wampanaug Lake,** where canoe rentals are available at the state park. If you like to fish while on the water, a couple of good places to check out are **Twin Lakes,** in the far northwestern corner of the state, **Mudge Pond** near Sharon, and **Tyler Lake** near Goshen.

Squantz Pond is a terrific place to go for a paddle in October. Along the western shore, the forest spills right down to the water's edge, and if you go early enough, the foliage appears to be set on fire by the morning sun. **Burr Pond** north of Torrington is a good place to take the

family; in addition to pleasant paddling, you can hike around the pond's perimeter or have a picnic at the state park on the pond's shores.

Farmington River

Allow 2–3 hours. Moderate. Access: From Riverton, take Rte. 20 north about a mile to Hogback Rd. (look for a boat launch sign). Turn left and continue to Hogback Dam; look for a small turnoff on the left side of the road for the put-in.

The West Branch of the Farmington in northern Connecticut might very well be the perfect river in southern New England to run in a canoe. In 1994, 14 miles of the West Branch, from near the Massachusetts border south through New Hartford, gained "wild and scenic" status from the federal government. For the most part, the river indeed lives up to its wild and scenic billing.

The first 6 miles, from Hogback Dam to Pleasant Valley, are quite simply about as pretty as it gets in southern New England. For most of this first section, the land on both sides of the river is state forest and thus undeveloped. Roads run along either side of the river, and you'll come across the occasional fly fisherman. But otherwise, if you use your imagination, you might be able to visualize what it was like to paddle these parts in the pre-Colonial era of exploration.

You will likely need more than novice paddling skills here; in places, rapids on the first 2 miles approach a Class II level, depending on how high the water is. There is nothing particularly tricky here— no complicated bends in the river to negotiate or big rocks or sweepers to avoid. But the water can move fast and the waves can buck up, so you need to be confident in handling a paddle.

How long a trip you make is pretty much your call. Your decision should be based on your stamina and paddling skills. As mentioned, the first 6 miles are probably the most beautiful stretch, but the next 10 miles or so are no slouch either. You'll encounter a few rapids that might rise to Class II level until you reach the Route 44 bridge, about 13 miles down river. This is a good place to take out, but if you want a real thrill, keep on going through Satan's Kingdom.

In addition to the inherent difficulty of running the Satan's Kingdom rapids—Class III in medium to high water—this is a popular tubing spot. So while you're trying to avoid rocks, you might also find yourself trying to avoid folks running the rapids in inner tubes. Look on the bright side: If you flip here, at least you'll have plenty of people to rescue you and help right your canoe. After this, the river gradually mellows out on the way to Collinsville Dam.

Housatonic River

Allow 4–5 hours. Easy–moderate. Access: Put in below the covered bridge (for Rte. 128 in West Cornwall. Takeout 20 miles downriver before the dam at Bull's Bridge.

The Housatonic, rising near Dalton, Massachusetts, flows southward for about 140 miles before emptying into Long Island Sound near Stratford. It is a river of many characters: a meandering stream in places, a serious whitewater challenge for short stretches, and a wide, slow-moving giant, feeding a series of lakes in its final stages before entering the Sound.

Dams regulate the river's flow, and in some places have essentially regulated it to a standstill. Three narrow lakes—from north to south, Lake Lillinonah, Lake Zoar, and Lake Housatonic—exist because of the damming. All these lakes are easily navigable by canoe, although you won't have any noticeable current to help carry you along. The canoeing is pleasant enough, but the best stuff lies farther to the north, between West Cornwall and Bull's Bridge.

This roughly 18-mile stretch starts at one covered bridge and ends (more or less) at another. In the high water of early spring, there may be some sections that are too much for novice paddlers to handle. But otherwise, the flow rate of the river is just about perfect for canoeists of all abilities. For the first half of the trip, the water moves along at a quick enough pace that you really don't need to do much paddling if you don't want to, except to correct your direction. After that, the pace slows—just right for a tranquil drift on a summer afternoon.

The first half of the run is through Housatonic Meadows State Park, a good place to pull off for a picnic lunch. This is also a trout management area (see "Fishing," below), so you can expect to see fly fishermen casting their lines out over the water. Be careful not to get fouled up in their lines—or better yet, join in the festivities. The state of Connecticut keeps the river well-stocked and this is catch-and-release territory, so there should be plenty of fish in the river for everyone. Another good place to pull off for lunch is at the Route 341 bridge in Kent. Or you can simply call it a day in Kent, as many people who canoe the river do, forgoing the last 3 or 4 miles to Bull's Bridge.

Gear, Rentals & Outfitters

The place to go for rentals, instruction, gear, and guided trips in the Housatonic River area is **Clarke Outdoors** (163 Route 7, Cornwall; ☎ **860/672-6365**). In the Farmington River area, head instead for **Collinsville Canoe and Kayak** (41 Bridge St., Collinsville; ☎ **860/693-6977**).

CROSS-COUNTRY SKIING

Cross-country skiing in western Connecticut is a good news/bad news deal. The good news is that there is some fine, varied terrain here. The rolling hills of the northwest are well suited for extended backcountry tours of 5 to 10 miles. You won't find the long, arduous climbs you might encounter in the hills of Vermont, and steep, technically tricky downhills are also rare. Most state parks permit cross-country skiing; for a list of those that do, contact the **Department of Environmental Protection,** Office of State Parks and Recreation (79 Elm St., Hartford, CT 06106; ☎ **860/424-3200**).

The bad news is that snow here is always an iffy proposition. In a typical winter, you can count on three or four decent storms to provide adequate trail coverage. But particularly at lower elevations, and particularly in the south, the snow isn't apt to last long, or it turns into the kind of icy mess that can make for tough going on skis without metal edges. Not surprisingly, then, the best skiing usually comes after a storm, and when in doubt, the farther north you go and the higher up you go, the better conditions you're likely to find.

For backcountry skiing, the **White Memorial Foundation** south of Litchfield is a popular spot, and deservedly so. Trails wind through the forest, around ponds, and over gently rolling terrain. If you don't like sharing your backcountry trails with anyone, try **Mohawk State Forest** west of Goshen. The trailhead can be hard to find (it's off Toumey Road, 4 miles west of Goshen off of Route 4), but there's a nice, 2-mile loop through the woods here—a great complement to a day of downhill skiing at nearby Mohawk Mountain. If you insist on steep climbs and descents, head for **Steep Rock Reservation** south of Washington Depot (see "Mountain Biking," below). The trails along the Shepaug River are gentle enough and good for a warm-up. But once you decide to venture off on the trails that lead away from the river, you'll quickly discover that when they say steep, they mean it.

For groomed-track skiing, the most reliable place to go as far as snow is concerned is **Pine Mountain Ski Touring Center** (Route 179, East Hartland; ☎ **860/653-4279**). Pine Mountain is 1,391 feet tall, and just a couple of miles south of the Massachusetts border, so the snow is preserved both by the northern latitude and higher elevation. The

15-kilometer trail network also connects with a challenging, 6-mile backcountry trail through Tunxis State Forest.

Winding Trails Cross Country Ski Center (50 Winding Trails Dr., Farmington; ☎ **860/678-9582**) has the largest groomed trail network—20 kilometers (12.42 miles)—in the state. Laid out mainly on old forest roads, the trails ease over gently rolling terrain. Low elevation, however, can be Winding Trails' downfall. Snow just doesn't last long here. The same goes for **Cedar Brook Cross Country Ski Center** (1481 Ratley Rd., West Suffield; ☎ **860/668-5026**), where 10 kilometers (6.21 miles) of trails wind through a working horse farm. What both ski areas lack in reliable snow coverage, they make up for in location, both being an easy drive from Hartford.

Gear & Rentals

In addition to gear and clothing for sale, **Backcountry Outfitters** (Kent Green, Kent; ☎ **860/927-3377**) rents cross-country skis and snowshoes. The **Wilderness Shop** (85 West St., Route 202, Litchfield; ☎ **860/567-5905**) also rents cross-country gear and snowshoes.

DOWNHILL SKIING/ SNOWBOARDING

If you plan to do any downhill skiing in Connecticut, it is important to have your priorities straight. If you think you're going to plunge down long, steep runs in knee-deep powder, you are in for grave disappointment. This is Connecticut, after all, where the hills are low and the climate just warm enough to prevent big snows from accumulating. In a typical winter, the hills of northwestern Connecticut get about 60 inches of natural snow, only a fraction of the snowfall received by ski areas in northern New England.

That said, there are a few things Connecticut skiing has going for it. There is plenty of snowmaking, so snow coverage is pretty reliable despite a dearth of the natural stuff. The atmosphere is generally low-key, so kids and beginners don't have to worry about being intimidated by swarms of fast-skiing, macho experts. And the relatively small size of the ski areas can be advantageous. There's none of the resort sprawl you'll find at the larger areas in the north; instead, the parking lot, the rental shop, and the base lodges are all close by.

Mohawk Mountain and Ski Sundown are the most noteworthy ski areas in the state. But if you happen to be in the neighborhood and need a quick, snow-sliding fix, you can also check out **Mt. Southington** (near Southington) and **Woodbury Ski Area** (near Woodbury), with vertical drops of 425 feet and 300 feet, respectively.

Mohawk Mountain

46 Great Hollow Rd., Cornwall, CT 06753. ☎ **860/672-6100** or 860/ 672-6464 for snow conditions. 24 trails (20% advanced, 60% intermediate, 20% novice); 1 triple chair, 4 double chairs; 540-foot vertical drop. Full-day tickets $29, night $17.

If nothing else, Mohawk Mountain has earned its place in history. In 1949, Walt Schoenknecht, who went on to develop Mount Snow in Vermont, developed the first rudimentary snowmaking system, using an ice pulverizer and fans. The result was a skiing surface more comparable to a skating rink than a ski slope, but an idea was born. Today, using vastly improved technology, most eastern ski areas can cover at least three fourths of their terrain with manmade snow, and Mohawk, with 95% coverage, is no exception. This is purely an intermediate's mountain and, at just over 600 vertical feet, not a particularly large one. Still, it is easily the best ski area in Connecticut, a decent place to take the family for a day if you don't feel like driving several hours north to Vermont.

Ski Sundown

Rte. 219, New Hartford, CT 06057. ☎ **860/379-9851** or 860/379-SNOW for snow conditions. 15 trails (20%

advanced, 45% intermediate, 35% novice); 3 triple chairs, 1 double chair; 625-foot vertical drop. Full-day tickets $32, night $22.

With plenty of easygoing terrain, Ski Sundown is a good place to learn to ski. For advanced skiers, Gunbarrel, which runs straight down the fall line, provides a reasonable challenge.

FISHING

Trout fishing is one of the true highlights of the outdoor life of western Connecticut. Mention the Farmington River or the Housatonic River (both described below) to any knowledgeable fly fisherman, and you're likely to get an enthusiastic and poetic response. Yet, while these two rivers are justifiably the most renowned fisheries in Connecticut, they are hardly the only places to fish.

When the water levels are relatively high, the fishing on smaller rivers can also be very good. The **Blackberry River** near Canaan and the **Ten Mile River** near Gaylordsville are considered by local fishermen to be among the most productive for those anglers trying to hook rainbow or brown trout.

For stillwater fishing, **Twin Lakes** in the northwestern corner of the state has a reputation for producing trophy-sized trout. **Tyler Lake** in Goshen is also considered a trout hot spot. You'll probably have a harder time figuring out how to pronounce **Wononskopmuc Lake** near Lakeville than you will figuring out how to catch the bass and pike in its waters. For largemouth bass, try **Mudge Pond** near Sharon.

Farmington River

Access: Various pull-offs along East River Rd. between Pleasant Valley and Riverton and along Hogback Rd. north of Riverton.

The Housatonic River might have a more widespread reputation, but the West Branch of the Farmington is no slouch. Over a 30-mile stretch, beginning in southern Massachusetts and extending into Connecticut, are more than 40 pools and runs. The active Farmington River Anglers' Association supplements the stocking done by the state of Connecticut. That means not only are the brown trout in the river plentiful, but there are a few big ones, running up to 28 inches long.

One of the reasons fishing on the West Branch is so good is that this is a well-protected river. In 1994, 14 miles of the West Branch—an area extending southward from the Massachusetts border through New Hartford—gained "wild and scenic" status from the federal government. Two "trout management areas," from Pleasant Valley to New Hartford and from Collinsville to Unionville, further add to the protection and nourishment of fish life in the river. The first of these is a catch-and-release area, so if you're looking for big fish, that's probably the place to head first.

Then again, catching fish on the West Branch may almost be beside the point. This is an exceedingly pretty place to simply stand knee-deep, look around you, and watch your line roll out across the water. It was for good reason the river got its wild and scenic designation, and an additional boost to the scenery comes from the state forests abutting the river between Riverton and Pleasant Valley.

The prime season for fishing the Farmington is probably late spring, when the water temperature rises into the 50s and trout suddenly become very interested in feeding. But this is a year-round fishery (although some sections of the river are closed to fishing for parts of March and April). So if you're willing to spend a few hours in water that's barely above freezing in January and February, the Farmington is a good place to come to catch a fish when all your friends are off skiing.

Where are the hot spots and what are the fish feeding on? The man in the know is Dave Goulet, proprietor of the Classic & Custom Fly Shop in New Hartford (see "Gear & Guides," below). Check in with Dave, pick up a license if you don't have

one, and head out to the river. Even if you don't catch a fish, the inherent beauty of the river won't leave you disappointed.

Housatonic
Access: Various pull-offs along Rte. 7 between Falls Village and Kent.

Of all the outdoor activities possible in western Connecticut, fishing the Housatonic stands perhaps at the pinnacle of the pyramid. Harold McMillan of Housatonic River Outfitters says, "This is probably New England's premier trout fishery. It's just a beautiful place to fish."

Why is that so? For starters, the state of Connecticut goes to great lengths to ensure that the Housatonic's reputation endures by keeping the river well stocked with brown trout and smallmouth bass. In addition, only catch-and-release fishing is allowed between Falls Village and Cornwall Bridge, a 10-mile stretch of "trout management area." The configuration of the river, with its numerous holes and pools (each, of course, with a clever name attributed to it by local fishermen), creates an ideal environment for trout to live and feed.

With essentially no industry in the immediate area, the water is relatively clean, although there remains some residual PCB contamination in the riverbed from years of industrial abuse in Massachusetts. And finally, as McMillan says, "This may be the most prolific river in New England as far as insect life is concerned." That might not be something that appeals to the average person, but to fish and fly fishermen, a healthy insect population is exceedingly good news.

During the course of the changing seasons, a river changes its character. Water temperatures rise and fall, as do water levels. Insect hatches vary. As a result, fish feeding habits change. In some rivers, this can cause long dry spells for fishermen, but not so in the Housatonic, primarily because of the sizeable populations of both trout and bass. Trout prefer colder, deeper water, whereas small-mouth bass prefer warmer, slower moving water and are willing to feed in the shallows that trout avoid.

As a result, the trout fishing in the Housatonic is usually best in the spring, when the water is still in the 50s. As the temperature rises and the water level typically drops in the midsummer months, the bass fishing shines. Then the cooler days of fall re-energize the trout. The rise and fall of the water level, of course, are due as much to dam releases as natural phenomena, but when the water is too high for wading, the float fishing can be superb.

In short, this is river fishing as good as it gets in New England. Check in at Housatonic River Outfitters (see "Gear & Guides," below) for tips on fishing hot spots and hatches, and if you want to be accepted as one in the know, don't call the river the *House*-a-tonic. It is pronounced *Who*-sa-tonic, and the real insiders simply call it "the Hous."

Gear & Guides

Classic & Custom Fly Shop (532 Main St., New Hartford; ☎ 860/738-3597) specializes in guiding on the Farmington River. **Housatonic River Outfitters** (Route 128, West Cornwall; ☎ 860/672-1010) specializes in guiding on the Housatonic, but offers guiding service on the Farmington and other streams in the area as well. Housatonic River Outfitters also has gear rentals available; both shops, of course, offer a wide range of gear for sale, as well as licenses.

Instruction

Housatonic River Outfitters (see "Gear & Guides," above) conducts 2-day weekend clinics on the Housatonic. **Marla Blair's Flyfishing** (18 Letendre Ave., Ludlow, MA; ☎ 413/583-5141) specializes in instruction for the whole family on the Farmington River.

HIKING & BACKPACKING

Connecticut's blue-blazed trail system is renowned, and deservedly so. There are few states in the country that can claim as extensive and well-maintained a trail network as can the state of Connecticut. Throughout the state, 700 miles of well-blazed trails are maintained by more than 90 volunteer organizations. The trail system was born in 1929 with the creation of the **Quinnipiac Trail,** a 23-mile route from New Haven to Cheshire. Among the most noteworthy of the trails in western Connecticut are the **Tunxis Trail,** which runs from Plymouth north to Tunxis State Forest; the **Mattatuck Trail,** which runs from Black Rock State Park to the Litchfield area; and the **Metacomet Trail** (see "Metacomet–Monadnock Trail," below).

So the hiking in western Connecticut can be surprisingly good, given the area's considerable development and population. In addition to the hikes described below, you might also want to check out **Peoples** and **Tunxis** state forests north of New Hartford. Long walks in the woods and outcroppings offering sweeping panoramas are the highlights of hiking in this relatively wild part of the state.

Bear Mountain

Allow 4–5 hours. Moderate–strenuous. Access: From the junction of Rtes. 44 and 41 in Salisbury, take Rte. 41 north for 3 miles. Look for the parking area on your left. Map: USGS Bash Bish Falls.

Through hikers on the Appalachian Trail sometimes look at the trail's relatively short jaunt through Connecticut and figure they'll have something of a respite before encountering the real mountains that begin in Massachusetts. Then they encounter the steep slopes of Bear Mountain and are either surprised or aggravated to discover that hiking through Connecticut was more work than they expected.

As a day hiker without a 40-pound pack to lug around, you should find the

THE HILLS ARE HOWLING

Just when you thought it was safe to go to sleep in the woods, look who's taking dead aim at your peace of mind. Coyotes, so firmly entrenched in the lore of the American West, are now alive and well, and increasing in number in New England states. The existence of coyotes in the East is not an especially new phenomenon. Coyotes began migrating to New England from Canada in the 1950s. But they are now so comfortably established that there have even been coyote sightings in New York's Central Park.

Why are coyotes thriving in New England? There could be many reasons, say wildlife experts. One is that deer populations are also thriving, and like any self-respecting creature of the wild, a smart coyote migrates toward a plentiful food source. The gradual reforestation of parts of New England has also been an encouraging factor. The relative absence of human predators—not many people make a living or habit of hunting for coyotes—have further allowed populations to flourish. And coyotes are remarkable opportunists, able to adapt their habits as their habitat and food sources change.

There are some people who imagine coyotes will help reduce an overpopulation of white-tail deer in the Northeast. Wildlife experts, however, tend to discount that theory. There are simply too many deer, and coyotes tend to hunt those deer that are most easily tracked—sick or ailing deer unlikely to survive much longer anyway. There has been some evidence in Connecticut, however, that coyotes have thinned out the populations of smaller mammals—red fox, rabbits, and woodchucks.

Of course, the presence of coyotes in close proximity to humans has sounded an alarm in many small towns in western Connecticut. Concerns about coyotes preying on livestock and pets have grown as reports of coyote attacks on sheep, dogs, and cats have grown. Nature, of course, is simply taking its course—the adaptable coyote taking advantage of the available food sources in its northeastern environment. But the realities of natural law are hard to accept when you see your beloved Dachshund swept away in the jaws of a coyote.

Backcountry travelers have little to fear when it comes to coyotes. It is not in the coyote's constitution to attack humans, although as opportunistic scavengers, coyotes are apt to treat themselves to campsite food that has not been properly stowed. What coyotes are very able to do, however, is add a good dose of eeriness to the backcountry night. The mournful howling that descends on a campsite as night closes in is the sort of thing that can give rise to the telling of ghost stories—and a long restless night.

extra work simply part of the fun and the challenge. Start on the Undermountain Trail heading west, a gentle walk through the woods at first. Soon, however, the trail begins to climb up the southeastern flank of Bear Mountain. When, after about a mile of walking, you come to the junction with Paradise Lane, turn right, head north, and continue to climb for a short time before the slope eases off. Notice in particular the mountain laurel that is the undergrowth of the forest; mountain laurel has the distinction of being the state flower of Connecticut.

When you come to the junction with the Appalachian Trail, turning left (south) will lead to the climb up Bear Mountain. But if you've got the energy, turn right instead and head into beautiful Sages Ravine (just over the border in Massachusetts), with waterfalls and placid pools beneath the steep, wooded slopes of the ravine.

Now retrace your steps and continue past the Paradise Lane junction. Take a deep breath and steel yourself—it's now time for a steep climb. Don't be shy about using your hands to steady yourself as you work up and over the rocks, and take your time. The climb to the summit is only about .5 mile, and when you arrive there, you'll realize the effort was well worth it. To the northwest are Mt. Everett and Race Mountain in Massachusetts. To the west is Mt. Frissel, which straddles the Massachusetts–Connecticut border, and farther west are the Catskills. Turn around and look south and east to Twin Lakes and Canaan Mountain. It is quite the view.

When you're ready to keep on going, follow the Appalachian Trail as it descends the south shoulder of Bear Mountain. Views to the southwest continue to open up before eventually the forest swallows you up again. In about a mile, you'll come to a junction with the Undermountain Trail. Turn left here, and in 2 miles you'll be back where you started from; it's about 8 miles of hiking in all, if you take the side trip into Sages Ravine.

Macedonia Brook State Park

Allow 3–4 hours. Moderate. Access: From Kent, take Rte. 341 west to Macedonia. Turn right onto Macedonia Brook Rd. to enter the park. The trailhead is at the picnic area about .5 mile along the road after crossing Macedonia Brook. Map: Trail map available at park headquarters.

A mellow walk in the woods, a little climbing, good views, picnicking beside a gently flowing brook or lunching in a pretty New England town—what else could you possibly want in a hike? It wouldn't be quite right to call 2,300-acre Macedonia Brook State Park undiscovered, but it is just far enough off the beaten path in northwestern Connecticut to avoid heavy use. That doesn't mean you'll have the trail to yourself on a summer weekend, but you won't encounter crowds either.

The Ridge Loop through the park is pretty easy to follow. And if you don't feel like doing the complete 7-mile loop, there are a couple of bailout trails that lead back down to Macedonia Brook Road, which you can take back to your car. You

can hike the trail in either direction—clockwise or counterclockwise—but by going counterclockwise, you'll have a tricky climb up Cobble Mountain. In the other direction, you would end up descending this particular pitch, which can be treacherous if it's wet.

The trail begins through a dense forest, climbing gradually to a north-south running ridge. Once you've gained the ridge, the trail meanders northward through the forest, passing by occasional feeder streams that lead down to Macedonia Brook. Depending on the time of year, ferns and wildflowers cover the forest floor.

After descending from the ridge, you'll come to a crossing with Keeler Road, virtually the halfway point of the hike. You cross a couple of more roads and pass by pretty Hilltop Pond as the loop begins its turn to the south. Soon the trail begins to climb, reaching a couple of lookouts with views of the Macedonia Brook drainage.

You've now come to the moment of truth—the climb up Cobble Mountain. If you're not game for this scramble, you can simply take the trail that descends to your left, leading back to Macedonia Brook Road. But what the heck? The Cobble climb is the one real challenge on this hike, so you might as well go for it. It's less than .25 mile before you reach the crest, and if you take it slow, using your hands to stabilize yourself when necessary, you shouldn't have any problem.

From the Cobble Mountain summit, the views to the west, of the Catskill and the Taconic Mountains, are terrific. Pause for a drink and a snack, regain your breath and stamina, and then begin the gradual, 2-mile descent through the forest back to the trailhead.

Ragged Mountain

Allow 3–4 hours. Moderate. Access: From Berlin, take Rte. 71A south for 1.2 miles and turn right on West Lane. Look for the trailhead in about .5 mile, where West Lane ends. Map: USGS Meriden and New Britain.

The cliffs of Ragged Mountain are well known to rock climbers, but you can get to the top and appreciate the spectacular views without having to scale a vertical face. This is also a very accessible hike. If you happen to be passing by on Interstate I-84 on your way to Hartford or Boston and are in the mood for a few hours of hiking, Ragged Mountain is only a couple of miles out of your way. Once you come to the top of the rocky mountain, however, you'll probably feel you've discovered a whole new world.

The loop is marked by blue blazes with red dots (and simply blue blazes where the Metacomet Trail joins in), so stick with the blazes and you won't get lost. From the trailhead, bear left for a clockwise loop. After some initial climbing, you'll eventually encounter views from the cliffs on the southeastern flank of the mountain. Below is Hart's Pond and, in the distance, the Hanging Hills of Meriden, another popular climbing area. Continue past the intersection with the Metacomet Trail as the loop begins turning northward, leading over the summit of Ragged Mountain. The going here can be as much of a scramble as a hike, over the rocky and—yes—ragged terrain. Now the cliffs face west, and the views in this direction are over Wesel Reservoir. Don't be surprised if you bump into a climber emerging over the edge of the cliffs, but also be careful in nearing the edge—it's a long way down if you make that fateful last step.

After the Metacomet Trail bears left, stay on course with the blue blazes and red dots to continue your loop. The trail leads through mixed forest and past a tree-lined swamp before turning southward again, sometimes following dirt roads as it makes its way back to the trailhead.

Overnight/Long-Distance Hikes
Appalachian Trail
From the south, the trail enters Connecticut by crossing the New York border just north of Bull's Bridge. In the north, the trail continues into Massachusetts after crossing over Bear Mountain in the northwestern corner of the state.

The famous Georgia-to-Maine Trail cuts a 52-mile path through the northwestern corner of the state, passing over Bear Mountain, as described above. Campgrounds and shelters are spaced at regular (about 8-mile) intervals along the trail, but don't expect anything elegant. If you decide to do the complete, 52-mile Connecticut section, you might as well tack on a few extra miles and continue north over Race Mountain in southwestern Massachusetts. This is one of the most scenic sections of the AT in southern New England (see "Hiking & Backpacking" in chapter 3, "Central Massachusetts").

Metacomet–Monadnock Trail
From the south, the trail begins in Meriden and runs north to the Massachusetts border at Rising Corner, west of Suffield. The trail continues through Massachusetts to Mt. Monadnock in New Hampshire.

Technically, this is known simply as the Metacomet Trail in Connecticut. But it subsequently becomes the Metacomet–Monadnock Trail upon entering Massachusetts, so don't be confused. You might hear it called the Metacomet Trail, the Metacomet–Monadnock Trail, or simply the M-M; in Connecticut these names all refer to the same trail.

Originally conceived in the early 1950s by Professor Walter Banfield of the University of Massachusetts, the trail is more of a routing than it is a true trail, often following roads through well-settled areas as a means of connecting trail sections through the woods. The fact that it exists at all, however, is a real tribute to the cooperation among private hiking clubs; state, local, and federal agencies; and private landowners.

Because it does pass through some well-settled territory, the Connecticut section of the trail is generally considered less scenic than the Massachusetts section. It is not lacking in scenic moments, however, particularly as it passes through Talcott Mountain and Penwood parks west of Hartford. And anyone who wants to be considered a true M-M through hiker—someone, that is, who has hiked the trail's full length—can't in good conscience leave out the Connecticut portion of the trail.

If you want to see a few scouting reports before setting out, you'll find them, and pictures of the trail, at **http://people.ne.mediaone.net/hiker 6/index.html.**

Gear

Backcountry Outfitters (Kent Green, Kent; ☎ 860/927-3377) has a wide variety of hiking and camping gear available. The **Wilderness Shop** (85 West St., Route 202, Litchfield; ☎ 860/567-5905) also sells hiking and camping gear and topographical maps.

HORSEBACK RIDING

In the Litchfield area, **Lee's Riding Stable** (57 E. Litchfield Rd., off Route 118, Litchfield; ☎ 860/567-0785) offers rides on trails through the surrounding woods as well as riding lessons, both English and Western style. Farther south, check out **Chance Hill Equestrian Center** (☎ 203/762-3234), which offers trail rides and lessons in Wilton.

MOUNTAIN BIKING

Mountain biking in western Connecticut suffers from the problem that seems to plague most of southern New England—plenty of great places to ride, but little guidance on how to find them or make the most of them.

The situation is improving, however. Local clubs, the New England Mountain Biking Association, and the Appalachian Mountain Club are not only helping get the word out about good places to ride, they're also organizing group rides that are usually open to anyone of the appropriate skill level. Local riders are trying to blaze trails in some areas, although the blazing effort in general must still be considered a work in progress. And local bike shops often have hand-drawn maps of nearby areas, although you shouldn't expect Rand McNally accuracy.

Still, there are no mountain-biking schools or outfitters in a region with much to offer riders of all levels. Even bike shops with quality mountain bikes to rent can be a hard find. To enjoy riding in the region to its fullest, you'll probably need to bring your own bike, and should make an effort to pick up good bits of local biking knowledge.

For novice riders, a couple of good places to find easy, double-track trails with relatively little climbing are **Huntington State Park** southeast of Danbury and **White Memorial Foundation** near Litchfield.

Nepaug State Forest

Allow 2–3 hours. Moderate–strenuous. Access: From the junction with Rte. 44, head west on Rte. 202 about 3 miles and look for the state park sign on your right. Map: Ask for a map at the Summit Mountain Bike Shop in nearby Canton (see "Gear & Rentals," below).

Skilled local riders wax poetic about Nepaug, which offers up some of the best single-track riding in the state. Challenging climbs, screaming downhills, easily negotiable fire roads if you're not a single-track enthusiast, good views—Nepaug has much to recommend it. It's not a big place, but 5-mile loops are possible, and there's enough variation for you to ride two or three loops in one ride with only minimal redundancy.

Finding your way around here isn't always easy. Trails and roads wind around without any apparent rhyme or reason, so getting lost is a very real possibility. That's the bad news. The good news is that this is a relatively compact state forest, covering just 1,200 acres, so if you do get lost, you won't get that lost. Furthermore, this is a mountain-biking hot spot, so you can expect to encounter other riders who can steer you right if you happen to go wrong.

The easiest thing to do in the forest is simply to stick to the dirt roads. The most significant of these is probably Satan's Kingdom Road, which runs north toward the Farmington River. By sticking to the dirt roads for a while, you can get a feel for the lay of the land. After that, go out for an assault on the single track.

Steep Rock Reservation

Allow 1–2 hours. Easy along the river; strenuous in the hills. Access: From Washington Depot, take the road across from the **Hickory Stick Bookshop** (☎ **860/868-0525**). Bear right and continue about 1.5 miles to the parking area for the reservation. Map: A map of the area is available for a nominal charge at the Hickory Stick Book Shop.

The great thing about Steep Rock is that it can be all you want it to be—no more or less. The reservation covers both banks of the Shepaug River south of Washington Depot, and if you stay on the dirt roads and a rail trail that run close to the river, you can enjoy a gentle, scenic ride. You'll even get a chance to ride through an old railway tunnel along the way, and when you've had enough riding, you can take a dip in the river to cool off.

If you decide to venture away from the river on the single-track trails— something like 20 miles of trails in all— you'll quickly discover how Steep Rock earns its name. The hills do indeed climb steeply and are rough and rocky in places, so good fitness and skills are called for. If you need a specific destination as an inspiration to carry you up the arduous climb, you might as well make it the Steep Rock Lookout, with its great view out over the river and the hills beyond. Just remember that what goes up must come down. If the climbs are an aerobic challenge,

you can bet on the descents being technically tricky.

One nice thing about Steep Rock is that it is a fairly difficult place to get desperately lost. A river runs through it, and you shouldn't have much trouble finding your way back to the river to reorient yourself.

West Hartford Reservoir

Allow 2–4 hours. Moderate. Access: Take exit 39 from Rte. 84. Take Rte. 4 east about 2.5 miles to the entrance to the reservoir complex, on the left. Map: Available at the administration building.

This is where mountain bikers from the Hartford area who are in the know come to ride. With 35 miles of trails and roads, there's something here for everyone. Come here on a weekend, and you'll have plenty of other riders to share in your experience and to offer guidance on suggested rides.

In fact, popularity might be the area's drawback, too. In addition to being popular among mountain bikers, the place is popular among hikers, and in recent years confrontations have been so heated, there was talk of closing the place to riders. That hasn't happened, but to ensure that the open-door policy remains in effect, be careful to play by the rules when riding here. Don't ride on trails that are clearly marked as being closed to bikes, and wear a helmet, as mandated by the Metropolitan District Commission, which is in charge of the place.

That said, go for it. Loops of 8 to 10 miles with varying degrees of difficulty are possible, so it's up to you how far and hard you want to go. Climbs max out at about 500 vertical feet, but do that three or four times in a 10-mile ride and you'll feel it. The reward of climbing, of course, is usually fast, fun descending, but be wary. Mountain riders here are known to ride together in sizeable packs, and barreling down a hill right into a six-pack of ascending riders is nobody's idea of a fun day on the trail.

Gear & Rentals

The Cycle Loft (25 Litchfield Commons, Litchfield; ☎ 860/567-1713) rents and sells mountain bikes. **Summit Mountain Bike Shop** (Route 44, Canton; ☎ 860/693-8891) is a good source for gear and local information on places to ride.

ROAD BIKING

It would be misleading to say there is no good road biking south of Route 84 in western Connecticut. Plenty of people ride the roads in this populous corner of the state, particularly as you move away from the coast toward **Ridgefield, Redding,** and **Wilton.** But the reality is simple: A lot of people live in this area, and a lot of people means a lot of cars. Even on back roads, traffic can be fairly heavy and shoulders not always substantial, so if you choose to ride in these parts, be prepared to deal with plenty of cars passing by, ofttimes at close range.

That's why the better riding is in the far north, where the state's population, and the traffic associated with it, dwindles. Hills present the greatest challenge in the north—marked less by their length or steepness, but rather by their frequency. This is lumpy countryside where long, extended stretches of flat road are rare. This doesn't make profound cardiovascular fitness a prerequisite—what goes up must come down, after all—but you must be willing to do some uphill pedaling to appreciate western-Connecticut riding to its fullest.

Back roads abound, providing plenty of opportunities for leisurely exploration. Most (but not all) back roads are surprisingly well marked, usually with weather-beaten wood signs directing you toward some town or major roadway should you get lost. Somewhat surprisingly, **Route 44,** the main east-west route through the northwest, is actually a fairly pleasant road to ride, particularly between **Winsted** and **Canaan.** While traffic can be considerable, the shoulder is wide in most places and the scenery is first-rate.

Farmington River Ride

Allow 2–3 hours. Easy–moderate; mostly flat, with one hill. Access: From Winsted, take Rte. 44 east to Rte. 318. Turn left and continue into Pleasant Valley and look for a convenient parking spot. Map: Any good state roadmap will do.

If ever there were an opportunity to combine cycling and fishing, this is it. Fishing tackle is, of course, not exactly the easiest equipment to transport on a bike. But if you can figure out some way of doing it—by strapping your rod to your top tube or by some other means—go for it. This ride essentially passes up one side of the West Branch of the Farmington River and then down the other, through the dense, undeveloped woodlands of American Legion and Peoples state forests.

Start in Pleasant Valley (how perfect a name is that?) and head north, along the western bank of the river, on West River Road. You're bound to see cars parked in roadside turnoffs and fly fishermen in waders, standing in the river in pursuit of the fish of their dreams. The road is flat and narrow and the riding easy, so take your time and enjoy the tranquility of the place.

After about 4 or 5 miles, West River Road ends at a T with Route 20. Turn right here, and cross over the river into the tiny town of Riverton. About .5 mile north of the town, look for a public boat launch sign, where you'll turn left onto Hogback Road, another narrow way along the banks of the river. Soon the road will begin climbing as you near West Branch Dam. You'll be able to spot the concrete facade of the dam through the trees, the indicator that the climbing portion of your ride is about to begin.

The steady climb lasts about a mile as the road angles to the east, away from the river. Reaching a T, turn right onto Mill Street for one short, final, uphill stretch before beginning the downhill run back toward Riverton. After a steep downhill (take this one slow), Mill Street comes to a T with Route 20. Turn right and continue the descent. This can be a rousing fun and fast downhill, but be careful, too. The shoulder is not particularly wide, there are a couple of blind turns in the road, and passing traffic tends to move at a healthy rate of speed.

After Route 20 levels off and you come back into Riverton, continue straight on East River Road, following the sign to Peoples State Forest, when Route 20 bears right over the river. Once again, the main theme of this ride reasserts itself—narrow road, dense forest, and the river passing alongside. If you've got enough energy, and you're disinclined to fish, lock up your bike and try one of the hiking trails that lead uphill into the forest. Peoples State Forest is one of the better places in western Connecticut for a good walk in the woods.

The road here resembles a roller coaster for a while, with quick ups and downs, before flattening out as you near the end. Eventually you arrive at a T with Route 318. Turn right, pass over the bridge, and you'll be back in Pleasant Valley, concluding a very pleasant ride of roughly 20 miles.

Falls Village Double Loop

Allow 2–5 hours. Moderate–strenuous; rolling, sometimes extended hills. Access: From Canaan, take Rte. 7 south to Rte. 126 west and Falls Village. In Falls Village, follow signs to the river; after crossing under the railroad tracks, look for a parking area on your left. Map: Any good state roadmap will do.

How can a ride last either 2 hours or 5 hours? It can when it is really two rides in one. This ride forms a rough figure-eight, so if you start at the crux of the eight, you can ride either loop or both loops together. You shouldn't have any problem completing either loop in 2 hours, but if you decide to go for the whole enchilada, budget 5 hours for your trip.

And plan to do some climbing. There are no long, grueling lung-busters here, but there are definitely a couple of hills that will get your heart pounding. If you end up doing the complete figure-eight,

the effort required to get up those hills in a 40+-mile ride will begin to take its toll on your legs. In short, don't be intimidated, but do be prepared.

The ride begins in tiny Falls Village. From the parking area, turn left (away from the village) and almost immediately cross a one-lane bridge. Just over the bridge, turn left onto Dugway Road, riding through archetypal Litchfield Hills countryside—woods, meadows, a rolling landscape, and the occasional elegant clapboard home. Eventually you come to a T and to something atypical of this area—Lime Rock raceway, where the race-car action is fast, furious, and serious on summer weekends. It might not be something you'd expect to encounter in this bucolic world, but there it is.

Turn right here onto Route 112, and soon you'll begin a steady climb to open farm fields, with views of hills and forests in the distance. The road leads past the Hotchkiss School, one of Connecticut's most exclusive boarding schools, before coming to a junction with Route 41. Here you'll turn right, riding into the village of Lakeville to briefly join Route 44 for the ride into Salisbury.

Salisbury is just what a town in western Connecticut ought to be, with its clapboard homes, church, and mix of antiques galleries and restaurants. All of it is painstakingly tasteful; if you were so much as to whisper a word like, say, McDonalds, you'd probably be immediately escorted out of town. This is a good place to stop for a snack and to browse.

From Salisbury, take Route 41 north (not Route 44, which heads east), and look for Beaver Dam Road on your right about 2 miles out of town. Turn here, then make a left on Taconic (at a T), and then bear right at the next fork. One more right turn, onto Twin Lakes Road, will take you along the edge of the lake, where you can expect to see fishermen drifting lazily on the water.

At the next T, turn right, followed shortly by a left (at the next T) onto Route 44. In about a quarter of a mile, you'll come to an intersection with Route 126, where you'll turn right to head back into Falls Village.

At this point, you will have completed the first loop, traveling a little over 20 miles in all. If you've had enough riding for the day, now's the time to call it quits. But for a second loop of roughly the same distance, stay on Route 126 as it makes a short, steep climb out of town. Continue across Route 7 to Route 63, bearing right to begin a clockwise run around Music Mountain.

After a couple of miles on Route 63, turn right onto Route 43. This is a strangely lumpy road, looking as though the pavement had been laid over a series of frost heaves. So don't expect smooth riding; just take it easy and appreciate the scenery of cattail-filled marshes and tree-covered mountainsides.

In about 4 miles, you'll come to an intersection with Route 128. Turn right, and get ready to do a little climbing. The climb is steady and tough enough to remind you that you've already put in more than 30 miles of riding, but it comes with a reward—a long, swift descent into the town of West Cornwall. The perfect New England ride would, of course, be incomplete if you didn't ride through a covered bridge, so here's your opportunity. In fact, this is a rare opportunity; the covered bridge in West Cornwall is one of the last of its kind in Connecticut.

Once through the bridge, turn right on Route 7, so the Housatonic River is on your right. This is a pretty section of road as it winds through the woods and along the river, but be mindful of traffic; Route 7 is an important north-south thoroughfare in western Connecticut. When you come to the intersection with Route 112, turn left, and then, after about .5 mile, turn right onto Dugway Road, which leads back to your starting point. You'll have logged in a fair amount of riding, more than 40 miles in all. But for a complete sampling of the best of the region, from tranquil back roads to clapboard villages with a covered bridge thrown in, it's a hard ride to beat.

Gear & Rentals

The Cycle Loft in Litchfield (see "Mountain Biking," above) has equipment for sale and to rent.

Outfitters

The Bicycle Tour Company (Box 381, Kent, CT 06757; ☎ **888/711-KENT**) offers 3-day weekend trips in the Litchfield Hills. Also, the **Connecticut Bicycle Coalition** (One Union Plaza, Hartford; ☎ **860/527-5200**) is a good resource for information on organized rides in the area.

ROCK CLIMBING

It might come as some surprise that some of the best rock climbing in southern New England can be found in western Connecticut, but it is. For whatever reasons of glacial and geological history, traprock—the hard, igneous subsurface of the western-Connecticut landscape—has been left exposed in the form of cliffs ranging from 50 to more than 100 feet high. You're not going to find 500-foot 5.13s out there, but if you can be content with 80-foot 5.10s, you can have a field day.

The premier climbing spot in the state is probably **Ragged Mountain** (see "Hiking & Backpacking," above) near Southington, which has a rich climbing tradition that dates back to the 1920s. The Main Face at Ragged rises about 100 feet, and includes such challenging routes as the wonderfully named Unconquerable Crack. **Craghole Pass** near Meriden is another popular traprock wall, with routes ranging in difficulty from 5.6 to 5.12.

At one time, the Chin of **Sleeping Giant** in Hamden (see "Walks & Rambles," below) was *the* place to climb in Connecticut. Students from nearby Yale University would come here to test their mettle after trips to the Alps inspired their climbing interests. But a fatal accident in the 1950s closed the Giant to climbing for many years, and it has only recently been reopened. The word on climbing the Chin is to be cautious about blithely using pre-fixed implements; some may be 70 years old and unreliable.

Guides & Instruction

Go Vertical (727 Canal St., Stamford; ☎ 203/358-8767) offers group and private instruction, both on an indoor climbing wall and in the outdoors. **Connecticut Mountain Recreation** (119 Jessica Dr., East Hartford; ☎ 203/569-3113) also offers climbing instruction, both indoors and outdoors.

SAILING

Sailing in Long Island Sound can be a tricky business. Winds can do funky things, picking up or shifting for no apparent reason, swirling and gusting, and sometimes simply disappearing altogether. This has much to do with the fact that the strong southwestern winds that kick up in summer in places like Cape Cod and Rhode Island are blocked out by Long Island. Long Island Sound is not a wide body of water—less than 10 miles across between Stamford and the island—which is not a lot of open water to allow wind to build up a head of steam.

This is not necessarily a bad thing, however. Because you're not likely to encounter big winds and big seas, the sound is a good place to learn how to sail, and there are some fine sailing schools in the area (see "Instruction," below) to teach you how. It also makes entering and exiting the many small harbors along the coast somewhat easier; a smooth, gentle cruise through a narrow channel is a lot more enjoyable than a roiling roller coaster ride in heavy winds.

If you've been dreaming of an extended cruise up the East Coast, the major harbors of western Connecticut, from Stamford to Fairfield, are great places to start. A number of charter companies are based here (see "Rentals & Charters," below), and there are plenty of small harbors to explore along the Connecticut shore as you work your way eastward out of the Sound.

Rentals & Charters

Both **Longshore Sailing School** and **Norwalk Sailing School** (see "Instruction," below) offer day-sailing boats for rent. For larger boats, there are a number of yacht-charter companies in Stamford, Norwalk, and Fairfield. To get started, you might try **Russell Yacht Charters** (404 Hulls Hwy., Fairfield; ☎ 203/255-2783) or **Soundwaters** (69 Dyke Lane #13, Stamford; ☎ 203/323-1978). But if you don't find the kind of boat or price you're looking for, don't hesitate to check elsewhere. There's plenty of competition.

Instruction

Longshore Sailing School (260 South Compo Rd., Westport; ☎ 203/226-4646) and **Norwalk Sailing School** (Calf Pasture Beach, Norwalk; ☎ 203/852-1857) are well-reputed institutions with both adult and children's programs. **Women's Sailing Adventures** (39 Woodside Ave., Westport; ☎ 800/328-8053 or 203/227-7413) is, as the name should obviously imply, a school for women only. Start with a 4-hour beginner's class and build up to a 2- to 7-day program on boats up to 44 feet long.

SEA KAYAKING

Poking around the many small coves and harbors of the southwest can be entertaining enough, but don't expect solitude while you are doing it. This is a busy boating world, and opportunities for pulling up on a secluded beach for a quiet picnic lunch are essentially nonexistent. One good place to launch from is the beaches of **Sherwood Island State Park,** south of Westport. From here, it is a fairly easy trip out to the **Norwalk Islands. Silver Sands State Park** in

Milford is another good launching spot, particularly if you're interested in exploring **Milford Point.**

One of the best ways to experience sea kayaking in this region is to join a guided, day-long trip to the Norwalk Islands with the people from the **Small Boat Shop** (144 Water St., South Norwalk; ☎ 203/854-4223). Several of the islands are included in the Stewart B. McKinney National Wildlife Refuge, and the bird-watching as you circle around these tiny islands can be excellent. Don't worry if you've never been in a sea kayak before; instruction is offered to those who need it, and it won't take beginners long to pick up everything they need to know.

SWIMMING

Along the coast, private land eats up much of the shoreline, and many public beaches aren't really public at all. They're town-owned, so if you don't have a parking permit—acquired through membership in a local association or by paying taxes—you're out of luck. The one major exception is **Sherwood Island State Park,** located south of Westport. The 2-mile stretch of sand is a perfectly decent place to hang out on a towel or bring the kids. Don't expect any surf, of course. This is Long Island Sound, which during the warm summer months can resemble a big, placid puddle.

In the northwest, perhaps the nicest place for a swim is **Lake Waramaug State Park.** Inns along the picturesque lake's shores also have private beaches reserved for their guests. **Burr Pond State Park** is another popular place to take a dip.

Tubing in the **Farmington River** isn't exactly swimming (unless you tip over), but it's still a great way to get into the water and get wet. Join up with **Farmington River Tubing** (Satan's River Recreation Area on Route 44 in New Hartford; ☎ 860/693-6465 or 860/739-0791) for a ride through the rapids of **Satan's Kingdom Gorge.**

WALKS & RAMBLES

Western Connecticut may lack a single, enormous tract of undeveloped land, but there's no lack of opportunity for a short walk in the woods. A map of the state is freckled with state forests, parks, and reserves, particularly north of Interstate 84. It is hard to drive for more than a few miles without passing some place to pull off the road and get lost in the woods for an hour or two.

Furthermore, the state's blue-blazed trail network is legendary (see "Hiking & Backpacking," above). Trails can be found everywhere, and for the most part they are well maintained. Outdoorsmen in Connecticut take pride in the blue-blazed network, and rightfully so. Despite the encroachments of development in this compact state, the network is vivid proof that the great outdoors can still find a place in the land-use mix.

In addition to the walks described below, you might want to check out **Penwood State Park,** which runs along a high ridge between Avon and West Hartford. South of Litchfield, the **White Memorial Foundation,** a 4,000-acre preserve, has 35 miles of trails that lead through marshland, old-growth forest, and to the shores of Bantam Lake. The trail network at **Kettletown State Park** is much smaller, but wandering through the woods here, and crossing the free-flowing brooks that feed Lake Zoar, makes for a satisfying half-day diversion.

Devil's Den

Allow 2–3 hours. Easy–moderate. Access: Take exit 42 from the Merritt Parkway (Rte. 15) and follow Rte. 57 north for 5 miles. Turn right on Godfrey Rd., and in .5 mile turn left on Pent Rd., which leads to the parking area. Map: There is a large board with a map at the trailhead. For more information, contact **Lucius Pond Ordway—Devil's Den Preserve,** Box 1162, Weston, CT 06833; ☎ 203/226-4991.

The official name is Lucius Pond Ordway—Devil's Den Preserve, but it's generally referred to as Devil's Den or, by those who are really in the know, simply as the Den. By whatever name, it is a godsend in heavily populated southwestern Connecticut—1,700 acres of undeveloped land owing its existence, in large part, to the efforts of the Nature Conservancy.

Being close to such a large concentration of humanity (New York City is just a half hour away) means, of course, that the 20 miles of trails in the preserve are well used. Still, this is a big enough place that you can manage to get away by yourself for a while, if that's your intention. Easy 3- to 5-mile loops pass through woods, by a small pond, and along a rocky ledge that affords views of the surrounding countryside. Depending on the time of year, wildflowers can be prolific; about 500 different species have been recorded in the preserve.

But perhaps what's most interesting about hiking in Devil's Den are the scattered remnants of another era of human habitation and industry. Sawmill sites dating back to the early 1700s, stone foundations, old mill implements, and charcoal-burning sites can be found throughout the preserve. Walking among these vestiges of a bygone era, all surrounded by a forest now reasserting itself, is a vivid reminder of how completely a way of life can come and go in a century or two. The sawmills of Devil's Den seem almost prehistoric artifacts amid fast-paced urban Connecticut, which presses in along the perimeter of the preserve. A walk in the woods and a walk back in time—Devil's Den offers a rare getaway in a part of Connecticut where you might least expect to find it.

Guided hikes and nature walks are offered on a regular basis and can only help add to your appreciation and understanding of the preserve. They're also popular, so you'll need to make a reservation by calling the preserve headquarters (☎ 203/226-4991).

Sleeping Giant State Park

Allow 2–3 hours. Moderate. Access: From Hamden, take Rte. 10 north about 3 miles. Turn right on Mt. Carmel Ave. The entrance to the park is on the left. Map: Should be available at the park gate.

How sweet it is in such a well-settled part of the state to come upon this haven of relative tranquility. Sleeping Giant thrusts up prominently from its surroundings with the approximate profile—a vivid imagination is helpful here—of a giant in repose. According to one Native American legend, massive indigestion forced the giant to lie down after consuming an enormous portion of Long Island oysters.

It is helpful to keep the giant image in mind when discussing trail options with other hikers or in reading trail guides. At least then, when you encounter references to the giant's knee, chest, or chin, you'll have some idea of what is being talked about.

The main hike here is along the Tower Trail, a gently graded, wide path that leads after about 1.5 miles to a stone tower at the top of 739-foot Mt. Carmel. While the vertical rise is about 600 feet, the trail climbs so gradually that it barely seems a climb at all. It begins with a series of switchbacks that pass through a mixed forest of maple, oak, ash, and mountain laurel.

In less than a mile, you'll find yourself confronting a magnificent, multicolored cliff rising more than 100 feet from a bed of rubble. This is the giant's chin, and if it weren't for the reality of being in southwestern Connecticut, you'd swear you had just been transported to a small bit of western mesa. Fortunately, you aren't obliged to climb the cliff; instead, the trail angles away, reaching the summit of Mt. Carmel in about another .75 mile.

The four-story stone tower at the summit has a castle-keep look to it. If you again allow your imagination to wander, you might envision yourself as some robber baron along the Rhine. The view to the south of Long Island Sound in the distance is sweeping, and there is enough forest in the surrounding landscape to create the illusion of minimal human settlement, even though you might know the reality to be otherwise.

From here, the easiest thing to do is simply to retrace your steps to the parking area for a round-trip hike of about 3 miles. But there are 30 miles of well-blazed trails in the park, passing up and over all parts of the giant's body. If you have the energy, keep on going. A full day's outing is easily possible, and who could expect that while at a site just 15 minutes from downtown New Haven?

WHITEWATER RAFTING & KAYAKING

For a truly thrilling whitewater experience, you need a lot of water moving at a high rate of speed. Two things can cause this to happen on the Farmington and Housatonic rivers, western Connecticut's whitewater hot spots: dam releases or heavy rainfall. Dam releases occur primarily in the spring months as a means of relieving water build-up resulting from melting snow. As a result, guided whitewater trips in the area are generally offered only in the spring months.

Rainfall, of course, is less predictable. But in an average summer, there are probably 6 or 7 days when rain causes a powerful enough surge to raise the whitewater level on choice sections of the two rivers to Class III and higher. Obviously, that makes for a very hit-or-miss proposition, but look at it this way: When everyone else in the neighborhood—hikers, bikers, fishermen, and so on—is moaning about the rain, anyone with a kayak is literally in over his or her head in thrill-a-minute fun.

On the Housatonic, the faster-moving water is in the north. By the time the Housatonic reaches New Milford, its flow rate is comparable to that of cold molasses. The Farmington in

Connecticut is generally a slow-moving river, although there are sections of Class II water between Riverton and New Hartford. The Farmington does pick up steam at Tariffville Gorge (described below), before mellowing out on its way to joining up with the Connecticut River.

In early spring, there are a couple of other smaller rivers where rapids can briefly build to levels approaching Class IV. **Sandy Brook,** which runs through Algonquin State Forest north of Winsted, provides a wild ride of roughly 3 miles of continuous rapids—a good test of skill for experienced kayakers. The **Shepaug River** north of Washington Depot is a little tamer, but when the water is high (usually early March), it can still provide a good, fast ride.

Bull's Bridge, Housatonic River

From Bull's Bridge, turn left at the sign for the covered bridge. There is ample parking on the other side of the bridge. The takeout is about 3 miles downriver, just north of Gaylordsville. There is a pull-out off Rte. 7.

"Any time it rains heavily," says Frank Dzubak, "every local kayaker heads for Bull's Bridge." Dzubak ought to know, seeing as he is one of those local kayakers. The reason they all congregate here is that this is, simply, the best and most challenging whitewater run in the state. When the river is running fast and furious, the 3 miles between Bull's Bridge and Gaylordsville offer up everything you can handle, and maybe more.

Hardcore hotshots start the run just below the dam upriver of Bull's Bridge. Part of this short section of rapids is known as Stairway to Hell, and for good reason. If you aren't an expert paddler, Stairway to Hell can really ruin your day. A 7-foot drop, with big whitewater hiding the dangerous rocks lurking beneath the surface, verges on Class VI when the water is high. It all flushes out into a pool beneath the bridge.

South of the bridge, the rapids are less ferocious, but still intense enough to reach Class IV in high water. From the bridge to Gaylordsville, a series of four or five rapids in the Class III to Class IV range are generally negotiable by confident intermediates, except in extremely high water. Of these rapids, probably the most challenging, according to Dzubak, is Pencil Sharpener, a long series of ledges. "It's long, technical, and has a lot of hydraulics," says Dzubak. For some that might sound ominous, but for thrill-seeking whitewater enthusiasts, it is as good a reason as any for playing hooky on a rainy day.

Tariffville Gorge, Farmington River
Put-in at the Rte. 189 bridge in Tariffville. Takeout about 2 miles downriver at the Rte. 187 bridge.

Upriver, the Farmington flows gently, with occasional Class II rapids. Downriver, rapids pretty much disappear altogether. In between is Tariffville Gorge, where the river gets squeezed through a narrow opening and, for a brief stretch, kicks up to Class III and higher. The rapids here are substantial enough, and the flow, in spring, is reliable enough for the gorge to have hosted elite slalom races in years past.

One of the highlights of the trip comes early, as the river bends around a concrete wall on the right. When the water level is high, a perfectly shaped wave—known as Cathy's Wave—forms here, and anyone with decent surfing skills can ride this wave all day without going anywhere. Here you will also find a section of rapids called Pencil Sharpener, apparently a popular Connecticut name for rapids. There are a number of challenging sections as you work your way through the gorge, but in many cases there are easy (or easier) routes so you can avoid technical difficulties.

Tariffville Gorge is a popular spot, so don't expect to have the place to yourself on a spring weekend. At the same time,

company can be a convenience; it's usually not too difficult to hitch a shuttle ride back to your put-in point.

Gear & Rentals
Clarke Outdoors (163 Route 7, Cornwall, CT 06796; ☎ **860/672-6365**) offers a full selection of boats and gear for sale and rental.

Instruction
Clarke Outdoors (see "Gear & Rentals," above) offers beginner and advanced-beginner lessons throughout the summer in Class I and II sections of the Housatonic.

Outfitters
Clarke Outdoors (see "Gear & Rentals," above) leads rafting trips in spring on the Housatonic below Bull's Bridge, as well as trips throughout the summer on the gentler section of the river between Falls Village and Kent. **North American Whitewater Expeditions** (Box 64, West Forks, ME 04985; ☎ **800/RAPIDS-9** or 207/663-4430) offers a similar rafting program.

Campgrounds & Other Accommodations

CAMPGROUNDS
Burr Pond State Park
Take exit 46 from Rte. 8 to West Highland Lake Rd. Continue to Burr Mountain Rd. and look for the campground entrance on the right. ☎ **860/379-0172**. 40 sites, no hookups. Tables, fireplaces, rest rooms.

Campsites here are set back in a dense forest. Burr Pond is known as a good place for swimming and fishing.

Housatonic Meadows State Park

From Cornwall Bridge, take Rte. 7 north. The entrance to the park is about a mile north on the right. ☎ **860/672-6772.** 95 sites, no hookups. Tables, fireplaces, showers, rest rooms.

If you are into canoeing, kayaking, or fishing along the Housatonic River, this is an excellent place to set up camp. The campground is located in the heart of the river's trout management area. You'll find Clarke Outdoors, which runs guided canoe and raft trips on the river, just down the road.

Lake Waramaug State Park

From New Preston, head north on Rte. 45 for about a mile, then turn left on Lake Waramaug Rd. ☎ **860/868-0220.** 77 sites, no hookups. Tables, fireplaces, showers, rest rooms, canoe rentals.

Lake Waramaug is one of the prettiest spots in northwestern Connecticut. There are several country inns along the lake's shores, but if you don't feel like paying top dollar for an inn room, this campground is an excellent alternative. Canoe rentals at the campground make it easy to get out on the water and appreciate the surrounding scenery.

Macedonia Brook State Park

From Kent, take Rte. 341 west to Macedonia and turn right on Macedonia Brook Rd. to enter the park. ☎ **860/927-4100.** 84 sites, no hookups. Tables, fireplaces, pit toilets.

Campsites are set in the woods along the banks of Macedonia Brook. The park is a first-rate spot for hiking, mountain biking, and bird-watching.

White Memorial Foundation

From Litchfield, go 2.5 miles south on Rte. 202 and look for the entrance to **White Memorial Foundation and Conservation Center** (☎ 203/567-0857) on the left. Two campgrounds with 65 sites, none with hookups; 18 are for tent camping only. Fireplaces, pit toilets, convenience store, ice.

The tent sites on wooded Windmill Hill are particularly attractive. The campground is in the heart of a 4,000-acre preserve along the shores of Bantam Lake. There are 35 miles of trails for hiking, horseback riding, and mountain biking.

INNS & RESORTS

Country inns and bed-and-breakfasts, most dating back to the 18th and 19th centuries, are probably more abundant in western Connecticut than in any other region in the country. The inns described below represent just a small sampling; for a more complete listing, contact Connecticut Tourism (☎ **800-CT-BOUND**).

The Boulders

East Shore Rd. (Rte. 45, New Preston, CT 06777. ☎ **800/55BOULDERS** or 860/868-0541. Room rates from $175 with breakfast included to $395 with breakfast and dinner included.

Stay during the fall in one of the inn's lakeview cottages, adorned with antiques and a fireplace, and you won't be disappointed. There's a private beach on Lake Waramaug, tennis courts, a hiking trail on the property, and canoeing, fishing, horseback riding, hiking, and cross-country skiing are all close at hand. Dine here at night and you'll understand why the place is called the Boulders; boulders are an integral part of the restaurant's decor. The imaginative, ever-changing menu is superb.

Hopkins Inn

22 Hopkins Rd., New Preston, CT 06777. ☎ **860/868-7295.** Room rates $69–$150.

Built in 1847, this handsome, Federal-style inn overlooks Lake Waramaug. A private beach makes for easy lake access, and the Housatonic River is just minutes away for fishing, canoeing, and kayaking. Perhaps the best thing about the inn is its restaurant. After a full day of exercise, sit out on the terrace overlooking the lake and fill up on the Austrian-influenced cuisine and a bottle of wine from neighboring Hopkins Vineyard.

Inn at Longshore

260 South Compo Rd., Westport, CT 06880. ☎ **203/226-3316.** Room rates start around $130.

This former country club has been reborn as a country inn. The beaches of Sherwood Island State Park and the sailing schools of Westport are close by.

Old Riverton Inn

436 East River Rd. (Rte. 20), Riverton, CT 06065. ☎ **800/378-1796** or 860/379-8678. Room rates $80–$175, including full breakfast.

Most country inns in New England were once private homes or farms that have been converted to inns. Not so in the case of the Old Riverton Inn, which opened in 1796 as a stagecoach stop on the route from Albany to Hartford. Riverton is one of those blink-or-you'll-miss-it kind of towns, a great spot to get away from it all. The West Branch of the Farmington River is basically right out the front door for fishing and canoeing, and there is excellent hiking in nearby Peoples and Tunxis state forests.

Under Mountain Inn

482 Undermountain Rd. (Rte. 41), Salisbury, CT 06068. ☎ **860/435-2379.** Room rates $150–$195, including full breakfast.

This 18th-century farmhouse has been converted into a stylish seven-room inn. With its orderly, white-clapboard architecture, Salisbury is a quintessentially New England town, and the Under Mountain Inn fits right in. This is an excellent area in summer to set up base camp for bicycling or horseback riding and in winter for cross-country skiing.

Chapter 7

Eastern Connecticut

In order to pay eastern Connecticut a compliment, I am almost obliged to do so in a backhanded way. The most outstanding thing about eastern Connecticut, unkind as it might seem, is that there is almost nothing outstanding about it. The Berkshires have mountains, Rhode Island and Cape Cod offer spectacular beaches and the lure of the sea. The Litchfield Hills of western Connecticut have an aura of in-country chic. So, on what can eastern Connecticut stake its claim to fame?

The answer is nothing, and that is a very good nothing indeed. Most of eastern Connecticut has managed to fly below tourism's radar, allowing it to settle into a state of placid, unaffected bucolia. Leafy forests, small towns, tranquil farmlands, free-flowing streams, winding back roads—all are part of the patchwork quilt that is northeastern Connecticut, which calls itself, with pride and considerable justification, "the Quiet Corner." Towns farther south along the Connecticut River, including Essex, Hadlyme, and Chester, ache with such rural 18th- and 19th-century authenticity that it is almost inconceivable the cities of Hartford and New Haven are less than an hour's drive away.

I am like most New Englanders—I know eastern Connecticut mostly from the times I have passed through it, or over it, during my travels. I remember once looking down on the area while on a flight from Washington to Boston, and marveling at the expanse of unbroken forest. How, I wondered, was such a thing possible in the hyper-developed northeast corridor? I also remember passing through the region in the middle of the night while on a train to Vermont. According to the conductor, we (the passengers) could expect to see an overweight woman emerge from a track-side strip joint in Willamantic to bare all for the passing train. In eastern Connecticut, that's about as wild as things ever get.

Once you pass through the Interstate-91 corridor from west to east, urban Connecticut all but vanishes. Hartford, New Haven, Stamford, Bridgeport, Waterbury, Danbury—all of Connecticut's largest cities lie in the west. According to the 1990 census, Groton is the only eastern Connecticut community with a population exceeding 40,000.

Of course, it would be misleading to characterize all of eastern Connecticut as rural and undiscovered. Along the shore, sun-and-water worshippers come by the thousands to Hammonasett Beach and Rock Neck state parks. Mystic, with its aquarium and re-created 19th-century seaport, is one of Connecticut's leading tourist destinations. And in 1992, the Pequot Tribal Nation's opening of Foxwoods Resort Casino in Ledyard threatened to disrupt eastern Connecticut's pervasive tranquility. The ensuing construction of three resort hotels with a combined 1,400 rooms suggested that a complete transformation of the region was at hand.

Yet so far that hasn't happened. While there has been an increase in traffic, and some increase in crime, "casino sprawl" in the surrounding communities of Ledyard,

North Stonington, and Preston has yet to materialize. The casino industry has become a $1-billion-a-year business, yet it has remained surprisingly self-contained, and most of eastern Connecticut has gone on about its business characteristically unaffected. Just 15 minutes from the casino lies the heart of Pachaug State Forest—at 22,938 acres, Connecticut's largest tract of undeveloped land.

Pachaug is not alone. Even as the lure of gambling bumps up visitor numbers and increases traffic, Pachaug, Cockaponset (15,652 acres), and Natchaug (12,935 acres) state forests reaffirm the rural essence of the quiet east. Well-marked hiking trails weave throughout the region, giving rise to Connecticut's distinction (in this case, in both the eastern and western parts of the state) of having one of the best recreational-trail systems in the country despite the density of its population. The back roads of eastern Connecticut, light on traffic and full of spirit, make for some of the best road cycling in southern New England.

This is popular country, too, for horse-borne travelers; both Natchaug and Pachaug state forests have camping areas specifically designed for people with horses. Where else in New England can you find something like that?

There are drawbacks. Because travelers commonly pass up eastern Connecticut, it is overlooked by outfitters as well. If you're looking for someone to lead the way on a cycling, canoeing, fishing, or hiking expedition, the pickings are pretty slim. Only near the coast, which attracts tourists in sizeable numbers, does the outfitting business pick up, primarily for such water-based sports as sailing and sea kayaking. Otherwise, in eastern Connecticut you'll be left to your own devices to find your way and to make your own discoveries.

And that's not necessarily a bad thing. It helps to keep the Quiet Corner quiet, and thank goodness for that.

The Lay of the Land

A geographer dividing Connecticut into two parts would certainly select the **Connecticut River,** which bisects the state on a north-south axis, as the line of demarcation. Not so in this book. **I-91,** which also traverses the state on a north-south axis, defines two parts of the state in more human terms. To the west (see chapter 6, "The Litchfield Hills & Western Connecticut"), the state is more settled, with the cities of **Hartford** and **New Haven** lying on the I-91 boundary. To the east—the territory covered in this chapter—the big cities and highways give way to smaller towns and fewer major thoroughfares. So for the purposes of this book, I-91 is the dividing line.

The most important highway that passes through the region is **I-95,** which runs along the shore of **Long Island Sound** and stretches 70 miles from New Haven to the Rhode Island border. It is *the* major automotive channel between Boston and New York, and points in between, and so is one of the most heavily traveled highways in America. It is also the main route used on summer weekends to access the beaches of Connecticut and Rhode Island, as well as Cape Cod, exacerbating traffic problems.

Route 9, which generally parallels the Connecticut River as it flows in a southeastern direction from Hartford into Long Island Sound, is also a major route used by beachgoers coming from Hartford and points north. It also provides access to the river and the small towns that cling to its banks.

Two other interstate highways traverse the region. **I-84** runs from Hartford northeast to the Massachusetts border, where it eventually connects with the Massachusetts Turnpike in Sturbridge. **I-395** runs north from the New London

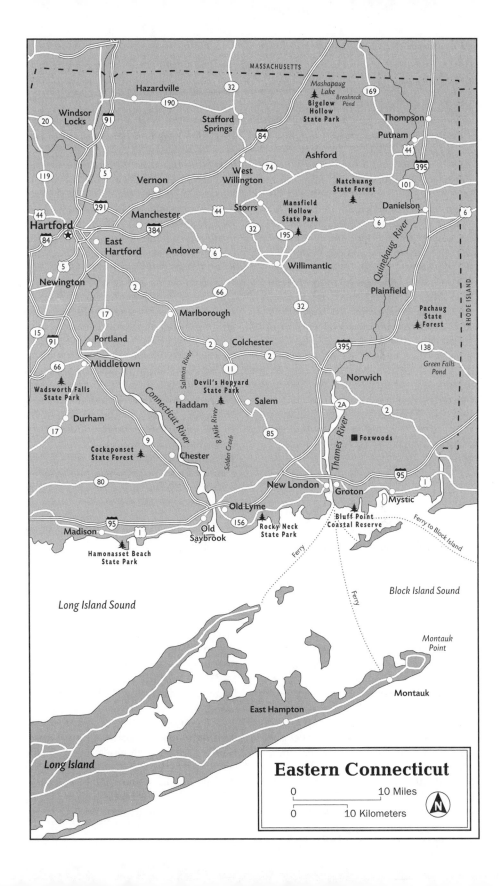

Eastern Connecticut

0   10 Miles

0   10 Kilometers

area along Connecticut's eastern edge, exiting in the northeastern corner of the state on its way to Worcester, Massachusetts. Within the rough triangle created by I-84, I-395, and Route 9 lies the heart and soul of rural eastern Connecticut, although the state's largest tract of public land, **Pachaug State Forest,** lies just east of I-395.

There are three other key points of reference that visitors often use in orienting themselves in eastern Connecticut. One is **Storrs,** home of the University of Connecticut, which lies approximately 25 miles due east of Hartford on **Route 44.** Another is **Foxwoods Casino,** which is in Ledyard, in the southeastern corner of the state. For better or for worse, Foxwoods generates more tourism revenue than any other attraction in the region. Finally, there is **Mystic** and its re-created seaport, which before the emergence of Foxwoods was the tourism hub of the east. It is still a focal point on the eastern shore.

Orientation

Forests, rolling hills, two major rivers, and a heavily indented shoreline—in sum, that's eastern Connecticut. The hills are not substantial enough to be called mountains—not one measures over 1,000 feet—yet they are everywhere, forming a kind of lumpy landscape that caches water in its pockets and folds. Hence, this is a region of numerous ponds, small lakes, and rivers.

The Connecticut, of course, is the river of greatest significance. Flowing out of the mountains of New Hampshire, it is fed by other rivers while it becomes a broad, syrupy swath of water ambling toward Long Island Sound. Over its 410-mile length, the river drops a total of 1,600 vertical feet, yet in its last 75 miles—from Springfield, Massachusetts to Long

Island Sound—it drops just 40 feet. That makes for a very slow-moving river.

It is also, relatively speaking, a clean river. Historically, it has been used mainly as a transportation corridor, a source of energy, and a source of water for agriculture. The industrial activity that heavy polluted such rivers as the Millers to the north, the Housatonic to the west, and the Blackstone to the east, was not as prevalent along the Connecticut. To the east, also flowing south into the sound, is the Thames River, a wide but short receptacle for smaller rivers, including the Shetucket and Quinebaug, which feed it from the north.

Deciduous trees predominate in eastern Connecticut's forests, chief among them are maples, birches, and beeches. Toward the south, near Long Island Sound, the tree and plant life are characteristic of milder, maritime environments, in the form of cedars, oaks, and rhododendrons, among others. These forests are, in places, remarkably dense; a walk in the woods in eastern Connecticut can seem, in midsummer, like a walk through a tunnel of foliage. This can make the color changes in fall a remarkable sight, made all the more so by the fact that leaf peepers don't tend to come here in droves as they do to Litchfield Hills, the Berkshires, or Vermont.

Coves, harbors, and rivers make the eastern Connecticut coastline look like a piece of ragged cloth. The occasional rocky headland separates marshlands and sand beaches that remain relatively well protected from severe weather, given the sheltering presence of Long Island just a few miles to the south.

While eastern Connecticut's weather is mild by New England standards—no surprise given that Connecticut is the most southern of New England states—there are still four distinctive seasons. Hartford's average temperature in January is 28°, but rises to 73° in July. This is, in fact, a shade cooler than Boston, so Hartford sees more snow in an average winter than Boston does.

In the fall, of course, the hillsides glow with color, as they do elsewhere in New England. Yet unlike northern New England, where winter and summer tend to collide without much of a noticeable spring in between, Connecticut can claim a real spring. Beginning in April, flowers, rhododendrons, and dogwoods bloom, a pageant of annual rejuvenation that continues well into May.

Parks & Other Hot Spots

Bigelow Hollow State Park
From I-84, take exit 73 for Union. Go east on Rte. 190 for 2 miles, then turn right on Rte. 171. The entrance to the park is on the left, about 1.5 miles down the road. Headquarters: **Department of Environmental Protection,** Office of Parks and Recreation, 79 Elm St., Hartford, CT 06106; ☎ **860/424-3200.**

Located in the far northeast, the state park teams with adjoining Nipmuck State Forest (8,000 acres) and Mashapaug Lake to form one of the most enticing outdoor areas in the state. The canoeing and fishing in the lake and neighboring Bigelow Pond are superb, as are the trails for hiking, which include the Nipmuck Trail.

Bluff Point Coastal Reserve
Take exit 88 from I-95 and go south on Rte. 117. Turn right on Rte. 1 and drive 0.3 miles to Depot Rd. Turn left and continue under the railroad tracks to the parking area. Headquarters: **Department of Environmental Protection,** Office of Parks and Recreation, 79 Elm St., Hartford, CT 06106; ☎ **860/424-3200.**

Private property covers the vast majority of the Connecticut coastline. Bluff Point provides rare public access to coastal forests and marshland. This is a great place for easy hiking and for bird-watching.

Cockaponset State Forest
Take exit 8 on Rte. 9 and turn east on Beaver Meadow Rd. Turn right on Ranger Rd. to the state forest headquarters. (The forest is also accessible from the south via exit 6 from Rte. 9.) Headquarters: **Department of Environmental Protection,** Office of Parks and Recreation, 79 Elm St., Hartford, CT 06106; ☎ **860/424-3200.**

At 15,652 acres, this is the second largest tract of undeveloped land in the state. A system of dirt roads makes this forest one of the prime areas in eastern Connecticut for mountain biking.

Connecticut River
Flowing toward the southeast, the river enters Connecticut from the north at Thompsonville and empties into Long Island Sound at Old Saybrook. There are numerous access points along the river. Connecticut's Department of Environmental Protection (79 Elm St., Hartford, CT 06106; ☎ **860/424-3200**) is a good source for river information as well as fishing and boating licenses.

The river runs southward for about 70 miles, broadening as it nears Long Island Sound. Powerboat traffic on weekends can be considerable, but there are still a number of fine coves and feeder streams for canoeists to explore. There are three camping areas reserved primarily for canoeists. Bird-watching along the river, particularly as it nears Long Island Sound, is excellent.

Hammonassett Beach State Park
From I-95, take exit 62, then head 1 mile south. Headquarters: Box 271, Madison, CT 06443; ☎ **203/245-2785.**

In summer this is a major beach scene; bring your towel, your Coppertone, and a good spy novel. Any other time of year, this is a good bird-watching area. Wading marsh birds—herons, egrets, etc.—are regular visitors, and waterfowl are abundant during fall migrations. The state's largest campground, with 558 sites, is located within the park.

Mansfield Hollow State Park
From Storrs, take Rte. 195 south. Just after the intersection with Rte. 89, turn left onto Bassetts Bridge Rd. Look for a parking lot on your left at Mansfield Hollow Lake. Headquarters: **Department of Environmental Protection,** Office of Parks and Recreation, 79 Elm St., Hartford, CT 06106; ☎ **860/424-3200.**

Mansfield Hollow Lake, a 500-acre reservoir, is a popular canoeing spot among flatwater enthusiasts from the nearby University of Connecticut. The fishing—for large- and smallmouth bass and trout—is said to be some of the best in eastern Connecticut. Mountain bikers are regular users of the trail network that winds through the 2,500-acre park.

Natchaug State Forest
Take Rte. 198 south from Phoenixville. Continue 4 miles to the main park entrance, on the left. Headquarters: Pilfershire Rd., Eastford, CT 06242; ☎ **860/974-1562.**

Despite its size (12,935 acres), Natchaug is sometimes eastern Connecticut's overlooked state forest, for no particularly good reason. For backpackers, camping at designated backcountry sites is (with a permit) allowed—a rarity in southern New England. The forest includes another rarity—a campground specifically for horseback riders. There are 55 miles of trails in the forest, as well as several paved and unpaved back roads.

Pachaug State Forest
From Voluntown, take Rte. 49 north. Continue about a mile to the main forest entrance, on the left. Headquarters: Box 5, Voluntown, CT 06384; ☎ **860/376-4075.**

At 22,938 acres, this is the king of Connecticut's state forests, but it is only part of a larger region of wilderness. Adjacent Arcadia Management Area, across the border in Rhode Island (see chapter 8, "Rhode Island & Block Island"), adds another 13,000 forested acres to the

package. There are about 40 miles of trails for hiking and horseback riding and seven stocked lakes for fishing. With limited campground facilities (just 40 primitive sights in two areas), the forest is rarely crowded despite its size.

What to Do & Where to Do It

BALLOONING
There may be no better way to view the fall foliage of northeastern Connecticut than to take to the air. **Brighter Skies Balloon Company** (119 Roseland Park Rd., Woodstock; ☎ **800/677-5114** or 860/963-0600) takes passengers up for 1- to 1½-hour rides at sunrise or sunset, when winds are usually calmest. Those are also the times of day when the light is at its most dramatic, so bring along a camera and lots of film. Fall is not the only time to go—the company operates year-round.

If you're feeling more adventurous, **Mystical Balloon Flights** (40 Forest Dr., Salem; ☎ **860/537-0025**) combines balloon flights with bungee jumping from the balloon. In either case, expect champagne to come with the deal; it's a part of ballooning tradition.

BIRD-WATCHING
The marshlands of the Long Island Sound shoreline and the small islands just offshore are great spots to see a mix of wading birds (egrets, herons, ibises) and shore birds, including terns, gulls, and plovers. **Bluff Point Coastal Reserve,** with its hiking trails, is one of the most accessible areas for getting close to shore and marsh habitats. The **Stewart B. McKinney National Wildlife Refuge,** a collection of dispersed land parcels, includes (in Westbrook) Salt Meadow, the

first national wildlife refuge, so designated in 1971. Over 200 species have been sighted here, and it is a good place to spot ospreys. Two-and-a-half miles of hiking trails wind through the refuge.

The **Great Island** area, where the Connecticut River flows into Long Island Sound, is a popular stopover for migrating waterfowl. In winter, bald eagles have been seen nesting here. To appreciate this habitat fully, you'll need some kind of boat. Bald eagles may also be seen wintering farther upstream, at **Hamburg Cove.**

Although **Hammonassett Beach State Park** sees serious crowds in the summer, it is the beach that is the overwhelming attraction. The crowds dwindle considerably as you head inland to the marshes along the Hammonassett River, and you might be surprised by the diversity of bird life and the relative serenity here. In spring and fall, migrating birds flock here by the thousands.

Field Trip Organizers

The Audubon Shop (871 Boston Post Rd., Madison CT 06443; ☎ 203/245-9056) organizes trips to Hammonassett Beach State Park, particularly in spring and fall. **The Hartford Audubon Society** (Box 270207, West Hartford, CT 06127; ☎ 860/644-7343) invites the public and beginning birders to join regular trips to hot spots throughout the region, particularly along the Long Island Sound shore.

CANOEING

If you're someone who likes river paddling, your best bet in eastern Connecticut is to come in spring, when water levels in the numerous rivers and streams are fairly high with runoff from melting snow and ice. Depending on how snowy a winter it has been, even some of the smaller streams, such as Eight Mile River below Chapman Falls in Devil's Hopyard State Park, may be runnable.

More reliably, though, the **Quinebaug River** makes for a good spring outing on

the 12-mile stretch from Route 205 to Butts Bridge Road. Another reliably good stretch of quick water is the 14-mile stretch of the **Willimantic River** from Route 32 to Eagleville Dam.

For stillwater paddling, you might want to check out **Uncas Pond** in Nehantic State Forest near North Lyme or **Green Falls Pond** in Pachaug State Forest. Small, undeveloped, and relatively undiscovered, Uncas is a great getaway spot. The same might not be said for Green Falls, which can draw a crowd on weekends. But with a small campground, it's a good spot to bring along the whole family for a couple of days of canoeing, hiking, and exploring.

Mashapaug Lake

Union, in Bigelow Hollow State Park. Access: From I-84, take exit 73 for Union. Go east on Rte. 190 for 2 miles, then turn right on Rte. 171. The entrance to the park is on the left, after about 1.5 miles. Continue past Bigelow Pond to Mashapaug Lake and the boat-launch area.

Just when you think Connecticut is about to come to an end, as you head northeast on I-84, you discover in Mashapaug Lake one last gem. There are some homes and docks along the northern shore of the 1.5-mile-long lake, but a state forest and a park surround the rest of the lake. The forest seems to tumble right to the water's edge, so paddle along the southeastern shore and keep your eyes open for birds and wildlife. Bring along a fishing rod as well; a state-record largemouth bass was caught in the lake. Return then to the picnic area in Bigelow State Park, where the view up to the lake shields out the development along the north shore, creating the illusion of an almost perfectly pristine body of water and surrounding forest.

If you listen carefully, you might be able to hear the sounds of traffic along I-84, which passes about a mile to the west. But if you hug the shore, trees seem to block out almost all but the sound of your paddle dipping into the water. After a picnic lunch, you might also want to check out Bigelow Pond, Mashapaug's tiny neighbor. Its coves are filled with water lilies, and except for the rare fisherman, you're likely to have the pond entirely to yourself.

Selden Creek

Hadlyme. Access: From East Haddam, head south on Rte. 82. In Hadlyme, turn right on Rte. 148, at the sign for the Connecticut River ferry. There is a parking area for boaters on the right, next to the ferry port.

This exploratory outing is actually divided in three parts. Part One is the Connecticut River. Part Two is Selden Creek. Part Three is Whalebone Creek. Taken together, they form one of the most enchanting canoe excursions imaginable along the Connecticut River.

Whalebone and Selden Creeks are oddities of a sort in that they are freshwater tidal marshes. As the level of the Connecticut River rises and falls due to tidal activity occurring downstream at the confluence with Long Island Sound, so too does the water in these creeks rise and fall. Look for the signal lights along the eastern shore of the river, just south of the ferry, indicating the entrance to Whalebone Creek. This is a special place, a world of marsh grasses and wild rice, and birds by the hundreds, from tiny songbirds to the imperial great blue heron. Poke around in the small inlets that branch off the main channel, exploring and taking your time, but remaining alert to water levels that could leave you stranded at low tide.

Returning to the main channel, head back to the open river and then downstream to Selden Creek, less than a mile away on the eastern shore. Powerboats are permitted here, although the 6 m.p.h. speed limit helps keep the peace. The creek, which runs southward and eventually reconnects with the Connecticut, essentially creates an island, the most prominent feature of which is Selden

Neck, a small hill. The modus operandi here is just as it is in Whalebone Creek—explore inlets off the main creek, while being mindful of water levels.

As you re-enter the Connecticut River, head northward to return to the launch area. Yes, you'll be going upstream, but the flow of the river here is so slow that it's of little concern. More of a concern, particularly on weekends, is motorized boat traffic, so it's best to stick near the shore, well away from the main river channel, and to be prepared to negotiate the occasional upthrust wake. This is an easy day trip, but there is no reason not to extend it if you have time. There are campgrounds for boaters only in Selden Neck State Park (see "Campgrounds," below), so if you have a reservation (which is required), spend a night along the river shore, and go right back to exploring the marshes the next morning.

Gear & Rentals

Down River Canoes & Outfitters (Route 154, Haddam, CT 06438; ☎ 860/345-8355) sells canoes and accessories and also offers guided outings on the Connecticut River. **North American Canoe Tours** (65 Black Point Rd., Niantic CT 06357; ☎ 860/739-0971) rents canoes at state parks throughout Connecticut, including Hopeville Pond and Quaddick Pond. Overnight rentals are available at Hopeville Pond.

Outfitters

Approach Adventure Travel (Box 65175, Burlington, VT 05406; ☎ 888/277-7622) organizes 1- to 3-day trips, both guided and self-guided, in eastern Connecticut.

CROSS-COUNTRY SKIING

The almost total absence in eastern Connecticut of a legitimate cross-country skiing center, complete with groomed tracks, rentals, instruction, etc. is something of a mystery. This might not be the land of the big snows, but an annual snowfall exceeding 60 inches isn't exactly a spit in the bucket, either. Nevertheless, groomed-track skiing pretty much gets the cold shoulder. Your one choice is **Quinebaug Valley Ski Touring Center** (☎ 860/886-2284) in Preston. Otherwise, if you want to go cross-country skiing in eastern Connecticut, you'll have to be content with heading for the woods and making your own tracks.

So where are the best places to go for doing just that? A 4.5-mile loop circles Mansfield Lake in **Mansfield Hollow State Park** (☎ 860/455-9057), and sees a good deal of action from skiers coming from the nearby University of Connecticut. **Gay City State Park** in Hebron (☎ 860/295-9523) features two well marked loops, one 2.5 miles, the other 5 miles long, and both through relatively flat woodlands. **Pachaug State Forest,** set on a relatively high plateau, often has decent snow cover when there is little snow at lower elevations. Be prepared, however, to share trails with snowmobilers. The **Connecticut Department of Environmental Protection, State Parks Division** (79 Elm St., Hartford, CT 06106; ☎ 860/424-3200), produces a brochure on ski touring in the state.

DOWNHILL SKIING

The lack of big mountains and big snows limit the opportunities for downhill skiing in eastern Connecticut. With the bigger, snowier mountains of Vermont and New Hampshire just a couple of hours away, Connecticut skiers are more likely to hop in the car and drive to better skiing than to hang around home, where the pickings are minimal.

Eastern Connecticut's one lift-serviced ski area is **Powder Ridge** (☎ 877/754-7434 or 860/349-3454) in Middlefield, which makes ends meet because: a) it's about halfway between Hartford and New Haven, two large population bases, and b) there are a lot of devoted Connecticut skiers who need a quick, close-to-home

fix from time to time. Powder Ridge is not, of course, big by northern New England standards, but with an elevation of 500 vertical feet, it's not a complete pancake, either. There are 14 trails, four chairlifts, and two lifts specifically designed for snow tubing—all respectable numbers. Toss in snowmaking and night skiing, and you've got a decent, pocket-sized ski area.

FISHING

Eastern Connecticut could easily be considered a solitary fisherman's paradise; its waters are teeming with fish. This is due in part to the numerous lakes, ponds, streams, and rivers that mark the region, as well as the bays, inlets, and coves reaching out from Eastern Connecticut into Long Island Sound. It is also due to the efforts of the Fisheries Division of the state's Department of Environmental Protection, which has one of the most aggressive stocking programs of any state in the country. Each year, roughly 800,000 trout are released in Connecticut waters (east and west), along with various other species, including salmon and bass.

Many of these fish, of course, end up in the bountiful waters of the east, but you wouldn't know it judging by the manner in which outfitters and guides are distributed throughout the state. It is as though a slippery slope has deposited virtually all of the state's guides and outfitters west of I-91. This may or may not be a good thing. On the plus side, eastern waters are fished less. On the down side, you're pretty much on your own finding hot spots and figuring out what the fish are biting on. Even tackle shops—great sources of advice and information—are few and far between.

Perhaps the obvious thing to do is head for a place with a fish name. The **Salmon River,** flowing through the state forest of the same name, is stocked with trout as well as salmon, of course. The state has been make a concerted effort to reinvigorate Atlantic salmon in its rivers, and the Salmon River has been a primary recipient of the state's attention. So, too, has the **Eight Mile River,** which flows through Devil's Hopyard State Park and is also stocked with trout. *Note:* To protect the salmon, the state enforces a strict catch-and-release policy.

There is excellent trout fishing to be had in the far northeastern corner of the state, far from any major population centers. Among the rivers favored by local flycasters are the **Mount Hope** and the **Natchaug.**

Near Winchester, **Pickerel Lake**—another fish-named body of water—does indeed have pickerel, but its primary game fish is largemouth bass. When it comes to largemouth bass, **Mashapaug Lake,** accessible from Bigelow Hollow State Park, can lay at least statistical claim to being number one; the state-record largemouth bass was caught here.

Major-league brown trout fishing is what attracts fishermen to **Rogers Lake** near Old Lyme. And for a complete smorgasbord of fishing possibilities, **Mansfield Hollow Lake** is loaded with trout, bass, pickerel, and pike.

As for saltwater fishing, keep in mind that Long Island Sound is, recreationally speaking, one of the most heavily used bodies of water in the country. Fishermen come not only from Connecticut harbors, but also from harbors along the north shore of Long Island. Do not go fishing in the sound with great expectations of being alone or chancing upon a school of fish that no one else knows about.

That said, there is still some good fishing to be had in the sound, particularly for bluefish and striped bass (stripers). Some Connecticut-based charter boats will take you farther afield (or asea, as it were) to go after bigger game fish, including tuna and shark. This, however, means leaving the sound, and technically leaving Connecticut waters.

The principal harbors for charter activity along the coast are **Branford, Clinton, Old Saybrook, Niantic,** and **Mystic.** Steer clear of so-called party boats, the larger and less expensive cousins of charter boats. The general definition of a charter boat is one that carries six clients or fewer. Expect to spend somewhere in the neighborhood of $800 to charter a boat for the day. That might sound like a lot, but when you divvy the cost up with five of your best fishing buddies, you come in at a somewhat reasonable $125 per person.

For a list of charter-boat operators, contact the **Connecticut State Tourism Office** (☎ **800/CT-BOUND**) and ask for the *Connecticut Vacation Guide.* For information on licenses and regulations, call the Department of Environmental Protection's Fisheries Division (☎ **860/ 424-3474**). Licenses, as in most states, are available at marinas and tackle shops.

Gear

North Cove Outfitters (75 Main St., Old Saybrook, CT 06378; ☎ **203/388-6585**) is well supplied for fishing, as well as other outdoor activities. **Cubeta's Field and Stream** (157 Meriden Rd., Rte. 66, Middlefield CT 06455; ☎ **860/347-4353**) is a certified Orvis dealer.

HIKING & BACKPACKING

When it comes to hiking, Connecticut is an amazing place, where the seemingly impossible becomes possible. It is a most settled state, with many cities, towns, and roads, and a population density of almost 700 people per square mile. The existence of an extensive, well-marked, and, for the most part, well-maintained trail network defies common sense. Yet there it is, for hikers and, to a more limited degree, for backpackers to enjoy.

Lacking the mountainous topography of points farther north in New England, eastern Connecticut's trail network lacks the kind of grand vistas that might reward a hiker upon reaching a mountaintop. And to hike, or take an extended hike, in Connecticut means you'll have to occasionally pass by private homes and lands or through nodes of civilization. But

A SCOURGE IN CHECK?

If there is one thing that eastern Connecticut can lay unequivocal claim to, and it is a dubious distinction, it is that Lyme disease (from the area of the same name near the coast) was first discovered here. The notorious disease, borne by tiny deer ticks, has been blamed for a host of symptoms, ranging from fatigue to central nervous system disorders. Fear of the disease has turned tick checking—inspecting exposed parts of the body for the nasty critters—into a summer ritual throughout southern New England.

In 1998, however, two pharmaceutical giants, SmithKline Beecham and Pasteur Merrieux Connaught, each announced they had come up with a Lyme-disease vaccine. In tests, the vaccines were reported to be 75% to 95% effective. By the end of the year, the SmithKline Beecham product, LYMErix, received approval from the Food and Drug Administration. Vaccination is carried out through three injections over a 12-month period.

The news of a vaccine is welcome in Connecticut, which has the highest rate of Lyme disease in the country. It is particularly welcome in Windham County in the heart of the Quiet Corner, which has the highest rate of infection in the state.

The end of the scourge, it might seem then, is at hand. Yet the good news must be tempered with caution. Officially, the effectiveness rate of the vaccine is reported to be 78% after three injections. That means there is still a 22% chance it won't work. Furthermore, for those who are not vaccinated—and for the time being, that means the majority of people who head into tick habitats—the risk of infection remains an ongoing issue.

Doctors stress that the vaccine is not for everyone. It is aimed at high-risk people, those who spend a considerable amount of time in wooded, brushy, or overgrown grassy areas, where the ticks flourish. If you expect to do a lot of spring and summertime hiking, mountain biking, bird-watching, etc., the vaccine might be for you. Otherwise, simple precautionary measures and common sense may be adequate protection.

For starters, avoid tick habitats if possible, particularly from April through July, the prime tick season. Second, cover exposed areas of the body, particularly your legs. Pulling your socks up over long pants might look incredibly dorky, but it keeps ticks out. Third, after spending time in an area where you might have been exposed to ticks, check not only your body, but also your clothing for the insects. And finally, if you are bitten, get treatment as quickly as possible. It takes 24 hours for the bacteria to invade the bloodstream after a bite. Nip the spread of the disease at the bud, and you should be in the clear.

for the most part, hiking in eastern Connecticut is a true revelation; despite the encroachments of civilization in the Northeast, deep forests and free-flowing streams still do exist.

Much of the credit for the existence of Connecticut's great trail network must go to the **Connecticut Forest & Park Association** (16 Meriden Rd., Rockfall, CT 06481; ☎ 203/346-2372), a 70-year-old association that organizes volunteer trail-maintenance crews and has done much to persuade private landowners to cede their rights of way in areas where public lands don't exist.

Bluff Point

Allow 3 hours. Easy. Access: Take exit 88 from I-95 and go south on Rte. 117. Turn right on Rte. 1 and drive 0.3 miles to Depot Rd. Turn left and continue under the railroad tracks to the parking area. Map: May be available at the trailhead; otherwise, contact the **Department of Environmental Protection,** Office of Parks and Recreation, 79 Elm St., Hartford, CT 06106; ☎ 860/424-3200.

Getting to the Long Island Sound shoreline without tramping uninvited through someone's backyard is a difficult endeavor indeed. Private land proliferates. You can head for the state-park beaches—Hammonassett and Rocky Point—but hiking opportunities are minimal, and solitude (except during off hours or the off-season) is an unlikely prospect.

Then there is Bluff Point, hugging the shore of the Poquonock River estuary as it reaches southward to Long Island Sound. Looking out from the parking area at the trailhead, you might be dubious about its value as a hiking location. Across the estuary, planes take off and land at the Trumbull Airport. It seems an unpromising start for a quiet walk in the woods, marshlands, and beaches of the coast. But the sound and fury of air traffic fades quickly to a drone, and then only to the occasional distant rumble, before the magic of the coast forest asserts itself.

This is a good place to go for a hike with kids. The going isn't difficult—the 5-mile trail is almost completely flat—meaning that it could have been classified, for this book's purposes, as a walk rather than a hike. It is a trail you could run (as some local aerobophiles do) and complete in a half hour. But it is also a place to spend time, to beachcomb, to keep an eye out for birds and wildlife, and to appreciate the transitions in the landscape, from forest to marsh to beach to water.

From the trailhead, bear right along the trail as it skirts the river shore before entering the forest. Ospreys frequently work the river, so keep your eyes open. As you head briefly into the woods, there is a junglelike quality to the tangle of trees, brambles, and wild grape. In a little over a mile, you'll reach Bluff Point itself, a 20-foot rise from which views sweep southward over Long Island Sound to Fisher's Island.

From here, turn right to walk along the spit of land that leads to Bushy Point. Along the beach, particularly at low tide, look for the sorts of prizes that beachcombers treasure—a shard of frosted sea glass or some strangely beautiful shell. When you reach Bushy Point, retrace your steps back to Bluff Point, and then turn inland to loop back to the trailhead. Along the way, you'll pass the foundations of the home of Governor Fitzjohn Winthrop, who in 1700 lived here and worked the land. The forests now close in, and soon you'll return to your starting point.

Breakneck Pond

Allow 3–4 hours. Moderate. Access: From I-84, take exit 73 for Union. Go east on Rte. 190 for 2 miles, then turn right on Rte. 171. Look for the entrance to Bigelow Hollow State Park, on the left after about 1.5 miles. Continue to the second parking area, at the end of Bigelow Pond. Map: Contact the **Connecticut Department of Environmental Protection,** Office of Parks and Recreation, 79 Elm St., Hartford, CT 06106; ☎ 860/424-3200.

It is rare in southern New England to come upon a lake or pond of any size that bears no trace of development. Breakneck Pond, a narrow dagger of water that pierces the border with Massachusetts, brings together two adjectives that are music to any hiker's ears—accessible and remote. The trail that loops the pond passes through a relatively undisturbed world of lily pads and beaver dams and forests crowded with mountain laurel.

From the parking area, take the East Ridge Trail (blazed in white) that leads directly to the pond. When you reach the southern edge of the pond, bear left onto the Breakneck Pond Loop Trail, marked with white blazes and blue dots, that connects to the orange-blazed Pond Vista Loop. The trail runs tight to the shore, and it is as if you are walking the knife's edge separating two environments—the pond on your right, the forest on your left. Watch carefully for birds; herons and kingfishers are known to work these waters.

You'll reach a trail junction as you near the Massachusetts border, but you should simply stick close to the pond. Soon you'll reach the border, marked by a monument, and loop back southward on the blue-blazed Nipmuck Trail along the pond. You'll encounter the occasional trail junction, but when in doubt, keep the pond close to your right to find your way back. Listen as you walk for the sound of frogs; this is their world, and they are known to announce their appreciation of it.

When you come to the southern terminus of the pond, turn right to rejoin the East Ridge Trail that leads back to the parking area. You'll have hiked a total of 6 to 7 miles with little climbing (although the trail close to the pond might in places require a little scrambling). You should have some energy still stored up and, if so, hike the short loop around Bigelow Pond. It is less than a 2-mile walk, but it's well worth the effort, as you'll pass through a pretty forest, come upon the occasional impressive boulder, and view the lily pads near the pond shore and perhaps a fisherman quietly trying to lure bass to the end of his line. When you finish the hike, settle in at the picnic area at the edge of Bigelow Pond for a well-earned lunch.

Overnight/Long-Distance Hikes

It might come as a surprise that backpacking, or some semblance of it, is possible in eastern Connecticut. Both **Natchaug** and **Pachaug** state forests have backcountry camping sites and are large enough to make an overnight backpacking trip a worthwhile endeavor. For more information on sites, reservations, and regulations, contact the **Connecticut Department of Environmental Protection** (79 Elm St., Hartford, CT 06106; ☎ **860/424-3200**).

Gear

North Cove Outfitters (75 Main St., Old Saybrook, CT 06378; ☎ **203/388-6585**) sells a wide variety of outdoor gear, including hiking and camping equipment.

HORSEBACK RIDING

To the west in Litchfield and Fairfield counties, the horse show, with all the attendant pomp and social pressures, is an institution. It is probably fair to say that nowhere in America is show jumping more of a big deal than in western Connecticut. But what about the east?

There are still plenty of stables and plenty of great riding terrain. Two unique finds in eastern Connecticut are the horse camps of **Pachaug** and **Nachaug** state forests. The campgrounds are reserved for people with horses only, providing a great opportunity for an extended exploration of the back roads and trails in both state forests. For more information on the horse camps, contact the **Connecticut Department of Environmental Protection, State Parks Division** (79 Elm St., Hartford, CT 06106; ☎ **860/424-3200**).

Other hot spots for riding include **Coventry, Willington,** and **Woodstock,** where stables offering instruction and guided rides are concentrated.

Instruction & Outfitters

Coventry Riding Stables (☎ **860/742-7576**) in Coventry, Woodcock Hill Riding Academy (☎ 860/487-1686) in Willington, and **Woodstock Acres Riding Stable** (☎ **860/974-1224**) are good choices for guided rides and instruction.

MOUNTAIN BIKING

Eastern Connecticut may lack big hills for rugged climbing or wild, technical descents, but it certainly doesn't lack for good terrain to ride. In fact, one of the attractive things about eastern-Connecticut riding is that it is not all rough-and-tumble riding, for which only dedicated mountain-biking jocks need apply. There is plenty of tough single track to be sure, but eastern Connecticut can also claim more than its fair share of easy, dirt-road, and double-track riding that can take you deep into the woods.

Another eastern-Connecticut plus is that trails tend to be well marked. Well-blazed trails, for both hiking and biking, are a Connecticut hallmark. This doesn't mean, of course, that you'll never get lost. On the down side, many of the maps of state forests and state parks are not much more than adequate. When it comes to mapping, the forests-and-parks people in Massachusetts do a much better job than the folks in Connecticut do.

As is the case in most areas of southern New England, mountain bikers in eastern Connecticut have yet to jump in to fill the mapping void. That leaves you to the usual resources—local bike shops, where you will not only find out where to ride, but also find people to ride with.

In addition to the rides below, you might want to check out **Shenipsit State Forest** in Somers for some fairly challenging single-track riding, as well as some lung-expanding climbing, at least by eastern-Connecticut standards. You might also want to check out the trails at **Wadsworth Falls State Park** in Middlefield. It's a good place to go if you have only a short time to ride; the trail network here isn't extensive, but what you will find is quality.

Cockaponset State Forest

Various trails. Spend an hour or all day. Moderate; short, but sometimes steep hills. Access: From Rte. 9, take exit 6 and head west (right) on Rte. 148. Approximately 1.5 miles later, turn right onto Cedar Lake Rd. Turn left at the Pattaconk Lake sign 1.5 miles later and continue past the lake to a parking lot on the right. Map: Available at forest headquarters on Ranger Rd. (take exit 8 from Rte. 9 and turn left on Beaver Meadow Rd. to Ranger Rd., on your right).

Thirty miles of single-track, double-track, and unpaved roads would be a conservative estimate for Cockaponset, which at 15,652 acres is the second largest state forest in Connecticut. That not only makes for a lot of riding, it creates a lot of opportunity for rides and loops of various lengths and difficulty. Here, mountain biking should more accurately be called forest biking; the deep green of the dense, mostly deciduous forest is interrupted only as you near the two major reservoirs, Pattaconk and Turkey Hill, within the forest boundaries. Otherwise, you'll be surrounded the entire time by trees and more trees.

From the parking area, turn right (on Filley Road), and then turn right again on the first dirt road you come to. There are plenty of opportunities to get lost, but if you stay alert to your position in relation to Pattaconk Lake (or reservoir, as it is also known), you can loop around the lake to return to your starting point.

Or you can stay on Filley Road instead, avoiding the more technical riding, but staying alert to traffic, and head north to Turkey Hill Reservoir. All the while, you'll notice trails branching off the road. Pick the trail that looks good to you; you can always retrace your tracks to Filley Road, the main drag bisecting the forest from north to south.

One thing you should keep in mind is that, at least in theory, the blue-blazed Cockaponset Trail and the red-blazed Pattaconk Trail are off-limits to riders. The policy, however, seems flexible, designed primarily to prevent potentially injurious biker-hiker encounters. During weekdays, when the trails are lightly used, park personnel, if they are out monitoring trail use at all, tend to look the other way.

Mansfield Hollow State Park

Five-mile loop. Allow 1 hour. Easy; mostly flat. Access: From I-84, take exit 68 to Rte. 195 south through Storrs. After Mansfield Center, turn left on Bassetts Bridge Rd. Look for a parking area on the left at the boat-launch area for Mansfield Hollow Lake. Map: Available from the **Department of Environmental Protection,** Office of Parks and Recreation, 79 Elm St., Hartford, CT 06106; ☎ **860/ 424-3200.**

Here's a great ride for novice riders interested in bumping up their skill level. At 5 miles, the loop around Mansfield Hollow Lake is relatively short, so supreme fitness isn't a prerequisite. The ups and downs are short, and the technical sections just tricky enough to challenge, but not to intimidate. And it is a relatively easy trail to follow, blazed with blue marks and used in winter as a cross-country ski trail.

From the parking area, head toward the edge of the lake (away from the road) to pick up a wide trail that enters the woods before running along a rocky dike. Keep following the blue blazes; unless you choose to veer off on a couple of single-track options, the trail is wide enough to accommodate riders whose bike-handling skills and confidence aren't quite up to negotiating narrower channels through the woods. The surface varies, from easy-going, soft pine needles to the occasional nest of roots—again, nothing killer here, but there's just enough challenge to toy with your balance and confidence. There are a couple of stream crossings, but in both cases there are bridges, so there will be no macho bashing across stream beds in hopes of reaching the other side before getting swamped.

Meanwhile, the dense forest closes in all around the trail, although you'll occasionally find views of the lake, where drifting boats carry fishermen casting their lines out across the water. The fishing here is first-rate, so when you're done riding you might want to try your own luck with a rod and reel. Swimming, alas, is not permitted—the lake is a secondary drinking-water supply.

Natchaug State Forest

Various roads and trails. Allow as much time as you can afford. Moderate; some extended climbing. Access: From Rte. 44 in Phoenixville, take Rte. 198 south. The main entrance to the park is on your left, in about 3 miles. Map: Available at forest headquarters.

Mountain biking usually can be divided into two separate categories of riding. Category one involves technical, single-track riding filled with anaerobic bursts and changes of speed. This is the type of mountain biking where bike handling is the main name of the game. Category two involves faster, more continuous riding on smoother, more open surfaces—riding more akin to road riding, where aerobic fitness is the main thing.

Natchaug riding tends to favor mountain biking of the category-two style. The dirt (and occasionally paved) roads of the forest are also popular with horseback riders for the same reason they work for mountain bikers—they're easy to follow, the woods resound with tranquility, and there is little or no motorized traffic.

There are hills in Natchaug. Not big hills, though, since eastern Connecticut simply doesn't have the topography for long, arduous climbing. But there are a few climbs here that are long enough to elevate your heart rate, and keep it elevated for a while. In fact, you can start with a climb right off the bat. Park at the picnic area just inside the forest entrance, and climb the half-mile paved road until you reach an intersection. Turn right, onto unpaved Kingsbury Road, and from there just think left all the way. Bear left after you pass the horse camp entrance, then turn left again at the next dirt road.

In a couple of miles, you'll come to an intersection with Pilfershire Road, where you'll bear left again. The dirt road soon gives way to pavement, and you'll start climbing again. At the next intersection, make a sharp left. This will lead you past the forest headquarters, and soon, on your right, you'll see the road that will lead back down to the picnic area from which you started.

That's Natchaug in its simplest terms. Once you've completed this ride—about 7 miles in length—head out again and start exploring. Get off the road and try out some of the trails that lead into the heart of the forest. And once you've done this, head south into neighboring James L. Goodwin State Forest for more dirt roads and even better single track. In all, there are well over 60 miles of roads and trails in the two forests; you could spend a week here and almost never have to ride the same trail twice.

Pachaug State Forest

Various trails. Spend an hour, all day, or a couple of days by overnighting in the Mount Misery Campground. Easy to moderate; mostly flat terrain, but because of the size of the forest, rides can be fairly long. Access: From I-395, take exit 85 to Rte. 138 east. Before Voluntown, turn right (north) on Rte. 49. Look for the forest entrance on the left. Map: Available at forest headquarters.

The riding in Pachaug is, in many ways, much like the riding in Cockaponset State Forest. There are fewer hills in Pachaug, which more or less sits atop a plateau. But in terms of the trail mix—narrow, unpaved roads and a large network of interconnected double- and single-track trails—and in terms of the dense forestation, the riding in the two large state forests is quite similar.

You can do an easy, non-technical route of about 10 miles by taking Trail Road north from the Mount Misery parking area toward Phillips Pond. You'll start off at the tiny pond, an enchanted place of lily pads and overhanging trees, where you may want to stop for a break or a snack. From here the road continues north until it reaches paved Hell Hollow Road.

Turn left here, then take the next dirt road on your left. Turn left at the next intersection onto Lawrence Road, then make a right at the next intersection, and then a left onto Cutoff Road. This leads back to your starting point for a total loop of about 7 miles. But if you're eager to continue, head south on Firetower Road, which turns into a double-track road after you pass Mt. Misery. This eventually meets Trail Road, where you'll take a sharp left to return to the starting point.

That's Pachaug in simplest terms, terms that even beginning mountain bikers should be able to handle easily. More expert riders will be tempted to explore the numerous single tracks that depart from the dirt roads. Go for it, with just two precautions: First, trails aren't always

well marked (or mapped), so keep aware of how you got to where you are. Second, Pachaug is a popular horseback-riding area. Horses have been known to be spooked by fast-moving mountain bikes, particularly on narrow trails, so stay alert for riders you might encounter.

Gear & Rentals

Cycle Center of Vernon (Route 30, Post Road Plaza, Vernon; ☎ 860/872-7740) is a good place for equipment and ride information. **Scott's Cyclery** (1171 Main St., Willimantic, CT 06226; ☎ 860/423-8889) has a particular bent toward mountain biking.

ROAD BIKING

Of all the activities possible in eastern Connecticut, road cycling may reign supreme, particularly as you move inland and more deeply into the Quiet Corner. Back roads abound, and heavy traffic recedes on all but a few main roads. There are enough hills and rolls in the terrain to make things interesting, but there are few killer steeps and long, lung-destroying climbs. Small, well-kept towns with Colonial roots add vibrancy and a sense of history, while the omnipresent forests simply add color. The hard thing here is not finding a good route, but choosing a good route from among many.

In fact, it is somewhat surprising that eastern Connecticut remains relatively undiscovered by touring cyclists. The major bicycle-touring companies don't come here, and the few riders you might meet along the road are likely to be locals. Perhaps this is simply in keeping with eastern Connecticut's undiscovered character, and perhaps it is best kept that way.

East Haddam/Hadlyme Loop

Allow 2–3 hours. Moderate; one steep hill. Access: Rte. 148 in Hadlyme, at the Chester-Hadlyme ferry port. Map: Any good state roadmap should do.

Could there possibly be a perfect 20-mile ride in Connecticut? Probably not, but this ride must certainly be nominated for the award. There is, after all, a little bit of everything that characterizes a classic New England ride: storybook villages, smooth roads with little traffic, deep forests, open marshlands, streams running alongside the road, antiques stores, and even a short ferry ride.

In fact, probably the best way to start this ride is by taking the ferry. (*Note:* On weekends, the ferry runs only between 10:30am and 5:00pm. For schedule information, call ☎ 860/443-3856.) Park next to the ferry port in Hadlyme; there's a large parking lot there used primarily by boaters heading out onto the Connecticut River. Once across the river, head west on Route 148 into the town of Chester, one of the many small towns along the river that seem misplaced in the 20th (or 21st) century. Sleepy, unaffected, and quintessentially New England, Chester seems also to have been missed by the paintbrush of tourism that has touched up towns like East Haddam and Essex.

From Chester, backtrack a mile to Route 154, and head north to Tylerville. If you're going to encounter traffic on the ride, this is where you'll find it. In Tylerville, turn east on Route 82, crossing the river into East Haddam, with its almost movie-set-perfect Victorian and Colonial houses. If you get the urge to shop or grab a bite to eat, do it here.

Continue from East Haddam on Route 82 for about a mile, keeping an eye out for signs to Devil's Hopyard State Park. Bear left on Devil's Hopyard Road, and be prepared to climb. For the next 2 miles or so, the road climbs steadily, with a couple of steep pitches, as it winds through the woods toward the tiny crossroads of Millington. Take your time and appreciate the scenery—this is the only real climbing you'll have to do on this ride.

The road finally levels off in Millington, where the only hint there's some kind of town at all is a roadside welcome sign. Continue following signs to Devil's Hopyard as the road begins to descend, then make a right turn into the state park. Now the road narrows and the trees close in, and after the climbing you've done, this is a great place for a break. Check out 60-foot Chapman Falls (just off the road on your left), and then stop for lunch or a snack at the streamside picnic area.

From here, the road wends narrowly through the cool, dense forest, eventually leaving the state park and intersecting with the combined Routes 82 and 156. Turn right and make sure, about a half mile later, to stick with Route 82 where the two routes diverge. This eventually takes you toward the pretty homes, stately trees, and resounding quietude of Hadlyme.

At this point, having ridden between 15 and 20 miles, you might want to assess your fitness. If you feel you've had enough riding, simply descend on Route 148 from Hadlyme to the ferry, passing beautiful marshlands along the way. But if you're still game to do more riding, head north for a few miles on Route 82 toward East Haddam and Moodus, passing antiques shops, a neat carriage museum, and handsome homes along the way. Go as far as you want—5 miles, 10 miles—and then simply turn around and retrace your route back to Hadlyme.

Mansfield Hollow Loop

Allow 2–3 hours. Moderate; rolling terrain. Access: From Storrs, take Rte. 195 south. Just after the intersection with Rte. 89, turn left onto Bassetts Bridge Rd. Look for a parking lot on your left at Mansfield Hollow Lake. Map: A detailed map of Connecticut should be adequate; the more detailed, the better.

You might expect that a ride through an area known as the Quiet Corner would be mellow, and so it is. Most of this ride is on minimally used back roads, with just a few miles on busier thoroughfares. Yet as you pass through such small towns as Windham and Hampton, you get the sense that life here, even on the busiest of highways, is never rushed.

From the state park parking lot, turn left on Bassetts Bridge Road, soon bearing right onto South Bedlam Road. After a bridge, bear right again, then cross Route 6 to Route 203, which leads, in a couple of miles, to Route 14. Turn left here and stay on Route 14 as it leads to Windham, postcard-perfect with its white clapboard homes, stone walls, and church.

Less than a mile east of Windham, keep an eye out for Back Road (how perfect is that name?) on your left. Turn left onto what is, indeed, a back road, then after 1.5 miles bear right on Bass Road (which turns into Kemp Road), and in another 2.5 miles, turn left onto Brook Road Extension. After 2 miles, turn right onto South Brook Road. During the time you spend on this 5-mile stretch, you may find yourself wondering whether you have remained in the densely populated state of Connecticut or have been beamed up to the back woods of northern Maine.

Soon you'll come to an intersection with Route 6, where you'll turn right (to the east) and ride its wide shoulders to the intersection with Route 97, where you'll turn left (north) and into the town of Hampton. This is another of those tiny communities, dating back to the 1700s, for which the word *quaint* seems inadequate. North of Hampton, look for Station Road, where you'll want to bear to your left. The road, passing between James L. Goodwin State Forest and Natchaug State Forest, dips so deeply into the woods that you'll feel at times as though you're riding through a tunnel of foliage.

In a little over 4 miles, you'll come to an intersection with Route 198. Turn left here, and after about 4 miles, turn right onto Bedlam Road. In about 1.5 miles, turn left onto South Bedlam Road, then right onto Bassetts Bridge Road, which leads back to your starting point.

Mystic

Allow 2–3 hours. Easy–moderate; some rolling hills. Access: From I-95, take exit 90 into the town of Mystic. Map: Check at the tourist information center in Mystic.

Mystic, with its renowned seaport and aquarium, attracts flocks of tourists during the summer months. On some roads, particularly Route 1, traffic can get heavy. But that still leaves plenty of lesser-traveled routes to explore in the town of Mystic itself, and in the north, away from the shore, where traffic (other than on Route 2, with cars and buses coming from and going to Foxwoods Casino) recedes the farther inland you go.

From the center of Mystic, head west on Route 1, cross the drawbridge, and take a right on Gravel Street. Across the river, the grand old ships of Mystic Seaport stand in waiting. Another left on Eldredge and a right on Pearl brings you into the heart of Mystic's historic district, a bustling place during the heyday of whaling in the mid-1800s.

Head right onto River Road, and ride along the Mystic River. This is a good place to slow down and do some bird-watching; the wonderfully athletic osprey, one of the great fishing birds of the world, has been making a comeback in recent years in New England in general and along the Connecticut coast in particular.

Go under I-95 and cross Route 27 before continuing straight onto North Stonington Road. Then bear left onto Lantern Hill Road, passing through farmlands. Turn right on Route 214, and you'll end up at Foxwoods Casino, a sudden burst of parking lots and development in what looks like the middle of the woods. At last report, the casino had not made any special accommodations to look after the bikes of touring cyclists who come in to drop some change in the slots or big bills at the baccarat tables, but who knows—maybe things have changed.

At the casino, turn right (south) onto Route 2, the main route used by the gambling crowd for its comings and goings. You can expect plenty of traffic here, and perhaps a snoutful of tour-bus exhaust, but at least the shoulder is wide. And this stretch won't last long. In about a mile, you'll turn right onto Route 201 and will be back in the heart of Connecticut farmland.

At Route 184, go straight onto Old Stonington Road past the old Mystic Fire Station (not onto Route 27), which leads back to River Road and back to Mystic. If you're looking for a meal to replace the calories expended on your ride, Mystic does not lack for places to eat. Try **Mystic Pizza** (56 W. Main St.; ☎ 860/536-3700), the inspiration for the movie of the same name that launched the career of Julia Roberts.

Gear & Rentals

Mystic River Kayak Tours, Bike & Moped Rentals (18B Holmes St., Mystic; ☎ 860/572-0123) rents bikes and leads guided tours in the Mystic area. Gear tending toward the high end is available at **Groton Cyclery** (1360 Rte. 184, Groton; ☎ 860/445-6745). **Clarke Cycles** (4 Essex Plaza, Essex; ☎ 860/767-2405) is a good source for equipment and ride information in the Connecticut River valley.

Tour Organizers

The **Connecticut Bicycle Coalition** (One Union Place, Hartford, CT 06103; ☎ 860/527-5200) organizes numerous rides in eastern Connecticut, some free, some requiring a fee. The **Pequot Cyclists** in southeastern Connecticut are also active in organizing rides, and non-members are usually welcome. Check at bike stores in the Mystic area for club and ride information.

SAILING

Long Island Sound, well protected by land and particularly well protected from the southwesterly winds that typically prevail in summer, is generally known among sailors for light winds and smooth waters. Experienced sound sailors learn to adapt to variable and changing winds, unlike the steadier breezes that blow farther out to sea. The eastern part of the sound is also known in places for strong currents, particularly where tidal flows enter and exit. Strong currents are infamous through the Race, where the tides must squeeze between Fisher's Island and the Connecticut coast.

While the sailing in the sound may, on an average day, be less rugged than sailing in the more open waters elsewhere along the New England coast, this is still a popular area for cruising yachtsmen. Connecticut's well-indented shoreline lends itself to a number of small, attractive harbors, from **Stonington** in the east to **Guilford** and **Branford** as you near New Haven. Smaller boats can also explore inland from the coast along the several rivers that empty into the sound, particularly the **Connecticut, Mystic,** and **Thames.**

Instruction

Womanship (☎ 800/342-9295) has schools in several locations around the country, including Mystic. As the name of the school implies, the 3- to 7-day instructional programs are designed specifically for women. **Yachting Services of Mystic** (31 Water St., Mystic, CT 06355; ☎ 800/536-9980) has instructional programs for beginners to advanced sailors, and is certified by the American Sailing Association. **Coastline Sailing School & Yacht Charters** (8 Marsh Rd., Eldridge Yard, Noank, CT 06340; ☎ 800/749-7245 or 203/536-2689) also offers lessons for all experience levels.

Charters & Rentals

Both **Yachting Services of Mystic** and the **Coastline Sailing School** (see "Instruction," above) charter cruising yachts for day sailing or extended periods of time.

SEA KAYAKING

There may be no better way to experience the Connecticut coast than in a sea kayak. Land-bound folk must face the fact that private land limits access to much of the coast, while larger boats—cruising yachts and the like—are limited to the water depths they can safely navigate. Neither of these restrictions applies to sea kayaks, which make the myriad coves, inlets, and shoreline marshes a grand world to explore. If you are into bird-watching in particular, it is hard to imagine a better way of going about it than in a sea kayak.

The **Great Island** area, where the Connecticut River enters Long Island Sound, is a great place to poke around and keep on the lookout for birds. So too are the marshlands of the **Barn Island Wildlife Management Area,** south of Pawcatuck in the southeastern corner of the state. And there's always **Mystic,** with its bustling harbor and river. You won't be alone, as boats of all shapes, sizes, and means of propulsion come and go here. But with Mystic Seaport and other sights, there is a lot to feast your eyes on.

In addition to the usual nautical charts, you might want to get a copy of the **Connecticut Coastal Access Guide,** a freebie distributed by the state's Department of Environmental Protection, Long Island Sound Programs (☎ 860/424-3034). The detailed map includes information on boat-launch areas, shore restrictions, points of interest, and other details of interest to the coastal kayaker.

Gear & Rentals

North Cove Outfitters (75 Main St., Old Saybrook, CT 06378; ☎ 203/388-6585) sells kayaks and accessories.

Instruction

Mystic River Kayak Tours, Bike & Moped Rentals (18B Holmes St., Mystic; ☎ 860/536-8381) guides instructional trips on the Mystic River. Lessons can also be arranged through **North Cove Outfitters** (see "Gear & Rentals," above).

Outfitters

Collinsville Canoe & Kayak (41 Bridge St., Collinsville, CT 06022; ☎ 860/693-6977) leads day trips in Little Narragansett Bay, the mouth of the Connecticut River, and the Mystic River. Expect a little new-age spirituality to come with the deal; the company also offers a program called "Healing Through the Art of Kayaking." **The Sea Kayaking Company** in Meriden (☎ 203/333-3998) leads trips on Long Island Sound.

SWIMMING

With Long Island acting as a barrier between the Connecticut coast and the ocean, surf and rough water are essentially nonexistent at the beaches of Long Island Sound. Thus, **Hammonassett Beach** and **Rocky Neck State Park,** the two principal beaches along the sound, are reasonably good places to bring small kids. They can get crowded, of course, although the younger crowd—the surf-minded crowd—tends to head either to the beaches of Rhode Island or to Cape Cod.

There are a number of inland ponds and lakes for fine freshwater swimming. At **Beach Pond** in Pachaug State Forest, you can experience a rarity—swim from one state to another. The pond lies on the border between Connecticut and Rhode Island. A few other good places to take a dip are **Hopeville Pond,** just west of Pachaug State Forest; **Alexander Lake,** off Route 101 near Dayville; and **Wadsworth Falls State Park,** off Route 157 near Middlefield.

On the down side, don't even think of swimming in the Connecticut River, even if you're out there on a canoe with the hot sun beating down. The river is relatively clean as major northeastern rivers go, but it's not *that* clean. Of more concern is the fact it's a heavily used waterway by motorized boats of many sizes. Swimmers and powerboats do not mix comfortably.

WALKS & RAMBLES

Given Connecticut's extensive trail system (see "Hiking & Backpacking," above), you will rarely find yourself far from an opportunity to take a short stroll, no matter where you are in the state. In a small state with reportedly more than 700 trail miles, trailheads are literally everywhere.

Devil's Hopyard State Park

Allow 1–2 hours. Easy. Access: From East Haddam, take Rte. 82 east 1 mile, then bear left after a mile onto Hopyard Rd., following signs for Devil's Hopyard. The park entrance is on your left after about 8 miles. Map: Available at the campground.

What a wonderful name for a park, and the image from which the name is drawn is even better. According to legend, the potholes at the bottom of Chapman Falls came from the hooves of the devil as he hopped around from one rock to the next. In fact, the grinding of waterborne rocks carved out the holes, but that seems a prosaically scientific explanation.

Chapman Falls is the park's chief highlight, a 60-foot rush of water that steps down in three tiers. A short set of stairs and a trail lead down to the base of the falls. Descend so you can examine the cascading water and appreciate the way it has sculpted the surrounding rock, then return to the trailhead to embark on a more extended outing.

The longest trail in the park is the Vista Trail, which begins in the main picnic area. Cross the covered bridge—yes, a covered bridge for hikers—and then bear right to begin a counterclockwise loop. For the Vista Trail, orange blazes are your guide. These blazes lead you, after about a mile, up to the viewpoint that gives the trail its name. Below you are meadows; in the distance, wooded hills. It is a view enhanced by just emerging from a dense forest, and the sudden openness, in its contrast, is impressive.

From here the trail turns northward, leading to an impressive, old-growth oak tree before descending back down toward the stream. The sound of the falls, heard faintly at first, begins to build to a rumble and then a roar as you draw nearer. Soon you'll arrive back at the bridge, completing a loop of about 2.5 miles.

Gay City State Park

Allow 1–3 hours. Easy. Access: From Manchester, take I-384 east to exit 5. Head south on Rte. 85 for about 4.5 miles and look for the entrance to the park on your right. Map: A map should be available at the park entrance, or you can contact the **Department of Environmental Protection,** Office of Parks and Recreation (79 Elm St., Hartford, CT 06106; ☎ **203/424-3200.**

Here's your opportunity to walk through the woods of a park that comes with its own curious bit of history. The park gets its name from a religious group that in 1796 settled here in what was essentially a commune. Most of the commune's 25 families were members of the extended Gay clan—hence the name. With the income from a succession of mills, they were able to make a reasonable go of things for a while, until after a variety of misfortunes (fire, deaths in the War of 1812 and the Civil War), the community collapsed. What is left today of the commune are a few cellar holes, mill foundations, and the occasional headstone.

Just 12 miles from downtown Hartford, the park gets a fair amount of use from hikers, bikers, horseback riders, fishermen, and swimmers. Still, the hiking trails rarely seem crowded. The two principal trails here, both well marked, are the 2.5-mile Pond Loop and the 5-mile Outer Loop. The Pond Loop is just as advertised—a trail that circumscribes the pond. You'll pass ruins of the old Gay City mill, walk on old roads and trails, pass by a beaver lodge, and generally ramble through the mostly deciduous forest.

The Outer Loop, also as its name implies, simply makes a much larger loop around the pond. It is more of a woodlands walk, twice crossing the Blackledge River—the stream that the Gay City settlers dammed to power their mills. A highlight of the walk is a small, lilypad-covered pond, where frogs croak and birds mingle. It is an image that could have come straight out of a children's book, an idyllic little tableau of nature.

Rhododendron Sanctuary & Mt. Misery

Allow 1 hour. Easy. Access: From Voluntown, take Rte. 49 north. Continue about a mile to the main entrance to Pachaug State Forest, on the left. Continue past forest headquarters on Headquarters Rd. to the parking area. Map: Available at forest headquarters. Make sure to get the Chapman area map, not the Green Falls area map.

Much longer hikes are possible in this, the largest of Connecticut's state forests. But for a quick taste of the forest—a kind of greatest hits of Pachaug—this short walk is hard to beat. The best time to go is late spring or early summer, when the rhododendrons are in bloom. The brief walk into the sanctuary—less than .25 mile—brings you into a beautiful jungle world that seems somehow out of place in New England. The surrounding cedar swamp only enhances the eerie, tropical feel of the location.

If conditions are relatively dry, you can leave the boardwalk that leads into the sanctuary and continue on the narrow foot trail that wends through the swamp and back to the road. If conditions are wet, simply retrace your steps to the road and turn right, while looking for the beginning of the trail to Mount Misery on your left. The trail leads through a dense forest of hemlock, oak, and mountain laurel, and after about a mile, you arrive at a rock outcropping and are treated to a view of the surrounding forest.

Mount Misery is a mere 441 feet, not much of a mountain, really. Yet sit here while munching on a picnic lunch, with the forest rolled out like a carpet below you, and you'll feel about as on top of the world as you ever will in eastern Connecticut. From here, you can simply head back the way you came. But for a slightly longer walk, continue on as the trail descends to Firetower Road. Turn right and walk along the road until you reach Cut-off Road, where you'll turn right again to return to your starting point.

WHITEWATER KAYAKING

Lacking the dramatic elevation changes that make rivers run fast (and white), eastern Connecticut can claim few whitewater hot spots. A rare exception is the **Salmon River,** which can produce rapids approaching Class III. But that fast-moving water is a short-lived phenomenon. Be there in early spring, when snowmelt and icemelt flood the river, or you'll have to head to the western half of the state for whitewater.

Campgrounds & Other Accommodations

CAMPGROUNDS

Attention, canoeists: Three campgrounds along the Connecticut River are reserved primarily for you. **Selden Neck State Park,** the most southerly of the three, allows campers in any kind of boat, while **Gillette Castle State Park** and **Hurd State Park** are for canoeists only. Hurd, with 12 sites, is the smallest; Selden Neck, with 46 sites spread over four separate areas, is the largest. In each case, the facilities are fairly primitive—no flush toilets and no tables—which seems appropriate for riverside camping. Reservations are a must; call the same number (☎ **203/526-2336**) to reserve a site.

Devil's Hopyard State Park

From East Haddam, take Rte. 82 east 1 mile, then bear left after a mile onto Hopyard Rd., following signs for Devil's Hopyard. The campground is on your left after about 8 miles. ☎ **860/873-8566.** 21 sites, no hookups. Water pump, primitive toilets, tables, fireplaces.

The one drawback to this campground is that some of the sites are close together, without much of a barrier (in the form of trees or bushes) to protect privacy. Yet this is such a peaceful and generally secluded place that those staying here tend to mellow out and not intrude upon their neighbors. The relatively primitive facilities—no hookups or flush toilets— also tend to discourage the RV crowd. The opportunity to hike in the neighboring forest and to explore the nearby Eight Mile River, including 60-foot Chapman Falls, makes this one of the best eastern-Connecticut public campgrounds for getting away from it all.

Hammonassett Beach State Park

Take exit 62 (for the park) from I-95 and follow the connecting road to the park entrance. ☎ **860/245-1817.** 558 sites, no hookups, flush toilets, showers, snack-concession stand, tables, fire rings.

If your idea of going camping is sharing a relatively small space with 558 (or more) of your best buddies, this is the place for you. Some semblance of privacy might be possible on weekdays; on weekends, forget about it. The beach is the draw, of course, meaning a generally young, beach-worshipping crowd.

Mount Misery Campground

From Voluntown, take the combined routes 138 east and 49 north, and then turn right on Rte. 49 north when the two diverge. Continue 1 mile and look for the Pachaug State Forest entrance on the left. Follow signs to Mt. Misery campground. ☎ **860/376-4075.** 22 sites, tables, primitive toilets, fire rings.

The campground, near the Nehantic and Pachaug trails, is geared toward hikers and horseback riders using the forests' trail system. There is also camping to the east, at Green Falls Campground, with 18 sites. Given a choice, you'll probably prefer Mt. Misery, at least on a summer weekend. Green Falls Pond attracts a fair amount of day-use traffic to the Green Falls area.

Rocky Neck State Park

From I-95, take 72 and continue south to Rte. 156. Turn left and look for the entrance to the park, on the right. ☎ **203/739-5471.** 160 sites, no hookups. Tables, showers, flush toilets.

This is the mellower of eastern Connecticut's two main public beaches— Hammonassett being the other—although it's all relative. Like its counterpart to the west, it can get crowded on summer weekends. Stay through the week or come any time other than summer. The bird-watching and saltwater fishing can be excellent.

INNS & RESORTS

Griswold Inn

36 Main St., Essex, CT 06426. ☎ **860/767-1776.** Rooms $90–$185, including breakfast.

The decor in this late 18th-century house evokes the sporting life of a bygone patrician era. One room features a collection of antique firearms; others are adorned with Currier & Ives prints and marine art. It all feels like the kind of place where the good old boys might gather for refreshments after the hunt. The 31 guest rooms put you right on Main Street in Essex, one of the Connecticut River Valley's characteristically charming towns. There is great road cycling in the area (see "Road Biking," above).

Inn at Woodstock Hill

94 Plaine Hill Rd., South Woodstock, CT 06267. ☎ **860/928-0528.** Rooms $90–$155 a night.

It doesn't get much quieter in the Quiet Corner than in Woodstock, way up in the far northeastern corner of the state. The inn, which dates back to the early 19th century, is surrounded by the soul-soothing greenery of rolling farmland, much of it still owned by the original family that settled here in the late 1600s. Hiking and horseback riding are the activities of choice, especially in nearby Natchaug State Forest and Mashasmoquet State Park.

Lighthouse Inn

6 Guthrie Place, New London, CT 06320. ☎ **888/600-5681** or 860/443-8411. Rooms, including continental breakfast, start at $120.

Steel tycoon Charles Guthrie had this Mediterranean-style mansion built in 1902, and it seems a bit out of place on the New England coast. There is an air of California about it, and indeed some of the Hollywood crowd, including Bette Davis and Joan Crawford, have stayed here and strolled the grounds designed by Frederick Law Olmsted. Included within the grounds is a private beach for those who prefer not to do their swimming and tanning in the company of the thousands who come to Connecticut's public beaches on summer weekends.

Norwich Inn & Spa

607 W. Thames St. St. (Rte. 32), Norwich, CT 06360. ☎ **800/275-4772** or 860/886-2401. Rooms from $115, low season; up to $245, high season. Packages including use of spa facilities, tennis courts, etc., may run considerably higher.

Note that this is an inn *and* a spa. That means you aren't obliged to commit yourself to some disciplined fitness-and-diet program to stay here. You can overnight in the Georgian-style inn or one of the surrounding villas, and dine extravagantly if you want. Or you can go the full spa route: working out in the exercise room, getting a massage or a facial, playing a game of tennis, or even delving into astrology classes if that's your thing.

Randall's Ordinary

41 Norwich Westerly Rd. (Rte. 2), North Stonington, CT 06359. ☎ **860/599-4540.** Rates $75–$195 double, including breakfast.

This 1685 farmhouse is on the National Register of Historic Places, and the people in charge here seemed determined to do everything possible to turn back the clock 3 centuries. You can overnight in a four-poster bed in one of the three guest rooms in the farmhouse, or you can opt for one of 12 guest rooms in the relatively modern barn, which dates back only to 1819. The big deal here is the $39 prix-fixe dinner, cooked over an open hearth with authentic Colonial cookware, and served by people dressed in authentic Colonial attire.

Spa at Grand Lake

1667 Exeter Rd. (Rte. 207), Lebanon, CT 06249. ☎ **800/843-7721** or 860/642-4306. Two-night weekend packages, including 3 meals a day, massage, and use of spa facilities, start at $300.

Only a half hour from Hartford but light years away in spirit, this spa in the heart of the Quiet Corner is a true retreat. Guided hikes, aerobics, yoga, and so-called aquarobics are the sort of physical activities that fill the day. Meals are conceived as healthy—hence, light on fat and calories. For those seeking pampering, there's plenty of the usual spa stuff to choose from, from facials to pedicures.

Chapter 8

Rhode Island & Block Island

Rhode Island is fascinating, maddening, crowded, wide-open, stunningly wealthy, and pervasively working class all at the same time. It is a world of contrasts and contradictions, the smallest state in the country and at the same time the second most densely populated, narrowly edged out by New Jersey for that title. Sixty percent of the state is forested, yet 87% of the population is classified as urban. So urban is Providence, in fact, that its skyline, considered archetypal of metropolitan America, was used as the backdrop for the "Superman" TV series of the 1950s.

Given Rhode Island's 420 miles of coastline, a figure disproportionate to the state's size, the freedom of open water—Narragansett Bay, the Sakonnet River, Rhode Island Sound, and Block Island Sound—forever beckons. Yet the open water has itself become, in a manner of speaking, urbanized. There are said to be more boats per square mile in Narragansett Bay than anywhere else in the world.

What is one to make of all of this? Until recently, I had driven through Rhode Island many, many times without stopping for as much as a look-see on my way to Cape Cod. I had thus seen Rhode Island in its most congested light, as a passing blur of pavement and Providence, where interstate highways converged in an implosion of urbanization. This viewpoint at least enabled me to witness, from the detached perspective of my car, the evolution of Providence as something of a Renaissance city. Providence, with its booming downtown and a popular TV drama sharing its name, has become a hot ticket among American cities at the turn of the millennium.

But where was the great outdoors of the state? That was the Rhode Island I didn't see. Where were the refuges and retreats and the forests—all that undeveloped land that supposedly composed more than half the state? In passing through, I had little sense of their existence, and when I finally came to spend some extended quality time in Rhode Island, I came to understand why. The "great outdoors" of Rhode Island is not easy to find, particularly if you are without a boat. Water divides and subdivides the state, making getting from one place to another, even in a state where distances are obviously small, a complex and sometimes frustrating endeavor. To get, for example, from Providence to Tiverton, your best bet is to go through Fall River, Massachusetts.

Open land, despite the acquisitional fervor of such organizations as the Rhode Island Audubon Society, is relatively rare, and widely dispersed in mostly small parcels. The largest tract of undeveloped land, Arcadia Management Area, is, at about 13,000 acres, roughly four times the size of the next largest. Less than 10% of the land is public, and private ownership seems particularly prevalent along that extensive coastline. According to the Sierra Club, there is no marked hiking trail in the state longer than 8 miles.

Yet despite such discouraging numbers, I discovered there is still something approaching a great outdoors in Rhode Island. The Sierra Club's statistic, for example, strikes me as either incorrect or misleading. Rhode Island might not be the state you'd come to for a multiday wilderness backpack, but shorter trails do connect together to form longer trails, such as the recently conceived (and still evolving) North-South Trail, which traverses the state. Hikes of longer than 8 miles are possible.

From Watch Hill to Point Judith, and along the shores of Block Island, are great sandy beaches for swimming and, when storms stir up the ocean water, for surfing. These beaches are part of a barrier of sand separating the open water from inland ponds—Ninigret, Green Hill, Trustom, and Point Judith ponds on the mainland, and Great Salt Pond on Block Island—that teem with bird life and are ideal for canoeing and sea kayaking.

Head for the northwestern quadrant of the state, and you will discover a rural Rhode Island. You don't have to head very far, either, because once you've slipped out of the bounds of Providence and Warwick, it is clear that coastal land is where development is concentrated. Move inland, and rural Rhode Island quickly reveals itself in places like the Great Swamp, a complex amalgam of dense forests, berry bushes, wetlands, and meadows, where wildlife congregate in great numbers.

And of course, there is all that open water. Sailing has a long and worthy tradition here—Newport is the original and still spiritual home of the America's Cup—and has been joined in popularity by its latter-day soulmates: boardsailing and sea kayaking. Yes, there is a high concentration of boats, under sail and motor, in Rhode Island's waters, but it doesn't take that much imagination or exploratory initiative to find room for yourself out there.

Rhode Island, of course, has a rich history (figuratively and literally) as a seaside refuge from the whir and dither of urban life. In the 1890s, the barons of New York society's wealthy elite—with names like Astor, Vanderbilt, and Belmont—built their "cottages" in Newport. These cottages, some with as many as 70 rooms, were fashioned after French châteaux and palaces. If you could afford one, the price tag might range up to five million dollars, an astonishing expenditure in 1890 currency. And it was all for no more than a few weeks of country living, rich-and-famous style, each summer; for close to 50 weeks of the year, these grandiose structures stood largely unused, perhaps American history's greatest display of conspicuous and disposable wealth.

Newport made history in sporting circles as well, in ways befitting the upper-crust lifestyle of the wealthy folk who summered here. In 1876, the first polo match in America was played in Portsmouth, just north of Newport. In 1881, the first U.S. lawn tennis championship was played in Newport. Polo and tennis—not exactly the sports of the common, working-class American.

I had assumed that the extravagant Newport lifestyle quickly ran its course, and in many ways it did when the 1929 stock market crash eviscerated the great wealth that had made the mansion-building possible. Yet evidence of seaside wealth still exists on Rhode Island's shores in the small pockets of Watch Hill, Little Compton, Block Island, and, yes, Newport. These newer homes might not be a match for the palatial digs of yesteryear, but by any other standard they are mansions. Yacht clubs, tennis clubs, golf clubs—all the things that go along with the privileges of being able to afford a multimillion-dollar home—are in evidence, too. Rhode Island might have become widely urbanized, but that has not deterred those of great wealth from still considering it an ideal summer retreat.

The rest of us who live by more modest means must be content with Rhode Island's many other enticements. The beaches, the sea, the coastal ponds, the smattering of forested lands—there is

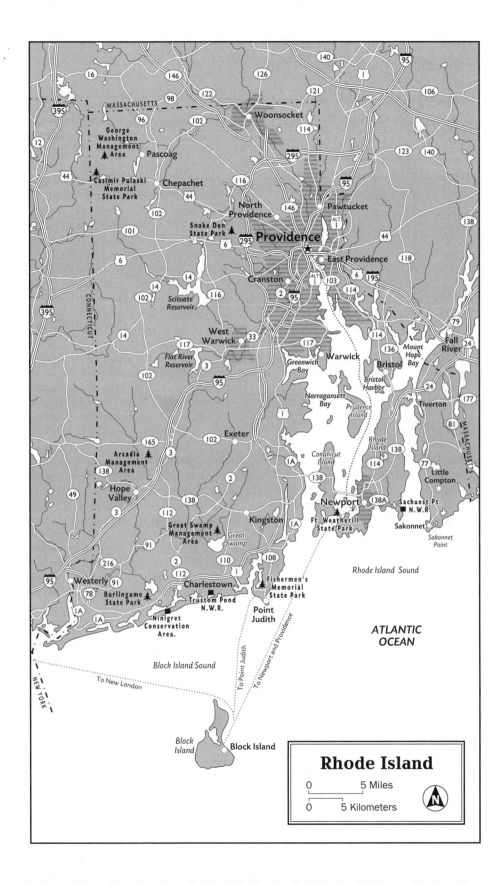

Rhode Island

0   5 Miles

0   5 Kilometers

much to discover here, even if it is the smallest state in the country.

The Lay of the Land

The most distinctive geographical feature of Rhode Island is not the land itself, but the sea, which cuts sharply into the heart of the state in the form of Narragansett Bay (and, to a lesser extent, the Sakonnet River). The major land masses within the bay—Rhode Island itself, upon which Newport rests; Conanicut Island; Prudence Island, etc.—are those remnants left untouched when glaciers of the last ice age, 10,000 to 12,000 years ago, swept the rest of the land out to sea.

The coastline alternates between fine, sandy beaches, most notably along the southern shore, and rugged rock, found in places like Watch Hill and, most famously, Newport, where mansions stand high above the water's edge. All of this has at least some connection to glacial history. The sand is the residue of the grinding, pulverizing effect of the ocean movement's glacial retreat; the rock remains as either bedrock impervious to the powers of ice and ocean, or as the depositing of material left behind by the glacier in its rapid dissolution.

The water off Rhode Island's coast is often referred to as the ocean, which is technically incorrect. In fact, two bodies of water—Rhode Island Sound to the east and Block Island Sound to the west—lie between the coast and the Atlantic Ocean. Just what is a sound? In the dictionary, it is defined rather vaguely as "a long, relatively wide body of water." These two bodies of water are very wide (unlike, for example, narrow, protected Long Island Sound to the west), allowing ocean swells and the accompanying surf to reach Rhode Island's shores.

Moving inland, the flora of Rhode Island is mixed, as upland forests characteristic of Connecticut to the west comingle with maritime forests more common to Massachusetts and Cape Cod to the east. The former are primarily deciduous forests of maple, birch, beech, and oak; the latter, growing in sandier soil, are characterized by scrub oak and pine. What hills there are in Rhode Island are found in the northwest, but even they are meager by New England standards. The high point of the state, at 812 feet, is Jerimoth Hill, just a few miles from the Connecticut border.

The World Almanac calls Rhode Island's climate "invigorating and changeable." Indeed, the parts of the state that are close to the water—which is to say, much of the state—are cooled in summer by ocean breezes and, because of their proximity to the water, remain relatively mild (by New England standards) in winter. The normal temperature in January in Providence is 29°F, rising to 73° in July. In an average winter, Providence gets close to 40 inches of snow, a fairly hefty amount for a city so near the sea. The snow, however, rarely lasts long due to the damp, above-freezing air drifting in off the ocean.

Whatever you might think of Rhode Island's landscape as a human being, you'd find it close to perfect if you were a bird. With many varied habits—coastal ponds, islands, meadows, wetlands, forests, and rivers—there is something here to attract almost any kind of bird, migratory or resident. Bird sanctuaries here typically report impressive sighting lists—250 species is a common number—and dedicated birders flock to places such as Block Island and the southern coast ponds in the fall to witness the spectacle of migration.

Orientation

Rhode Island is, as is oft repeated, the smallest state in the country, just 40 miles from east to west and 50 miles from north

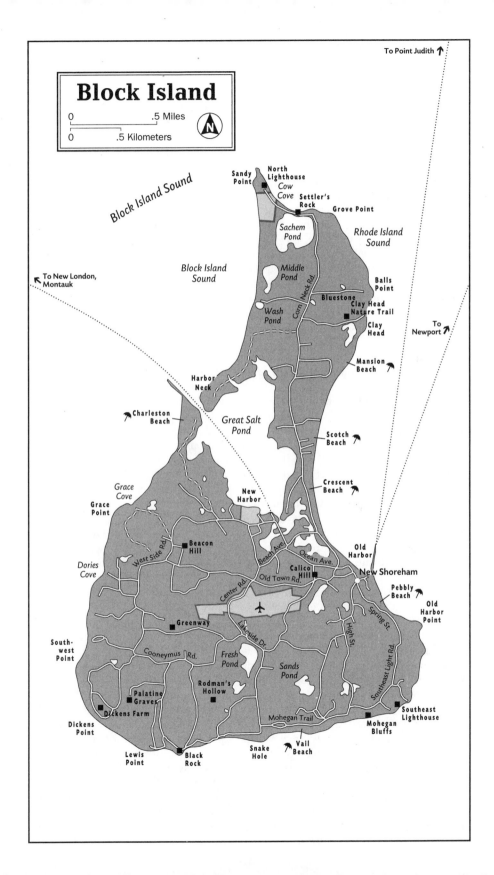

to south. Roads are everywhere—there are, for example, more miles of paved roadway in Rhode Island than in Alaska. Even so, getting from one place to another in Rhode Island is not always easy. Water, of course, presents a major obstacle, but all those roads, even through inland Rhode Island, tend to meander.

You'll find no tidy grid here; instead, the major roadways form radial spokes emanating from **Providence,** the capital of the state and its governmental, economic, and spiritual hub. Providence, actually, is more than just Providence. **Cranston, Auburn, Pawtucket, Pawtuxet,** and other cities and communities crowd around the capital, and you must be very local (that is, know to whom you're paying your property taxes) to know where one community begins and the other ends.

The most important of the roadways in and out of Providence is **Interstate 95,** which traverses the state from southwest to northeast. In Providence, **Interstate 195** spurs off to the east and is the principal route to Cape Cod. The major east-west routes are **Route 6,** which approximately bisects the state, and **Route 44,** which bears northwest from Providence toward Hartford, Connecticut.

Continuous north-south routes are few, although **Route 1** is the main way to get from Providence to the beaches along the southern coast. Route 1 passes through such small cities as **Wickford** and **Narragansett** before veering westward toward **Watch Hill** (home, for those with a bent for trivia, of the country's oldest carousel). Watch Hill is the affluent neighbor of appropriately named **Westerly,** the commercial hub just to the north. Watch Hill, the most southwestern point in Rhode Island, marks the end of roughly 20 miles of sandy beach that stretch from **Point Judith,** which juts out into the water as the point where Rhode Island Sound, Block Island Sound, and Narragansett Bay meet.

Rhode Island itself—the piece of land that lent its name to the state—is the large island separating Narragansett Bay to the west and the Sakonnet River to the east. It is a well-settled island dominated by the city of **Newport** on its south end. Newport might be famed for its turn-of-the-century mansions and America's Cup yacht racing, but it is also a vital entity in Rhode Island's economy (tourism, of course, being a major contributor) and is home to a naval base.

In quiet contrast is minimally developed **Prudence Island,** accessible only by ferry (☎ 401/253-9808 for times) from **Bristol.** The Narragansett Bay National Estuarine Sanctuary covers the northern third of the island, while South Prudence State Park covers the southern third. In between lies bucolic farmland.

The southeastern corner of Rhode Island, home to the small communities of **Tiverton** and **Little Compton,** might as well be an island, too, at least as far as state geography is concerned. It has no land connection to the rest of the state (although driving over two bridges from Bristol will get you there), but is instead attached to Massachusetts. If you're seeking a low-key, rural area along the coast, the southeast is where you'll want to be.

You'll also find a rural landscape inland, to the west and northwest of Providence. This is where the largest tracts of open land can be found in the state; significant among them are **Arcadia Management Area, Great Swamp Management Area,** and, in the far northwest corner, **George Washington Management Area.**

Finally, sitting out there on its own roughly 10 miles offshore, is **Block Island,** which is to Rhode Island what Martha's Vineyard or Nantucket is to Cape Cod. A lamb chop–shaped island just 20 square miles in size, Block Island is a quiet, getaway kind of place, for at least two reasons. First, it is accessible only by ferry, with the ferry from **Galilee** (☎ 401/783-4613 for times) providing the shortest ride at 70 minutes. In other words, to get to Block Island, you really have to want to go there. Second, it is so small that a car for most visitors is a luxury rather than a necessity. No one comes to Block Island to rush through life.

Parks & Other Hot Spots

Arcadia Management Area
From I-95, take Exit 5a to Rte. 102 south. Turn right onto Rte. 3 south and right again, at the blinking light, onto Rte. 165 west. Headquarters: Arcadia (☎ **401/789-3094**).

At roughly 13,000 acres, this is Rhode Island's largest tract of undeveloped public land. For deep-woods recreation, from mountain biking to hiking to cross-country skiing, this is the premier spot in the state. Just west, across the Connecticut border, is contiguous Pachaug State Forest, Connecticut's largest tract of undeveloped land, with more than 22,000 acres. There is a world of backcountry to roam around in here.

Burlingame State Park
From Charlestown, head west on Rte. 1. Within a mile, look for signs for the exit to Burlingame State Park. Headquarters: Johnston (☎ **401/277-2632** or 401/322-7337 at the park).

The campground of this state park has an astonishing 755 sites, primarily because popular beaches are just a few miles away. In other words, this can be a tent city on a summer weekend. The park itself is only a part of a jumble of undeveloped (or semi-developed) land totaling more than 2,500 acres. There is the contiguous, state-managed Burlingame Management Area and the tiny (30-acre) Kimball Wildlife Preserve, managed by the Rhode Island Audubon Society. Watchaug Pond is very popular for swimming and canoeing, and roughly 10 miles of hiking trails wind through the park and management area.

George Washington Management Area
From the junction of Rtes. 44 and 102, head 5 miles west on 44. Headquarters: West Gloucester (☎ **401/568-2013**).

If you're looking for anything approaching mountains in Rhode Island, this is the place, with hills rising up to nearly 800 feet. (Jerimoth Hill, the state's high point, is just to the south.) Bowdish Reservoir, a popular swimming and fishing spot, is the management area's most notable feature, although there are also well-marked trails for hiking and cross-country skiing.

Great Swamp Management Area
From I-95, take exit 3A to Rte. 138 east toward Kingston. Before the junction with Rte. 110, turn right onto Liberty Lane. Headquarters: West Kingston (☎ **401/789-0281**).

The Great Swamp, at just over 3,000 acres, is not all swamp. It is a landscape of dense deciduous trees combined with a thick underbrush of berry bushes and dogwoods. And yes, of course there are wetlands and bogs, as you should expect in a swamp area. This is a prime bird-watching area, full of everything from tiny thrushes to athletic osprey. The dirt and grassy roads that crisscross the area also make for excellent mountain biking. Worden's Pond (on the south edge of the management area), along with tiny rivers—the Chipuxet, for example—that feed it, is a first-rate spot for canoeing and flatwater kayaking.

North–South Trail
The trail enters Rhode Island from the north through Buck Hill Management Area in the far northwestern corner. It terminates just west of Ninigret Conservation Area on Block Island Sound. For trail information, contact the **North–South Trail Council,** c/o the R.I. Department of Environmental Manage- ment, 235 Promenade St., Providence, RI 02908; ☎ **401/222-2776,** ext. 4309.

This 70-mile trans-state route is a creation of the 1990s, springing forth from the efforts of dedicated Rhode Island hikers eager to have a trail in their state that is comparable to the Metacomet–Monadnock and the Midstate trails that run through Connecticut and Massachusetts respectively. This is, of course, not purely a wilderness route. The trail passes over a mix of backcountry hiking trails, abandoned back roads, and paved roadways, and veers briefly into Connecticut to avoid the private property of an insurance company that, not surprisingly, envisioned all sorts of insurance risks in allowing hikers onto its land. With the mapping of the North–South Trail completed in the mid-1990s, it is now possible, by connecting with Massachusetts's Midstate Trail and trails in New Hampshire, to hike from New England's southern coast to the Canadian border.

Sachuest Point National Wildlife Refuge/Norman Bird Sanctuary

From Portsmouth, take Rte. 138 south, turn right on Mitchell's Lane, and continue on to Third Beach Rd., following signs to the Sanctuary. For the refuge, turn right on Hanging Rock Rd., then left onto Sachuest Point Rd., which leads to the sanctuary. Sanctuary headquarters: Middletown; ☎ **401/846-2577.** Refuge visitor center: Sachuest Point; ☎ **401/847-5511.**

There's not an enormous amount of land—only 500 and 800 acres, depending on who's doing the counting—in the bird sanctuary and the national wildlife refuge. But with the greater Newport area so developed, it just seems like a lot of land. Sachuest Point juts out as a rocky spit into Rhode Island at the end of the Sakonnet River. Inland, the bird sanctuary, with open fields, wetlands, and forest, is considered one of the best bird-watching areas in the state.

What to Do & Where to Do It

BIRD-WATCHING

Perhaps the best location in the state for birding is **Norman Bird Sanctuary,** a few miles east of Newport. Here, and at neighboring **Sachuest Pont National Wildlife Refuge,** more than 200 species have been recorded, and as many as 70 species use the area as a nesting ground. It is a popular stopover for migrating birds, if you happen to come in the fall. It is .also a popular spot in the summer for human visitors, so don't necessarily expect to do your birding alone.

Trustom Pond National Wildlife Refuge, east of Green Hill Beach, sees much less human visitation. Reportedly 300 species have been spotted here at one time or another, in part because there is some kind of appealing habitat—meadows, forest, wetlands, pond—for every bird, no matter what the species. This is a good place to spot ospreys.

Block Island is similarly blessed with a variety of habitats, including grasslands, wetlands, and saltwater and freshwater ponds. Thanks to the active stewardship of organizations, from the U.S. Fish and Wildlife Service to the Nature Conservancy to local groups, many of these habitats have remained protected and therefore attractive to a wide variety of species, particularly fall migrants.

Outfitters

The **Audubon Society of Rhode Island** (12 Sanderson Rd., Smithfield, RI 02917; ☎ **401/949-5454**) organizes numerous birding outings at various locations throughout the state. Most are open to non-members for an additional fee. There are numerous outings at the **Norman Bird Sanctuary** (583 Third Beach Rd., Middletown, RI 02842; ☎ **401/846-2577**) particularly geared toward families and children.

BOARDSAILING

Among the coastal ponds, **Ninigret Pond,** as the largest, is probably the best. The sailing is particularly good when the wind is onshore, as it typically is in the afternoon in July and August. For more open water, you might want to try **Narragansett Town Beach.** When the wind picks up straight out of the south and steamrolls into Narragansett Bay, the bay sailing conditions can be spectacular near **Warwick Neck,** situated at the top of the bay's West Passage.

When the wind is out of the north or the south, **Fogland Point** (west of Tiverton Four Corners), where the Sakonnet River squeezes between steep banks on both sides, can feature some great wave action. If the wind is out of the east or west, however, the upper Sakonnet can be a dud. Head instead for **Third Beach,** near Sachuest Point east of Newport, which is less sheltered from easterly blows.

Rentals

Rental equipment is available at **Island Windsurfing** (86 Aquidneck Ave., Middletown, RI 02842; ☎ **401/846-4421**).

Instruction

Island Windsurfing (see "Rentals," above) also offers lessons for all ability levels. **Sail Newport** (60 Fort Adams Dr., Newport, RI 02840; ☎ **401/846-1983**) conducts 1-week classes for young people during July and August.

CANOEING/FLATWATER KAYAKING

Canoe or flatwater kayak? In many cases in Rhode Island, the latter may be preferable. Some of the best spots in the state for flatwater paddling involve fairly large bodies of water that might be exposed to wind. Under such conditions, a kayak might be more manageable, but the choice is yours.

Among Rhode Island's outdoor highlights are the ponds immediately within the barrier beaches along Block Island Sound. **Point Judith Pond, Green Hill Pond, Trustom Pond, Ninigret Pond,** and others are great areas for exploring marshes, wetlands, and open water, although in some cases access (or the difficulty thereof) is a problem. What might seem to be the best launching spots are often on private property, so you must be careful to avoid trespassing.

Inland, there are many small ponds and lakes to explore. **Bowdish Reservoir** in the George Washington Management Area is a popular canoeing spot, although with a large campground and beach, it is a popular spot in general. **Watchaug Pond** in Burlingame State Park is similarly well populated, although heading to the marshes and Poquiant Brook on the pond's northern shore, and away from the crowds, can provide some fine paddling and exploration.

Finally, there is the **Great Salt Pond** on Block Island. You might have to share it with a number of other craft—large and small—but given some of the sleek, handsome yachts that pull into the harbor, paddling around in that kind of company is part of the fun.

Ninigret Pond

Allow 4–6 hours. Access: From Charlestown, head east on Rte. 1A and bear right onto Mattunuck School Rd. Turn right on Charlestown Beach Rd. There is a small parking area on your right just before crossing the bridge as you near the beach.

As mentioned, the ponds just inside the barrier beaches of Rhode Island's southern shore are well worth exploring, and Ninigret Pond, at 1,700 acres, is the largest of the bunch. Yet size alone is not the reason to choose Ninigret over the others. Rather, it is that most of its shoreline is undeveloped, with Ninigret National Wildlife Refuge lying on the northern shore and Ninigret Conservation Area—which includes some of the wildest ocean beach in Rhode Island—on the southern shore. On other coastal ponds you might feel like you're trespassing (as indeed you might be) as you explore the shoreline; the sense of intrusion on Ninigret is minimal.

Take East Beach Road from Charlestown almost to the end, and pull off in the parking area on your right. Put in here and let your imagination run wild. If you're exploring the north shore, be sure to bring binoculars. The wildlife refuge is a popular hangout for birds of all sorts; roughly 250 species have been sighted here. Just keep in mind that beaching your boat on refuge shores is not permitted in order to protect nesting species.

That's not the case on the south shore, where in several places it's possible to pull up your craft and scramble over to the ocean beach. You won't encounter anything like the crowds you'd find at the height of summer at public beaches to the west, but don't be surprised to see four-wheel-drive vehicles cruising up and down the strand.

Poking around the coves, inlets, and marshes of Ninigret can consume the day. Take your time. Explore. Have a picnic lunch on the beach. Relax. But stay attuned to potential hazards. The winds can blow, the tides can change, and currents, especially near Charlestown Breachway, can be strong.

Worden's Pond, Chipuxet River

Allow 4–6 hours. Access: From West Kingston, head south on Rte. 110. After about 4 miles, turn right at the blinking light onto Worden's Pond Rd. Look for a small boat-launching area on your right.

This isn't a trip you'll enjoy on a windy day. The pond is generally shallow (less than 10 feet), so it doesn't take much of a breeze to whip up some nasty waves. But if conditions are reasonably calm—morning is best—exploring the shores of this pond and the tiny rivers that feed it is about as enjoyable as inland canoeing gets in Rhode Island.

Paddle northward, heading across the pond toward the mouth of the Chixupet River, which enters the pond from the northeast. Again, be alert to wind conditions; if the wind starts picking up strongly out of the south, you'll face a rough crossing to return to your starting point.

The pond has a long and curious military history. It was the site of a brief (and quickly quashed) rebellion of Native Americans against English colonists in 1675, appropriately dubbed the Great Swamp Fight. Many years later, in the 1940s and 1950s, the pond was used as a target for bombing practice by American warplanes. In the cove between Case Point and Stony Point, which jut out into the north end of the pond, there is an old, abandoned seaplane hangar.

As you near the north shore, however, the real attraction is the natural environment as the pond and the Great Swamp meet. Head a ways up the Chipuxet River into the swamp, where red maples, a common, water-resistant tree in the area, and cattails crowd the shore. Yes, you'll be paddling upriver, but the current is slow and not hard to defeat, and you can turn around almost any time you feel like it, as the width of the river permits. (You can also start this trip from Taylor's Landing in West Kingston, following the river about 3 miles downstream into the pond.)

Explore, explore, and explore—again, being ever mindful of the wind, should it kick up from the south. And be sure to bring along a fishing rod—the bass and pike fishing is said to be superb.

Gear & Rentals

Those heading out to Ninigret Pond should try **The Kayak Center's** (☎ 401/364-8000) small rental facility at Charlestown Beach. **Oceans & Ponds**

(Ocean and Connecticut aves., Block Island, RI 02807; ☎ **401/466-5131**) rents kayaks for exploring the Great Salt Pond and beyond.

Outfitters

Group outings are organized by members of the **Rhode Island Canoe/Kayak Association** (☎ **401/725-3344**).

CROSS-COUNTRY SKIING

In an average year, it snows about 40 inches in Providence, a figure that is surprisingly high. It is, for example, higher than the average annual snowfall in Hartford, Connecticut, which is farther inland and closer to the mountains. Nevertheless, a healthy cover of natural snow is not something to count on in Rhode Island, making cross-country skiing very much a hit-or-miss proposition.

The only groomed trail system in the state is in **Pulaski Memorial Park,** in the northwestern corner of the state. From Providence, take I-295 north to Route 44 west. For non-groomed touring closer to the heart of a metropolis, there is pleasant, gently rolling terrain through the woods in **Goddard Memorial Park** (☎ **401/884-2010**) in Warwick. You might also want to check out the **East Bay Bike Path** (see "Road Biking," below). The surface might be a little lumpy from foot traffic, but after a fresh snowfall, you ought to have a pretty smooth ride on the relatively flat trail.

Farther afield for backcountry skiing, there is **Arcadia Management Area,** where the 4-mile Tripp Trail leads up Heartbreak Hill. Arcadia is also popular with snowmobilers, so be prepared for the possibility of a motorized encounter. For information, call ☎ **401/789-3094.**

DOWNHILL SKIING

Rhode Island is not prime skiing country: Snowfall is not abundant, the hills are barely hills (the state's highest point is Jerimoth Hill, at 812 feet), and the coastal climate is not conducive to snowmaking. Yet, surprise!—there is a ski area, one with an enticingly odd name. **Yawgoo Valley** (160 Yawgoo Valley Rd., Exeter, RI 02822; ☎ **401/295-5366**) is a ski area of Rhode Island dimensions, with a vertical rise of just 245 feet. Still, there is a fair amount of action packed in here: 12 trails, the longest of which is 2,200 feet, four lifts, night skiing, a sizeable ski school, and a snow tubing park. If you need a downhill skiing fix in Rhode Island, this is the place, and on a Friday, even under the lights, with swarming packs of kids from nearby Providence, it can be quite entertaining.

FISHING

Any place called the Ocean State must have a lot of water, and wherever there is a lot of water, you can expect to find a lot of fish. For anything from freshwater perch to deep-sea tuna, there is some place in Rhode Island (or off Rhode Island's shore) to satisfy you.

It probably goes without saying, however, that in the Ocean State, saltwater fishing takes precedence over freshwater fishing, if for no better reason than there is a lot more salt water than there is fresh water. Bluefish are notoriously voracious creatures known to bite on shoe leather when engaged in a feeding frenzy. When they run in large schools close to Rhode Island's shores, surf casters line up at places like **Ninigret Conservation Area,** a prime spot because access is limited to those in four-wheel-drive vehicles or those willing to walk a few miles.

The coves, harbors, and open waters of **Narragansett Bay** attract a variety of game fish, including striped bass, sea trout, bluefish, and flounder. You can join shore-based fishermen on jetties at places like **Sakonnet Point.** But you're likely to have better luck chartering a boat with an experienced captain who knows where the hot spots are. Of course, if you want to go "blue water" fishing—fishing in deep water well off-shore for tuna, shark, or other big-game fish—you'll have to charter a boat if you don't own your own.

On the mainland, the **Point Judith** area is charter-boat central, although charter boats are based in numerous other spots around Narragansett Bay as well, including **Newport, Narragansett, Wakefield,** and **Warwick. Block Island** is also a prime spot for chartering an offshore fishing vessel. You'll probably want to steer clear of so-called head boats, which may carry over 100 fishermen hanging over the railings, and look for charter boats, which are licensed to carry six passengers or fewer.

Freshwater fishing may play second fiddle to saltwater fishing in Rhode Island, but there are still a few hot spots you might want to check out. **Worden's Pond** in the Great Swamp area and **Watchaug Pond** in Burlingame State Park are considered prime bass-fishing waters and play host to a number of bass-fishing tournaments every summer. **Beach Pond,** on the Connecticut border in Arcadia Management Area, is also a good place to cast for bass.

Fly-fishing on the **Blackstone River,** which flows south from Massachusetts into the Seekonk River and Narragansett Bay, is gaining new momentum. The Blackstone, at least as a river to fish, has a less than distinguished history. With, at one time, more mills per square mile along its banks than any other river in America, the Blackstone has been called "the first polluted river in America," and at one time was one of its most polluted.

Yet the river is recovering. In 1986, the National Park Service created the Blackstone River Valley National Heritage Corridor, part of a drive to replace polluting industry with tourism. Local efforts to clean up the river water have been productive (although the river's sediments remain contaminated). Local fly fishermen tend to head for the falls in **Albion,** a Blackstone hot spot. One other river in the state favored by local anglers is the **Clear River** in the northwest, near Burrillville.

Gear

Fin & Feather Lodge (95 Frenchtown Rd., East Greenwich, RI 02818; ☎ **401/885-8680**) is a good place to go for freshwater fly gear. **Oceans & Ponds** and **The Saltwater Edge** (see "Outfitters & Instruction," below) also feature a wide variety of gear and tackle, particularly for saltwater fly-fishing.

Outfitters & Instruction

Oceans & Ponds (Ocean and Connecticut aves., Block Island, RI 02807; ☎ **401/466-5131**) is Block Island's headquarters for salt pond fishing, surf casting, and blue-water charters. There is also a saltwater fly-fishing school. On the mainland, **The Saltwater Edge** (561 Thames St., Newport, RI 02840; **401/842-0062**) specializes in saltwater fly-fishing instruction and guide services and conducts week-long summer fishing camps for kids. **White Ghost Guide Services** (43 York Dr., Coventry, RI 02816; ☎ **401/828-9465**) specializes in Narragansett Bay fishing.

Charters

Where to start . . . perhaps simply by recommending that you contact the **Rhode Island Party and Charter Boat Association** (☎ **401/737-5812**), which can put you in touch with a charter operator to match your interests, objectives, and budget. With so many experienced and able captains operating out of Rhode Island's harbors, it would be misleading to recommend just one or two here.

HIKING & BACKPACKING

Don't expect to find long stretches of pristine countryside in Rhode Island, but don't expect to find a landscape completely devoid of hiking possibilities, either. On the western border, **Arcadia Management Area** abuts Connecticut's Pachaug State Forest. At 13,000 and 23,000 acres respectively, they are the largest public land areas in each state. The **North–South Trail** is a relatively

JERIMOTH HILL

There are the fearsome massifs of Alaska's Mt. McKinley and Washington's Mt. Rainier, able to daunt even the most experienced, most fearless climbers. There are California's Mt. Whitney and Colorado's Mt. Elbert, both over 14,000 feet. But among the high points of the nation's 50 states, perhaps none is more of a challenge to reach than Jerimoth Hill in Rhode Island.

Of course, at 812 feet, Jerimoth Hill is anything but a high-alpine monster. The problem for climbers is not what's there but getting there at all. The hill is surrounded by privately owned land. So if you want to attempt to reach the summit of Jerimoth Hill, at least via the most direct route, you must trespass. This is a transgression that the landowner whose property you must cross has not taken kindly to.

Stories of hikers being harassed, chased away, or having cameras ripped from them have become Jerimoth Hill legend. All attempts at negotiating some kind of truce have failed. In fact, the situation has become so unpleasant and confrontational that the Highpointers Club, whose approximately 1,200 members seek to bag all 50 state-high summits, officially gives credit for reaching the Jerimoth summit to those who simply come close. A sign along Route 101 near the hill reads JERIMOTH HILL, STATE'S HIGHEST POINT, 812 FEET. Have your picture taken alongside this sign, and you are considered by the Highpointers to have made it to the top.

Of course, there is something unsatisfying about this solution. Some of the more determined Highpointers manage to get atop the real thing by negotiating with friendlier landowners, through whose property more circuitous routes to the top are possible. They bushwhack through the woods and may indeed reach the summit. Or maybe not—there is no marker designating the top spot on the undistinguished hill, so the exact location of the high point is not completely clear.

And you thought summiting Mt. McKinley was hard . . .

recent development, a product of the 1990s, during a period of considerable growth in mapping and developing trails for both hikers and cyclists.

North–South Trail
The trail enters Rhode Island from the north through Buck Hill Management Area in the far northwestern corner. It terminates just west of Ninigret Conservation Area on Block Island Sound. Map and trail information: **North–South Trail Council,** c/o the R.I. Department of Environmental Management, 235 Promenade St., Providence, RI 02908; ☎ **401/222-2776,** ext. 4309.

The North–South Trail is one of those projects born of enthusiasm—in this case, for hiking—and then brought into reality by more than a considerable amount of cooperation among individuals, private organizations, and public entities. Creating a 70-mile trail (or 72-mile or 78-mile, depending on who is measuring) along the western edge of Rhode Island, linking several large tracts of public land, was not really a matter of trail cutting. Instead, it was a matter of piecing together existing routes, blazing them uniformly, and, most critically, getting landholders along the way to buy into the idea.

The first section of the trail, consisting of 7 miles running through Arcadia Management Area, was designated as part of the North–South Trail in 1992. Other trail segments soon followed, with private landholders agreeable (for the most part) to granting rights of way. Of course, there has been—and continues to be—some reluctance. For example, the trail briefly enters Connecticut to skirt past land owned by Factory Mutual, an insurance company uncomfortable with the liability issues involved in having hikers walking around (and possibly tripping and hurting themselves) on its property. Other landholders grant access only in spring, when a group hike is organized along the length of the trail, after which those sections of the trail are closed to the public.

So hiking the full length of the trail on one's own still remains a hit-or-miss proposition. Access issues may or may not have been resolved by the time this book is published.

What can you expect? The trail is obviously a mixed bag. You might find yourself deep in the forest, as you would when hiking along sections through Arcadia, George Washington, or Buck Hill Management Areas. You might also find yourself walking along paved roads through well-settled areas. If you head off on an extended trip, you can overnight in a backcountry shelter, a public campground, or a motel. This is only a partial walk on the wild side; there is plenty of civilization along the way as well. And if you really want an extended trip, there's no reason to stop at the Massachusetts border. Keep going north on the Midstate Trail, which leads to New Hampshire, where trails can take you all the way to Canada.

Tippecansett Trail

Allow 5–6 hours. Moderate–strenuous. Access: Take Exit 4 from I-95, turning north on Rte. 3. At the intersection with Rte. 165, head west 7 miles to Beach Pond. Pull in to the parking lot on the right side (north side) of the road. Map: For Arcadia, maps are available at the management area headquarters. Maps for the Connecticut portion of the trail are available at Pachaug State forest headquarters (see chapter 7, "Eastern Connecticut").

All right—so much of this hike is in Connecticut, in Pachaug State Forest. Much of it is in Rhode Island, too. And since it begins and ends in Rhode Island, and since you won't have any idea when you're crossing state borders as you hike through the woods, the hike is listed in this chapter of the book. A note of

caution: There are places along this route where blazes might be hard to follow, so you'll probably want to go over the hike with knowledgeable folks at the state forest or management area headquarters before heading out.

The 12-mile hike begins at the east end of the parking area, where yellow blazes (for Rhode Island's Tippecansett Trail) and blue blazes (for Connecticut's Pachaug Trail) are your guides. Climbing up stone steps, the trails diverge at about the .5-mile point; bear left onto the Pachaug Trail for a clockwise tour.

For the first 5 miles, the trail rises and falls gradually as it passes through dense deciduous forest and past impressive cliffs and boulders. At about the 3-mile mark, you'll come to the shore of Beach Pond, pass through a boat-launch area, and continue on almost due north and back into the woods again.

Reaching a small dirt road, the Pachaug Trail heads left, but to continue your circuit, you'll bear left on the road on the Canonicus Trail, marked with white blazes, which leads back into Rhode Island on its way to Escoheag Hill. Trail blazes through this section can be hard to follow, so be vigilant, since roads and trails come and go, and at times the trail follows old roads. While the forest has re-established itself here, there is clear evidence that at some time in the past, people made an effort to establish farms in this area. When you reach paved Escoheag Hill Road, turn right and follow the road past a cemetery, where you'll pick up the yellow-blazed Tippecansett Trail on your right. Stick with those blazes—they're your guide back to the parking area and the trailhead.

HORSEBACK RIDING

Can there be anything that evokes a more romantic image than horseback riding on a beach? If that's your idea of an ideal way to spend time outdoors, then you've found the right place in Rhode Island.

Around Newport, the top spot for riding is the **Newport Equestrian**

Academy (287 Third Beach Rd., Middletown; ☎ **800/8HORSES** or 401/848-5440). In addition to rides on the beach, trail rides and instruction for all ages and abilities are on the program here. And when the weather fails to cooperate, there's also an indoor riding ring. On Block Island, **Rustic Rides Farm** (on West Side Road; ☎ **401/466-5060**) is where you want to head for beach rides and instruction, and is open year-round.

Farther inland, **Casey Farm** (on Route 1A in Saunderstown; ☎ **401/295-1030**), an 800-acre working farm overlooking Narragansett Bay, is a great place to go with kids. The farm dates back to the mid-1800s, and not much seems to have changed in the passing years. Plan to leave with bags stuffed with the farm's organic produce.

MOUNTAIN BIKING

In a state where the high point is just 812 feet in elevation, "mountain" biking might seem a misnomer. Indeed, there are no grueling, 2,000-foot climbs, nor are there similar whacko descents. Nevertheless, you might be surprised—in areas to the northwest, **Arcadia Management Area** and **George Washington Management Area** in particular, the ups and downs can be considerable.

Also, it would probably be incorrect to reidentify the sport as off-road riding. Some of the best riding in the state is in fact on back roads or the remnants of back roads. For example, there's great riding on **Prudence Island,** that isle of refuge amid bustling Narragansett Bay. But almost all of it is on dirt, gravel, and even paved roads.

If Rhode Island mountain biking has a shortcoming, it isn't a shortage of trails or roads, but rather a lack of adequate maps. Prime spots, such as Arcadia Management Area and **Big River Management Area,** feature sensational riding, but finding your way through the maze of trails and roads can turn into an unsolvable puzzle. This leaves two reasonable choices: Keep track of where you've come from so you can double back if necessary, or join up with locals who know where to go. Or you can just wing it, go where you feel like, and maybe or maybe not end up back where you started from. Rhode Island isn't that big a state, so it's hard to get that lost.

For more information on places to ride, trail information, group rides, etc., contact the **New England Mountain Biking Association** (☎ **800/576-3622**) or its Rhode Island chapter (☎ **401/397-8127**).

Arcadia Management Area

Allow 2 hours to all day. Moderate; short but sometimes steep hills. Access: Take exit 5A from I-95 onto Rte. 102 south. Go 1 mile to Rte. 3 south. Turn right, then a mile later turn right again onto Rte. 165 west. Within a mile, you'll see a sign for the management area on Arcadia Rd., on your left, which leads to the area headquarters. Various trailheads are along Rte. 165. Map: Available at management area headquarters (260 Arcadia Rd., Richmond; ☎ **401/539-2356**).

In the world of Rhode Island mountain biking, this is the big kahuna, offering many miles of single track, double track, and old roads. Loops of greater than 20 miles are possible, and it is for good reason that local riders sometimes refer to the area as "Single-track Central." By some estimates, there is something like 40 miles worth of single track here. On a typical Saturday, cars with bike racks fill the pull-offs along Route 165.

In fact, if there is a drawback to Arcadia, it is that there may be too many routes. In this complex trail-and-road network, getting lost is a very real possibility, and the trail map produced by the management area is a rough sketch at best. At various trail junctions are signs with destinations and mileage information, which are of some help.

What might a typical ride in Arcadia look like? Start by parking your car near the white church at the end of Frosty Hollow Road; it's on your right, about a mile west of the turnoff for the management area headquarters. Ride back east on Route 165 about .25 mile to the trailhead for John B. Hudson Trail, on your left. Here you'll dip into the woods for about 1.5 miles of challenging single track, while making your way toward Breakneck Pond. At times, the area's rocky underpinnings are exposed, demanding good bike-handling skills.

Riding around the eastern shore of the pond, pick up the Breakheart Trail, marked with yellow blazes. Within about a mile, the trail crosses the extension of Frosty Hollow Road, and if you've already had enough riding, simply turn left here to return to your car, about a 2-mile jaunt on a wide-open road. But if you're up for more riding, continue as the Breakneck Trail loops around toward the west, past Penny Hill—at 370 feet not much more than a bump—and you'll eventually meet up with the Escheat Trail. Turn left here to reach Escoheag Road, where a left turn brings you back to Route 165. A couple of miles of road riding brings you back to your car.

If this description sounds confusing, consider that a few trail and road crossings you pass along the way are not well marked. If you are blessed with good orienteering skills, keep in mind that Route 165, the aortal line through the heart of the management area, is never far to your south. When in doubt, head south. Or join up with someone who knows where they're going. The trail system here is complex, but well worth the effort.

Big River

Allow 2–3 hours. Moderate. Access: Take exit 6 from I-95 left onto Rte. 3 south. At your second left, turn onto Burnt Sawmill Rd. Look for a paved parking area on the left. Map: Ask for directions and ride descriptions at Coventry Mountain Bikes (982 Tiogue Ave., Coventry; ☎ 401/826-8030).

The Big River area, just a few miles from Arcadia, is less well known and its trails are not as clearly marked. Nevertheless, it is a spot favored among local mountain bikers for at least two reasons. One, the trails are less populated than those at Arcadia (not that Arcadia is crawling with humanity). Two, the going is generally faster and less rocky—good terrain for training racers trying to build up some cardiovascular oomph.

There are about 30 miles of trail here, almost all single track, and the location has its drawbacks. Before the area became popular with mountain bikers, it was popular with motorcross riders, as evidenced by the big sandy patches you'll find throughout the area. Also, much of the area is mud-prone, meaning you'll want to steer clear after a heavy rain. Still, when the conditions are right, local riders insist this is about as good as it gets if you're looking for single track that combines technical challenges with pure speed.

There has been some talk in recent years among local riders to improve trail blazing and signage, but don't count on it. Your best bet in getting to know this area is to join up with local riders. That failing, bring a long ball of string to trail behind you, so that you can backtrack and find your way back to the trailhead.

Great Swamp

Allow 2 hours. Easy, 6-mile loop, almost completely flat. Access: From I-95, take exit 3A to Rte. 138 east toward Kingston. Before the junction with Rte. 110, turn right onto Liberty Lane. Follow the road to the end, where there is a parking lot and a barred gateway. Map: Available at management area headquarters (☎ 401/789-0281).

If the rides described above sound like they might overburden your bike-handling and route-finding skills, here's the antidote. In fact, here's the ride on which to bring the kids. At 6 miles it's relatively short, it's flat, and the wide, grassy-road surface demands skills no greater than the ability to stay upright and pedal forward.

The ride basically circles the Great Swamp, one of Rhode Island's natural gems. Thick vegetation crowds the swamp, and in fall, the foliage colors of the trees bordering the swamp can be breathtaking. Make that early fall—later in the season, this is a popular spot among hunters.

You could probably blast through this ride in less than half an hour, but to rush is to miss the point of being here. Think of this as a combined mountain-biking and bird-watching outing, because this territory is held dear by a wide variety of species, particularly wading birds such as herons, ibises, and waterfowl. You might as well pack along a fishing rod, too; a short spur from the main loop leads to the edge of Worden's Pond, considered one of the top bass-fishing ponds in the state. If you go fishing, you probably won't be alone—ospreys work these waters, too.

Gear & Rentals

For riders heading to Arcadia or Big River, **Coventry Mountain Bikes** (982 Tiogue Ave., Coventry, RI 02816; ☎ **401/826-8030**) is about the closest, full-service bike shop. In the Providence area, **East Providence Cycle Company** (414 Warren Ave., East Providence, RI 02914; ☎ **401/434-3838**) is conveniently located just off Exit 6 from Interstate 195.

ROAD BIKING

Plenty of roads and plenty of traffic—for most of Rhode Island, the blessing and curse are inseparable. **Newport** is often mentioned as a place for cycling, and indeed you'll see many riders meandering through the mansion district and along Ocean Drive. This is certainly one way to see the sites, but traveling by car is still the way most people go, so traffic can be heavy. Perhaps more noxious are the small motorbikes, available for rent at various locations in Newport, that weave in and out of traffic and present more of a hazard to cyclists than less maneuverable cars. Try Newport if you want, but don't expect a peaceful ride.

The same cannot be said for the **East Bay Bike Path,** a paved, 14.5-mile route between Providence and Bristol. Passing over wooden bridges, through state parks, and along the shores of Narragansett Bay, the only traffic you'll face is in the form of other, non-motorized users, including cyclists, in-line skaters, and pedestrians. There is better news for the future, too. Under development is the **Blackstone River Bikeway,** which will connect with the East Bay Bike Path and stretch northward along the Blackstone River for 17 miles to the Massachusetts border. Put them together, and you'll have more than 31 miles of dedicated bike path. The Blackstone River Bikeway is scheduled for completion by 2002.

Rhode Island is making an effort to be bicycle-friendly, and the state produces a map showing designated bike routes. These routes—theoretically, if not always in fact—feature ample shoulders and relatively little traffic. For a copy of the map, call **401/222-4203,** ext. 4042.

Block Island

Allow 2–3 hours. Easy; flat and rolling terrain. Access: Take the ferry from Galilee (☎ **401/783-4613** for schedules and fares). Ferries also depart from Newport and New London, Connecticut. Map: Any decent roadmap of Block Island will do.

Given that the entire island amounts to only about 7,000 acres—7 miles long and 3 miles wide at its widest point—a bicycle on Block Island is not just a recreational vehicle, but a sensible means of transportation. Indeed, unless you plan to spend several weeks or more, the cost of bringing a car on the ferry is prohibitive (the passenger car rate, one-way, is $26.30, plus $8.40 per adult and $4.10 per child), so a bicycle is probably the *most* sensible means of transportation. It is also the most sensible means for taking a leisurely tour of one of the real gems of Rhode Island.

To Native Americans, Block Island was *Manisses,* "Island of the Gods," a name attributable to its considerable natural beauty. Historically, to those piloting ships at sea, it was known as the "Bermuda of the north," and not because of its allure as a vacation destination. Shoals and ledges, similar to those encircling Bermuda, made Block Island one of the great navigational hazards of the New England coast, particularly when the island was enshrouded in fog. During the 1800s, shipwrecks were common for boats headed for New Bedford or Providence by seafarers because of its similarly dangerous shoals and ledges.

As you explore the island on a bike, both sides of Rhode Island's character—its natural beauty and its ruggedness—are revealed. If you arrive on the ferry from Point Judith (at 70 minutes, the shortest ferry ride to the island and the best choice for day-trippers), you'll arrive in Old Harbor. Bear left on Spring Street, heading south toward Southeast Lighthouse and Mohegan Bluffs. The redbrick lighthouse occupies a spectacular perch overlooking the ocean, although that is not its original perch. In 1993, with the shoreline eroding, the lighthouse was moved back about 200 feet to ensure it wouldn't tumble into the sea.

Continuing onward, as the road begins to curve westward, you'll see a parking lot for Mohegan Bluffs on your left. Walk up the short path to the edge of the bluffs and soak in the spectacle of the land falling abruptly below your feet—200 feet to the sea.

Continue on from here past Center Road to Cooneymus Road. Turn here, looking for a sign for Rodman's Hollow, a ravine formed 12,000 years ago by glacial activity. Ditch your bikes here for a while and take a walk through the ravine (see "Walks & Rambles," below) to Black Rock Beach. When you return to your bikes,

keep in mind there's no reason to rush. Explore some of the back roads of the southwestern part of the island, passing shingled cottages, ponds, wild berry bushes, and the kind of seaside landscape that is quintessentially Block Island.

Eventually you'll find your way to New Harbor, on the edge of the Great Salt Pond, a popular stopover for cruising yachts, which sit impressively and abundantly in the harbor. Grab a bite to eat—there are plenty of options in New Harbor—then make your way to Colt Neck Road, the main route to the north end of the island. This leads past Crescent Beach, a popular swimming and surfing spot, and a turnoff for Clay Head, where a nature trail winds over red-clay cliffs.

Soon you'll reach the north end of the island, notable for two attractions. One is North Lighthouse, built in 1867; the other is Settlers Rock, inscribed with the names of the original settlers who came to Block Island in 1661. From here, you have no choice but to retrace your route down Colt Neck Road to catch the evening ferry. Or, if you wish, you can stay for a day or two or more (making sure you have a reservation in the busy summer months). There is no good reason to hurry anything when you come to Block Island.

Great Swamp Loop

Allow 2 hours. Easy; flat and gently rolling terrain. Access: West Kingston, at the junction of Rtes. 110 and 138. Map: Any good state roadmap will do.

It's a hot summer's day along the Rhode Island coast, and you don't feel like spending every minute of every hour hanging at the beach. Head just a few miles north, then to the Great Swamp area, and immerse yourself in the area's dense forests. In fact, so thick is the tree canopy over sections of this roughly 15-mile loop, that for most of the summer, sunlight will likely never reach the ground.

Start in West Kingston and head south on Route 110. It should quickly become clear what a magnet the beaches can be; on rural routes just a few miles inland, the flow of traffic dwindles to near nothing. After about 4 miles, turn right at a blinking light onto Worden's Pond Road, passing on your right the pond by the same name. There is a pull-off on your right that leads to the pond's edge, and here's a good place to stop for a rest and to cool off in the breezes drifting off the pond.

As you leave the pond behind and the forest begins to close in again, look for Biscuit City Road, on your right. Turn here and continue on until you see a sign for New Biscuit City Road and Route 2. Turn left and then right at the junction with Route 2. This might be considered a major thoroughfare, but it is still pleasant riding. The road surface is smooth, the shoulder space considerable, and traffic surprisingly light.

Keep an eye out for Liberty Lane—you'll reach it after less than 2 miles—which branches off to your right. Here you'll find yourself diving deeply into the forest foliage, with the northern perimeter of the Great Swamp Management Area on your right. This narrow lane eventually leads to Kingstown Road (Route 138), where you turn right to return to West Kingstown. So a 15-mile ride seems barely to have raised your heart rate? Well, then go ahead—the summer days are long. Do it all over again.

Tiverton–Little Compton

Allow 3–4 hours. Moderate; mostly flat and rolling terrain; wind may be a factor, particularly near Sakonnet Point. Access: From Interstate 195 in Fall River, Massachusetts, take Rte. 24 south. Take Exit 5 for Tiverton and Rte. 77 south. Map: Any good roadmap of Rhode Island will do, although all back roads may not be identified on the map.

You've passed through the congestion of Providence and its environs, and you were alarmed by the number of people crowding the roadways in and around Newport. You're wondering why you strapped your bike to your bike rack when all of Rhode Island seems like one giant, traffic-filled parking lot. Then you veer toward the southeast, toward Tiverton and Little Compton, and all at once it becomes abundantly clear why you brought your two-wheeler. The traffic dies away. Rural roads pass farms and farmstands, and seemingly endless stretches of meticulously built stone walls. An air of quiet settles in. The bike comes off the bike rack, and you can't wait to ride.

You can start this ride in Tiverton if you choose, but starting a few miles south in Tiverton Corners is probably a better option. For whatever reason, what little traffic there is in this part of the state seems to end here; much of the riding southward to Sakonnet Point is as close to traffic-free as Rhode Island riding gets. A small-business center on your right, just after the Tiverton Corners intersection, is a good place to park.

Route 77 is your central route, stretching 9 miles from Tiverton Corners to Sakonnet Point, and that's probably the 9 miles you'll want to ride first. Below to your right, the Sakonnet River glistens beyond verdant farm fields. Depending on the time of year, you'll be hard-pressed to keep yourself from stopping at vegetable stands selling plump ears of corn and tomatoes. You'll also be hard-pressed to pass by the Sakonnet Vineyards in Little Compton without stopping for a wine-tasting tour.

Little Compton must surely be the stone-wall capital of America. Two- to 4-foot-high walls are everywhere, pieced together expertly to form crisp, squared-off angles. Behind these walls are elegant summer homes; wealth here is far more understated than it is in Newport and even Watch Hill, but it is clear a few folks in this neighborhood have some cash in the bank.

SERVING UP WINNERS AT THE NEWPORT CASINO

When fellow members of a snooty Rhode Island social club didn't take too kindly to a prank instigated by James Gordon Bennett, Jr., the wealthy publisher of the *New York Herald,* he did what any other self-respecting Newport millionaire would have done—he built his own club.

In 1879, he commissioned the distinguished architectural firm of McKim, Mead, and White to build a private club and playground for the wealthy summer residents of Newport's fabulous Gilded Age. The result was the Newport Casino, a shingle-style edifice of lavish proportions, with turrets and verandas and an interior piazza designed to host lawn games, equestrian shows, and a sport that had recently arrived in the United States—tennis.

Eventually, the interior space was turned into a permanent grass court—one of the few still in existence in the United States—and the Casino now houses the recently renovated International Tennis Hall of Fame (194 Bellevue Ave.; ☎ 401/849-3990), which is chock-full of memorabilia and interactive exhibits. The pavilion, a National Historic Landmark, hosts professional tournaments several times a year, and every July it hosts the induction ceremonies for new Hall of Fame enshrinees. More important for the active sportsman, however, are its 13 courts, which are open to the public from May to October, and offer tennis players an extremely rare opportunity to play on a grass court. Reservations are essential, so call in advance if you'd like to try serving a game or two on the grass. The Casino is open from 9am to 5:30pm daily, except Thanksgiving and Christmas; admission to the Hall of Fame costs $8 per adult, $20 per family.

—Naomi P. Kraus

Arriving at Sakonnet Point, you'll find the air filled with the powerful aroma of fish, and for good reason. While sport fishermen cast out their lines from the rocky jetty that angles out to seal off the harbor, commercial fishermen bring in larger catches from deeper waters. Meanwhile, kids of various sizes scramble to raise sails and secure sheets and halyards during sailing-school lessons.

Heading northward again, take time to explore. Take a right on Swamp Road and then a left onto South Commons Road, which leads into Little Compton and its Vermont-like village green. At the center of Little Compton, turn left onto Meeting House Road, which leads back to Route 77, or take your time rambling around the back roads of Little Compton. Getting lost here is not only possible, but likely; fear not—you're never too far from Route 77, and the few people you're likely to encounter are also likely to be more than happy to help with directions. Lost but cheerful cyclists are a common site in these parts.

While returning to Tiverton Corners on Route 77, assess your energy level. If you're up to riding 4 or 5 more miles, turn left onto Neck Road (Route 179), which soon joins Pond Bridge Road as it winds north toward the Emily Ruecker Wildlife Refuge. This is a serene landscape of marshlands, narrow channels, and salt ponds. Continue on from here on Seapowet Avenue to the intersection with Route 77, where you'll turn right to head back to your starting point.

Gear & Rentals

There are several places on Block Island to rent bikes. **Esta's Bike Shop** (53 Water Street; ☎ 401/466-2651) is as good as any. If you feel compelled to ride around Newport, you can rent a bike from **Ten Speed Spokes** (18 Elm St.; ☎ 401/847-5600) next to the transportation center.

ROCK CLIMBING

Rock climbing? In Rhode Island? Unlikely as it might seem, there is a fairly active rock-climbing community in the state. No, there is nothing approaching Yosemite's El Capitan, but there are a few climbs of up to 60 feet that are enough to challenge the skills of deft, experienced climbers.

The cliffs of **Snake Den State Park,** due west of Providence, top out at around 40 feet, but with routes rated as hard as 5.12, this is considered some of the most technically challenging climbing in the state. The rock at **Fort Wetherill State Park** south of Jamestown is loose in places, and the climbing—in the 5.6 to 5.7 range—is not as challenging as the climbing at Snake Den. But there is something particularly thrilling about hanging on a wall of rock that drops straight into the sea. **Pettaquamscutt Rock,** off Route 1A north of Narragansett, is, at 60 feet, about as big as a rock wall gets in Rhode Island, although it is not considered a particularly rigorous climb by aficionados.

Gear & Rentals

Rhode Island Rock Gym (210 Weeden St., Pawtucket, RI 02860; ☎ **401/727-1704**) has a limited supply of climbing equipment for sale and rent.

SAILING

If Rhode Island were ever to declare an official state sport, it would have to be sailing. Sailing is ingrained in the state's life and lore. It is a part of growing up as a Rhode Islander; everywhere you go in summer, you'll see kids scrambling aboard small boats for sailing classes.

Narragansett Bay, as previously mentioned, is home to more boats per square mile than any other body of water in the world. The shoreline of Narragansett Bay itself is pocked with coves, inlets, and harbors—enough to keep even the most avid explorer entertained for years. And should that fail to satisfy, sailors can turn their eyes to the open seas and the considerable cruising opportunities to the north and the south. On weekends, the bay seemingly turns into one giant regatta, with racers competing on everything from sailboards and up.

In summer, winds in the bay are generally reliable, driven in from the south and southwest by high-pressure systems off the coast. The prevailing wind here—as it is to the east in Buzzard's Bay and along the shores of Martha's Vineyard—is what's known as a "smoky sou'-wester," given its smoky character by summer humidity and the moisture drawn off the surface of the ocean. When the wind is out of any other quadrant, the going in Narragansett, while sailing through its many sheltering islands, can best be described as fluky.

Beyond Narragansett Bay, Rhode Island's most popular cruising ports include **Watch Hill** and Block Island's **Great Salt Pond.** Rhode Island is nicknamed the Ocean State, which is technically inaccurate since the ocean lies beyond Block Island and Rhode Island Sound. In highlighting the state's attachment to the sea, however, the nickname is absolutely appropriate.

Gear

The Ship's Store (East Passage Yachting Center, 1 Lagoon Rd., Portsmouth, RI 02871; ☎ **401/683-0457**) has everything from charts and foul-weather gear to rigging and dinghies.

Rentals & Charters

Sail Newport (53 America's Cup Ave., Newport, RI 02840; ☎ **401/849-8385**), with 14 boats ranging from 19 to 22 feet, is a good place to go for day sailors who want to explore Narragansett Bay. **East Passage Sailing** (1 Lagoon Rd., Portsmouth, RI 02871; ☎ **401/683-5930**) has a 16-boat, bare–boat-charter fleet (there's no crew) for exploring Narragansett Bay and beyond.

Instruction

J World, with "campuses" in Annapolis, San Diego, and Key West as well as Newport, is consistently rated one of the top sailing schools in the country. Two- to 5-day courses (with 6 hours a day of on-water time) are offered for everyone from the landlubber novice to the blue-water expert. Contact J World, Box 1509, Newport, RI 02840; ☎ **800/343-2255**). **Newport Sail School & Tours** (Goat Island Marina, Dock 5A, Newport, RI 02840; ☎ **401/848-2266**) offers 5- to 13-hour courses for beginning, intermediate, and racing sailors.

Outfitters

Offshore Sailing School (16731 McGregor Blvd., Fort Myers, FL 33908; ☎ **800/221-4326**) operates out of several harbors around the country, including Newport. While it bills itself as "the Ivy League of sailing schools," Offshore is really as much a luxury-tour operator as a school. The 3-day "Live Aboard Cruising" course mixes instruction with tour stops on islands from Block Island to Martha's Vineyard, where fine dining, shopping, and other non-instructional enticements are part of the package.

SEA KAYAKING

Exactly what is sea kayaking? It is certainly not just "sea" kayaking, because a boat technically considered a sea kayak has almost universal flatwater applications. Hence, those bodies of water singled out in "Canoeing/Flatwater Kayaking," above, are perfectly navigable by someone in a sea kayak. If there is any noteworthy difference at all between a sea kayak, a flatwater kayak, and a canoe, it is that a sea kayak is usually steered by a pedal-controlled rudder, which can sometimes snag in shallow water or reeds. Also, sea kayaks are typically bigger and heftier and might not be as maneuverable as a canoe or flatwater kayak in tight conditions.

Most sea kayaks, however, are designed to withstand rougher, open-water conditions as well. In fact, many skilled sea kayakers deliberately seek out rough water and surf, considering the thrills that go with riding waves to be the ultimate in sea-kayaking fun. In some ways, then, a sea kayak has broader applications than a canoe or flatwater boat. That's noteworthy in Rhode Island, with everything from freshwater ponds to bays to saltwater ponds to the open sea.

So where to go? **Narragansett Bay** is an obvious place to start, with its many coves and beaches. You might want to paddle out from Bristol Harbor to **Potter Cove** on Prudence Island, to come ashore and explore Narragansett Bay Estuarine Sanctuary. It's a fair amount of paddling, though—about 10 to 12 miles round-trip—and much of it over open water, so you'll need to be in reasonably good condition. A much shorter option is to put in at **Easton Beach** in Newport and head south past the mansions that line the shore. In essence, this is the water-based equivalent of walking the Cliff Walk (see "Walks & Rambles," below).

Sakonnet River, with less boat traffic than Narragansett Bay, is also popular with sea kayakers. Paddle in for a picnic at Sandy Point Beach, or poke around the Emily Ruecker Wildlife Refuge. Take care here if the wind is strong and directly out of the south; under such conditions, the going can be rough when crossing the river.

Of course, the coastal ponds—**Ninigret, Green Hill, Point Judith,** and others (see "Canoeing/Flatwater Kayaking," above)—are all worthy sea-kayaking destinations. So is the **Great Salt Pond** on Block Island. But if you're near the coast and conditions are right, you might want to try your hand at surf riding. Rhode Island surf rarely gets huge and unruly, so on most summer days, even a paddler of modest skill should be able to do reasonably well. You'll probably want a smaller, more maneuverable boat than the standard sea kayak, which can also be hard to roll should you get flipped over by the waves. Take a lesson (see "Instruction," below), and go for it. There's nothing quite like the thrill of surfing a wave with a paddle in hand.

Rentals

The Kayak Center (9 Phillips St., Wickford, RI 02852; ☎ **401/295-4400**) rents both single and double kayaks at Wickford Cove on Narragansett Bay, as well as on Charlestown Beach Road at Ninigret Pond. **Oceans & Ponds** (Ocean and Connecticut aves., Block Island, RI 02807; ☎ **401/466-5131**) is the place to rent kayaks on Block Island.

Instruction

The Kayak Center (see "Rentals," above) conducts clinics in open-ocean paddling and surf riding, as well as basic kayaking technique. **Sakonnet Boathouse** (169 Riverside Dr., Tiverton, RI 02878; ☎ **401/624-1440**) conducts clinics in rolling, open-water paddling, and basic paddling technique.

Outfitters

Sakonnet Boathouse (see "Instruction," above) conducts half-day and full-day tours of nearby areas, including Seapowet salt marshes, Bristol Harbor, and Newport Harbor. **The Kayak Center** (see "Rentals," above) leads 1- and 2-day trips in Narragansett Bay, including tours of Newport Harbor and the sea around Newport's famous mansions.

SKY DIVING

If you've never jumped from a plane before, here is your chance. The **Boston-Providence Sky Diving Center** (North Central Airport, 6 Albion Rd., Lincoln, RI 02865; ☎ **800/SKYDIVE**) will take you up to 10,000 feet, and from there it's 35 seconds to terra firma. Inexperienced jumpers go in tandem with an instructor and free-fall about 5,000 feet before the chute is opened. There are just two

restrictions—you've got to be older than 18 and lighter than 230 pounds.

SURFING

Killer waves are uncommon on Rhode Island's shores. More typical are 2- to 3-foot cruisers that roll in on the southern beaches. From time to time, when storms at sea roil the ocean waters, waves may reach 6 feet and even higher, but consider that the exception.

Nevertheless, Rhode Island, probably because it is a state linked so closely with the sea, has an active surfing community. First-time visitors head for the obvious spots, including **Misquamicut, Mattunuck,** and **Narragansett Town** beaches. After that, it's time to venture to more secluded places, such as **Ninigret Conservation Area,** or to breaks such as the **Trunces,** held in high regard and semi-secrecy by local surfers. The local folk (that is, the surf-shop crowd) are your best source of information on where the best breaks are. Given the shifting nature of beach sands and the ocean floor, and the variables of weather and wind, yesterday's good break might be today's dud.

For the hard-core, Rhode Island surfing is not just a summer sport. Dedicated surfers have been known to come here even in midwinter, insisting that winter waves tend to be bigger. That's something only a rare few will ever want to find out.

Gear, Rentals & Instruction

The Watershed (396 Main St., Wakefield, RI 02879; ☎ **401/789-3399;** surf phone ☎ 401/789-1954) offers rentals and free lessons every summer Wednesday at noon. **Warm Winds** (26 Kingstown Rd., Narragansett, RI 02879; ☎ **401/789-9040**) is also a good source for gear and surf information.

SWIMMING

The state officially lists 95 public beaches, both saltwater and freshwater. For body surfing, the best beaches are along the southern coast—**Misquamicut Beach,** the beaches of **Mattunuck, Roger W. Wheeler Memorial Beach,** and others. If you are willing to swim without a lifeguard present, take a long walk down the beach of **Ninigret Conservation Area** for privacy. Another place to escape crowds is **Little Compton Town Beach,** in the far southeastern corner of the state. If you're looking for more of a social scene (and less surf), check out prosaically named **First, Second,** and **Third Beaches** near Newport.

One of the appealing aspects of Rhode Island swimming is the water temperature. While temperatures to the north and east—along the Cape Cod, New Hampshire, or Maine coast—rarely break above the just-tolerable 60° mark, Rhode Island water in the summer often hits 70°. That's just about right for cooling you off on a hot summer's day.

WALKS & RAMBLES

With 420 miles of coastline, taking a walk on the beach must certainly rank as a Rhode Island highlight. Of course, many of the popular public beaches—notably Misquamicut, Mattunuck, and Wheeler beaches—are crowded during the peak summer season, but there are still a few places to get away from it all.

Head west, past Charlestown Beach, from the parking area at Charlestown Breachway, and you've got the 3-mile beach of **Ninigret Conservation Area** to explore; you'll be disturbed only by the occasional four-wheel-drive vehicle transporting the surfers or fishermen who come to surf-cast here. Another fine stretch of sand stretches from Watch Hill to **Napatree Point,** which separates Watch Hill harbor and Block Island Sound. In places, you might have to scramble around fences cordoning off private beach areas, but once on the beach, you've got about a mile of sand and dunes stretching to the point. Go early in the morning, when the sun is rising over the sound and plovers are scurrying about the sand.

To explore the pond and wetland environment just inland from the beaches, head for **Trustom Pond National Wildlife Refuge** off Mattunuck School Road in Green Hill. Trails lead through meadows, seaside scrub, and trees to the pond's edge, where if you're lucky you might spot that most athletic of fishing birds, the osprey, hard at work. Otherwise, the three walks described below—a diverse collection indeed—are your best bets.

Cliff Trail

Allow 2 hours. Easy. Take Rte. 138 south to Rte. 138A south. Turn right on Memorial Ave. and park at Easton Beach. The walk starts behind nearby Cliff Walk Manor. Maps and tours are offered by the **Cliff Walk Society** (☎ 401/849-7110).

A place to get away from it all? Hardly. On an average summer day, hundreds of people walk the 3.75-mile walk—or portions of it—with rugged cliffs dropping to the sea on one side and the grand mansions of Newport lore on the other. Despite the heavy use, this is still a pretty walk, squeezed as it is between sea and wealth. It is also a chance to be an unabashed voyeur; you can get a taste not only of how the rich and famous once lived, but how, in some cases, they continue to do so. Not all the homes and mansions along the Cliff Walk have become historic museum pieces; many are relatively new and still inhabited.

As you begin your walk, heading southward, it will soon become clear that not all the residents here appreciate being the subject of unabashed voyeurism. Hedges, wood fences, and vine-covered metal fences block the view—and protect the privacy—of many homes here. But don't feel too deprived. Things get better as you move along, and many of the great mansions that have brought lasting fame to Newport remain grandly in view.

This is an out-and-back hike, so go as far as you want before turning around, although keep in mind that some of the most impressive homes are those at the walk's southernmost point. Stories of the great extravagance that went into these mansions—or "cottages" as their owners modestly called them—abound. For the mosaic work in the Marble House, for example, William K. Vanderbilt imported a team of Italian specialists who spent a year on the job. In other words, nothing was done on the cheap. It is stories like this one that make taking a guided tour along Cliff Walk a worthwhile venture.

The Greenway Trail (Block Island)

Allow 3 hours. Easy. Access: From Old Harbor, take Old Town Rd. and turn left onto Center Rd. The parking lot is on the right side of the road, across from the airport at Nathan Mott Park. Map: Available from the **Nature Conservancy** on Ocean Ave. in New Harbor (☎ **401/783-4613**).

The island might be only 7 miles long and (at most) 3 miles wide, but somehow there is still enough room for 25 miles of hiking trails. Their existence is a testament to cooperation—among private organizations (such as the Nature Conservancy), public organizations (such as the U.S. Fish and Wildlife Service), and private landowners. All deserve a nod of appreciation.

The 12 trail miles that constitute the Greenway run through forest, meadow, former farmland, and a curious geological feature called Rodman's Hollow. Depending on the time of year you go, nature will likely be showing off in one way or another. In May, the shadbushes (flowering berry bushes) bloom brightly. In mid- to late summer, wild berry bushes bear fruit. In fall, migrating songbirds arrive by the thousands.

Head from the trailhead through a four-way junction into the appropriately named Enchanted Forest, where a thick copse of pine, spruce, and maple trees blocks out the sun. Bear right around Turnip Farm, an area where you'll find northern blazing star and bushy rookeries—rare finds in Rhode Island—blooming. Continue on from here as the trail leads to Rodman's Hollow.

This ravine was cut by glaciers some 10,000 to 12,000 years ago. If you use your imagination, you might be able to envision the movement and melting of glacial ice, making its way to the sea, and using Rodman's Hollow as a kind of sluiceway. When the trail splits, head right to a knoll that affords a terrific view of the rugged, seaside landscape. Return to the junction, take the other fork, and you'll find yourself walking through open meadows along the shores of Fresh Pond.

If you've still got some hiking energy after backtracking to the trailhead, head north to the Clay Head Trail, at Colt Neck Road on the north end of the island. Winding above bluffs that, in characteristic Block Island style, tumble into the sea, the singular trail splits into a series of smaller trails that wind into the brush, away from the sea. It is for good reason that this area is locally known as the Maze.

Drop by the Nature Conservancy in New Harbor, grab a map and hiking recommendations, and go exploring. On such a small island, there is a surprisingly large bounty waiting to be found.

Sachuest Point

From Portsmouth, take Rte. 138 south and turn right on Mitchell's Lane and continue on to Third Beach Rd., following signs to the Sanctuary. For the refuge, turn right on Hanging Rock Rd., then left onto Sachuest Point Rd., which leads to the sanctuary. Sanctuary headquarters: Middletown; ☎ **401/846-2577**. Refuge visitor center: Sachuest Point; ☎ **401/ 847-5511.**

Leave busy Newport to reinvigorate your imagination of what this seaside world might have been like before it became so thoroughly settled. Although this 242-acre refuge was once home to a naval communications station, there is little evidence of naval activity left. Instead, a trail network winds through meadows, bayberry bushes, beach roses, and wildflowers, with the mixed sound of songbirds and waves washing up on the point's rocky shores. Don't be surprised when, as you walk by, swarms of tiny thrushes or swallows rise up from the meadow grasses in a sudden cloud.

None of the walks here are long; if you were to walk every inch of every trail, you would walk less than 4 miles, all on almost perfectly flat ground. As you make your way around the trail that skirts the shoreline, views unfold, particularly to the west. The churches, stone walls, and manicured lawns of nearby Middletown sweep down to the edge of the sea, creating an image similar to that of the English or Irish seaside. Farther to the west, the roofs of Newport's mansions glisten in the sun.

If you still feel inspired after completing the Sachuest Point loop, make the short drive to Norman Bird Sanctuary, where trails wind through inland meadows, forests, and wetlands. And don't think of this as just a place to visit in summer. In late fall, this area is considered a prime spot by birders to view migrating waterfowl.

Campgrounds & Other Accommodations

CAMPGROUNDS

Burlingame State Park

Located off Rte. 1 4 miles west of Charlestown. ☎ **401/322-7994.** 755 sites, no hookups. Showers, rest rooms, grocery store, phone, tables, grills, firewood.

If 755 sites sounds like a lot, it is. Because of its proximity to Rhode Island's most popular beaches, the campground is almost always full on summer weekends. If size is a deterrent, there are some attractive compensations—Wachaug Pond for swimming and canoeing, and hiking

trails that wind into the woods, far away from the camping area.

Fishermen's Memorial State Park

Located on Old Point Judith Rd. (Rte. 108) south of the intersection with Rte. 1. ☎ **401/789-8374.** 182 sites, 40 with full hookups, 107 with water and electric. Showers, rest rooms, tables, tennis and basketball courts.

This is a tidy place with paved roads connecting the sites. There are beaches within walking distance, but the real attraction of this campground is that it is relatively close to the ferry in Galilee, a bonus if you're planning an early start for a day trip to Block Island.

George Washington Management Area

Located in Gloucester, off Rte. 44, 5 miles west of Rte. 102. ☎ **401/568-2013.** 45 sites, no hookups. Non-flush toilets, tables, fireplaces.

The primitive nature of this campground in the northwestern corner of the state tends to discourage the big-RV crowd. With a nearby boat ramp leading into Bowdish Reservoir and with hiking trails leading into the management area, this is a popular spot for canoeists, fishermen, and hikers.

Melville Ponds Campground

Located at 181 Bradford Ave. in Portsmouth, off Rte. 114. ☎ **401/849-8212.** 123 sites, 33 with full hookups, 33 with water and electric. Handicapped rest rooms, showers, phones, tables, fireplaces, firewood.

Convenience is the strong selling point here. This is the closest campground to Newport, and sea kayakers will appreciate the easy access to Narragansett Bay.

Ninigret Conservation Area

From Charlestown, head south on Rte. 1 for approximately 5 miles. Turn left on East Beach Rd. and continue to the end. Access to the campground is on the left. For information and reservations, contact the Rhode Island Department of Parks and Recreation (☎ 401/322-0450). 20 primitive sites. No fresh water; you must pack in your own.

Tent camping is, alas, not permitted here. You need to be in a "self-contained unit." So if you've got a four-wheel-drive vehicle that can double as your home unit, you're in business in one of the finest camping spots in the state. What else can be better than a remote beach, with the waves crashing at your doorstep and Ninigret Pond in your back yard? For surfcasters and sea kayakers, it doesn't get much better than this in Rhode Island.

INNS & RESORTS

Castle Hill Inn & Resort

Ocean Dr., Newport, RI 02480. ☎ 888/466-1355 or 401/849-3800. Double rooms $95–$250; suites $125–$325.

If you want to get some feel for what it was like to rough it in the grand Newport style, you might want to stay in this small mansion, situated on a bluff separating Newport Harbor and Rhode Island Sound. Built in 1874, the inn has played host to the likes of Grace Kelly, Montgomery Clift, and Thornton Wilder, who wrote of his stay here, "I could see at night the beacons of six lighthouses and hear the chiming of as many sea buoys." You can stay in one of the inn's 40 rooms, or in one of the more modern, outlying Harbor Houses, but if you really want a flavor of manorial splendor, the inn is the better choice. The restaurant, high-end all the way, is excellent.

Champlin's Hotel & Resort

Great Salt Pond, P.O. Box J, Block Island, RI 02807. ☎ 401/466-7777. Rates $85–$250, depending on the season.

Block Island is known for its soulful inns and B&Bs, but this resort certainly does not fit into that category. Accommodations are in 30 familiar, modern-American motel-style rooms. But if recreation is your primary interest, this place is hard to beat, with on-site bike and kayak rentals, tennis courts, a swimming pool, and a private beach. It even has its own 220-slip marina for visiting yachtsmen.

Green Hill Beach Motel

Green Hill Ocean Dr., South Kingstown, RI 02879. ☎ 401/789-9153. Rates start around $70.

A pint-sized motel with just 17 units, there is nothing particularly special about this place. Staying here, however, does allow you access to a private beach, which you need share only with other motel guests and a few local residents. If you're someone who likes to spend your beach time away from the crowds, and you aren't fussy about accommodations, this is a good place to set up camp.

Hotel Manisses

1 Spring St., Block Island, RI 02807. ☎ 800/626-4773 or 401/466-3162. Rates from $65, off-season; $180 and up, peak season.

This is considered the grand old lady of Block Island hotels. The Victorian-style hotel has 25 guest rooms, named for shipwrecks—an appropriate theme for Block Island. The rooms vary widely in size and decor, but most feature antiques and lots of wicker. Animal lovers will be delighted at the site of llamas, emus, goats, geese, black swans, and a Scottish Highland Ox grazing on the property. What might it have been like to summer on the island at the turn of the century? Stay at this time-capsule hotel and find out.

Rockwell House Inn

610 Hope St., Bristol, RI 02809. ☎ 401/253-0040. Rates start at $85.

At one time, Bristol was one of the most important seaports in New England. Those days are gone, but the aura of history remains on Hope Street, where this bed-and-breakfast, housed in an 1809 Federal-style building, is located. The inn is close to the East Bay Bike Path and the ferry to Prudence Island. And, if it's a rainy day, you might want to check out the Herreshoff Museum in Bristol. From 1893 to 1934, Herreshoff was the builder of eight defenders of the America's Cup, and more impressive racing yachts are hard to imagine. Or, if it is a rainy day, you might just want to hang at the inn and feast on the excellent breakfast of homemade muffins and granola.

Sakonnet Vineyards
162 West Main Rd., Little Compton, RI 02837. ☎ 800/91WINES or 401/635-8486. Rooms $85–$95 per night, including breakfast.

If you're a cyclist, staying here puts you in the heart of some of the most enjoyable riding in Rhode Island. If you are a wine lover, staying here puts you in the heart of Rhode Island's most distinguished vineyard. If you are both a cyclist and a wine lover, this approaches nirvana.

Accommodations are in a tiny, renovated three-bedroom inn, known as The Roost, that was the original farmhouse on the vineyard. For a group of touring cyclists able to fit comfortably in three rooms, this is an ideal stopover, although you can expect to leave the place with your panniers overburdened with fine wine.

Shelter Harbor Inn
10 Wagner Rd., Westerly, RI 02891. ☎ 800/468-8883 or 401/322-8883. Doubles $100–$136 in summer, including breakfast.

This restored 18th-century farmhouse offers comfortable accommodations and excellent food, but for lovers of sea and sand, the real attraction is the 2-mile private beach just outside the inn's back door. There's also a rooftop whirlpool, two paddle-tennis courts, and a croquet green.

Index

NOTES

NOTES

NOTES